BOTTOM LINE

PERSONAL

BOOK OF BESTS

BOTTOM LINE
PERSONAL
BOOK OF BESTS

INSIDE INFORMATION FROM AMERICA'S LEADING EXPERTS

by the Editors of *Bottom Line Personal*

Introduction by Martin Edelston

Foreword by Ken Glickman

St Martin's Griffin 🕮 New York

R

Bottom Line Personal Book of Bests

Production Editor: David Stanford Burr

Designed by Michael Mendelsohn of MM Design 2000, Inc.

Library of Congress Cataloging-in-Publication Data

Bottom line personal book of bests: inside information from America's leading experts / Bottom line personal newsletter staff.
       p.   cm.
   ISBN 0-312-15069-5
   1. Life skills — United States.   I. Bottom line / personal.
 HQ2039.U6B666   1997
 646.7 — dc21   96-29543
                                             CIP

First St. Martin's Griffin Edition: February 1997

10 9 8 7 6 5 4 3 2 1

Table of Contents

INTRODUCTION
BY MARTIN EDELSTON

This book is dedicated to you.

My life for the last quarter century has been dedicated to you. I have been working to help millions of Americans do well and be well in these increasingly challenging and complex times.

There are so many ways to do better and to protect yourself as things change . . . and change . . . and change. This book contains thousands of ways—some small, some big. All are important.

This all started when I realized the great need for better information for the top management of American businesses. I also knew a wide array of experts who could be helpful to those businesses. In 1972, I brought management and those experts together via *Boardroom Reports*.

One expert recommended another expert and my network expanded and expanded.

And, I continually read cutting-edge books and a myriad of publications in constant search for new experts with the new ideas and new ways of dealing with the continuous changes in health, family, taxes, laws, overseas competition, changing value of the dollar, changes in the workforce, etc. *Boardroom Reports* (now *Bottom Line/Business*) has grown to become one of the largest business newsletters in the United States.

It became obvious that individuals needed assistance in dealing with multiplying personal changes and *Bottom Line/Personal* was born. It has grown to be the world's largest newsletter with millions of people reading each issue.

All the hard work, seven days a week—without vacation—is so well worth it, when I read letters from our subscribers thanking us for saving their lives.

Our information has helped women solve orgasm problems, men solve impotency problems, families solve money problems, children solve college problems, young people heal colitis, and many people solve retirement problems. The information helped me make a back problem disappear without the surgery recommended by one of the country's leading orthopedic specialists. I also put an end to the agony of my dehabilitating asthma that the specialists could not cure.

I love the letter from the Las Vegas showgirl who, recognizing that she could not be a showgirl forever, used *Bottom Line/Personal* as her guide for starting a second career and investing her hard-earned money wisely.

Through continuous reading of useful material, meeting with the experts and talking, listening, and thinking, new publications and books developed and the most effective business system of all . . . I-Power.

I-Power began with a suggestion from the great Peter Drucker. His suggestion was to make my meetings more interesting by asking each attendee for two suggestions on how they can operate more effectively. Using the simple system that grew out of those few words, we changed our whole operation. High employee turnover became zero turnover, a $20 million per year business became a $100 million per year business.

I have come to truly understand the value of time . . . and it is much too valuable to be wasted. Key: regularly ask yourself—*Who Am I? Where Do I Want to Go? How Am I Going to Get There?*

If you tune into the right information, it is amazing how much you can accomplish.

Recognize that life is confusing and it is your job—and mine— to bring order to it. The *Who Am I* questions help bring order. Keeping a journal helps shape the order and—believe it or not—improves your health, too. I figured this out decades ago and recent research has confirmed it.

It is helpful to prepare *To Do* lists and set your priorities in the evening. You will accomplish more the next day. We only live this life once, make the most of it.

Many years ago, I met one of the country's highest paid executives. I asked him what he did with all the money he made (about $100 million that year). His reply: "Life is a game and the money is how you keep score." My response— there are other games, many very good, helpful games. We cannot take our money with us but we can do much good and *that* legacy lives on and on. That rich man has gone on to accumulate a huge amount of money. The price— continuing aggravation, an ugly divorce, and a triple bypass operation.

Evaluate everything and everyone carefully. *Genuine? Baloney?* I learned to use this incredibly powerful tool long ago from one of the smartest people I have had the privilege to know. I use it regularly.

It is really amazing to see that you can indeed, do anything that you want to do . . . if you want to do it hard enough and you are willing to pay the price. This principle helped me to become one of the best Yellow Page salespeople ever (almost fifty years ago), one of the best mail-order salespeople, an amazing soda jerk in my teens, a peerless swimming instructor, a super-fast dishwasher in my early teens, and a black belt in karate at the tender age of fifty-seven.

Good health is the foundation. The health rules are simple and the key ones are in this book.

You do not have to be a genius to do it all. Anyone can do well with the right knowledge. Einstein said that we operate at 2 percent of our brain capacity. Other estimates run up to 10 percent. So imagine what happens if your brain is full of useful information—rather than information with no relevance. It makes a huge difference.

This is your book. It is dedicated to you—someone has dedicated the best part of his dedicated life to bring it to you. Thousands of other dedicated people have helped, too, through the years.

Special thanks for their assistance in putting this book together go to Boardroom's Nancy Crowfoot, Catherine Dolan, Peter Goldmann, and Ray Holland . . . to John Hawkins & Associates' Warren Frazier . . . St. Martin's Press's Matthew Shear . . . design consultant, Barbara Marks . . . and master illustrator, Alexi Tani.

FOREWORD
BY KEN GLICKMAN

Now You Can Do Everything Right

You have great golden opportunities in your hands right now—the ideas for a wonderful life.

Now you can be healthier, wealthier, and even wiser, too.

Here are the best thoughts from thousands of experts around the country. There are experts here for every aspect of your life.

It all works. I hear how well it works over and over again every week . . . for I meet with hundreds of *Bottom Line/Personal* subscribers every week as I travel all around the country teaching Time Management and I-Power to *Bottom Line* subscribers.

Their enthusiasm is awesome . . . for *Bottom Line* has helped millions, too—in so many ways.

Big articles, little articles . . . all have helped in one way or another. Things that may seem insignificant to you now can change your life tomorrow, next month, or next year.

The magic words that change family fights to hugs and kisses . . .

The bill that is okay to pay late if one big bill must be paid late . . .

The way to get an ambulance fast . . .

The simple basics of team work . . .

The very simple essentials of time management . . .

The big, big difference between time management—and life management . . .

The new jobs . . . the better jobs.

And—I hear so many better-health stories, too. One person recently whose life we saved by writing about when to get a third opinion . . . and the woman who almost died because she loved grapefruit—and didn't know the dangers of taking a very popular antiallergy drug, too.

Better bottom lines are all over now—at big companies and small government, including the military . . . and in schools, too.

You're in for a real treat now . . . a book full of great golden opportunities. Take advantage of them. Any questions—write to me at Greenwich Institute, 55 Railroad Avenue, Greenwich, CT 06830.

Bottom Line did wonders for me as I moved through life from lawyer to college instructor, to business manager, to marketing vice president . . . and now to the best work of all, Director of the Greenwich Institute for American Education.

There is a lot of very useful information in this book for you and your family. Read it carefully, please. It will be very helpful to you. To make the most of it, have a pencil handy and make notes. Especially helpful are small Post-Its for marking pages.

Best Ways to Test-Drive a Car

David Solomon

Before you buy a new car, take full advantage of your test drive. Make sure the dealer lets you drive the vehicle where you can give it a thorough workout . . . on bumpy roads . . . in stop-and-go traffic . . . and on highways, especially the entrance and exit ramps. Pay special attention to how the car matches up to your expectations for comfort, drivability, interior layout, and power.

COMFORT

Engineers call the science of fitting the car to the person *ergonomics*. You'll soon see how well they did when you climb in behind the driver's seat.. Don't forget that the "feel" of the car should suit your co-drivers and frequent passengers.

Clearance: Can you get in and out without hitting your head?

Headroom: Your hair shouldn't touch the ceiling. If it does, and you love the vehicle, consider ordering it with a sunroof. This will give you another inch or two.

Seat height: Does it give you good road visibility?

Headrest: Will your head, neck, and back be comfortable after driving for a while?

Leg room: Does the seat move far enough forward and back not only for you but for all drivers?

David Solomon, editor of *Nutz & Boltz®*, Box 123, Butler, MD 21023.

SAFETY SECRETS

■ **Safest car colors:** Greenish-yellow is best . . . then cream, yellow, and white. *Least-safe colors:* Red and black. *General rule:* Light-colored, single-tone cars are safer. They have significantly fewer accidents than dark cars because it is easier for other drivers to distinguish them from the surroundings.

Lemon Book: Auto Rights for New & Used Cars by Ralph Nader and Clarence Ditlow. Moyer Bell, Ltd.

■ **Exposure to nitrogen dioxide from car exhaust** doubles the chance that a hay fever sufferer will develop the classic symptoms—sneezing and a runny nose. This chemical appears to damage the mucous membranes lining the nose, making them more sensitive to airborne pollen. *Self-defense:* When pollen counts are high, hay fever sufferers should avoid city streets during rush hour.

Robert Davies, M.D., professor of respiratory medicine, St. Bartholomew's Hospital, London.

■ **The most dangerous driving day is Friday.** *Most dangerous time of day:* Late afternoon to early evening. *Most dangerous month to drive:* November. The safest month is March . . . safest day, Sunday. *Caution:* Medium and heavy trucks make up less than 4% of registered vehicles but are involved in nearly 10% of fatal accidents.

National Safety Council statistics, Itasca, IL.

SHREWDER PAPERWORK

■ **Register a car** in the name of the primary driver only. *Reason:* If the car is owned jointly and one spouse has an accident, the victim can go after both spouses' incomes and assets in a lawsuit. In most states, if the vehicle is owned only by one spouse, the other's assets are protected.

Bert Whitehead, Franklin, MI, tax attorney and fee-only financial planner.

■ **Remove a dealer logo decal** from a car by heating it a bit with a hand-held hair dryer set to low. This should soften the glue enough for the decal to be gently peeled off. *Better:* When buying a car, get the dealer to agree—in writing—that the car will not have any dealer identification when you take delivery.

Used Cars: Finding the Best Buy by Chicago Tribune auto editor Jim Mateja. Bonus Books, Inc.

■ **Cheaper car insurance.** Discounts are available in many states if drivers complete a defensive driving course. Ask your insurer if discounts apply in your state . . . call the National Safety Council, 800-621-6244.

Auto Insurance Alert! by financial writer Andrew Tobias. Simon & Schuster.

■ **Secret car warranties.** Secret factory warranties cover repairs of problems common in particular car models—long after *official* factory warranties run out. Owners are not usually notified of secret warranties, called *special policy adjustments.* To find out if there are such warranties on your vehicle, send a stamped, self-addressed, business-sized envelope to the Center for Auto Safety, 2001 S St. NW, Washington, DC 20009. List the year, make and model of your vehicle.

Mark Eskeldson, author of What Auto Mechanics Don't Want You to Know. Technews Publishing.

DRIVABILITY

Test-drive the car at night to make sure that the headlights are powerful enough for your comfort.

Power: Does the car run smoothly and accelerate adequately? *Hint:* Make sure the car you test has the engine size, transmission type, or gear ratios that you want.

Rear visibility: Can you see adequately with the exterior rearview mirrors? If they're too small, be aware that replacements don't exist.

Noise: Does engine exhaust or wind noise bother you?

Fuel type: Does the car need expensive high-test gas? High-performance, multi-valve, super- and turbo-charged models all do.

INTERIOR

Instrumentation: Can you read the gauges easily?

Controls: Do you hit the wiper switch and put the radio on?

Door handles: Can you find them in the dark?

BOTTOM LINE

If you're satisfied with your test drive, don't assume the car that the dealer delivers to you will be as good.

Check out the finish of the car you want to buy to make sure you haven't been sold a vehicle that already has been driven . . . or damaged in transit. Look for telltale signs of repainting . . . like paint traces on the rubber stripping or trim, mismatched colors, and misfit panels. And take a good look at the undercoating. It should look slightly weathered—not sparkling clean and still soft.

Insist on a test drive of your new car before you accept delivery. *Also:* Never take delivery at night. You want to examine your car carefully in broad daylight. You may also want to have the car looked over by a good mechanic.

How to Make Your Car Last Twice as Long

David Solomon

T he best way to save money on a new car is to put off buying one for as long as possible. Motorists can easily double or even triple the life span of their present cars simply by performing proper maintenance, practicing good driving habits, and avoiding the kinds of mistakes that send most cars to the junkyard.

MOST COMMON MISTAKES

• *Mistake:* **Failing to observe the "break-in" period.** Drive gently during a new car's first 50 miles—and be sure to vary your speed for the first 1,000 miles of the car's life. Failing to do so results in improper seating of the piston rings, which leads to increased oil consumption for the life of the car. Also, change the oil promptly after the first 1,500 miles to eliminate bits of metal and grit found in a new engine.

• *Mistake:* **Making sudden starts and stops.** Accelerating aggressively only to slam on the brakes at the next traffic light does little to save time—but does cause needless wear to your engine, transmission, suspension and brakes—and wastes gas. *Better:* Anticipate traffic patterns to keep your speed as constant as possible. Emulate good truck drivers—they tend to be very gentle on their vehicles.

• *Mistake:* **Downshifting needlessly.** In the early days of automobiles, brakes were so unreliable that prudent drivers always shifted into a lower gear when descending hills or approaching busy intersections. Today, brakes are very reliable . . . and far less costly to repair than engine and transmission components. *Rule:* Use "engine braking" only when

David Solomon, editor, *Nutz & Boltz*®, Box 123, Butler, MD 21023.

EMERGENCY BASICS

Accident Checklist

• **Move all involved cars safely off the main roadway.** Many injuries can occur *after* an accident as people mill around on a busy road.

• **Call for medical help for the injured people.** If someone appears to be injured but says he/she is okay, call for help anyway.

• **Call the police and stay put until they arrive.** *Important:* Never admit guilt or negligence. Just relay the facts and let the police determine who—if anyone —was at fault.

• **Get data from each driver involved**—no matter how minor the accident. *Important:*
  • Name
  • Address
  • Phone number
  • Driver's license number
  • Insurance information
  Also: Get names, addresses, and phone numbers of the witnesses, including passengers in the cars that were involved.

• **Write down the details of the accident** while they're still fresh in your mind. *Describe:* Car directions, speed, whether signal and brake lights were functioning and used, etc.

• **Draw a map of the accident.** Note the location of any stop signs, traffic lights, objects in the road, etc.

• **If you carry a camera in the car**, photograph the accident from all angles and get good shots of any damage to each car.

• **Remain calm** and follow all police instructions.

Reality Check Gazette®, 8667 Sudley Rd., MS-270, Manassas, VA 22110.

Selling Your Car Yourself

Paul Brand

Selling your car yourself makes you more money than you would get selling or trading it in to a dealer . . . but it is also riskier.

Trap I: The prospective buyer could steal your car during the test drive.

Self-defense: Get information—name, address, phone number—on him/her before handing over your keys . . . go on the test drive or hold his car keys and another item, such as a credit card or driver's license . . . turn away anyone who makes you uncomfortable.

Trap II: Erroneous problems identified by the buyer's mechanic to lower the car's value.

Self-defense: Know what is wrong with your car . . . be there for the mechanic's inspection.

Trap III: In many states, the license plate stays with the car. If the new buyer doesn't transfer the title right away, you are still the legal owner and he is driving under *your* insurance policy—you could be liable for any violations or accidents.

Self-defense: Go with the buyer to the county registrar's office or Department of Motor Vehicles to make the title change.

Paul Brand, a former racing-car champion, instructor in emergency driving, and automotive columnist for the *Minneapolis Star/Tribune* and many automotive magazines.

descending a long, steep grade. At all other times, use your brakes.

• *Mistake:* **Driving with a cold engine.** Engine wear occurs most swiftly not during high-speed driving but in the first moments after a car has been started, when the cylinders are starved for oil. *To avoid trouble:* Before driving off, let your engine idle with your foot *off* the accelerator pedal for one minute—*no more and no less.* Once you're under way, drive slowly and avoid using your heater, wipers, and other power-hungry accessories until the engine reaches its proper operating temperature—usually about three minutes.

Special danger: **Accelerating briskly with a cold engine** causes head gaskets to fail. Premature use of accessories speeds wear of engine bearings.

• *Mistake:* **Shifting gears haphazardly.** Manual transmissions cost less and are cheaper to maintain than automatics—if you learn proper shifting techniques. Picking too high a gear for a given speed "lugs" your engine. Picking an excessively low gear causes it to "over-rev." Both practices waste fuel and damage your engine bearings. *Better:* Shift so your engine speed remains between 2,000 and 3,000 revolutions per minute (RPM). Use overdrive settings only for speeds greater than 45 miles an hour.

Common problem: With many manual transmissions, shifting from neutral to first gear causes an audible grinding of the transmission's synchronizer rings.

Remedy: Avoid shifting directly from neutral to first. Instead, move the shift lever briefly into second, then shift into first gear. And—never rest your hand on the shift lever or rest your foot on the clutch pedal. Use your right foot for both accelerator and brake. Use your left foot for the clutch.

• *Mistake:* **Driving with dirty and/or worn-out oil.** To many motorists, oil maintenance means simply adding the occasional quart of 10W40. In fact, 10W30 offers far more protection against engine wear. And by the time you're a quart low, it's time for another oil change.

Change conventional motor oil once every three months or 3,000 miles, whichever comes first. *Better:*

Switch to synthetic oil. It costs a few dollars more but offers superior protection for up to 12,000 miles.

To keep oil clean between changes, select the biggest oil filter that will fit under the hood. (Most cars accept either a "tall" or "short" filter. The tall one always provides better filtration.) If you live in a dusty environment, bolting on a bypass oil-filtration system provides an extra measure of protection without voiding your car's warranty. *Cost:* About $80, plus labor.

Avoid oil additives: Despite manufacturer's claims, they neither reduce engine wear nor boost performance.

Switch from a disposable pleated-paper air filter to a more effective—and reusable—wetted-foam filter. *Cost:* $20 to $40. To help lock out dirt, apply a thin layer of grease to the seal between the filter and the filter housing.

• *Mistake:* **Driving with dirty fuel.** Although owners' manuals often give it short shrift, clean fuel is essential for long engine life. Replace your fuel filter every 10,000 miles or two years, whichever comes *last. Cost:* $12 to $50.

In either case, stick to the recommended fuel. Using regular in a car designed to run on premium causes "knocking," which can quickly destroy an engine. Using premium gas in a car designed to run on regular wastes gas, money, and causes drivability problems.

If your car has fuel-injection, never let your tank drop below one-quarter full. Cornering on an almost-empty tank can momentarily disrupt the flow of fuel to the fuel pump, thus damaging or destroying it.

• *Mistake:* **Failing to guard against weather damage.** To reduce exposure to sunlight and other environmental threats, keep your car garaged or at least covered. If your car must remain outdoors without a cover, put a dashboard-protecting sunscreen in your windshield and park so that it faces a different direction each day. (This helps "spread out" sun-induced damage.) To preserve weather-stripping and other rubber surfaces, use silicone spray. Wash your car by hand or in a "dancing chamois" car wash. Avoid car washes that use rotating brushes.

CAR-CARE ESSENTIALS

■ **Don't rustproof a new car** *after* you buy it. Rustproofing may invalidate the new car warranty, leaving you unable to collect the cost of repairs if rust damage does occur. *Best:* Wait until the original warranty lapses before rustproofing. And make sure the rustproofer solidly stands behind the job.

Bert Holtje, editor, *Agency Sales,* Box 3467, Laguna Hills, CA 92654.

Cold Weather and Your Car

George Giek, AAA

Regularly check to make sure battery cable connections are tight and there is no corrosion on the terminals . . . in batteries where the fluid levels can be checked, make certain fluid covers the battery plates . . . to prevent fuel lines from freezing, consider adding a commercial additive containing isopropyl alcohol to the gas tank when filling up before and during extremely cold weather.

Important: Never attempt to jump-start a weak car battery that has frozen because of extremely low temperatures.

George Giek, managing director, AAA Automotive Services, Heathrow, FL.

■ **Smart car care.** Don't drive with a gas tank less than one-quarter full, or "sloshing" of gas when cornering may damage the fuel pump . . . use the octane grade gasoline specified in the owner's manual—higher octane gas will not improve performance, and lower octane gas may damage the engine . . . keep antifreeze in your en-

CAR-CARE ESSENTIALS

gine even if you live in a climate where it never freezes—it contains valuable rust inhibitors. Use a 50/50 mix of antifreeze and water. *Best:* Distilled water that has been purified of minerals that could damage the cooling system.

Bert Holtje, editor, *Agency Sales*, Box 3467, Laguna Hills, CA 92654.

INSURANCE INSIGHTS

■ **Car insurance dilemma:** If you report an accident, your rates may go up or your policy may be canceled. If you *don't* report it and seek coverage—if you are sued, for example—your insurer may not protect you. *Safest:* Report any accident that involves another person—even if it seems to be his/her fault. If others are not involved, you can consider paying the claim yourself.

Robert Hunter, head of the insurance group at the Consumer Federation of America, 1424 16 St. NW, Washington, DC 20036.

■ **Car insurance trap:** Insurers in most states are not required to disclose their underwriting guidelines. *Result:* Applicants don't know why they're rejected . . . policyholders don't know what's required to stay insured. Many unwittingly lose coverage. If you've been treated unfairly, contact your state insurance commissioner. If coverage was suspended, ask that the commissioner have the company reinstate your policy until the dispute is resolved. *Car insurance strategy:* Take the highest deductible you can afford—and don't file small claims. View insurance as protection against only major damage or loss.

Robert Hunter, head of the insurance group, Consumer Federation of America, 1424 16 St. NW, Washington, DC 20036.

• *Mistake:* **Ignoring your antifreeze.** Antifreeze not only keeps your car working in cold weather but also helps prevent rust and corrosion. For optimal protection, use a 50-50 antifreeze-water mix. *Important:* Use distilled water, not tap water. Change annually.

• *Mistake:* **Cleaning your engine.** While an under-hood cleaning might make your engine look better, it can severely damage sensitive electronic sensors and connectors located there. Better to leave your engine dirty. If you insist on a clean engine, hire an experienced professional to do the job.

• *Mistake:* **Over-tightening your lug nuts.** Though it sounds trivial, improperly tightened lug nuts or bolts represent a big source of trouble for car owners.

Too much lug-nut torque, and your brake rotors will warp and cause your brake pedal to pulsate. Too loose, and your wheels will not be securely attached.

Problem: Many mechanics tighten lug nuts with air wrenches, which are notorious for over-tightening.

To avoid trouble: Get your own torque wrench. *Cost:* $15. Each time your wheels are removed for maintenance, use the wrench to check the torque readings on your lug nuts against your owner's manual.

• *Mistake:* **Failing to perform "hidden" maintenance tasks.** While owners' manuals usually specify how and when to perform the most crucial maintenance tasks, they often provide incomplete information about other key tasks.

Example: Manuals typically say nothing about brake fluid, which should be changed once every two years or 24,000 miles. Anti-lock systems' brake fluid should be changed annually.

Power steering fluid should be changed every three years or 30,000 miles, whichever comes first. Timing belts should be replaced every 60,000 miles, timing chains every 100,000 miles.

Note: Without regular use, certain systems quickly fall out of adjustment. *To avoid trouble:* Run your air conditioner and defroster at least once every two weeks. Release and reapply the parking brake daily.

• *Mistake:* **Failing to recharge or replace an old or weak battery.** Besides increasing the risk of leaving you stranded, a weak battery causes needless wear of both the alternator and the starter. Both need a good power source to operate properly.

To avoid trouble: Choose the biggest, most powerful battery that will fit under your hood.

• *Mistake:* **Rustproofing your car.** Aftermarket or dealer-applied rustproofing treatment is not only costly, in many cases, it can void your car's rust warranty.

Driving with Big Trucks

David Solomon

O
ne of the most stressful and frightening aspects of driving is sharing the road with big trucks.

But if you have better insight into the world as seen through truckers' eyes, you may understand more about the way they perform and can avoid tangling with them. Here's what you need to know.

SHARING THE ROAD WITH BIG TRUCKS

•*Mirrors:* Most trucks have a multitude of mirrors, both flat and convex. Because of their size, they can distort the picture or leave out whole sections of the lane beside the truck. For this reason, the most dangerous place to drive is beside a big rig. To get an idea of big-rig blind spots, try to see the trucker's face in his/her mirror. You'll quickly learn how limited his visibility is.

•*Lanes:* A trucker's turn signals are most important. Always watch for them. If a trucker signals to change lanes and you are in the way, move out of his way as fast as you can.

David Solomon, editor of *Nutz & Boltz®*, Box 123, Butler, MD 21023.

SHREWD CAR-BUYING

■ **Better car buying:** Shop during the late fall or winter, when sales are slowest—and deals are easiest to come by. And try to shop during the last week of the month, when dealerships are competing in contests or pushing to meet sales quotas. If possible, shop late in the day—at dinnertime or afterward—when salespeople and managers tend to be tired and more flexible about closing deals.

Have I Got a Deal for You! by Kurt Allen Weiss, consumer advocate and former car salesman, Clifton, NJ. Career Press.

■ **Odometer tampering on used cars** is still rampant. It is most common among cars previously owned by rental car companies and corporate fleets and those leased by individuals. These cars, while well maintained, are driven far more than average cars. *Self-defense:* When looking to buy a used car—whether from a dealer *or* an individual—always look at the car's service records. See if the current mileage makes sense compared with the mileage when the car was serviced. If records are not available, contact the car's prior owner, whom you can find through the Department of Motor Vehicles. Otherwise—*don't buy that car.*

David Solomon, an editor of *Nutz & Boltz®*, Box 123, Butler, MD 21023.

•*Escape:* Seasoned truckers know they must have an escape path if they need to get off the road quickly—in case the air pressure fails and the brakes suddenly lock up. If a trucker is in the left-hand lane, he will always be looking for a path to the right so he can get off the road before the brakes cause the truck to come to a skidding halt.

•*Blind spot:* One thing all trucks have in common is a blind spot directly behind the trailer. If you want to slip in behind a truck to save gas by being pulled along in the truck's wake, you'll find the trucker very uncooperative. Truckers hate it when a four-wheeler hangs back there. It makes them nervous. This is one of the reasons truckers like to drive in caravans, so the trucker behind can watch the "back door." They try to discourage you from slipping in between.

•*Passing:* Truckers hate passing. It is one of the most risky things they have to do. They have to plan their approach, speed, exit, and reentry back into their lane. Anytime they must change lanes, there is a risk of hitting someone hiding in the blind spot. So avoid passing, slowing down, and forcing him to pass you.

Consider how much energy a truck uses to speed up and pass. The trucker typically must break the posted speed limit to gain enough momentum to pass. In a trucker's mind, there are two rules to live by—deliver the load on time and use as little fuel as possible. When you get in his way, you become the enemy.

•*Hills:* Truckers like to gain speed while going downhill so they have more momentum to go up the next hill. If you are in their way, you either force them to pass you or to ride on your tail. Sometimes it is better to give up the right-hand lane so the truckers can speed up and slow down when going up and down the hills. *Remember:* Give them room—lots of room.

•*Wet roads:* The water splash from a truck can be overwhelming. Stay away from big rigs when it is raining hard or when there are large puddles in the road. The splash can blind you, especially at night. If your vehicle, trying to pass the truck, is covered with the spray, the truck driver won't be able to see you. Also, trucks have better traction than cars in the wet weather and can stop much faster than cars. Don't follow too closely.

•*Snow and ice:* Because of their awesome weight, trucks can drive on ice and snow long after four-wheel-drive vehicles have lost traction. Don't be deceived into thinking you can continue driving in this weather just because trucks are traveling. If anything, you might become a hazard when you spin out right in front of one.

DANGEROUS TRUCKS

Many trucks are loaded beyond their rated capacity and many have brakes that are not functioning properly.

The more axles and tires a truck has, the better its stopping ability. If you consider the actual amount of braking ability a truck has in relationship to the weight of its load, you can get an idea of how effective the truck's brakes are. Once the truck's front wheels lose traction, the truck becomes a huge, deadly projectile.

Because dump trucks (also known as "sand haulers") don't have to cross state lines, they don't have to stop at the weigh stations. Because they are not closely checked for overloading, some may exceed the safe gross vehicle weight limit by as much as they can.

A majority of the single-axle dump trucks in use are designed to carry a maximum of 16.5 tons. But most states do not limit them to the manufacturer's gross weight limit, allowing them to carry in excess of 20 tons. It is estimated that 95% of all single-axle dump trucks are running over the manufacturer's specified safe-load limit.

Some container haulers fit into this category. They run from the shipyard or railroad loading docks to local warehouses, and don't go very far on the highway.

In some states, container haulers are allowed to exceed the manufacturer's safe-load limits. Some owners of container haulers use old, run-down trucks with tires that are unfit for use. Their extra-heavy loads break up streets and bridges faster than anything else on the road.

■ **Learn the history of your company and its products.** The more you know about your product's background, the better you will be able to convey its strengths, the achievements your company has made over time, and the values the company stands for. *Helpful:* Interview the boss and "old-timer" employees. Read old company brochures. Ask the factory foremen and the vendors who supply the company what kinds of advances have been made in materials or procedures used in your product.

Arthur Rogen, sales and marketing consultant, Dix Hills, New York. He is the author of The Street Smart Salesman, Avery Publishing Group, Inc., 120 Old Broadway, Garden City Park, New York, NY 11040, $9.95.

■ **Hidden career assets** can be helpful to getting a new job in today's tough market for good jobs. Keep an inventory of all work- and nonwork-related learning experiences. Include complex skills, like learning to fly . . . and less-obvious ones, like organizing a church newsletter. Volunteer work, a hobby, or a special project in which you were once involved may contain the seeds of a new career.

Helen Harkness, Ph.D., career therapist, Garland, TX.

■ **Start a networking conversation** by asking open-ended questions instead of ones that can be answered *yes* or *no. Examples: What advice would you give someone just starting out in the field of X? How did you get started in X? Questions like these not only break*

How to Increase Your Productivity

Edith Weiner

At an almost breathtaking pace, medical science is discovering new insights into human biology.

Used the right way, much of this new knowledge can help managers heighten workers' job satisfaction and increase their own productivity. *Major discoveries . . .*

LIGHT AND COLOR SECRETS

Researchers have found that light has a profound effect on our bodies. Though not completely understood, the reason is probably linked to the effect light has on two vital areas of the brain—the hypothalamus and the pineal gland. Our moods, even those of color-blind people, are affected by the intensity and color of light around us.

Helpful: Use a consultant to help you decorate your office . . . and choose your wardrobe. The right color and lighting can raise output and make work more enjoyable. Wearing the right colors can also boost a sales rep's closing rate.

Where to find an expert: Most large management consulting firms can make recommendations. For color, try the Pantone Color Institute, 201-935-5501.

Also, bring more natural light into the workplace. Tests show that it has a positive impact on perfor-

Edith Weiner, president, Weiner, Edrich, Brown, Inc., futurists and strategic planning consultants, 200 E. 33 St., New York, NY 10016. She is also coauthor of the very useful and insightful new book, Office Biology. MasterMedia Ltd.

mance. There are lights available now that simulate natural light. For advice, consult a lighting engineer.

SOUND SECRETS

Women are far more sensitive to sound than men. They can also hear higher-pitched sounds. Some research suggests that women may even be subliminally sensitive to sounds beyond the conscious hearing range.

Example: Some scientists believe high-frequency tones given off by computer terminals can cause stress in women who use them. Harm may occur even though users aren't actually aware of the sound.

If your company has complaints from VDT users, consider hiring an acoustical engineer. The problem may be with the sound, not the light source.

Other research has discovered how we screen background noise from conversation that we want to hear.

Helpful: If you want someone's attention, don't talk more loudly, just move closer. Halving the distance quadruples the sound.

SMELL SECRETS

This may be the most exciting area of research. Science has discovered that odors have a profound effect on our moods and performance.

Examples: Exposure to apple-cinnamon may improve editing skills . . . fruit scents may induce women to make certain purchases . . . clove has a calming effect . . . and peppermint elevates mood and may relieve headaches.

Try scenting your office with various fragrances to find the ones that have the effect you want.

Helpful: Contact the Fragrance Foundation (212-725-2755). This organization tracks the latest research in the field and can put companies in touch with consultants.

BIORHYTHM SECRETS

Each individual has a natural rhythm to his/her activities, but in a typical business environment we're all expected to arrive, work, and eat at more or less the same times.

Helpful: Give yourself (and employees) more schedule flexibility. Experiment with having several

CAREER PSYCHOLOGY

the ice but also provide valuable information.

Wolf Rinke, Ph.D., CSP, president, Wolf Rinke Associates, Inc., human resource and management consulting firm in Clarksville, MD and author of *Make It a Winning Life: Success Strategies for Life, Love and Business.* Achievement Publishers, $24.95.

GETTING AHEAD

■ **Did you know that secretarial and receptionist jobs** are good stepping stones to higher positions—*including management?* Secretarial jobs often require word processing, spreadsheet, database, and on-line skills. Receptionists need excellent communication, organizational, and customer-service skills. These are important skills for higher positions in most companies as well. *Bottom line:* Jobs that have been thought of as dead-end positions in the past can be real career opportunities today—if taken seriously.

Kathryn Marion, editor, *The Reality Check Gazette,* 8667 Sudley Rd., Manassas, VA 22110. Six issues. $15/yr.

■ **Start your day by tackling your toughest task first.** You'll come into the office knowing exactly how you will start the day and what you will do. And—you will avoid the anticipation and anxiety associated with knowing there is a large task looming that you must handle later in the day.

How to Make the Most of Your Workday by Jonathan and Susan Clark, management consultants in Scottsdale, AZ Career Press, $16.95.

■ **Smart way to get ahead at work:** Become a powerful source of information by reading magazines, newspapers,

and periodicals. Busy schedules can make it difficult for others to read as much as they would like. As a result, they are more likely to overlook important articles. Sharing valuable information and critical clips with these people will help you stand out as an ally and as someone who stays informed.

Robert Half, founder of Robert Half International, Inc., and Accountemps, employment specialists in the financial, accounting, and information systems fields, Menlo Park, CA.

WORK-AT-HOME BASICS

How You Too Can Make Working at Home Work

Jack Nilles, JALA International

Working part of the week at home isn't working out if you're not getting all your work done . . . and you're feeling out of the loop.

Solutions: Make lists at night of what you must accomplish the next day—and for the rest of the week or month. Work with your manager to develop an output schedule. Handle feelings of being left out by spending more of each week at the office . . . or at least spending more time on the phone with colleagues to stay in touch and help them solve work-related problems.

Important: Listening to the grapevine for managerial changes is fine, but avoid gossiping about personalities. You'll only leave a negative impression.

Jack Nilles, president of JALA International, Inc., a management consulting firm that helps businesses establish telecommuting programs, 971 Stonehill Lane, Los Angeles, CA 90049. He is author of Making Telecommuting Happen: A Guide for Telemanagers and Telecommuters. Van Nostrand Reinhold, $24.95.

snacks instead of one long meal. Take a midday nap if it helps rejuvenate you in the afternoon.

As far as possible within the demands of the business world, tell employees you're more interested in results than in when they're achieved.

Biorhythms are also affected by sunlight. If you must start work before sunup, take an outdoor break as early in the day as possible. It can boost your mood and productivity.

Keep a chart of your own cycles of high and low energy levels. Try to schedule meetings and other tasks accordingly.

GENDER SECRETS

The latest tests confirm again that women are biologically equipped to process a wider range of sensory information than men.

Women are less obsessed with beating out rivals and getting super-rich than men are. They want to succeed for the sake of emotional fulfillment.

Men are more prone to tunnel vision—aiming at destroying their enemies quickly. Women, by contrast, see the broader picture and strategize better for long-term success.

Despite these differences between the sexes, managers don't have to plan one set of tasks for women and another for men. Instead, be attuned to using the assets of each to the best advantage.

Example: When assembling a project team, try to include a balance of men and women. If you don't, chances are greater that the team will overlook an important strategy, side effect, market, or other opportunity.

AGE SECRETS

As people grow older, their gender-hormone levels decline. In women, declining estrogen during menopause can bring on irritability and forgetfulness. In men, declining testosterone levels can cause low energy levels and loss of concentration.

If you manage people who show these symptoms, help them find support. And do the same for yourself if you're nearing 50.

Helpful: To increase productivity and job satisfaction among older workers, offer to redesign offices for them—provide softer colors, comfortably built chairs, equipment with large enough displays to be seen by someone with less than great vision.

BRAIN SECRETS

Science is rapidly discovering that while the brain has many similarities to a computer—which stores and processes information—the *brain* also *interprets* information.

Not appreciating this difference has led many companies to rely too heavily on computers.

The brain works in a way that usually makes it easier to remember what we read in a book than what we see on computer screens.

Recommended: Ask for advice from a neuropsychologist or neurobiologist at a local university whenever the company is developing or revising training programs. Their expertise about how people learn can be valuable in making training techniques much more effective.

How to Break Free from Corporate Bondage

Michael Dainard

It's never easy to leave a career in which you've spent much of your lifetime. It's even harder if you've reached a high level of success and are locked in by the golden handcuffs of a large salary, benefits, expense accounts, perks, and prestige.

Michael Dainard, former director of marketing for CBS television stations and, since 1986, president of Michael Dainard Associates, an international marketing agency in New York. He is the author of *Breaking Free From Corporate Bondage.* Dearborn Publishing Group.

WORK-AT-HOME BASICS

■ **Home/career option for some people**—working three 12-hour shifts each week rather than five eight-hour days. *Benefits to you:* Lower child-care and transportation costs . . . more quality time with your children. If such a shift is too drastic, consider working four 10-hour days per week instead. *Important:* Present the idea to your boss with an emphasis on its benefit to the *company*—an employee with longer office hours three days per week . . . computers and other office equipment won't be busy during the day . . . "rush" jobs can be completed more often without having to pay overtime.

Suzanne Smith, codirector, New Ways to Work, a nonprofit advocate for restructured work-time options, San Francisco, CA.

PERFORMANCE

Don't Work . . . Plurk

Teri-E Belf

Plurking means combining play with work. Use playful approaches for anything that feels like work.

Example: Turn grocery shopping with a child into a game. Split the grocery list, and have each of you get half the items. Whoever gets his/her half to the shopping cart first wins.

Plurking makes drudgery fun and has unexpected side benefits.

Example: In the grocery store, less impulse buying.

Teri-E Belf, success consultant in Annandale, Virginia, and author of *Simply Live It Up: Brief Solutions.* Purposeful Press, $16.95.

PERFORMANCE BOOSTERS

■ **Dissatisfied with your job?** Take a look at it from a fresh perspective—as if you were a stranger viewing it for the first time. *Ask yourself:* "What can I do differently?" . . . "What simple steps can I make today toward change?" . . . "Is there some aspect of this job that I haven't explored?" . . . "What's unique about my skills and/or personality that makes me stand out from the competition?"

Diamond in the Rough by Barry J. Farber, president, Farber Training Systems, Florham Park, NJ. Berkley Books, $12.

■ **Put yourself in a "peak state"** just before a big meeting by sitting or standing up straight, throwing your shoulders back, and lifting your head. This position pumps more oxygen through your body.

Also: Remember a time when you felt unstoppable. Re-create the feeling mentally. Set up a trigger to put you back in touch with that feeling—a finger snap, deep breath, or gesture. Just before the big meeting starts, use the trigger to put yourself in tune with high performance.

Tony Robbins, a motivational speaker and author of several books, including *Giant Steps*. Simon & Schuster, $10.

JOB-CHANGE SECRETS

■ **Before changing jobs,** determine what effect it will have on your pension benefits. It may pay to wait a while before making the change. Federal law says that employee benefits must be 100% vested—*nonforfeitable*—after five years of work for one employer . . . or be at least 20% vested after three years and increase to 100% vesting after seven years. But there are some exceptions—

But many people who seem to have it made are really unhappy. *Questions to ask yourself:*

- Do you harbor a secret dream of doing something else?
- Have you thought about your dream—really thought about it?
- Do you think you're too old to make a major change?
- Do you worry about your mortgage and other financial responsibilities?

Reality: In today's world of corporate restructuring and downsizing, more and more middle- and high-level managers are having the decision made for them. Whether or not you have a clearly identifiable dream, if you are in a corporate management position it is smart to seriously consider what you might want to do instead . . . and how you can go about doing it.

THE DREAM COMES TRUE

In my case, I wanted to be a writer, my dream since I was a child. I'm now following a ten-year path to realize that dream. Although I have several years to go along this path, I've already published two books and 14 screenplays, and I'm working daily on writing projects.

My family life is considerably richer. I'm even making a fairly good living between my writing, teaching continuing education courses about marketing, and running a successful international marketing agency.

I've never worked harder, but it no longer seems like work because I really enjoy what I'm doing. When you add up work-related items, such as preparation, travel time, and entertaining clients after hours, your job represents a huge segment of your life. Think how happy you would be if you could spend that time doing something you love to do.

WHERE TO START

Take a few days off to analyze and visualize how it would feel to actually live your dream. Is this what you really want?

Even if you eventually decide not to change careers, this is a valuable exercise. It refreshes your outlook, allows you to reexamine your strengths and weaknesses and lets you fine-tune your goals.

Caution: Be sure that you're not just experiencing mid-life hopelessness borne of extreme fatigue, stress, or career stagnation. Maybe it isn't really the industry or the job, but the particular company or people with whom you're working that have got you down or held you back.

Change for the sake of change, without any planning behind it, is dangerous and sometimes leaves behind a trail of family breakups, wasted dreams, substance abuse, and severe depression.

Whatever your age, if your dream is merely to become rich or famous as soon as possible, you're more apt to find restlessness and insecurity than happiness.

I find that most dreamers fall into three basic categories:

• **Daydreamers**, who are always fantasizing but find all kinds of reasons not to actually do.

• **Different drummers**, who don't talk much about their dreams but just make them happen (entrepreneurs, inventors, scientists, artists), in spite of obstacles and doubters.

• **Procrastinators**, who have what it takes in terms of skill and talent but keep putting off their dreams until tomorrow. These people need a push and a plan.

Helpful: Write down exactly how you arrived at where you are today, then make a written commitment to leave your job and try something new.

DREAM ASSESSMENT

Thorough research is essential to really know what this new career path would entail. It helps to evaluate whether you can live with the downside that accompanies any evolution.

Research is needed to succeed and understand how long attaining the success might take. To find answers to these questions, you'll have to visit the library—and talk to a lot of people who are in the same or similar businesses.

such as for public school teachers in many states. And vesting in your company may occur *faster* than the federally mandated minimum rate. Ask your employer's benefits administrator about the company's vesting schedule.

Your First Financial Steps by Nancy Dunnan, New York–based financial writer. HarperPerennial, $12.

■ **Seek lifetime *employability*,** not lifetime employment. The idea that a company would give an employee a job until retirement—lifetime employment—is dead. Instead, focus on building a successful career by making continuous efforts to improve your skills—and by learning to adapt and synthesize your knowledge and abilities for other positions. Adaptation will bring lifetime employability.

Lifetime Employability: How to Become Indispensable by Carole Hyatt, career consultant and marketing and social behavior researcher. MasterMedia Limited, $12.95.

■ **Don't rush into a new position** determined to "fix" everything your superiors have messed up. *Danger:* At best, co-workers will resent your inexperience and resist your efforts. At worst, they will sabotage your career. *Best:* Learn from those around you. Try to win them over with a friendly attitude, a desire to learn and any mutual interests you may share outside the workplace.

Hit the Ground Running: Communicate Your Way to Business Success by Cynthia Krueger, communications consultant in Wheaton, IL. Brighton Publications, $13.95.

YOU AND YOUR BOSS

■ **To get your boss to accept your great idea:** Never ask for a decision larger than what you need to go on to the next step in developing the idea . . . always under-commit and over-perform to gain credibility . . . avoid premature publicity about your idea, which can lead to internal jealousy . . . recognize your own weaknesses and enlist others to help you fill these gaps.

Zenas Block, a business professor at New York University and coauthor of *Corporate Venturing.* Harvard Business School Press, $14.95.

NEW-JOB NEWS

■ **Show motivation and enthusiasm** on a job interview by telling key things that you have done that prove you are self-motivated . . . volunteering a few ideas that might improve the company's product—and explaining how you would implement them . . . asking whether there would be a task force or team on which you could serve—to show your willingness to go the extra mile for the company . . . explaining why doing this kind of work is important to you.

The New Interview Instruction Book: A Guide to Winning Job Offers Using Proven Techniques Developed by Headhunters by Nicholas Corcodilos, corporate headhunter in West Trenton, NJ. North Bridge Press, $22.95.

To Avoid Job-Search Self-Sabotage . . .

• Don't think of yourself as just average.

• Do not assume the world knows you are talented.

THE RIGHT STUFF

Ask yourself—and a trusted friend or counselor, but not a member of your family, if he/she thinks you have the aptitude and talent to succeed at your dream. If so, you can always obtain additional education, training, and practice.

It's just a matter of analyzing what is lacking and then determining how you could go about acquiring it and how long it will take.

It's also useful to analyze your weaknesses—including any bad habits that may be bothering you.

Consider your family's financial needs (short- and long-term), such as living expenses, insurance, savings, and pension plans. Decide what you can cut out.

A certain amount of fear is healthy because it will force you to figure out how to deal realistically with financial problems and other hurdles. But don't let it paralyze you.

The most difficult fears to handle are those (often disguised) of your spouse, family, and friends who want to keep the comfortable status quo. Expect this opposition, and don't let it discourage you. If it does, you may not be ready to make the move.

SET A TIMETABLE

While it's important to set a timetable for your plans, don't expect to make your dream come true overnight. You might, for example, take night courses so you can keep working at your current job. If you've been laid off, you may have to take an interim job to tide you over.

If you are working with an outplacement firm, make it clear to the staff that your goal is to try the new endeavor, not repeat the old one. The staff of the outplacement firm may be able to help you assess your goals and get started on the new path.

As you spell out the various elements of your personal game plan, try to start on a self-improvement program that includes proper diet, rest, and exercise.

It is also a good time to concentrate on eliminating or reducing bad habits. Get help if necessary. You must be prepared to go after your dream with all of your determination.

Don't depend on luck. Luck requires being well-prepared when opportunity knocks. An action plan means setting specific programs of what, where, when, how, and costs. I suggest making detailed lists, even down to the type of new clothing you may need. Use a monthly calendar to schedule each of the activities required in your plan.

Map out one year. At the end of the first month, you will have a better idea of what you can accomplish on a daily and weekly basis without stretching yourself to the limit. You're striving for a lifetime program, not quick burnout.

At the end of six months and again at the end of a year, review your progress and reevaluate on the basis of your experience. Reassess your plan occasionally to make sure that you're not overloading yourself, neglecting your family, or lacking needed relaxation.

If events that are beyond your control have caused a temporary detour, don't panic. Write a new plan for the next 12 months, in which you add or delete parts of your original action program. Build on your strengths and cut down the weeds—those things that you no longer need to do.

Simple Ways to Reduce Job Stress

Samuel H. Klarreich, Ph.D.

Job-related psychological stress takes an enormous toll on Americans. It affects one of every five workers in this country . . . and costs our economy billions and billions of dollars a year in absenteeism, lost productivity, and medical expenses—including expenses caused by accidents and

Samuel H. Klarreich, Ph.D., vice president of Mainstream Access Corp., a Toronto–based consulting firm. He is the author of several books on stress, including *Work Without Stress: A Practical Guide to Emotional and Physical Well-Being on the Job*. Brunner Mazel Inc.

- Never complain about your present circumstances or your past employers.
- Avoid self-defeating behavior, like being late for interviews.
- Pay close attention to your personal appearance.
- Work to eliminate any personality traits that could distract potential employers—such as talking too much or too little or having poor posture.

Jobs for Lawyers: Effective Techniques for Getting Hired in Today's Legal Marketplace by Hillary Jane Mantis, Esq., director, career planning center, Fordham University School of Law, New York. Impact Publications, $14.95.

Better Interviewing

Go for the *Wow* factor. Give the interviewer what he/she doesn't expect in order to make you the unforgettable candidate.

Example: Bring along your own photo show detailing your accomplishments and goals on an interview.

Also: Read everything you can find about your prospective employer and its industry—including newspaper articles, annual reports, brokerage house analyses, etc. Use the information gleaned from this research during the interview to demonstrate your ability to meet the company's needs.

Sharkproof: Get the Job You Want, Keep the Job You Love . . . in Today's Frenzied Job Market by Harvey B. Mackay, chairman and CEO of Mackay Envelope Corp. HarperBusiness, $9.

SUCCESS PSYCHOLOGY

■ **Employees with drive** are sought by companies. But there are different kinds of drive. Individuals driven by a need to compensate for feelings of inadequacy may accomplish a great deal as entrepreneurs. But—they often do poorly in large organizations because they do not relate well to the concerns of others. People driven to identify with outside role models are much more likely to adopt the organization's concerns as their own, and to work with others for mutual success. *Key:* During the interview, ask questions that throw light on the source of the person's high drive.

Harry Levinson, Ph.D., publisher, *The Levinson Letter,* 404 Wyman St., Waltham, MA 02154, 24 issues, $98/yr.

■ **Beware of the charming job candidate.** Charm may result from a deep need to be liked. And it can be a sign of a self-centered personality. *To evaluate a charmer:* Ask about past job activities—a history of individual assignments may indicate a problem working with others. Note how often the candidate says "I." Ask the candidate to describe situations where he/she had to manage others, and deal with their problems and mistakes. Be wary if the candidate seems overly critical of peers and competitors.

Harry Levinson, Ph.D., writing in *The Levinson Letter,* 404 Wyman St., Waltham, MA 02154, 24 issues, $98/yr.

■ **The lack of a clear career objective** should not be held against a job candidate under age 30. Most people don't know what they want until they are well into their 30s, and build careers on circumstances that develop during that period. *Important to look for in a candidate under age 30*: Desire to succeed . . .

alcoholism, both of which often originate in stress. Stress produces a remarkable variety of emotional and psychological symptoms.

Typical: Rapid heart rate and/or breathing . . . stammering . . . a sense of isolation from colleagues . . . headaches, stomach aches, and chest pain . . . reduced sex drive . . . stomach upset, diarrhea, and other gastrointestinal problems . . . chronic fatigue and insomnia . . . sweating . . . proneness to accidents . . . ulcers . . . and even drug addiction.

If you suffer from one or more of these symptoms—or if a coworker or family member remarks that you seem irritable or ill—it's time to evaluate the stress in your work life . . . and, if necessary, take steps to alleviate it.

THE COSTS OF CHRONIC STRESS

Untreated chronic stress leads not only to burnout, but also to heart attack, stroke, and other deadly health problems.

Workers often try to control their job stress via nonpsychological approaches—exercise, hobbies, vitamin pills, special diets, vacations, etc. While these approaches are healthful and might afford temporary relief, they eventually fail. In fact, such approaches often wind up increasing stress levels.

Example: A man who jogs every day to reduce stress feels even more anxious than usual if for some reason he must forgo jogging even for a day.

Bottom line: Stress is a psychological problem, and it can be fully controlled only by a psychological approach. I believe that the best way to do this is to recognize the 12 types of myths that cause job stress . . . and to systematically replace these myths with attitudes that are healthy and more realistic.

STRESS-CAUSING MYTHS

Myth 1. **Something awful will happen if I make a mistake.** *Reality:* Mistakes in the workplace may be a source of embarrassment and frustration, but rarely do they lead to anything more dire than a reprimand. The lesson sounds trite, but it's wise—don't fear mistakes, learn from them.

Myth 2. **There's a right way and a wrong way to do everything.** *Reality:* What's right for one person or situation is often not right for another. Mistakes are common in business, and they seldom result in tragedy. In fact, many excellent business decisions appear at first blush to be enormous blunders.

Myth 3. **Being criticized is awful.** *Reality:* Criticism—of oneself and of others—is central to personal growth. Being criticized is not tantamount to failing, and the process should never be viewed as something to be endured. Instead, workers should welcome criticism as a learning opportunity. *Note:* Reject criticism that is abusive or disrespectful.

Myth 4. **I need approval from those around me.** *Reality:* While you might welcome praise for a job well done, you don't really need "positive strokes" to be a fulfilled worker. Expecting praise in a work environment where it is rarely forthcoming can lead to disappointment and frustration.

Myth 5. **I must always be viewed as competent.** *Reality:* No one is good at everything. Even if you were perfect, there is no guarantee that your co-workers would admire you. How others view you lies entirely within their control. Worrying about your image only sets the stage for anxiety and more frustration.

Myth 6. **People in authority must not be challenged.** *Reality:* Most superiors are willing to listen to their subordinates' complaints and criticisms—if these are presented fairly and constructively. In fact, many bosses welcome complaints because they suggest better ways to do things. If you're inclined to confront your superior, do so. Even if you don't get all you want, the act of speaking out releases emotions that might otherwise lead to anger.

Myth 7. **The workplace is essentially fair and just.** *Reality:* Hoping for total fairness at work is not only unrealistic, it's not even desirable. Some of the best and most productive business solutions result from controversy and argumentation, which may seem unfair at the time.

Myth 8. **I must always be in control.** *Reality:* The notion that you can easily meet every deadline and fill every quota is appealing, but it only sets you up for frustration and stress. Even the best routines and systems

SUCCESS PSYCHOLOGY

a track record showing achievement and the initiative to take on increasingly complex challenges . . . personality characteristics that match the company culture—such as ambition, honesty, and integrity.

Harry Levinson, Ph.D., editor, *The Levinson Letter*, 404 Wyman St., Waltham, MA 02154, 24 issues, $98/yr.

SHREWDER COMMUNICATIONS

■ **Link encouraging words with specific actions.** It is not enough to simply say, *You did a good job.* To boost the power of positive feedback, say, *You did a good job in making sure all of those people knew they had to come to the meeting with ideas on how to solve this problem.*

Heroz, by William C. Byham, Ph.D., Harmony Books, 201 E. 50 St., New York, NY 10022, $18.

■ **Keep telecommuters in touch** to preserve their psychological connection with the company and fellow employees. Build in as much human contact and interdependency as possible for each long-distance worker. *Examples:* Require visits to the office for meetings . . . give frequent feedback . . . encourage phone contact . . . make sure the person is included in celebrations and company social events.

Harry Levinson, Ph.D., editor, *The Levinson Letter*, 404 Wyman St., Waltham, MA 02154, 24 issues, $98/yr.

BETTER COACHING

■ **Most common criticism mistakes:**
Criticizing something personal about an individual rather than the person's work . . . trying to prove you are right and the other person is wrong, rather than trying to resolve the problem . . . using "made-up" examples to illustrate a point, rather than real ones . . . generalizing by saying "always" or "never," rather than pointing to specific instances . . . criticizing in public rather than in private . . . using obscenities.

Richard Kern, editor, Sales & Marketing Management, 633 Third Ave., New York, NY 10017, 15 issues, $48/yr.

■ **Beware of "reverse delegation."** This occurs when subordinates who are faced with tough decisions ask higher-ups to make the final call. *Trap:* A boss who starts making such decisions does the subordinates' work as well as his/her own—a common cause of managerial overwork. *Better:* When a subordinate comes in with a problem, say, *Yes, that's a problem. What do you propose to do about it?* This makes it clear that it is the responsibility of the subordinate to come up with a solution.

Ted Pollock, management consultant, Old Tappan, NJ, writing in Production, 6600 Clough Pike, Cincinnati, OH 45224, monthly, $48/yr.

■ **Performance evaluation mistake.**
Basing evaluations on opinions, such as that an employee "needs to improve" a certain skill. An employee will resent this and become defensive. *Better:* Illustrate any need to improve with specific examples of instances where the employee's behavior has led to customer complaints or other problems.

Don Schackne, employee relations consultant, Delaware, OH, quoted in Office Systems94, 941 Danbury Rd., Box 150, Georgetown, CT 06829, monthly, $36/yr.

break down occasionally. Rather than worrying about control, focus upon what you're doing . . . and what you want out of life.

Myth 9. **I must anticipate everything.** *Reality:* Surprises are inevitable on the job as in other parts of life. Sensing things before they happen and gauging colleagues' "vibrations" certainly make good sense—but remember, you are dealing with probabilities, not foregone conclusions.

Myth 10. **I must have my way.** *Reality:* Good salaries, beautiful offices, and prestigious positions don't come easily—in fact, they may never come. No doubt there will be setbacks along the way. Effective workers do their work conscientiously without insisting upon immediate realization of their goals. Certainly you can strive toward such goals. Just don't demand them as conditions of continued employment.

Myth 11. **Workers who make mistakes must be punished.** *Reality:* An effective workplace calls for effective teamwork . . . and teamwork is impossible when employees are continually trying to assign or escape blame.

Essential for workers: Acceptance, tolerance, patience, allowance for imperfections—in yourself as well as in others.

Myth 12. **I need a shoulder to cry on.** *Reality:* A compassionate coworker is often helpful in difficult times—but not essential. Workers who resent not having one only cultivate their own self-pity and dampen the morale of themselves and of people around them.

Best Ways to Avoid Sabotaging Your Own Success . . .

Steven Berglas, Ph.D.

Why do some seemingly sensible people act in ways that harm their own interests?

They set out to succeed but somewhere along the way they either misjudge how to achieve their goals . . . do not want to face criticism and failure . . . or defeat themselves with the intention of hurting someone else. *The most common types of self-defeating behavior and how to avoid them . . .*

DELIBERATE MISCALCULATION

Most of us go through life trying to overcome the hurdles set in our way. We avoid doing things that slow us down or increase the odds of failure. Those who exhibit self-defeating behavior choose strategies that will backfire.

Poor decisions are made either because of overconfidence or because the desire for a short-term gain is stronger than the appeal of a long-term goal.

Example I: Jane wanted to study clinical psychology in graduate school. After her initial application was rejected, she decided to show the school she was really a desirable prospect by taking a few courses as a nondegree student at her own expense . . . a good strategy if carried out correctly. But instead of demonstrating her prowess by taking subjects in which she could easily get A's, she took the hardest courses she could find and scored only C's . . . dooming her graduate school hopes.

Jane miscalculated because she was overconfident. Had she estimated her strengths and weaknesses

Steven Berglas, Ph.D., clinical psychologist and management consultant, Harvard Medical School, Boston, MA. He is coauthor with Roy F. Baumeister, Ph.D., of *Your Own Worst Enemy: Understanding the Paradox of Self-Defeating Behavior.* Basic Books.

MONEY SMARTS

How to Ask for a Raise without Getting Fired

Robert Half
Robert Half International

When I was in charge of an office of 250 employees, I had the same problems that all executives have, including one of the most difficult challenges—how to compensate employees. It's relatively easy to arrive at appropriate pay for the very best employees. On the other end of the spectrum, there are marginal employees—those who are at high risk for being let go when they ask for an increase in salary.

When I asked borderline employees why they thought they deserved an increase, their answers followed a pattern:

- *I haven't had a raise for more than a year.*
- *Others at this company who do similar work earn more money.*
- *Employees at other companies earn more.*
- *My expenses are going up all the time.*

All of these answers are inappropriate. Not only will they antagonize the person who grants such raises, they can also work against you—making you someone who is not worth promoting or even a layoff candidate. Here are some rules to avoid offending your employer when you ask for a raise:

- Don't threaten him/her or imply that you might resign—unless you're fully prepared to follow through.
- Don't compare your salary with that of others in your company or other companies. Your skills are probably unique, and presenting them as such

will improve your chances of getting that raise.

• Let management know that you like the company and your job. And add a true compliment to your boss, one that's not obviously flattery.

• List your achievements in the past 12 months. It might be difficult to remember them all—which is why it is important to write them down.

• Ask for what you want, and be prepared to compromise.

Key: Understand that *yearning* for a raise is not the same as *earning* a raise.

Robert Half is the founder of Robert Half International Inc. and Accountemps (Box 3000, Menlo Park, CA 94026), employment specialists in the financial, accounting and information systems fields. His new book is *Finding, Hiring and Keeping the Best Employees.* John Wiley & Sons, 605 Third Ave., New York, NY 10158. 800-225-5945. $22.50.

Jay Conrad Levinson

15 Ways to Earn Money without Having a Job If You Have No Capital

• **Teach.** If you're an expert, there is someone you can teach.

How: Contact the continuing education department of a local community college or private university.

• **Write ads for a local real estate agent.**

Strategy: Most house ads sound alike, so by writing ads that are different—warm, humorous, etc.—you can set yours apart from the others.

• **Be a ghostwriter.** Ghostwrite a newspaper column for a local

more realistically, her chance of success would have been much greater.

Example II: Gary was happily married and prosperous. For many years, he indulged his hearty appetite for eating, drinking, and smoking but avoided exercise. Not surprisingly, he suffered a heart attack while only in his early 50s. When the doctor told him he had to change his lifestyle, he did so . . . for a time.

But after just three months, Gary decided he couldn't do without his vices. Two years later, he had another heart attack . . . this one fatal.

While it doesn't always lead to such unfortunate results, the same kind of poor trade-off between present benefits and future costs is found in many kinds of self-destructive behaviors—drug addiction . . . excessive sun exposure . . . overdependence on credit cards . . . even procrastination.

To avoid miscalculation mistakes: Evaluate your strengths and weaknesses and the long-term costs and benefits of your actions as realistically as you can . . . and try to consider all the alternatives.

TRYING TO AVOID THE TRUTH

Many forms of self-defeating behavior occur because people don't want to admit their limitations. They sabotage their own success in ways like these:

• **Self-handicapping.** This occurs when successful people deliberately construct obstacles for themselves so they will have an excuse for failure.

Example: Whenever French chess champion Deschapelles played, he insisted on giving his opponent the advantage of removing one of Deschapelles's pawns and taking the first move.

Result: Deschapelles increased his chance of losing . . . but always had a good excuse if he lost.

• **Substance abuse.** Alcohol and/or drug abuse serves two purposes for self-destructive people. It helps them blot out their own faults and inadequacies . . . and gives them an external excuse for failure.

Example: Violinist Eugene Fodor was a national hero at age 24 after he won the Tchaikovsky Violin Competition in Moscow. But within a few years, his reputation sank as he turned to drugs and was eventually arrested after breaking into a hotel room.

Reason: Great fame at an early age creates great expectations in audiences . . . and great stress in performers. Drugs eased the stress Fodor felt and provided an excuse for his failure to perform adequately—but allowed him to believe in his musical ability.

To face the truth: Develop a sense of perspective on yourself, recognize your imperfections, and learn to accept criticism.

THE QUEST FOR REVENGE

Sometimes self-defeating behavior is a misguided attempt to redress emotional wounds inflicted in childhood.

Example: Despite obvious talent, Stuart, aged 36, would break rules . . . steal . . . drink on the job . . . in an obvious manner that was sure to be detected. Then his supervisor would reprimand him and threaten his job.

This replicated a pattern from Stuart's childhood, when his father would beat him. After the beating, while Stuart was sobbing, his alarmed mother would scream at his father until his father withdrew into a state of depression. Thus Stuart would enjoy the sweet taste of victory over his father . . . even though he was in physical agony himself.

I call this self-defeating strategy "Pyrrhic revenge," after the famous "victory" of the Greek king Pyrrhus, who won a battle against the Romans but almost wiped out his whole army in the process.

merchant who needs the exposure for his/her business.

Example: A gardening column that you write could run under the byline of a local nursery owner.

• **Lead walking tours** of your city's favorite tourist attractions.

• **Speak the language.** If you are fluent in a foreign language, you can teach it. If you speak only English, consider teaching English as a second language.

• **Take it all off.** Art and photography classes are always looking for nude models. *Good news:* You don't have to look like Kate Moss or Brad Pitt.

A Little Capital

• **Breed fish.** Contact area fish stores or local wholesalers about supplying fish that you breed. *Good idea:* Start with guppies—they breed quickly and are always in demand.

• **Clear snow.** If you already own a tractor or snowblower, offer to clear snow from parking lots, in front of stores, etc.

• **Develop a course.** If you know a lot about a specific subject and can reach the right audience, you can create and publish a course on the field. The course might consist of lectures, tapes, pamphlets, records, and/or books.

• **Be the life of the party.** Use your talent to entertain kids—and grownups—at parties.

Examples: Be a clown . . . puppeteer . . . magician . . . mime . . . story teller.

• **Talk about money.** If you have experience in financial management or have a financial background, hire yourself out as a financial planner.

• **Wash dogs**. Open a self-service dog wash where pet owners pay for the use of shampoos, washtubs, combs, etc., so they don't mess up their own homes.

Earn from Home

• **Bookkeeping.** If you've got a head for numbers, you can keep the books for local business owners.

• **Research.** With a computer and a modem, you now have access to a wealth of information that businesses will pay you good money to find.

• **Proofread.** Check the grammar and spelling of articles about to be printed by local newspapers, magazines, advertising agencies, etc.

Jay Conrad Levinson, a California-based marketing consultant and author of *Earning Money Without a Job: Revised for the '90s*. Henry Holt & Co., 115 W. 18 St., New York 10011, $9.95. And *Guerrilla Marketing*. Houghton Mifflin Co., 222 Berkeley St., Boston, MA 02116, $12.95.

Career Changing Planning Strategies

Key Questions and Answers

Joyce Schwarz

If you want to change your career, now's the time to do it. Employers today are more accepting of the idea of career change, new professions are emerging, and retraining opportunities abound.

But careful planning is essential. *Steps to take:*

• **Determine if your career is the real problem.** If you are less than satisfied with your current

Pyrrhic revenge is typically found in marriages in which one spouse suffered abuse as a child . . . often from an alcoholic parent. He seeks out a partner who has the same problem his parent had. He tries to correct the problem and, in doing so, cure his own childhood wounds. This usually doesn't work, so instead he ends up venting the repressed anger against the parent . . . and doesn't mind destroying himself as long as his spouse goes down, too.

To avoid self-destruction via revenge: Realize your own interests . . . judge whether you are acting to help yourself or to hurt someone else.

CHOKING UNDER PRESSURE

Choking is a self-defeating behavior that occurs when people under pressure, striving to do their best, fail because they try too hard to succeed and do not perform as well as they can.

Example: Beth, an outstanding student, had to recite a speech from Shakespeare in front of her high-school class. After memorizing it perfectly, she stood up to speak . . . and nothing came out.

Reason: Smoothly speaking memorized lines is an automatic process. Beth wanted so intensely to succeed that her self-consciousness prevented her memory from working naturally.

The same phenomenon causes sports champions to falter in important matches and winning teams to lose championship games.

To avoid choking under pressure: Develop perspective. Remind yourself that success in life doesn't depend on just one event.

Example: If it's the last minutes of an important event or presentation, and victory or defeat depends on your next move, remember that just being there shows that you already are a success.

Secrets of Great Second Careers

This decade has more opportunities for a second career than almost any other in history, thanks to changing lifestyles and a growing number of niche markets.

Important: Whether it's part-time or full-time work, don't rush into a new career without considering many alternatives. Today's large list of new careers gives you a chance to choose one that meets your resources, talents and expectations of profit. Best bets...

ANIMAL BREEDER

The 1990s have been boom years for exotic pets—llamas, pot-bellied pigs, miniature horses and a wide variety of parrots, for example. Though the fascination with some unusual pets is just a fad, others are probably here to stay.

Llamas, for instance, have lost some of their former popularity, but they've also gained a stronghold among people who want gentle, intelligent pets and have enough land to keep them. Start-up costs for raising birds can be as low as $1,000 for a breeding pair and equipment. Breeding llamas requires an investment of about $100,000 for five breeding pairs and a modest marketing campaign.

Advantages: If you enjoy animals, breeding them can be rewarding in itself. And profits can occasionally be high. Many hand-raised parrots, for example, cost more than $1,500 each. Male llamas sell for $500 to $5,000, females for $4,000 to $11,000 (and some fancy specimens for $50,000).

International Llama Association, 2755 S. Locust St., Suite 114, Denver, CO 80222. 303-756-9004.

NEW HORIZONS

work, your career itself may not necessarily be the cause of your anxiety. Instead, the problem could actually be with the job you're doing. *Questions to ask yourself* . . .

• **If I changed jobs—not my career—would I find the fulfillment I'm seeking?** An accountant I know was fed up with the restraints of corporate life. She couldn't get excited about the company's goals . . . and didn't even like wearing corporate business clothes.

Instead of changing careers, however, she found a similar job at a non-profit organization whose goals she shares . . . and where she can dress casually. Today, she is—very happily—the organization's controller.

• **If I kept my job but changed my lifestyle, would I be happier?** Many people who sit behind a desk and perform routine tasks all day have fantasies about having a more exciting career. One solution might be to find a job at a smaller company where you can do your same job but play a greater role. Another solution is to keep your job, but take up a hobby . . . or work weekends on other income-producing projects.

• **If you need a career change, research the day-to-day routine of the new career.** *Reason:* Many careers aren't exactly what they seem.

Examples: Nursing isn't just care-giving—it's dealing with stress . . . professional writing isn't nearly as solitary as it sounds . . . opening a business requires as much sales skill as financial acumen.

NEW HORIZONS

Helpful: Before rushing into a new career, subscribe to a professional journal . . . attend conferences or seminars where you can meet others in the profession . . . join a professional organization.

Those people who are successful in a new career do well because it matches their personality and values, regardless of how drastic the change may be.

• **Get great advice**. Large corporations don't change directions without getting the best advice they can find. Neither should you.

Helpful: Create your own "board of advisers"—a group of people whose judgment and experience can help steer you in the right direction. Advisers can include people who know you from work in your community . . . have extensive knowledge of the new field you're entering . . . appreciate your talents . . . have changed careers themselves.

Spell out your plans to members of this informal group and ask for honest feedback. They're likely to suggest ways that you can improve or fine-tune your plans.

Also ask for support and advice from your extended family. After all, they may have to bear the brunt of a temporary reduction in your income. Because family members know you better than most other people, they can often make useful recommendations.

Important: Don't take their advice as gospel. You're the one who has to make the ultimate decision.

• **To make the transition smooth, move slowly.** A slow transition makes sense when your finances are unstable or you're facing a personal crisis such as a divorce.

Disadvantages: If the species you raise isn't well known, marketing may be difficult. Animal raising is usually full-time work.

BOOKSELLER

Selling used books can be done from a modest store or even from your home. If you do it from home, start-up costs can be as low as about $5,000 for office equipment and a minimum of inventory.

Specialty bookstores—for children or computer buffs, for example—have much higher start-up costs because of inventory requirements and advertising.

Advantages: If you like books, you can indulge yourself and meet interesting people in the process. Disadvantages: Low profits, unless you have an eye for acquiring bargains and selling them to well-heeled collectors.

FINANCIAL CONSULTANT

You do not have to spend an entire lifetime in finance to be a financial consultant.

Reality: By taking courses in personal financial planning, you can become proficient enough to help many people who lack the basic knowledge.

Approved courses can be located through the Institute of Certified Financial Planners, 7600 E. Eastman Ave., Denver, CO 80231. This is an excellent resource to start with.

Advantages: Initial costs, including home office equipment and a study course, can be as low as $4,000.

Disadvantages: Difficult to launch. You may have to start by doing work at low or no cost.

IMPORTER

Importing can be a great second career now, thanks to an easing of worldwide trade restrictions and burgeoning free enterprise in a growing number of countries.

Initial costs usually run under $10,000, including a minimum of office equipment, one trip abroad and

The American Booksellers Association, 828 S. Broadway, Tarrytown, NY 10591. *How to Open a Used Bookstore* by Dale Gilbert, Upstart, 155 N. Wacker Dr., Chicago, IL 60606. $14.95.

Carl A. Nelson's *Import/Export: How to Get Started in International Trade*, McGraw-Hill Inc., 1221 Avenue of the Americas, New York 10020. $14.95.

making contacts with local retailers who may be interested in buying what you can import.

It's best to specialize in one or two types of products, such as handwoven woolens from Latin America or ceramics from Italy.

Advantages: Profits can be high if you find a product that's in demand in the U.S. Once you have a going business, you'll be able to write off part or all of your travel for tax purposes.

Disadvantages: Dealing with foreign agents and customs officials can be difficult and very expensive.

NONPROFIT ORGANIZATION FOUNDER

If you are dedicated to a cause, consider starting a nonprofit organization.

That might sound out of your reach, but it's really much easier than most people think, especially if you have a talent for raising money.

Advantages: If you have a personal cause, a nonprofit foundation can help fulfill your dreams. Ironically, you can often earn more from a nonprofit organization than from a for-profit business.

Reason: Though nonprofit groups rely on foundation grants and donations, people who work for them are usually paid a steady salary. That's more than can be said of many new business ventures.

Disadvantages: Start-up costs are about $10,000. You'll need natural sales talent to attract donors and professional advice in setting up a nonprofit corporation.

PET CARE

The market is growing fast in the 1990s for pet grooming, pet boarding and services such as dog walking. Even if you work from your home, start-up costs can run about $30,000 for a pet-grooming business since you'll have to take a course in the subject and buy special equipment. If you rent a

Society for Nonprofit Organizations, 6314 Odana Rd., Madison, WI 53719. 608-274-9777.

Most large cities have schools that teach pet grooming.

NEW HORIZONS

Example: Take a part-time job in your new profession to build up experience before you completely cut ties with your present source of income. Or, take a transition job in or outside of your targeted profession that gives you more time to prepare for the new career.

Joyce Schwarz, a career consultant whose corporate clients include AT&T, Walt Disney and IBM, 1714 Sanborn Ave., Los Angeles, CA 90027. Schwarz is author of *Successful Recareering.* Career Press, $12.95.

CAREER SAVVY

Winning Strategy for Job Interviews

Ask about a job's success factors early in the interview. Then show how those are precisely your areas of greatest strength.

Wrong approach: Asking interviewers to describe the perfect candidate for a job. Skillful interviewers will sidestep that question.

Right approach: Asking what factors are most important for success in the position. That's a more subtle way of asking the perfect-candidate question—and is more likely to be answered.

Knowing the success factors lets you show how your knowledge, skills and abilities prove that you have what it takes to succeed in the position.

Richard Beatty is president of Brandywine Consulting Group, a firm in West Chester, PA, that helps individuals find jobs, and author of *The Interview Kit.* John Wiley & Sons, $10.95.

When to Say "No" to a Job Offer

Nick Corcodilis

Say no when: Starting pay is low but you're promised a big raise "soon." Will the company put the date and amount of the raise in writing? Will it guarantee in writing a performance review in so many months? You have every reason to doubt the good intentions of a company that will do neither.

Say no when: You don't meet the person you'll be working for. The personnel department or a committee does the hiring, so you aren't able to measure your compatibility with the boss-to-be. If the company won't arrange a face-to-face meeting, it could mean the boss and your job are about to go out the window.

Say no when: The specifics of your job are not made clear. If all you get are vague answers when you ask about details, you may be headed toward a "broken job." The company may only want you for a short-term project or—even worse—to fill a head count.

Nick Corcodilos, president, North Bridge Group, management consultants and executive recruiters, 73 Old Mountain Rd., Lebanon, NJ 08833. He is author of The New Interview Instruction Book: A Guide to Winning Job Offers. *North Bridge Press, 800-792-3382, $25.95.*

space for a shop, initial costs can be double that amount.

Other pet services are less expensive to start, but you'll need insurance if you board or walk pets.

Advantages: Profits can be high in areas where there's not much competition for this work.

Disadvantages: Even if you really love and care about animals, it can be very hard and very demanding work.

PUBLICIST

If you are creative, enjoy working with people and are good on the telephone, there can be a real opportunity in getting publicity for people, businesses and organizations.

Simply stated, publicists make their living by persuading TV and radio stations, newspapers, magazines and newsletters to mention their clients.

Advantages: Start-up costs of less than $1,000 for a minimum amount of office equipment, plus letters to prospective clients. Profits can be high if you are successful.

Disadvantages: Getting your first client will be difficult. You may even have to start by doing volunteer publicity for a civic organization.

SEMINAR PRODUCER

If you have a skill or hobby that others would like to know about, there can be an opportunity in teaching at paid seminars.

You can rent space in a hotel or institution or even hold small seminars in your home. One-day seminar fees usually start at about $50 per person.

Start-up costs can be as low as $500 for a minimum amount of marketing, which usually includes placing an ad in publications read by people interested in the subject.

Advantage: Profits can be large if your specialty is popular.

Disadvantage: To succeed, you've got to be an entertainer as well as a teacher.

Mistakes People Make When Applying for College Financial Aid

Kalman A. Chany

Most parents need financial help when they are paying for their children's college educations. Unfortunately, many parents are not familiar with the best ways to apply for and receive financial aid.

Result: They pay more out of their own pockets and enroll their children in colleges that they can *afford*—rather than colleges that are ideal for their children.

Here are the most common mistakes people make when applying for financial assistance from a college:

• *Mistake:* **Assuming that you're not eligible for financial aid.** Many people don't even apply because they believe they are not eligible if they earn more than $75,000 a year or own their own homes . . . or they've heard that their neighbors applied and were turned down.

Reality: There is no real income cutoff. Sometimes families with incomes in excess of $125,000

Kalman A. Chany, president of Campus Consultants, Inc., a fee-based firm that assists families in maximizing financial-aid eligibility, 968 Lexington Ave., New York, NY 10021. He is the author of *The Princeton Review Student Access Guide to Paying for College.* Villard Books.

College-Cost Strategies

Mark Tuttle

Beware: Prepaid tuition plans have pitfalls. They accept an amount of money up front—in a lump sum or installments—and guarantee to cover tuition when a child is ready for college. If your child chooses not to go to college or doesn't qualify for a school in the plan, you will get minimal interest on the refund.

Many plans cover only tuition—but nontuition costs can be a big expense. The plans may affect financial aid eligibility...and can have tax consequences for parents and children.

Self-defense: Discuss plans with a financial adviser before investing.

Mark Tuttle, spokesperson, Institute of Certified Financial Planners, 7600 E. Eastman Ave., Denver, CO 80231.

■ **Beware of senior-year slump.** Instead of slouching toward graduation, high-school and college seniors should spend their senior years building their job-hunting momentum. Their résumés should show that, instead of simply puttering along during the final year of school, they revved up for entry into the world of work. *Helpful:* Increasing school activities...taking on short-term projects...acquiring new skills or polishing current ones. Many interviewers focus on senior-year activities because they feel that people who don't slack off have superior work habits.

Marilyn Moats Kennedy, editor, *Kennedy's Career Strategist,* 1150 Wilmette Ave., Wilmette, IL 60091.

COLLEGE COST-CUTTING

■ **Teaching children at home** does not make them social misfits. More than 300,000 U.S. families now educate at home—for religious reasons or from disenchantment with schools in their areas. A major argument against home schooling has been that it deprives children of peer contacts needed for social development. *New study:* There is no difference in adulthood between personal and social adaptations of home-taught and school-taught children.

Study of more than 50 adults who were taught at home by their parents, led by J. Gary Knowles, Ed.D., assistant professor of education, University of Michigan at Ann Arbor.

Better College Planning

Put extra money into retirement plans, rather than paying down your mortgage faster—if you want to cut your odds of taking out a tuition loan when kids reach college age.

Reason: Equity in your home is often counted as an asset by schools when determining financial aid. The lower your mortgage, the higher your equity—and the more these schools assume you will be able to contribute to your children's college education.

But money in retirement accounts is not counted when determining financial aid.

Eric Tyson, a personal finance counselor in San Francisco and author of *Investing for Dummies.* IDG Books.

receive financial aid. Financial aid is awarded based on a complex formula that factors in many variables, including the number of members in the household, the number of children in college and the age of the oldest parent.

• *Mistake:* **Failing to do any advance planning for the application process.** Eligibility is determined by taking a snapshot of your family's financial situation. If you are applying for your child's freshman year of college, the year that is scrutinized is from January 1 of your child's junior year in high school to December 31 of his/her senior year. Any financial transactions you make during that year could help—or hurt—your child's chances of getting aid.

Example: If you had accumulated some stock investments to pay for college and sold them during the first half of your child's senior year in high school, the capital gains on the stock would increase your income and reduce your eligibility for aid.

To give your child the best chance of receiving financial aid, you must plan ahead to accelerate income into earlier years and minimize discretionary income items during the key tax years that affect your eligibility for aid.

• *Mistake:* **Missing the deadlines.** Many people believe that the time to apply for financial aid is after the child has been accepted to a college.

Reality: It's crucial to apply for aid at the same time that your child is applying to colleges. There is a limited amount of aid available, and priority is given to those who meet the deadlines. Deadline extensions are rarely granted.

The best source of information about deadlines is the school itself. Be certain to find out if the material is to be postmarked, received or processed by the deadline.

• *Mistake:* **Not keeping track of the process.** Many families simply fill out the financial aid forms and hope for the best. They are not assertive enough and do not keep track of things. They also don't check in with the colleges.

Reality: You have to assume that things are going to go wrong. Check with the school and make certain it has everything it needs. Find out if there is anything else you could send to improve your chances. Make photocopies of all the forms in case you are asked any questions.

Important: Although instructions on the application forms will tell you not to send them by certified mail, I recommend you do so for your own protection. If your forms are lost or misplaced, the processing center of the college may try to claim that you never filed them. Using certified mail/return receipt requested gives you proof of mailing and delivery.

• *Mistake:* **Assuming the college will help you get the most financial aid possible.**

Reality: It's important to understand that the college is apportioning a pot of money . . . and demand exceeds supply. Therefore, it is not in the school's best interest to help you figure out how to maximize your child's financial aid.

• *Mistake:* **Assuming financial-aid packages are set in stone.**

Reality: It is often possible to negotiate a better package than the one you are initially offered by the college. One of your strongest bargaining chips could be a better financial aid package from a comparable school. You might say, "I'd really love to have my child attend your school, but money is an issue. We've been offered a more generous package from College X." Be honest about this, though, since you may be asked to provide a copy of that package.

Trend: The first offer that a college makes to parents is often not its best offer. The college wants to see if you will blink—and it is leaving room for bargaining. College officials will deny this vehemently, but every year I see colleges change the sizes of their awards.

• *Mistake:* **Rejecting student loans when they're offered as part of a package.** Many parents say "I don't want my child to borrow or to have debt when he/she graduates from school." Meanwhile, these parents have thousands of dollars in credit-card debt outstanding.

Reality: Student loans are great deals and compare favorably with other borrowing options.

Better: Take the student loans, use current income to pay off other debt and then, if you want to

■ **Make your babies smarter** simply by talking to them. *Example:* As you hand a child a wooden spoon, tell him/her what it is, how it feels, what it's used for. *Also:* Don't use baby talk. Speak correctly, in complete sentences. Speak face-to-face. Continually introduce new words. Once he begins speaking, correct verbal mistakes by repeating what he said, using the correct form. *Example:* If he says, "I doed it," say, "Yes, you did it!"

Starting Out Well: A Parents' Approach to Physical Activity and Nutrition by Lawrence A. Golding, Ph.D., director of exercise physiology, School of Health and Physical Education, University of Nevada, Las Vegas, NV. Leisure Press.

■ **Kindergarten basics.** There are two major and quite different approaches to kindergarten education. *Academic programs* stress intellectual skills through formal instruction. *Developmental programs* cultivate the whole child. Most schools emphasize one approach while including elements of the other. *Remember:* Five-year-olds are not ready to be chained to a desk. Young children learn best from hands-on activities. *Bottom line:* Choose a program that leaves a major part of the day free for play and child-selected activities.

Ready for School? What Every Preschooler Should Know by former teachers and syndicated newspaper columnists Marge Eberts and Peggy Gisler. Meadowbrook Press.

LIVING AND LEARNING

■ **Learn while you drive.** The average person drives from 12,500 to 25,000 miles each year. Translated into hours, that's one to two college semesters. *Helpful:* Use time spent behind the wheel listening to creative or self-help tapes or your favorite music. Avoid radio shows that cause you to think negatively.

101 Simple Ways to Be Good to Yourself: How to Discover Peace and Joy in Your Life by Oklahoma City stress consultant Donna Watson, Ph.D. Energy Press.

■ **Make learning easier** by not expecting to be perfect right away. Accept your mistakes until you learn to do things well. *Benefits:* You'll develop a solid foundation on which to build . . . you'll wipe out fear of failure . . . the more you learn about a subject, the easier it is to learn even more.

The Secret of Getting Straight A's: Learn More in Less Time with Little Effort by aerospace engineer Brian Marshall. Hathaway International Publications.

■ **Auditing classes.** You can still attend college even if you don't want a degree. Even the most prestigious, competitive colleges and universities will allow you to take two or three courses without actually applying to the school. Some let you "audit," or sit in on, classes. You pay a fee but do not have to complete exams or written assignments and, of course, you get no college credit. But auditing a course is a good way to see if you like a particular school, major or course.

College After 30: It's Never Too Late to Get the Degree You Need! by college and university consultants Sunny and Kim Baker. Bob Adams, Inc.

pay the student loans off in a lump sum after graduation, you can do so with no repayment penalty. In this way, you might save hundreds—or even thousands—of dollars in interest.

• *Mistake:* **Being unaware of other attractive borrowing options.**

Reality: Even if they don't qualify for need-based student loans, virtually all students qualify for *unsubsidized* Stafford Loans. The colleges' financial-aid offices can tell you how to apply for these loans.

Some colleges have their own loan programs, which may have very attractive terms. There is also the federal Parent Loans for Undergraduate Students (PLUS) program, which allows you to borrow the total cost of education less any aid offered.

Example: If the tuition costs $25,000 and your child is getting $10,000 in financial aid, he can borrow up to $15,000.

Borrowing strategy: Take out a Perkins Loan first, then a Stafford Loan, then a PLUS Loan.

• *Mistake:* **Assuming that outside scholarships are where the real money is.** People are always hearing about awards from fraternal associations, unions, and private foundations. They're told all they have to do is find these untapped resources.

Reality: These awards represent less than 1% of all financial aid available and, as many families find out, may not save you money.

Reason: The school reduces your aid package by the amount of the scholarship.

Strategy: If your child wins an outside award, try to convince the school to reduce the loan and work-study portions of the package rather than the grant money dollar for dollar.

• *Mistake:* **Misunderstanding the federal rules for divorced and separated parents.** Federal rules require that the parent with whom the child resided most during the 12 months prior to completing the application submit the financial information. Custody and dependency for income-tax purposes are not relevant.

Some colleges may also require disclosure from the other parent. Even in this case, state and some federal aid programs will still be based on only one parent's financial data.

• *Mistake:* **Misunderstanding the definition of an "independent student."** Many parents believe that if they don't claim a child on their income-tax returns for several years, the child will qualify as an independent student and the parent's financial situation will not be relevant for obtaining financial aid.

Reality: The parents may be paying several thousand dollars in additional taxes and accomplishing nothing. The requirements for independent-student status are straightforward. *The student must meet any one of the following criteria . . .*

• 24 years old as of January 1 in the academic year for which aid is sought.

• A ward of the court or have both parents deceased.

• A veteran of the U.S. Armed Forces.

• Married.

• A graduate-school or professional-school student.

• Have legal dependents other than a spouse.

• *Mistake:* **Failing to understand the implications of every financial decision you make** during the years you are seeking aid.

Reality: From January 1 of your child's junior year in high school to January 1 of his junior year in college, any decision you make could ruin your chances for aid the next year. *Common mistakes:*

• Withdrawing funds from a pension.

• Taking capital gains on securities.

• Overpaying state and local taxes so that you receive a large refund the following year.

Note: Widowed or divorced parents who remarry during a child's college years are sometimes unpleasantly surprised to find that the income of the new spouse is factored into the financial-aid formula.

EARLY LEARNING

■ **Children and reading basics.** Buy a bed lamp so children can read before going to sleep . . . play word games together . . . encourage them to contribute lines to letters you write . . . act out the stories you read together using different voices for different characters . . . give books as gifts . . . don't punish children by forcing them to read or write for a set period of time.

Child psychologist Lawrence Kutner, Ph.D., author of *Parent & Child: Getting Through to Each Other.* Avon Books.

COLLEGE CONNECTION

■ **Athletic scholarships** are awarded by even the smallest colleges. But these schools often don't have the budgets to recruit prospects. Assertiveness pays. *Helpful:* Ask high school coaches for leads . . . contact college coaches directly and let them know about your abilities . . . write a self-profile, including information about academics, family, athletic ability, honors. Apply during the 10th and 11th grades . . . senior year may be too late.

Marilyn Shapiro, editor, *College Financial Aid Strategies,* 14609 Woodcrest Dr., Suite 101, Rockville, MD 20853.

■ **Clever college-aid strategy.** Parents turned down for a federal Parent Loan for Undergraduate Students (PLUS) due to a poor credit rating have another financing option. Have your child apply to the Stafford Student Loan program. *Example:* A college freshman can borrow $4,000 over the normal $2,625 limit for dependent students. The student will be charged interest on the additional amount, but the variable rate is relatively low—now 7.43%.

Kalman A. Chany, president of Campus Consultants, Inc., a firm that advises families on financial-aid eligibility, 968 Lexington Ave., New York, NY 10021.

■ **Students do much better** in college when they form alliances with fellow students, faculty members and student advisers. *Recommended:* Enrollment in at least one small class every semester. The frequent interaction among students and between students and teacher helps counter the anonymity of large lecture classes.

Five-year study by Harvard University professors, led by Richard J. Light, professor of education, reported in The New York Times.

Secrets of Learning Any Language

Barry Farber

No matter how poorly you did when you had to study French or Spanish in school, you can still learn any foreign language now . . . *if you really want to.*

Teaching myself to speak 23 foreign languages during the past 46 years has helped me develop a method that maximizes language proficiency while minimizing the pain involved. It still takes a lot of work . . . but this method lets you have a lot of fun as well.

TOOLS TO LEARN A LANGUAGE

The secret of learning a language is to use all the tools available. Find a bookstore that offers a broad selection of learning materials in your chosen language. *Then acquire the following . . .*

• **Language textbook.** A basic text that covers grammar thoroughly. Before beginning any study of your new language, read the first five chapters over and over—until you understand as much as you can. If some sections remain incomprehensible, leave them . . . you will be able to understand them later.

• **Phrase book.** A phrase book for travelers contains many practical words and phrases . . . and tells you how to pronounce them.

• **Dictionary.** Get a two-way dictionary that has both English-foreign and foreign-English sections.

• **Language courses on cassettes.** The best are formatted courses that follow the Pimsleur method. This method doesn't simply repeat phrases in English and the other language, but it forces you to recall what you learned earlier.

Barry Farber, the nationally syndicated radio talk-show host and founder of The Language Club, Box 121, Times Square Station, New York, NY 10036. He is author of How to Learn Any Language. Citadel Press.

• **Flash cards** with English words and phrases on one side and translations on the other side provide a convenient method of rapid review.

• **Newspaper.** Get a copy of one newspaper in the language you are studying . . . preferably one from the country itself rather than one published in the U.S.

HOW TO LEARN A LANGUAGE

Spread out your newspaper and begin reading the first paragraph of the first article. Highlight every word you don't know with a marker. Look up these words in your dictionary.

Whenever you find a new word—or whole phrase—write it and the translation on opposite sides of a blank flash card.

If you find a word that looks similar to one that you already know, it is probably a different grammatical form of the base word found in the dictionary. Try to figure out the meaning in the newspaper from the context and the grammar you have acquired so far.

Put the dictionary word on a flash card. Write the words you don't understand on question cards to carry with you so you can ask their meaning from someone who knows the language.

Now go on and try to decipher the next paragraph.

If possible, set aside a block of time every day for language study. In addition to studying the grammar and the newspaper, start to learn the conversational phrases in your phrase book so you can try them out whenever you meet someone who speaks the language.

Listen to your cassettes . . . but not passively. Test yourself by hitting the pause button after an English phrase and trying to translate it yourself before you switch the cassette back on.

Wherever you go, carry a pack of flash cards. Review the cards in every spare moment—waiting for an elevator or phone connection, at the checkout counter, etc.

ELEMENTARY LESSONS

■ **Pick your child's classroom carefully.** Ask other parents and teachers, too—in the spring— before the next year's class assignments are made. You can then approach the principal with concrete information on why your child will work and learn better in a particular class. If the school doesn't respond, be persistent.

The Classroom Crucible: What Really Works, What Doesn't and Why by education-policy analyst Edward Pauly. Basic Books.

■ **Best time to meet teachers.** The start of the year, when your child's slate is clean and no problems have arisen. Open-house meetings usually take place six weeks after school starts. By then, a pattern has already been set—and these meetings are not for extended talk. *Better:* At the end of the first week of school, ask the teacher for a talk the following week. At the meeting, express general support and say that you will help if problems arise.

Save Our Schools: 66 Things You Can Do to Improve Your School Without Spending an Extra Penny by Mary Susan Miller, PhD, a former teacher and administrator who now teaches at William Patterson College, Wayne, NJ. Harper San Francisco.

■ **Help children learn to read** by giving them things they want to read. *Examples:* Write children notes instead of trying to get them to read from a plodding workbook . . . read aloud, even to older children . . . If a child is reading aloud and comes to an unfamiliar word, don't immediately ask him to sound it out. Ask, "What makes sense there?" This helps the child think about what word fits in with what he's reading.

Lawrence Kutner, Ph.D., child psychologist, syndicated columnist and author of Parent & Child: Getting Through to Each Other. Avon Books.

Help Kids Read Better

Richard Robinson, Ph.D.
University of Missouri-Columbia

Ask them questions that require thinking skills about what they've just read, not just recitation of specific facts and details.

Examples: Why did you like/dislike a character? . . . how is the character the same as or different from you?

Also: Before finishing the story, ask them to predict the ending. And use every opportunity to illustrate how reading is used in the "real world."

Examples: Describe how reading is important in your job . . . show how it is used in daily living—following recipe directions, reading the newspaper, looking up a number in the phone book . . . discuss how reading is necessary to stay informed about current political issues so you can vote in an educated manner.

Richard Robinson, Ph.D., professor of education, College of Education, University of Missouri-Columbia and author of *Twenty-Five Ways to Help Your Child Become a Successful Reader* (Language Arts Consultants).

How to Teach Yourself Anything—How to Do Well on Any Test

Adam Robinson

A super-high IQ is not essential to learn rapidly and efficiently. Whether you're in graduate school, taking continuing education courses or trying to assist a child in high school or college, there are studying techniques that will result in improved understanding, higher test scores and better grades.

Key: Take an active role right from the start. Don't approach the assigned reading passively and assume that if you simply pass your eyes over your textbook and notes enough times, you'll absorb it. Engage in an ongoing dialogue with the reading material.

KEY QUESTIONS TO ASK YOURSELF

• **Why I am reading this?** Before you begin reading, ask yourself if you are reading for general ideas or specific facts. And—how deeply you have to probe the material.

You can cut your reading time dramatically if you realize that you can skim much of the book—even skip parts that you will never need to know.

• **What do I already know about the topic?** Before you begin, spend a few minutes jotting down what you know already, what you think about it, and what you would like to know.

This will prime you to ask yourself relevant questions as soon as you begin to read the material and you will probably be surprised when you realize how many ideas come from your background knowledge.

Further, thinking for yourself before you give the

Adam Robinson, cofounder of the Princeton Review, a program that helps students do well on standardized tests, 2315 Broadway, Third Floor, New York, NY 10024. He is the author of seven books on education, most recently *What Smart Students Know: Maximum Grades, Optimum Learning, Minimum Time.* Crown Publishers Inc.

author a chance to influence you will improve your ability to form original insights and opinions.

Bonus: This exercise gives you practice at quick responses to new material, a valuable skill when you are faced with unexpected test questions or sudden real-life problems that you haven't studied.

After these preparations, skim the whole book. Pay particular attention, though, to the introduction, table of contents and chapter summaries and glance at the author's biography. All this information will help you answer the next question.

• **What's the big picture?** Once you begin reading, find out the main points and ideas conveyed by the book so that you don't get bogged down in details during the next stage, when you actually read the book in depth.

Your aim is to sustain an active dialogue that helps you learn as you read. Learning new material is often hard work that stretches your mind. The process becomes more enjoyable when you approach it like a game.

• **What is the author going to say next?** Try to anticipate the next step in the discussion. Even if you are learning something completely new, you can probably make a reasonable guess.

Example: If you are studying chemistry—a subject about which you know nothing—and you come to a section on "strong acid reactions," you can anticipate that the next topic will be something like "weak acid reactions"—even if it isn't, you will be more interested in following the discussion than you would if you were just reading passively.

Absorbing new material will become even easier when you answer the next question.

• **What are the expert questions?** These are the questions that are typically asked about the subject you are currently studying.

Example: Geology books repeatedly answer questions like "What is this made of?"; "What are its properties?"; "Where is it found?"; "By what process was it formed?" History textbooks deal with other questions like "When did it happen?"; "Who was involved?"; "What were the causes?"; "What were the effects?"

FOR BETTER READING . . .

Better Way to Read . . . for work or school

Brian Marshall

Read the book for four minutes, and divide by four to get your per-page rate for that book. Use the rate to calculate how much time the total reading assignment will take.

Add extra time before and after each assignment for previewing and reviewing the material.

Brian Marshall, a former aerospace engineer who worked on the space shuttle. He is now an entrepreneur and author of *The Secrets of Getting Better Grades: Work Smarter, Not Harder.* Park Avenue Productions, $12.95.

Seventh Grade

Laurence Kutner, Ph.D.

Seventh grade is a watershed year for most students.

Reason: School days are structured differently, with a different teacher for each subject. Many children have a hard time adjusting and grades may suffer. *When a child's grades slip:*

• Find out how your child perceives the situation and ask him/her to suggest solutions.

• Don't be surprised if he blames the teachers for being "too hard" or claims they don't "like" him.

• Explain that he has to do the work nonetheless.

• Talk to your child's teachers and ask for their thoughts on the problem.

• A child who forgets assignments or turns them in late simply may need a notebook to keep track of his schedule.

• Get your child to agree to a study schedule to complete each day's work.

• Instead of focusing on grades, focus on the quality of day-to-day work. If the work is done right, the grades will follow.

Laurence Kutner, Ph.D., child psychologist in Cambridge, MA, and author of Parent and Child: Getting Through to Each Other. Avon Books.

When you know the pattern of these questions, you can anticipate a lot of what will appear in tests.

• **What are my own questions?** To study more effectively, exercise your curiosity by asking general subject-related questions that interest you. Try to answer the questions; don't be afraid to guess.

Example: If you are studying financial planning and read that the amount available to a person in a case study for investment is the difference between earnings and expenditures, ask yourself when is it appropriate to increase earnings and when is it appropriate to reduce spending.

As you go further into the subject, you will find some of your answers are right, some are close and some are way off. Whatever the case, thinking inquisitively and comparing your ideas with the facts will help you master the material as it becomes more familiar and personally meaningful. As you read on, the next three questions will help you take notes that are useful to review the subject and study for tests.

• **What information is important?** That will, in large measure, depend on why you are reading the book. Don't waste time and effort compiling notes that are irrelevant to your real aim. In general, about 20% of the book contains 80% of the useful information.

• **How can I summarize this information?** The shorter you can make your notes, the more useful they will be, especially if you are preparing for a test.

Important: Use your own words. If you are just copying phrases from the text, there's a good chance you don't really understand it.

• **How can I organize the information?** Try grouping it in ways different from those of the text. See what connections you can find, play with the material, summarize with diagrams and sketches, acronyms, rhymes, and anything that makes sense to you and helps you remember it. The more you exercise your brain to organize the material, the better you will be able to understand and recall it. Aim to condense the whole subject you are studying until it fits on one page, then study that page until you can reproduce it from memory.

You are now ready for the big test. All the thinking and questioning you did while reading has prepared you to handle any question you are likely to get. Looking beyond the immediate payoff of passing the test, active learning stimulates your continuing intellectual growth.

How to Help Your Child with Schoolwork

Nancy Haug, M.S.

Many intelligent parents know surprisingly little about how best to help their children with their schoolwork. Prodded by guilt and ambition, these parents compensate for their limited time at home by putting enormous pressure on their kids to excel in school—and in extracurricular activities.

This maximum-involvement approach can be just as destructive as not helping your children at all. *Symptoms of maximum involvement . . .*

• Physically hovering over your child throughout the homework session.

• Chronically providing answers or dictating sentences.

• Thinking in terms of "my homework" or "my grade" . . . as if the teacher is evaluating you as well as your child.

DRAWBACKS

While maximum involvement may indeed produce higher grades, it is quickly counterproductive. A hovering parent creates an anxious, dependent child—one who is ill-equipped to cope in a class where many other children are vying for the teacher's attention.

Parents who keep children from making mistakes also prevent them from learning from those

Nancy Haug, M.S., a former elementary and junior high school teacher and the mother of five young children. She is the coauthor of Erasing the Guilt: Play an Active Role in Your Child's Education—No Matter How Busy You Are. *Career Press.*

Checklist: Sources of College Money

Laurie Blum

• **Corporations.** Employee tuition benefits are an underused resource for college money in the U.S. Thousands of companies have programs that support all or part of employees' tuitions . . . or of their employees' children.

• **Athletic scholarships.** Millions of dollars in college-sponsored athletic scholarships go unused each year, usually because too few students apply or qualify.

There is money available for archery, badminton, bowling, crew, handball, lacrosse—even synchronized swimming. The State University of New York at Purchase even has a Frisbee scholarship.

• **Special talents.** Students with unusual aptitude in any area of the arts or sciences may find a grant tailored to them.

• **Gender and ethnicity.** Many organizations specify funding for men, women or students of a particular ancestry. Some, such as the United Negro College Fund, are well-known. Others are not.

Examples: The Swiss Benevolent Society of Chicago . . . The Vatra's Educational Foundation, Boston, for students of Albanian descent.

• **Family affiliations.** Many unions, sororities, fraternities, religious and civic organizations give grants to members and their children.

• **Areas of study.** Countless grants are awarded in specific areas of study.

Examples: The National Press Photographers Foundation for students of photojournalism . . . the Quota International Fund for those studying education of the hearing impaired.

- **Personal circumstances.** There are scholarships for Jewish orphans, disabled students, daughters of deceased railroad employees, and children of those killed during military action or public service, among others.

- **College students.** Don't forget to apply if you are already in school or are returning to school. Many grants are for upperclassmen.

Example: The AT&T Undergraduate Scholarship for public relations students is for sophomores through seniors.

- **Smaller grants.** Don't neglect the smaller grants—several $500 grants can add up to make the difference between living at home or attending the college of your choice.

Laurie Blum, author of 20 *Free Money* books and a partner in Blum & O'Hara, a Los Angeles fund-raising firm. Among her most recent titles are *Free Money for College* and *Free Money for Foreign Study* (Facts On File) and *Free Money for Graduate School* and *Free Money for Athletic Scholarships* (Henry Holt & Co.)

mistakes . . . and confuse teachers as to what the children actually know.

Worst of all, these parents are sending a negative message to their children: "I don't think you're capable."

BETTER WAY

Fortunately, there is another way for busy parents to deal with homework . . . what I call *moderate involvement*.

The ultimate goal of homework is to help children develop the skills they need to be successful. Moderate involvement helps achieve that goal. It saves time, reduces guilt, and keeps the responsibility of homework and learning where it should be—with the child.

Moderate involvement with homework can be boiled down to two words: *Monitor* and *review*. What a moderately involved parent should do . . .

- **Establish a quiet, positive homework environment** . . . a set time and place out of range of television.

- **Find a convenient time to help the child.** If you're feeling rushed or preoccupied, you'll only get frustrated.

- **Confirm that the child can follow written directions.**

- **Avoid hovering** . . . especially with a child who feels dependent or indifferent about homework. After seeing the session off to a good start, say, "I'll be back in a while." Then back off for a fair amount of time before checking in again. *Trap:* Parents who stay in close proximity are tempted to give their children the answer . . . rather than letting them hunt for it.

- **Review the assignment after it is completed.** This lends added significance to the child's work.

STRATEGIES FOR SPECIFIC SUBJECTS

While moderate involvement keeps parents in touch with their children's studies, it also allows children to think for themselves . . . to develop responsibility and self-discipline . . . to reach their potential. This approach can be applied successfully to all subject areas. In each case, ask yourself: "What is the teacher trying to accomplish?"

• **Writing.** To encourage your child to express his/her own ideas—without being paralyzed by a blank page—start the session with some informal brainstorming. Toss around a few ideas with your child until he/she finds one that is attractive. Then help with the toughest sentence in any story or report—the first one.

If your child is capable of carrying on from there, assure him that you'll return . . . and retreat to another room.

After the report is finished, read it carefully. For beginning writers—first- or second-graders—it is inappropriate to harp on every error in spelling or punctuation. (This is especially true if your child is being taught with a "whole-language" approach, which stresses a free flow of ideas over perfect spelling.)

For all age groups, balance corrections with praise for whatever is positive in the work.

• **Math.** Monitor your child through the first one or two problems to make sure the correct process is in place. For the dallying student, set a 15-minute timer and announce, "I hope you'll be done with number 12 by the time I get back."

• **Science.** No homework is more prone to excessive parental involvement than science-fair projects. To avoid this trap, divorce yourself from the attitude that your child needs to win a blue ribbon. A science project should be a learning experience for the student—no more and no less.

To set the right tone, guide your child toward choosing a project that isn't too advanced or complicated for his age group.

If your school's science fair is already out of hand, with parents who are obviously doing much of the work, you might approach your child's teacher or principal, or the PTA. Propose a change in the fair's format—at least for the lower grades—to a less competitive "invention convention." This can relieve pressure on parents to compete . . . and return the projects themselves to their rightful owners . . . the students.

How to Do Well on Standardized Tests

Adam Robinson

Every year, about one million high school juniors and seniors take the Scholastic Assessment Test (SAT), the all-important college entrance exam.

While the SAT is the best-known, it is by no means the only standardized test. Most graduate schools and professions use them as qualifying tests.

Here's how anyone can do well...

Preparing for the Test

• **Allow at least six to eight weeks of active preparation.** Excellent preparation can raise a student's percentile ranking by 10 or more percentage points. On the SAT, such an increase can mean the difference between going to a state school or an Ivy League college.

Preparation courses offer advantages over private tutors and are less expensive. They drill you on the types of questions you'll see and create the same type of pressure-filled environment.

The quality of review courses varies. Sit in on a class and see the materials—too much can be just as bad as too little. Ask what is the documented average improvement . . . the nature of the guarantee . . . whether free tutoring is available.

• **The best materials are those prepared by the same people who publish the actual test.** Avoid computer software. Purchase books containing the actual exams given in previous years.

ONE STEP AHEAD

• **Just looking over practice questions is not enough.** Practicing 10 hours a day using the wrong technique makes you good at doing the wrong thing. Learn techniques for answering the different questions you'll face.

Examples: On standardized math tests, figures are drawn "to scale" and answers can often be estimated visually. Questions based on complex reading passages can often be answered using common sense.

Taking the Test

• **Show up early.** Position yourself for a good seat when the doors to the room open. When you enter the room, look for a wall seat near the back of the room—for more elbow room and fewer distractions.

• **When the test begins, don't leap into the first question.** Survey the exam for a minute or two to get a sense of the difficulty of questions.

• **Don't rush through the easy questions.** You'll make careless errors. And don't labor over difficult questions at the end—most test-takers are going to get those wrong anyway. Instead, spend most of your time on the medium ones, which tend to occur in the middle of any question type or any section.

• **Don't rush to finish.** Most standardized tests are designed to prevent all but the very best test-takers from finishing. Be willing to leave some blanks if you can't finish. Unless you're aiming for a near-perfect score, you really shouldn't push yourself to finish.

• **Trust your hunches on easy questions—but not on hard ones.** Answers to hard questions are

How to Win the Homework Wars

Lee Canter, *Canter and Associates*

Parents need not spend time helping their children with their homework if they create the proper learning environment. Here's how to win the homework struggle . . .

SETTING THE MOOD

• **Help your child find an appropriate place to study.** This must be a well-lit, comfortable place where there are few distractions. The place can be anywhere—even the kitchen table—as long as it is quiet and not cluttered. All necessary supplies should be close at hand.

The space should be respected by family members as a quiet zone. Post a *Do Not Disturb* or *Quiet Please* sign as a reminder during homework time.

• **Schedule homework into your child's life.** Just as your child may have a piano lesson at 3 P.M., he/she needs a set time each day when homework is to be done. When homework is scheduled in advance, you end discussions about when it will be done and put a halt to the child's stalling tactics.

Strategy: Show your child a schedule of the week's activities, and let him figure out the time for homework. By doing so, he accepts responsibility for doing his homework. The time scheduled depends on the amount of homework assigned.

HOW TO HELP

• **Do not do a child's homework for him.** If you do your child's homework, you send the message that he is not able to do it alone. You may also

Lee Canter, president of Canter and Associates, an educational consulting service for schools, 1307 Colorado Ave., Santa Monica, CA 90404. 800-262-4347. He also teaches assertive discipline classes and homework workshops to parents and educators.

Mr. Canter is coauthor of *Homework Without Tears* (Harper Perennial) and *Help: It's Homework Time* (Canter and Associates).

affect your child's learning experience. The teacher may use homework as a diagnostic tool and will receive a false impression of your child's abilities if the homework is really your work. Eventually, your child may reach a point when the material becomes too difficult even for you. At that point, your child could be left feeling helpless.

Better: Let children do their own homework from the start. Be sure to look over the homework, but resist the strong urge to correct it. Your corrections may defeat the purpose of the assignment.

Exceptions: If the teacher asks you to help your child . . . or if the child has done his best work and still has questions. Even then, you should help only occasionally.

• **Recognize a child's efforts.** Often parents yell when homework is not done—but say *nothing* when it is done. Paying attention only to bad behavior is a mistake because some children will then use unwanted behavior to get attention from you.

Better: Say *Great job!* when a child hands in homework on time or does a good job on something. Offer rewards such as *You did such a good job of starting your homework without arguing that you can stay up 15 minutes later tonight.*

TYPICAL PROBLEMS AND SOLUTIONS

• **Your child "forgets" his homework and leaves his books at school** . . . or he rushes through homework, leaving it full of mistakes and sloppy.

What it means: Your child may be forgetting to bring work home or racing through homework because he would rather be doing other things. The smart parent takes away all those other distractions.

Solution I: If books are left at school, the time he would have spent doing math and history homework should be spent doing something academic.

Solution II: If he is racing through homework, set a minimum time. If he finishes early, he must do another academic activity until the time is up.

• **Your child waits until the last minute to do assignments.** Help your child break down projects into parts, so they are not overwhelming. Put these tasks into the homework schedule.

never obvious. They usually appear in order of difficulty—easiest ones first and hard questions toward the end of a section.

• **Guessing rarely hurts—and can help significantly.** No standardized tests penalize guessing, including those that deduct a fraction for an error. Errors cost only a fraction more than "blanks"—which also count against test-takers.

Strategy: If errors are not penalized, guess. If errors are penalized, guess if you can certainly eliminate at least one choice.

• **Use process of elimination.** It is almost always easier to show why a choice is incorrect than to show why it's correct—especially for difficult questions.

Reviewing Your Performance

• **If you're *sure* you bombed, cancel your score.** If you guessed at most of the answers or couldn't answer many of them, your fear is probably justified.

To cancel, notify the test administrators at the conclusion of the exam or up to five days later.

• **If you are unhappy with your score and plan to retake a test, see whether you can request your original answer sheet.** Reviewing your answers and mistakes is highly valuable. A number of test publishers will make it available to you for a nominal fee.

Adam Robinson, education consultant and co-founder of the Princeton Review, a national program that helps students do well on standardized tests. He is author of seven books on education, including *What Smart Students Know: Maximum Grades, Optimum Learning, Minimum Time* (Crown Publishers).

Reading to Kids Is Great for All: How to do it best

Jim Trelease

Mistake: Insisting on reading books your children don't like—or don't understand. Many adults enjoy reading books that were their own favorites when they were children. The problem with many of these so-called classics—which were written 50 or more years ago—is that they often include words or phrases that are no longer used today.

Helpful: Review any older book in advance to be sure that these words do not slow down the tale. If the book is particularly special, translate the words before you begin reading it, so that you can explain what they mean.

Mistake: Reading all the words as they are written. There are many well-written books that don't lend themselves to being read aloud—at least not word for word. Passages used for descriptive purposes may slow down the action and excitement.

In other cases, stories may include sections that are inappropriately violent or too scary for a young child.

Example: In some traditional versions of *Little Red Riding Hood,* the huntsman at the end of the story slices open the wolf to release the little girl and her grandma, then puts rocks inside the wolf and drops the beast down a well.

With older children, this presents few problems—most know it is just a story. But with younger, more fearful children, improvise a similar but softer ending if your instincts tell you it is best.

Example: A research paper can be broken down as follows—pick topic...do research...write rough draft...edit draft.

- **Your child takes all night to finish his homework.** If the problem is that your child is not focusing on work, set a timer and have the child play "beat the clock." The child should try to complete his homework before the bell sounds.

HELP FOR YOU

Talk to the teacher if your child is having problems doing homework. There may be a problem, such as a learning disability or perhaps the teacher is giving inappropriate homework.

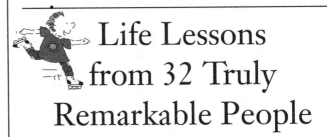

Life Lessons from 32 Truly Remarkable People

Guy Kawasaki, Apple Fellows Program

I have talked to some remarkable people in my life. But none were more remarkable than the 32 people I interviewed for my book.

INSIGHTS FOR EVERYONE

Some of these remarkable people were rich... some were poor. Some had achieved great success. Some had endured against overwhelming hardship. What struck me about all of these people was how their life experiences...their gains and their losses...heir triumphs and their traumas...had given them insights that could be shared with others.

Guy Kawasaki, former director of software product management for Apple Computer Inc., and now a participant in the company's prestigious Apple Fellows Program, Cupertino, CA. He is the author of *Hindsights: The Wisdom and Breakthroughs of Remarkable People* (Warner Books) and the current bestseller *How to Drive Your Competition Crazy* (Hyperion).

I asked many questions of these remarkable people. The most important question I asked was, *What have you learned from your life that you would like to share with the next generation?*

Here are the valuable lessons these people shared with me . . .

• **Most people give up when someone in authority—a boss or a bureaucrat—says *no*. *Be different*.** Don't listen when someone tells you to "sit down and shut up." Stand up instead, and shout "no."

If you come from a place of truth . . . if you align yourself with what is right and true and good . . . if what you seek will help others . . . then nothing can stand in your way.

Once you learn that lesson you will never be a victim again—instead, you will be a winner.

• **Persist against the conventional wisdom.** Just because the world says your idea isn't good doesn't mean it isn't. Trust that little voice inside you that tells you when an idea is good, even when everyone tells you otherwise.

There is never a right way or a wrong way to do anything. There is always a new and better way to do it. Beware of those who claim to be experts. They get so good at one way of doing things that they assume it is the only way to do it.

Go in the direction in which you think you ought to be going. Realize that your idea may *not* be very good if everybody tells you what a great idea it is. The opportunities for the big win aren't found where the crowds are, but where most other people are not looking.

• **Do it because you love it and you'll do it better.** Whether you're a truck driver or the chief executive of a *Fortune* 500 company, if you don't get a kick out of what you are doing you won't do it well. The world is filled with people who are smart and energetic. Unless you are, you won't succeed at what you're trying to do. But if you get a job that you love, you'll never *work* a day in your life.

• **If you want to succeed, be prepared to tolerate a lot of failure along the way.** You must accept failure as part of success—as long as you learn from each failure.

READING IS FUNDAMENTAL

Mistake: **Reading books with a lot of dialogue.** These stories are hard to read aloud. On the printed page, it is obvious who is speaking, but the listener can be confused—especially if the "he said/she said" doesn't come until the end of the line.

Strategy: Short of avoiding such books entirely, draw upon your acting skills and vary your voice with each character. But be forewarned—this requires a slower, more studied effort.

Mistake: **Lying down while reading.** Adults love to lie down with kids while reading because it makes the experience cozier and more intimate.

Problem: You will get drowsy and fall asleep. This is especially true of working parents who read to children in the evening. If you doze off, the result will be jabbing elbows from impatient kids . . . or kids who equate reading with boredom.

Solution: Read earlier in the evening, and always sit up straight. Shift from time to time to keep alert.

Mistake: **Ignoring a child's questions about the story.** Children react to readings with questions. They may not understand something or how it works . . . or they may want to know how you feel about the situation being described or if it ever happened to you.

Strategy: Don't become impatient or angry that you were interrupted. Stop reading, and take your time responding. Remind yourself there are no deadlines for finishing a book. Talk about the book for a few minutes after you close the cover. Ask what the child thought of the book and deflate possible areas of anxi-

READING IS FUNDAMENTAL

ety. You may, for example, need to re-mind a child, This is just a story that someone made up.

Mistake: Interpreting the book for your child. Always giving your opinion and explanation of the story may not leave much room for your child's opinions and interpretation.

Better: Discuss the book, but allow your children to view the story in their own ways.

Jim Trelease, one of the country's top experts on children and reading. He is author of *The Read-Aloud Handbook* (Penguin) and several other books that include read-aloud stories.

■ Talking at the dinner table boosts children's reading skills.

Kids who were exposed to interesting dinner-table conversation as preschoolers do better on vocabulary and reading tests in elementary school than those who were not. *Note:* Talking to kids about adult topics at any time increases their vocabulary and reading skills . . . but because of the pace of modern life, dinnertime is often the only opportunity parents have to talk at length with their children.

Catherine Snow, PhD, professor of education, Harvard Graduate School of Education, who led a study of 55 children.

If you try something but fail, think about what you did wrong and try it again. If you fail again, try a third time. Each failure brings you closer to success.

When you ultimately make it work, people will say, *What a success. This guy never fails.* What they don't see is all the misses before the hit.

Failure is horrible, but it happens and it's over, while success goes on and on. The only time failure is crippling is when you refuse to learn from it.

• **Don't let your personal misfortunes defeat you.** Everyone has handicaps. Some are just more visible than others. Whatever your situation, there are millions of people whose situations are worse. Whatever your problem is—physical or emotional—accept it and go on from there. Only you, and no one else, is responsible for changing that situation.

• **Always be ready to learn from others.** Your personality is there waiting to be developed. But how it develops depends on what you borrow from the world. All that we develop is borrowed from others—our parents, friends, relatives, teachers.

• **Don't accept society's judgment on who you are and what you can accomplish.** If you let the world cast you into a role, you never will go beyond that role.

Make your own definition of who you are and what you can accomplish. Above all, never see yourself as a victim. If you do, you truly have made yourself powerless.

Whatever hurdles to success you think you face can be overcome as long as you are willing to take responsibility for your own life and your own success.

• **Whatever else you have going for you, you need faith and spirituality to complete the package.** Great physical beauty or athletic prowess won't guarantee your success. Along with the physical and emotional sides of our being there must be a spiritual side. Don't see yourself trying things alone. See yourself trying them in partnership with someone who is greater than you.

That doesn't mean expecting miracles. You have to work hard. You have to take your own chances. You have to get up each morning and plan what you want to accomplish that day.

What Everyone Should Know about Estate Planning Now

Alexander A. Bove, Jr.

Most people think that by drawing up a will, they have done all that is necessary to get their estate and financial affairs in order. Nothing could be further from the truth.

Using a will to pass along property is one of the most expensive—and most vulnerable—ways to set up an estate. There are other, more advantageous and tax-effective ways to transfer property to your heirs. *What to consider when planning an estate . . .*

DON'T CONFUSE PROBATE WITH ESTATE TAXES

Probate is the legal process by which property in a deceased person's name can pass to his/her heirs or beneficiaries after debts and expenses of the estate are paid.

Probate property includes anything that is in the deceased's name alone at the time of death. It does not include jointly held property, assets that are payable to a named beneficiary at death, or assets in a living trust.

By itself, the probate process does not generate any revenue to the state or federal government in

Alexander A. Bove, Jr., a Boston estate lawyer and author of six books on estate and tax planning. His latest book is The Complete Book of Wills and Estates. Henry Holt and Company.

TRAPS TO AVOID

■ **Estate planning alert.** Be sure to update the beneficiaries of your IRA, 401(k), pension plan, and life insurance policies to reflect changes in your family's make-up—births, deaths, marriages, and divorce. You should review beneficiary designations in these assets—and in your will—at least every five years. *Best:* Make beneficiary changes promptly as circumstances change.

Laurence I. Foster, a tax partner in the personal financial planning practice of KPMG Peat Marwick, LLP, 345 Park Ave., New York, NY 10154.

■ **Think twice before selling** highly appreciated securities if you're seriously ill or getting on in years. *Reason:* You'll pay a capital gains tax unnecessarily. *Better:* Let your heirs inherit the securities. That way you'll beat the capital gains tax. *Another way to avoid capital gains tax:* Set up a charitable remainder trust. Give the securities to the trust. Let the trust sell them (with no capital gains tax). You'll get income for life from the trust without the capital being diminished by the taxes. *Bonus:* An income tax charitable deduction.

Laurence I. Foster, a tax partner in the personal financial planning practice of KPMG Peat Marwick, LLP, 345 Park Ave., New York, NY 10154.

■ **Do not underestimate the amount of your estate.** The $600,000 total that is exempt from federal estate tax may sound like a lot—but it is easy to exceed that figure without realizing it. *Why:* Your estate includes the value of your pension benefits, proceeds from life insurance, appreciation in the value of your house and similar items that you can't spend now but which will be subject to tax if you die.

Best: Avoid leaving part of your wealth to the IRS out of negligence. Survey your assets with an estate-planning expert and adopt a plan to avoid future taxes.

Irving Blackman, partner, Blackman Kallick Bartelstein, LLP, 300 S. Riverside Plaza, Chicago, IL 60606.

■ **An estate-planning diary** helps to document your assets . . . and provides a roadmap for your heirs. *Important:* Buy the right one. An estate diary, or organizer, serves as a one-stop aid for your heirs, who will need to quickly find vital information—funeral arrangements, location of safe-deposit boxes, list of investments, medical records, life-insurance policies, etc. *Trap:* Some organizers are more complex than they need to be. Others aren't complex enough. It all depends on what your needs are. *Self-defense:* Examine before you buy.

David Rhine, CPA, partner in the accounting firm of BDO Seidman, 15 Columbus Circle, New York, NY 10023.

■ **Living wills save money** during patients' last hospitalizations. Hospital charges for those Medicare patients who did not have living wills during their final hospital stays averaged more than $95,000. For patients with living wills, the average was $30,000. *Reason:* Living wills prevent patients from receiving any unwanted treatment—such as life-prolonging therapy.

Study of almost 500 Medicare patients, led by Christopher Chambers, MD, Thomas Jefferson University, Philadelphia, PA.

■ **Estate planning tool.** A durable power of attorney gives a person you choose the power to act as your agent and legal representative for specified

the form of taxes. But probate is a necessary process, and there are legal fees and expenses involved.

Estate taxes, on the other hand, are based on who had ownership and control of the property, regardless of whether that property had to go through probate. If there are estate taxes due, the probate court will not allow the beneficiaries to collect what is left of an estate until the taxes are paid.

INCLUDE A "NO CONTEST" CLAUSE

One way to discourage challenge to your will is to include an "anti-contest" provision. This provision states that anyone who contests the will automatically forfeits any bequest made to him/her. It does not mean that all contests are legally prohibited. It merely means that challengers will lose their share of your estate if they attempt to interfere with your wishes.

Of course, to make this clause work, you must leave potential challengers a meaningful amount . . . enough so that they will think twice before they rush to their lawyers and start running up legal fees.

PREPARE A DURABLE POWER OF ATTORNEY

This allows someone else to act for you in the event of your disability or incapacity. A regular power of attorney gives someone else the authority to act for you, but that authority automatically ceases if you become incompetent. In such cases, it is necessary to start probate proceedings in order to appoint a personal representative for you.

A durable power of attorney avoids the need to go to probate court because it survives your disability or legal incompetence. By naming someone to act as your "attorney in fact," that person is authorized to sign checks, enter contracts, buy or sell real estate, enter safe-deposit boxes, run your business, make transfers to your trust, and in some cases make health-care decisions on your behalf. Since this gives that person tremendous power, be careful about whom you select.

CONSIDER A "LIVING TRUST"

This is a trust you set up during your lifetime that can provide for your living expenses and other benefits while you are alive. Upon your death, it allows for the transfer of whatever property is left to your surviving spouse or other beneficiaries you name.

Since there is a lifetime transfer of the property to the trust and the trust specifies what is to be done with that property upon your death, the probate court does not get involved.

With most living trusts, you have the right to change or revoke the arrangement at any time. While this power to change the terms of the trust means you do not get any immediate income-tax benefits, it also means that the property placed in the trust avoids the costs, delays, and publicity of probate, and it can save estate taxes in the future.

A trust is very flexible and allows you to do just about anything, as long as it is not illegal. It can, for instance, run a business, provide for minors or elderly persons, pay medical bills, create a scholarship fund, and provide for retirement, education, marriage, even divorce. A trust can hold real estate, cash, securities, or any other type of property.

For the trust to become effective, you must actually "fund"—or transfer property to—the trust. All too often, people do not change the title on their existing holdings, so the trust has no substance.

If property is held in joint names, for example, those assets pass to the joint survivor. If property is held in your name alone, it must go through probate, and will go to the trust only if that is what your will provides.

Although some attorneys disagree, I think it is advisable for you to name yourself as trustee of a trust that you establish. This allows you to maintain full control over your property for as long as you wish and are able. You can also name a successor trustee to take over if you are ill or die.

PICKING THE RIGHT EXECUTOR

An executor's job is to collect and preserve all estate assets, pay all appropriate debts, expenses, and taxes, and distribute what's left according to the terms of your will. You are free to choose anyone

purposes in case you become disabled or incompetent. *Needed:* Language in the power of attorney document specifying that the holder of the power may continue to act on your behalf in case of your disability or incompetency. Without that language, a power of attorney automatically ends in case of disability or incompetency.

Retiring Right: Planning for Your Successful Retirement by Lawrence Kaplan, PhD, professor of economics, City University of New York. Avery Publishing Group.

■ **A shrewd way to save estate taxes** is to set up a family partnership to own assets. It is a way to move wealth to the next generation at low gift-tax cost. What you do is form a partnership with family members, with yourself as the general partner—you have 99% of the shares and the rest of the family has 1%. Every year you transfer parts of your interest to other family members.

David S. Rhine, a tax partner with BDO Seidman, CPAs, 15 Columbus Circle, New York, NY 10023.

■ **Proceed cautiously when making a gift** from a revocable trust. If you die within three years and the trust property is transferred directly to the recipient, the IRS may argue that tax liability is triggered on what would otherwise be a tax-free gift. To play it safe, the donor should first withdraw the property, and then make it a gift.

Assets, American Society of CLU & ChFC, 270 Bryn Mawr Ave., Bryn Mawr, PA 19010.

■ **Savvy estate planning.** List your miscellaneous personal property and the people you want to inherit it in a letter—not in your will—and keep it with your important papers. Then you can avoid the expense of revising your will each time your property changes. The executor must report all miscellaneous property to the IRS and pay any estate or gift taxes on them.

Martin Shenkman, an attorney in private practice in New York and New Jersey who specializes in estate, tax and financial planning.

Avoid Tax on Debts

Suppose your son owes you $10,000. Your will provides for cancellation of that debt upon your death. *Tax result:* Even though your estate does not collect it, the value of that debt is considered an asset of the estate that is subject to federal estate tax.

Better way: When the debt is first established, spell out that the payment obligation will cease at your death. *Result:* When you die, there is no repayment right for your estate to succeed to and there is no asset to be taxed.

Caution: The transaction establishing the debt should reflect the cancellation feature. *Example:* Your son is buying some stock from you. The stock is worth $100,000. If he gives you a note with a cancellation-at-death clause, the purchase price should probably be higher than $100,000. Otherwise, the IRS can argue that your son got more than he paid for and treat the transaction as partly a sale as well as partly a taxable gift.

Estate of Moss, 74 T.C. No. 91

you want to act as executor, and usually the probate court is obliged to follow your wishes.

But one other approval is essential to your selection of executor—that of the executor himself. So it is a good idea to discuss the matter with the person you choose, to be sure he/she will accept. After all, it is not an easy job, and if the person wishes, he can decline the appointment after your death.

Important: To guard against this occurrence or the possibility that your executor may die before you, make sure you name at least one successor executor in your will.

It is essential that you not name as executor someone who may be hostile to your heirs or beneficiaries. The problem is that, while the family may fume over such an appointment, there's usually very little they can do to overturn it after you die.

PICKING THE RIGHT ATTORNEY

Fashioning a plan to distribute your property after your death involves interrelated components, and a will is just one of them.

To find an attorney experienced in this field, see if there's an "estate-planning council" in your area. This is made up of professionals who specialize in this field. Request the names of two or three attorneys to interview. *Alternative:* Ask the trust department of a local bank for its best referrals.

Inform the people you call that you are interviewing attorneys to help you make your estate plan. *Some questions to ask . . .*

• **What are your feelings about avoiding probate?**

• **What are your recommendations about choosing an executor?**

• **Do you recommend that I act as trustee of my own living trust?**

• **Can you tell me how to transfer assets to my living trust?**

Ten Biggest Estate Planning Mistakes . . . and How to Avoid Them

David Gerson

A good estate plan can slash your estate-tax bill so you can leave more to your heirs and less to Uncle Sam. As you fine-tune your estate plan, watch out for these common mistakes:

• *Mistake:* **Failing to use the annual $10,000 gift-tax exclusion.** The IRS lets you give away up to $10,000 a year per donee free of gift tax to an unlimited number of people. Spouses who want to make joint gifts can give each donee $20,000 a year.

Solution: Set up an annual gifting program to reduce the size of your estate. Consider making gifts at the beginning of the year so that the income being produced by the sum will no longer be your tax problem.

• *Mistake:* **Overusing the estate-tax marital deduction.** The IRS lets spouses leave each other property free from estate tax. But leaving everything to your spouse increases the family's estate-tax bill. You forfeit one of the $600,000 estate-and-gift-tax exclusions available to you when you die.

Example: Jack leaves property worth $1.2 million to his wife, Mary. No estate tax will be owed because of the estate-tax marital deduction. When Mary dies, one-half of her property will be sheltered by her $600,000 exclusion. Taxes owed on the other $600,000 will be about $250,000.

David Gerson, tax partner and regional director of estate planning, and Charles R. Cangro, senior tax manager, Ernst & Young, 787 Seventh Ave., New York, NY 10019.

Plan Your Estate to Transfer Wealth Too

Irving Blackman

When you draw up your estate plan, focus on strategies that transfer wealth rather than just cut estate taxes.

Example: If you have large amounts in qualified retirement plans—such as a 401(k) plan, Keogh, or IRA—you may want to cash out and use the funds to buy life insurance.

Reason: Funds left in retirement accounts will first be included in your estate and subject to estate tax, and then subject to income tax when paid to your beneficiary. The combined tax rates can be as high as 73%.

But if you use the retirement funds to buy life insurance and place the insurance in a life insurance trust to remove funds from your estate, your heirs will receive the insurance proceeds free of both estate and income tax.

Thus, much more will be transferred to them—even if you pay income tax amounts taken out of the retirement plan to pay the premiums.

Irving Blackman is a partner, Blackman Kallick Bartelstein, LLP, 300 S. Riverside Plaza, Chicago, IL 60606.

Cut Estate Tax

John N. Evans

Significantly lower estate taxes on family-owned real estate by placing it in a family limited partnership (FLP).

How: A parent acts as the general partner and gives partial interests to children and grandchildren each year.

Tax breaks: Gift interests generally escape the parent's taxable estate...annual gifts valued up to $10,000 can be made free of gift tax ($20,000 if gifts are made jointly with a spouse) . . . FLP interests can be valued at a discount due to lack of marketability, so interests still owned by a parent who dies will incur less tax, and the underlying property is gifted at a discount.

John N. Evans, tax partner, enterprise group, Arthur Andersen LLP, 1345 Avenue of the Americas, New York, NY 10105.

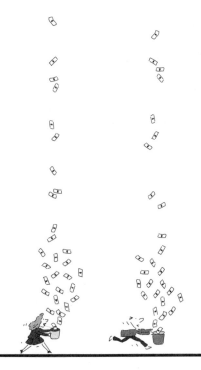

Solution: Jack puts $600,000 for Mary into a trust that does not qualify for the estate-tax marital deduction. When Jack dies, no estate tax will be owed because the $600,000 remaining in his estate will be sheltered by his $600,000 lifetime exclusion. Mary will receive income from the trust for life and when she dies, the children will receive the property in the trust. No estate tax will be due on Mary's estate because the $600,000 she owns outright will be sheltered by her exclusion.

• *Mistake:* **Making no plans to shelter taxable life insurance proceeds.** Many people are not aware that life insurance proceeds in their estate are taxable if they push the estate over $1.2 million. After taxes, your heirs receive the remainder.

Solution: Transfer ownership of the insurance policy to your children or other beneficiaries, or if you are planning to buy an insurance policy, make your heirs the owners. *Another option:* You can fund a trust with a life insurance policy. Your spouse can receive income for life, and the trust proceeds can pass to your children when your spouse dies.

Important: If you die within three years of transferring an insurance policy, that asset is still considered part of your taxable estate. So make any necessary changes as soon as possible.

• *Mistake:* **Making gifts to someone who uses the money to pay for medical or educational expenses.** When you pay a medical or educational institution directly on someone else's behalf, you can exceed the $10,000 annual limit on tax-free gifts.

Solution: By paying medical or educational costs yourself, you can reduce the size of your estate by more than the $10,000 allowance—without owing any gift taxes.

• *Mistake:* **Setting up a living trust to reduce your estate-tax bill.** Living trusts—trusts set up during your lifetime—have no impact on estate-tax liability.

Solution: Understand that estates of people who have living trusts bypass probate, thereby eliminating those costs. Living trusts also prevent the public inspection of your estate. But don't rely on them to save estate taxes.

• *Mistake:* **Saving the unified credit to shelter estate assets at your death.** The $600,000-per-person estate-tax exclusion also applies to gifts that are made during your lifetime.

Solution: In some cases, it makes more sense to make large gifts of property during your lifetime than after your death. This will shelter gifts from taxes by reducing the $600,000 lifetime estate-and-gift-tax exclusions.

The reason for making such gifts is that you can remove all future appreciation on the gifted property from your taxable estate. *Good assets to consider:* Interest in a family-owned business, partnership shares, real estate, growth-oriented stocks, and mutual funds.

• *Mistake:* **Not keeping your beneficiary designations up-to-date.** Beneficiaries must be named on many assets. *Examples:* Life insurance, retirement plans, bank and brokerage accounts. That's why it is easy to inadvertently leave valuable insurance proceeds to a former spouse, for instance.

Solution: Check beneficiary designations whenever there have been major changes in your life. *Examples:* Marriage, death, birth of a child.

• *Mistake:* **Holding all assets jointly.** Houses, brokerage accounts and other assets held in joint names pass by law to the survivor when one holder dies. As a result, carefully constructed estate plans are rendered ineffective.

Example I: When a married couple's jointly held assets pass automatically to the surviving spouse, the $600,000 lifetime exclusion for the deceased spouse is forfeited. *Better:* Set up a credit-shelter trust, which shelters this lifetime exclusion from estate taxes.

Example II: John has remarried, but wants his children from his first marriage to inherit his assets when he dies. If the accounts are held jointly, his second wife would automatically inherit them. John can set up a trust to give his second wife income over her lifetime and then distribute the assets to his children after her death.

Solution: Consider how assets are held before developing an estate plan and make changes, if necessary.

Five Key Estate Planning Documents

Sidney Kess, Esq.

Five legal documents that protect you and your family . . .

Will to direct how you want your assets to be distributed and to name guardians for your minor children. If you die without one, strangers may make these decisions for you—and charge your estate a hefty fee for doing so.

Durable power of attorney authorizing a trusted agent to handle your financial affairs if you are incapacitated.

Health-care power of attorney that gives your agent power to make medical decisions for you if you are incapacitated.

Living will directing whether you want to receive life-prolonging medical care if you are incapacitated and in a terminal medical condition.

Financial inventory listing all your assets and the locations of key documents, so they will be available to your agents or next-of-kin if needed.

Sidney Kess, Attorney and CPA, 630 Fifth Ave., New York , NY 10011.

■ **Estate tax trap.** Choosing the wrong executor for your estate can result in estate taxes being overpaid. *Worse:* They can be underpaid, which causes problems with the IRS. The person charged with the responsibility of being your executor should be financially knowledgeable and well-organized. *Best:* Name an executor who is used to dealing with finances.

Randy Bruce Blaustein, Esq., senior partner, Blaustein, Greenberg & Co., 155 E. 31 St., New York, NY 10016.

WILLS . . . WILLS . . . WILLS

All about Wills

James Jurinski, Esq.

What happens if I don't have a will when I die?

A. You will have died *intestate*. In such cases, the state in which you live makes one for you. State law dictates who will inherit your property and in what proportion. It will also be left to the state to decide who oversees your estate and who becomes the guardian for minor children.

Having a will allows you to make disproportionate distributions to heirs. It also helps avoid family conflicts by appointing an executor* to settle your estate. A will can be used to protect a surviving spouse by leaving sufficient property to maintain his/her current lifestyle. It also enables you to control death tax consequences.

*A person or bank trust department who will collect your property, pay taxes and debts, distribute assets to heirs . . . and receive a fee for so doing.

• *Mistake:* **Constructing an estate plan that uses the marital deduction to reduce estate taxes** when a spouse who is not a U.S. citizen inherits property. No estate-tax marital deduction is available for noncitizen spouses.

Solution: While the marital deduction does not apply, the annual exclusion for tax-free gifts is raised from $10,000 to $100,000 for noncitizen spouses. Consider a lifetime gift program or set up a qualified domestic trust, which would be eligible for the estate-tax marital deduction.

•*Mistake:* **Omitting foreign-owned assets from your estate plan.** Assets owned anywhere in the world by U.S. citizens are subject to the U.S. estate tax.

Solution: Review your estate plan, taking into account all assets owned worldwide. Look into the estate-tax credit for foreign taxes paid and the impact of any tax treaties between the U.S. and countries where you own property.

Trusts Are Not Only for the Rich

Martin M. Shenkman

F ew people realize how valuable trusts can be for their own estates. Too many mistakenly assume that trusts are only for the fabulously rich and not for those with just a family home, a company pension and a life insurance policy. But even these people can, benefit substantially from trusts.

Reason: Trusts save thousands of dollars in gift and estate taxes *and* provide a way to manage these assets when the original owners are no longer around. They also can protect assets from creditors and malpractice suits.

Martin M. Shenkman, a tax and estate attorney who practices in New York and New Jersey. He is author of several books, including *The Complete Book of Trusts*. John Wiley & Sons

Trusts need to be set up properly if they are to be effective, so be sure to consult an attorney. *Here are five of the most basic types of trusts and what they can do for you . . .*

LIFE INSURANCE TRUST

Let's say you own your home and have some modest investments, a pension, and a $500,000 life insurance policy. If your children are the beneficiaries of the insurance policy, your family could owe the government hundreds of thousands of dollars in estate taxes.

Reason: Life insurance proceeds, while not subject to federal income tax, are considered part of your taxable estate and are subject to federal estate tax with rates of 37% to 55%.

Solution: Create an irrevocable life insurance trust, which will then own the policy and receive the cash payout upon the policy owner's death. *Benefits:*

•**Income for the beneficiaries.** The irrevocable life insurance trust can be structured so that your survivors receive some or all of the annual income generated by the trust. The survivors can even receive the principal—subject to certain restrictions.

•**Avoidance of estate taxes.** If it's properly structured, such a trust ensures that insurance proceeds escape taxation in your estate as well as the estate of your surviving spouse.

In addition, because the proceeds are not included in your taxable estate or your spouse's taxable estate, they are not part of the public record and escape publicity. They also are not affected by probate costs.

•**Protection of assets.** The trust protects the insurance proceeds from creditors and malpractice actions.

•**Reliable management.** By naming a family member and an outsider, such as a bank or an accountant, to manage the trust assets, you eliminate the problem of inexperienced or incapable beneficiaries investing the trust's money.

CREDIT SHELTER TRUST

The primary purpose of a credit shelter trust is to preserve the $600,000 tax exemption—*the unified credit*—that all individuals get in their estates.

WILLS . . . WILLS . . . WILLS

If I have a living trust, do I also need a will?

A. Many people rely on a living trust** as a "will substitute." The trust is used to name a person—or trustee—to manage the trust's property, pay debts and death taxes, and distribute the assets to heirs according to the terms set forth in the trust instrument.

Setting up a living trust does *not* eliminate the need for a will. Not everything a person owns may be in the trust. For example, you may have a pending lawsuit that is settled after your death. The award, as an asset belonging to your heirs, is not in the trust. A will can say who will inherit the award.

Can I disinherit a spouse? A child?

A. You can't disinherit a spouse. All states have laws protecting surviving spouses. With community property laws and what is known as the right of election against a will, surviving spouses are entitled to share in a portion of the estate (from 25% to 50%, depending on state law).

However, a prenuptial or postnuptial agreement can be used to waive state-granted rights of protection to surviving spouses. Generally, for such an agreement to be valid (and override state law), there must be full disclosure of assets by both parties and each party must be represented by a separate attorney.

A child does not have the same protection as a spouse and can be disinherited. A will need not leave anything to a child, but should specifically mention the intention to disinherit.

**A revocable trust set up during one's lifetime which generally can be changed until death.

55

WILLS . . . WILLS . . . WILLS

Does having a will save estate taxes?

A. The will, by itself, does not save estate taxes. However, it can be used for this purpose.

Examples: A will can be used to make maximum use of the unlimited marital deduction (which allows spouses to leave each other an unlimited amount of property estate-tax-free). It can also be used to allow both spouses to make full use of their $600,000 estate tax exemption.

Do I need an attorney to write a will?

A. No, but it's a good idea to use one. An attorney will see to it that the will meets state requirements. He/she can also suggest tax, saving measures.

Generally, an attorney will charge under $500 for a simple will. You can save some of this cost by knowing what you want before you see the attorney. Decide who you want to inherit your property and who you want to name as executor.

James Jurinski, Esq., CPA and author of *Keys to Preparing a Will.* Barron's.

Under the law, everyone can give away $10,000 a year to individuals and $600,000 during his/her lifetime or upon death tax-free. Most couples own all their property jointly and have wills in which the husband leaves everything to the wife and the wife leaves everything to the husband. This may not be the best arrangement.

Example: Let's assume that a couple jointly owns an estate worth $1.2 million. When the first spouse dies, there will be no estate tax because of the unlimited marital deduction. But when the second spouse dies, the estate, which is now larger, will owe about $225,000 in estate taxes.

Solution: When your joint estate exceeds $1.2 million, divide all joint property equally between you and your spouse. For example, change a joint brokerage account into two separate accounts with half the assets in each. Then create a credit shelter trust under each spouse's will. The trust will allow the estate of each spouse to escape tax by taking maximum advantage of the $600,000 unified credit.

Example: Going back to the couple mentioned earlier . . . when the first spouse dies, $600,000 of his assets goes into a credit shelter trust for the benefit of the second spouse. (When the second spouse dies, $600,000 of her assets passes directly to the children or other heirs—with no estate tax).

Whichever spouse survives can have the right to receive all the income produced by the trust. That spouse also has the right to take principal from the trust to maintain his/her standard of living. It's almost like having the assets in your own name.

Important: It's not enough to just create the trust. You may also retitle your joint property in separate names so that upon your death the property can be transferred to the trust in order for it to save your family estate taxes.

Q-TIP TRUST

A *Qualified Terminable Interest Property (Q-TIP)* trust defers taxes and helps you attain a personal goal. Its aim is to ensure that after a spouse's death, assets exceeding the $600,000 unified credit pass first to the surviving spouse tax-free and then to the individuals for whom they were ultimately intended.

Without a Q-TIP trust, the assets could pass from the surviving spouse to his/her children from a different marriage.

Benefit: The trust is often used in second marriages to provide lifelong support for a current spouse. Then it funnels assets to the children from the first marriage after the stepparent's death.

Under this arrangement, your current spouse receives all of the income annually from the trust for life.

After your current spouse dies, *your* children—not your spouse's children from a previous marriage or any other beneficiary that your current spouse may have—inherit the principal. Even though your spouse's interest in the trust property terminates upon death, the initial transfer of property to the trust still qualifies for the unlimited marital deduction.

CHILDREN'S TRUST

This trust is designed to provide for your children and addresses a problem that occurs with gifts to children under the Uniform Gifts to Minors Act (UGMA) and Uniform Transfers to Minors Act (UTMA).

Problem: Under UGMA and UTMA, once children reach age 18 or 21, depending on the state in which they reside, they can do whatever they wish with the money in their custodial accounts.

Benefit: By transferring assets to any children's trust, such as a *Crummey trust*, the trustee can determine how the money in the trust is used and how much the child can receive.

GRANDPARENTS' TRUST

This is similar to the children's trust, except that the grandparents establish it to help pay for their grandchildren's college expenses.

A separate trust can be created for each grandchild. The limit that can be placed gift-tax-free in the trust each year is $10,000 per grandparent. Otherwise, the grandparent begins to eat into his $600,000 credit.

Important: Avoid setting up a single trust that names more than one grandchild as the beneficiary. Otherwise, you will run into the expensive generation-skipping transfer tax, which in many cases applies to transfers of more than $1 million.

WILLS . . . WILLS . . . WILLS

Estate Plan Redo

Robert Carlson

Change your estate plan when any of these events occur:

• Change in marital status.

• Birth or adoption.

• Serious illness, disability, or special support needs of an heir.

• An heir's request for gifts while you're alive instead of under your will.

• Forgiven loans.

• Change of residence.

Caution: Watch carefully for changes in estate value. If you are leaving specific amounts to some people and the balance to your surviving spouse, your spouse could be shortchanged if stocks or other assets drop in value.

Robert Carlson, editor, *Bob Carlson's Retirement Watch*, 8245 Boone Blvd., Suite 700, Vienna, VA 22182.

IMMUNIZATION CHECKLIST

Vaccinations: Is Your Child up to Date?

At what ages should children be immunized against childhood illnesses? For years, federal scientists and pediatricians affiliated with the American Academy of Pediatrics held different views. That left parents confused.

Now: There's finally widespread agreement over a single, straightforward schedule . . .

- **Birth to two months:** Hepatitis B.
- **Two months:** Diphtheria-tetanus-pertussis (DTP), Haemophilus influenzae type B (HiB), oral polio vaccine (OPV), Hepatitis B.
- **Four months:** DTP, HiB, OPV.
- **Six months:** DTP, HiB, OPV.
- **Six months to 18 months:** Hepatitis B.
- **12 to 15 months**: DTP or DTaP, HiB booster, measles-mumps-rubella (MMR).
- **Before kindergarten:** MMR. Or, this may be done at 11 to 12 years, depending on your doctor's recommendation.
- **Four to six years:** DTP or Dtap booster, OPV booster.
- **Eleven to 16 years:** Adult tetanus-diphtheria (Td).

Recommended Childhood Immunization Schedule for the U.S. Advisory Committee on Immunization Practices, the American Academy of Family Physicians and the American Academy of Pediatrics.

Better Familying . . . the Basics

Lawrence Balter, Ph.D.

By observing their parents, children learn how to cope with life—including how to deal with conflict. To be successful parents, fathers and mothers must learn to conduct their disagreements effectively. If this is done correctly, their children will learn a valuable lesson—that people who love each other can solve their problems in ways that satisfy both sides.

PARENTAL ARGUMENTS AND CHILDREN

No conscientious parent deliberately sets out to argue in front of his/her children. . . but in a family setting, it is virtually impossible to keep every disagreement hidden from them.

Even when they are too young to understand words, children are remarkably sensitive to the emotional signals of disagreement—such as facial expressions, body language, and tone of voice.

Children of all ages are distressed if their parents lose control when disagreeing. The distress is reflected in different behaviors as they develop.

Toddlers who witness shouting matches between their fathers and mothers may become fearful and agitated. Some begin to copy their parents' shouting

Lawrence Balter, Ph.D., professor of applied psychology at New York University. He is coauthor of *Not in Front of the Children: How to Talk to Your Child About Tough Family Matters*. Viking.

and table pounding . . . others suddenly burst into tears. They feel their own security is threatened when their parents show disunity.

Preschoolers understand more of the details of the argument. They may try to stop the fight by diverting their parents' attention to other matters . . . perhaps even by directing the anger toward themselves.

Example: Jane and her husband were in the front seat of the car bickering about the shortest route to the beach. Five-year-old Suzie started to hug her mother from behind while pointing out the beautiful flowers on the roadside. Meanwhile, three-year-old Sam began calling out in a loud voice, kicking the back of the front seat . . . and then punching himself.

School-age children are not only worried about their family security . . . they also feel socially embarrassed. They take sides in arguments.

Example: Martha was angrily accusing her husband of being stingy when eight-year-old Tom joined the fray, telling his father, " . . . and the last time I asked you for money for a new video game, you turned me down, too."

As Tom's case points out, sometimes children try to manipulate parental disagreements to their own advantage . . . and feel guilty later. More often, they blame themselves for the argument, inventing fanciful theories to explain how their actions caused their parents to quarrel.

It doesn't take an all-out screaming match to upset children. Hostility between parents that is expressed indirectly through sniping and sarcasm is also disturbing . . . and lays the foundation for children to develop the same style of behavior when they grow up.

HOW TO HANDLE DISAGREEMENTS

- **Don't deny that an argument occurred.** You can't fool children by pretending that you and your spouse are in agreement when obvious discord has upset the emotional atmosphere. They will figure out on their own that something is wrong and likely think it is worse than it actually is.

If parents deny their anger, children learn that anger is unacceptable and begin to bury their own

PARENTAL CHALLENGES

Saying No Is Not Enough

To help keep your kids away from drugs:

- **Boost their self-esteem.** Praise them every day . . . tell them how much you value them, and treat them in that way . . . suggest they make positive statements such as "I am a valuable person."

- **Encourage them to pursue activities they enjoy and excel at.** Support their choices—cheer them on at sports events and watch them perform in plays, concerts, etc.

- **Set a good example.** Don't smoke . . . use alcohol in moderation . . . practice constructive stress-management techniques.

- **Know your children's friends.** Make them welcome in your home so you can help guide your kids' activities.

If you suspect your children use drugs: Don't accuse them, but express your concern and reasons—poor grades, missed school, drugs found in the house, etc.—and get a professional evaluation to determine if there is a drug problem.

Lee Eggert, Ph.D., associate professor of psychosocial nursing, University of Washington, Seattle, WA.

■ **Children of single parents** are more likely to engage in early sexual activity, binge drinking, smoking, and attempted

PARENTAL CHALLENGES

suicide than children in two-parent households. But many single parents raise very healthy kids. *Keys:* Parental support and control, including rules to be followed and discipline when needed . . . community involvement . . . focus on education . . . teaching values, especially the value of helping others.

Peter Benson, president, Search Institute, a Minneapolis-based nonprofit research organization that focuses on youth issues. He led a study of more than 47,000 students in grades 6 through 12.

■ **Inaccurate portrayal of guns** in movies and on TV encourages kids to see guns as "cool," easily controlled weapons—and, therefore, as a good means of conflict resolution. *Reality:* It's very hard to hit anything with a handgun and even harder to kill someone with a single shot, we hear from James Boen, Ph.D. Bullets—even from powerful guns—cannot knock people over. And guns fired in enclosed spaces make ear-splitting noise. Explaining these inaccuracies to children helps discourage an unhealthy interest in firearms.

James Boen, Ph.D., is associate dean of academic affairs, School of Public Health, University of Minnesota, Minneapolis, MN.

■ **Less active students:** Only 36% of high-school students in grades 10 through 12 take part in vigorous physical activity for 20 minutes or more at least three times a week—down from 62% in 1984.

From a survey by Michael Pratt, M.D., M.P.H., medical epidemiologist at the Centers for Disease Control, Atlanta.

■ **Overcoming stereotyping.** Nontraditional fathering helps girls do better in school. Example: Fathers who encourage their daughter's athletic achievement

feelings rather than learn how to deal with them in positive ways.

What you should do: Acknowledge the argument and encourage your children to express their feelings about it. No matter how large or small the argument, tell the children who saw it that they can talk to you about it.

What to say: Tell your four-year-old child, "I know you just saw Mommy and Daddy yelling at each other. It was very upsetting for all of us. We're sorry. . . sometimes grown-ups lose their tempers. It wasn't your fault, and, of course, we still love you as much as ever."

• **Don't plead your case to the children or expect them to take sides.** It's not your child's job to be judge and jury over your disputes. And if you enlist a child to take your side, it threatens his relationship with your spouse.

What you should do: Explain the content of the disagreement in simple, neutral terms . . . give just enough information to reassure the child.

Example: Sara and Jeff had a heated argument over accepting Jeff's mother's invitation to dinner. The psychological origin of the dispute is Sara's resentment of Jeff's inability to refuse his mother's requests. Sara should tell the children, "You know how much Grandma likes us to come for dinner, but I would prefer not to go there tomorrow. I'd rather go next week instead."

• **Don't trivialize your spouse's anger**— or try to humiliate him/her. A child who sees that one parent repeatedly discounts the other's feelings and attitudes will conclude that the second parent need not be taken seriously. But children want two parents they can look up to . . . and they need to learn that adults take other people's concerns seriously.

What you should do: Find out why your spouse feels the way he/she does, and try to improve the situation with respect, not with ridicule.

• **Don't walk out of the house in anger.** A child who sees you leave may imagine that you will never come back . . . and think that if you can leave your spouse, one day you might leave him, too.

What you should do: If you feel so angry that you really can't take it any more, tell the child before you leave . . . reassure him you'll be back soon. Tell him, "I really must go out for a while, but don't worry. I'll be back to tuck you into bed."

   • **Don't resort to violence.** Dishes should stay in the cupboard . . . books on the shelves. Violence immediately destroys trust between people . . . makes it impossible to resolve disputes sensibly . . . threatens the physical safety of children caught in the middle . . . and teaches them to react to their own problems in the same way.

Important: Don't use profanity either . . . unless you want to hear your children imitating your performance.

What you should do: Learn to recognize the real source of your anger and tell your children about it.

TWO BASIC RULES FOR PARENTS

   • *Rule 1:* Learn to stop a developing argument in its tracks. Plan a strategy with your spouse when you feel a discussion is about to escalate into an angry exchange. One of you might say, "This isn't the place for us to argue. Let's stop now, and we'll discuss it later." Keep in mind, though, that despite your sincere efforts, you probably won't always succeed in avoiding arguments.

   • *Rule 2:* If you do have a major argument in front of your children—let them see when you make up. Show them that grown-ups aren't perfect . . . but when they make mistakes they own up to them and apologize. You want your children to learn these two rules of adult life.

PARENTAL CHALLENGES

help them to overcome passive female stereotypes and to function independently.

Repeated interviews with 240 fathers during a 40-year period by developmental psychologist John Snarey, Ph.D., Emory University, Atlanta, and described in his book, *How Fathers Care for the Next Generation.* Harvard University Press.

. . . AND MORE SAFETY

■ **Drowning prevention.** *For kids younger than four:* Never leave them alone near *any* source of water, including bathtubs, toilets, pails, spas, wading pools, irrigation ditches, etc. Swimming lessons do not "drown-proof" children— they may create a false sense of security. *For kids five through 12:* Teach them to swim, but be aware that swimming in a pool is very different than swimming in a lake or ocean. Make sure that they do not swim alone or without adult supervision. Insist that they use life preservers while boating or fishing. Know the depth of water in which your children swim. Make sure they know the dangers of jumping or diving.

Murray L. Katcher, M.D., Ph.D., professor of family medicine and pediatrics, University of Wisconsin Medical School, Madison, WI.

■ **Infants who sleep** on their backs are less likely to suffer sudden infant death syndrome (SIDS) than those who sleep on their sides or bellies. SIDS cases in Bristol, England, dropped from about 40 per year to none following a nationwide campaign to educate medical professionals and parents about SIDS and sleeping position. In the United States, the American Academy of Pediatrics has warned against putting babies to bed on their bellies. However, some pediatricians have criticized the Academy, saying the warning deflects attention from other SIDS risks, including bottle feeding, smoking, overheating or overexposing a baby, or using a too-soft mattress.

Study by Peter Fleming, M.D., pediatrician at the Institute of Child Health, Bristol University, England. Reported in *Medical Tribune*, 257 Park Ave. South, New York, NY 10010. 24 issues. $75/yr.

EYES, EARS, AND THROATS

■ **Can even a small amount of lead exposure harm a child?** Children exposed to lead early in life—even those with only slighty elevated levels of lead in their blood—can suffer impaired intellectual and academic perfomance in later years.

Study of 148 children conducted at the Harvard Medical School and Children's Hospital, Boston, led by David C. Bellinger, Ph.D., assistant professor of neurology, Harvard Medical School.

■ **Hearing problems** during infancy and early childhood can have a severe, negative effect not only on speech development, but also on learning and emotional growth—even an individual's vocational and economic potential. *Danger:* Hearing problems are usually not diagnosed until a child reaches almost three years of age—well past the critical period. *Better:* All infants should be screened for hearing problems during the first three months of life, ideally before leaving the hospital.

Ralph F. Naunton, M.D., director, division of communication sciences and disorders, National Institute on Deafness and Other Communication Disorders, Bethesda, MD.

■ **Regular eye exams** should begin at age four. This way, eye problems can be fixed *before* they become permanent.

Communication Lessons for Parents

Nancy Samalin

Even though our intentions are good, it's easy for parents to use words or phrases with children that are insensitive at best—hurtful at worst—and that actually work against the results we want.

This is especially true when we're annoyed, frustrated, tired, or stressed. We react automatically and don't even think about what we're saying.

One of the quickest and best ways to change this pattern is to watch out for red flag words. These are usually short, simple words that almost always escalate any conflict with a child—or a spouse or anyone with whom we have a close relationship.

By becoming aware of these words, we can substitute expressions that are more likely to result in cooperation and understanding.

WORDS TO AVOID

Most red flag words occur at or near the beginning of a sentence.

"If"—usually followed by "you"—when used as a threat.

- *If you do that again, you'll be sorry.*
- *If you don't get in that bathtub, there will be no story tonight.*
- *If you keep leaving your clothes all over the floor, I won't buy you any more this year.*

Many children perceive a threat as a challenge and may repeat the offense just to see what the parent will do.

These threats are often impossible to carry out. We make them when we're least rational—and often when we've lost control of the situation. And, if we don't follow through on the threat, the child stops

Nancy Samalin, founder and director of Parent Guidance Workshops in New York. She is consulting editor and columnist for *Parents* and author of *Loving Your Child Is Not Enough: Positive Discipline That Works* and *Love and Anger: The Parental Dilemma*. Penguin Books.

taking us seriously—we lose the ability to be authoritative.

In addition, a threat that is irrational or out of proportion relative to the offense doesn't teach the child anything about the realistic consequences of his/her behavior.

Better: "As soon as" or "when." These phrases are more positive and less punitive. They encourage you to stay rational—and make a statement that can be followed through.

 • *As soon as you've taken your bath, we'll have a story.*

 • *When you've hung up your jacket, we can play a game.*

"Who started it?" Obviously, this question applies to an argument or fight between two or more children. *But think about it:* Have you ever heard any child answer "I did?"

This question implies that we are looking for somebody to blame rather than trying to resolve the problem effectively. The result is likely to be even more fighting or finger-pointing.

Better: Take a neutral, problem-solving approach.

 • *You two have a problem. There's only one book here, and you both want it at the same time. What can you do about that?*

Instead of looking for a bad guy, you're helping the children work out a solution to the problem.

"Why"—especially when followed by "don't you," "can't you," or "won't you."

 • *Why don't you pick up your things?*
 • *Why can't you keep your hands to yourself?*
 • *Why won't you listen?*

These questions are unanswerable. In fact, we're not even asking why because we want a rational answer. Instead, we are really just blaming or making a critical statement. Children are not likely to cooperate when they feel they are being accused.

Another common use of the word "why" is "Why did you" . . . as in, "Why did you hit your sister?"

Children don't usually know why they do things. They're basically impulsive—and don't think before they act. You're likely to get a useless response such as, "I don't know, I felt like it," or, "Because she's a dork."

EYES, EARS, AND THROATS

Examples: Wandering eye, misaligned eyes, crossed eyes. These are usually correctable via simple outpatient surgery. Left uncorrected for more than a few months, however, they can progress to a condition known as *amblyopia* (lazy eye)—which can cause a permanent loss of visual acuity in the affected eye.

David Weakley, M.D., assistant professor of ophthalmology, University of Texas Southwestern Medical Center, Dallas, TX.

■ **Early eye exams for babies**—at the age of six months—can nip vision problems in the bud. Crossed eyes and focus problems can cause amblyopia (lazy eye). Loss of vision can be prevented by the diagnosis and treatment of these problems as early as possible.

L. Bruce Mebine, OD, president, California Optometric Association, Sacramento, CA.

■ **Infants and hearing loss**. Observe how your infant responds to sound. Infants should recognize the sound of a parent's voice . . . should look toward someone calling his name . . . and, by one year, understand common words like "no" and "bye-bye." If hearing loss is suspected, consult an audiologist. Hearing tests can be performed on infants as young as one day old. *Important:* The sooner hearing problems are detected, the better the chance that a child can be helped to develop normal speech and language skills.

Wende Yellin, M.S., director of communication and vestibular disorders, University of Texas Southwestern Medical Center, Dallas, TX.

COLLEGE BOUND

■ **Grades in college-prep courses** rate highest as a determining factor for college admissions. Eighty-two percent of surveyed admission counselors say this is a very important consideration. *Other key factors:* Admission test scores (46%), class rank (42%), grades in all subjects (39%), counselor recommendations (22%), teacher recommendations (21%), essay/writing samples (14%), interviews (12%), work/extracurricular activities (6%).

National Association of College Admission Counselors, 1631 Prince St., Alexandria, VA 22134.

■ **Better college application essays.** If you can choose your own topic, avoid academic ones unless you really know the material. Stay away from religion . . . and sex. Be careful of very personal topics or explanations of why you want to go to college. *Key:* Admissions people look for writing ability—not existing knowledge. Write clear, crisp prose. Avoid humor if there is any chance it could be misinterpreted. *Recommended:* Have your essay reviewed by someone who can write.

College After 30: It's Never Too Late to Get the Degree You Need! by college counselor Sunny Baker. Bob Adams, Inc.

■ **College success strategy:** Plot the coming semester on a calendar. Using the syllabus for each class, enter each test, paper and assignment date so you can prepare in time. *Helpful:* Note in particular those deadlines that fall within a day or two of each other so you'll know when to plan for extra working time.

College Survival by Greg Gottesman, a recent graduate of Stanford University. Prentice Hall, 15 Columbus Circle, New York, NY 10023. $11.

Better: Leave out the why and change the question to a clear, firm, nonaccusatory statement.

- *There will be no hitting.*
- *Those toys need to be picked up.*
- *I would appreciate your hanging up your jacket without my reminding you.*

"Never," "ever," and "always."

- *You never think about anybody else.*
- *When will you ever learn?*
- *You're always such a slob.*

These words can become self-fulfilling prophecies. They hurt a child's self-esteem and discourage him from trying to change. What they really say to the child is, "You're a disappointment . . . you're hopeless."

Better: Be concrete—describe your expectations clearly and specifically.

- Instead of "You never do anything I ask," try, "It's your job to take out the garbage, and that needs to be done this afternoon."
- Instead of "You never pick up after yourself," try, "I expect the blocks to be put in the toy box."

"You" . . . plus a negative adjective, noun, or phrase.

- *You're impossible.*
- *You're selfish.*
- *You're spoiled.*
- *You're a clod.*
- *You're acting like a baby.*

At worst, these are global statements about a child's character, which he can't change, as opposed to statements about his behavior, which he does have some control over. Even when they address his behavior, the statements are perceived as accusatory and negative. Accusations put people—children and adults alike—on the defensive, and a defensive person isn't likely to be reasonable.

"You" statements can be destructive to a child's self-esteem. Like "always" and "never," they can be self-fulfilling prophecies and are not likely to encourage your child to cooperate.

Better: Instead of telling your child what's wrong with him, talk about yourself, and keep it short. Try "I'm mad," which is much more effective than

"You're bad." An "I" statement encourages the child to take your feelings seriously—and respect them.

Beware: "I think you're bad" does not qualify as an "I" statement—it's still a "you" statement that happens to start with "I."

Another alternative is a brief, impersonal reminder about house rules, such as, "The rule is no TV until you've finished your homework."

How to Teach Kids Responsibility

Nancy Samalin

Responsibility in children—or anyone—is much more than just remembering to do chores or being obedient. It means caring about how your actions make other people feel and understanding why rules are important.

TO TEACH RESPONSIBILITY

•**Set an example.** Kids may not always listen when we lecture them, but they watch us carefully and draw conclusions about appropriate behavior from our actions.

Example I: You and your son are rushing to get to a store before it closes. You stop to help a woman carry her baby stroller up the stairs. Your child learns—it's good to go out of your way to help other people.

Example II: At the movies, you lie about your daughter's age so that her ticket is cheaper. Your daughter learns the nonresponsible message—*it's okay to lie.*

• **Whenever your kids take responsibility**, notice it—and express your appreciation. Re-

Nancy Samalin, founder and director of Parent Guidance Workshops, 180 Riverside Dr., New York, NY 10024. She is author of *Loving Your Child Is Not Enough: Positive Discipline That Works* and *Love and Anger: The Parental Dilemma.* Penguin Books.

YOUNG EMOTIONS

■ **Childhood depression signs**: Increased irritability . . . tearfulness . . . withdrawal from previously enjoyed activities . . . changes in appetite . . . sleep disturbances. If symptoms occur, consult a doctor. *Danger:* Untreated childhood depression is likely to persist—or recur in adolescence and adulthood. *Usual treatment:* Psychotherapy and, if necessary, medication.

Christopher Hodgman, M.D., professor of psychiatry and pediatrics, University of Rochester School of Medicine and Dentistry, Rochester, NY.

■ **Prepare kids for parent's surgery** by videotaping the parent reading one bedtime story for each day in the hospital—then playing one videotape at home each night. Also, have the kids color pictures for the hospitalized parent, and send a picture to them each day for posting in their room.

From Luella Gillispie, R.N., B.S.N., St. Mary's Hospital, Huntington, WV.

■ **Ease kids' visits after divorce** by having clothes at both parents' homes . . . using a neutral drop-off and pickup place, such as a parking lot or school . . . displaying the child's art, even if his/ her visits are infrequent. If practical, have the family pet travel with the child. Also, let him take along a security blanket or pillow. *Useful:* Let him carry personal belongings back and forth in his own backpack—and make his own decisions about what to take.

Linda Sartori, editor, *Kids Express,* 220 Eye St. NW, Washington, DC 20002.

HEALTHIER BABIES

■ **Hearing problems in newborns**—often overlooked—can now be detected via a new three-minute test. *How it works:* A probe containing a tiny loudspeaker and a tiny microphone is inserted into the ear. Faint sounds from the speaker stimulate the inner ear, causing it to produce its own faint sounds, known as osteoacoustic emissions. The microphone measures these sounds to determine if there is any hearing impairment. *Advantages:* The new test is accurate . . . faster and easier to do than current tests . . . and tests the full sound spectrum. Current tests only measure high-frequency response.

F. Joseph Kemker, Ph.D., chief of audiology, department of communicative disorders, University of Florida College of Health-Related Professions, Gainesville, FL.

■ **Bedtime baby bottles** containing juice or formula may promote dental cavities in infants. *Safer:* Cow's milk. It ranked last in a survey of tooth decay risk factors, from tooth-cleaning practices to fluoridated water exposure. Children too young to drink cow's milk should instead be given a bottle containing expressed breast milk or water. *Caution:* Take the bottle away once the baby falls asleep. Sucking on a bottle all night long increases risk of tooth decay and—because the eustachian tube linking the throat to the inner ear is short in infants—of ear infection.

Samantha Stephens, M.S., dental hygienist and acting dental director, San Francisco Department of Public Health. Her survey of mothers of 48 children older than six months was reported in *The Medical Post,* 777 Bay St., Fifth Floor, Toronto, Ontario M5W 1A7. 44 issues. $105/yr.

■ **Iron is the leading cause** of fatal ingestion poisoning in children three years of age and younger. *Important:* Keep all

warding desirable behavior encourages this. People often overlook these occasions or take them for granted. Worse, many parents only comment when their kids forget to be responsible.

Parents need to remember to say, "Thanks, that was a big help." Be especially careful to acknowledge behavior that's important to you but that may not be important to your child. *Examples:*

1. "I noticed that you put your books in your room instead of leaving them on the table. That's great—now I can set the table for dinner."

2. "I appreciate that you hung up your jacket when you came home."

3. Give kids choices. Adulthood consists of one choice after another. Making good decisions is a prerequisite to responsible behavior. Therefore a kid who is simply told what to do all the time never learns to make informed choices.

Suggestion: Instead of simply assigning chores to family members, make a list of everything that needs to be done and call a family meeting to decide who will take care of each task. Together, you may be able to divide the duties so that each person is assigned tasks he/she doesn't mind . . . or work out a rotation system so that no one is always stuck with the most difficult or tedious chores.

Involving your kids in this process shows them that their opinions are valued and gives them experience in finding practical solutions. It also reminds them that they're part of a team, with each member dependent on the others to keep the household running smoothly.

• **Help your kids connect privilege with responsibility and vice versa.** Too many children believe that they're entitled to whatever advantages they have—as though their parents were here to serve them. These kids have a hard time becoming responsible adults.

A parent who attended one of my workshops uses an ingenious system to prevent this problem. Her family has an annual ritual—each year, each child gets a new privilege and a new responsibility. One is contingent upon the other. The kids get to discuss their choices with their parents, who then take their concerns seriously.

Example: Your daughter has wanted a dog for several years. She agrees to baby-sit for her brother once a week. For this, she will earn the privilege of getting a dog.

• **Impose appropriate consequences.** Don't be too quick to "rescue" your children when they make mistakes. Parents often nag and then bail out their children anyway. One of the best ways kids learn is through the impact of reasonable consequences. You need not be overly punitive about mild oversights. Let the consequences speak for themselves . . . and your child will be less likely to forget next time.

Example I: You asked your son to pick up a carton of milk on his way home from school and he forgot. Instead of rushing to the store yourself, you serve dinner with no milk . . . and the next morning there's none to put on his cereal.

Example II: Your daughter leaves the house late several times a month and misses the school bus . . . despite your attempts to get her out the door on time. Each time, you drop everything to drive her to school—lecturing her on punctuality during the trip. Actually, she'll be more likely to change if you stop talking and let her walk to school. If this is not a safe option, tell her you will drive her when you're ready—after you've showered and done your chores. Few kids want to arrive in the middle of the second period.

• **Give kids a chance to fix their own mistakes.** Let errors be an opportunity for learning and a chance to do better next time. You may be tempted to blow up at your children's failures. But yelling rarely accomplishes anything and is likely to make you, as well as your children, feel even worse. If, instead, you help your kids find ways to set things right, they'll learn much more than they would from scoldings . . . and you'll feel better, too.

Example: It's your son's turn to make dinner. He forgets, stays late at school to play football and doesn't get home until 6 P.M. Instead of snapping at him or starting dinner yourself, try saying, "We have a problem now. What do you think we can do about it?" He may decide to make scrambled eggs . . . whip up a quick tuna salad . . . or trade shifts with the per-

iron supplements and iron-containing pills out of reach of young hands. Use the child-resistant packaging features on these products.

Patrice Wright, Ph.D., manager of pharmacology and toxicology, Nonprescription Drug Manufacturers Association, 1150 Connecticut Ave. NW, Washington, DC 20036.

FAMILIES TALKING

■ **Communicate the good things about your marriage.** Most couples express feelings effectively when angry or upset—but not when happy. *Helpful exercise:* Write three items that your mate does that please you . . . three things you would like him/her to do more often . . . three things you think he would like you to do more often.

The Ultimate Marriage Builder by David and Claudia Arp, family-life educators, Knoxville, TN. Thomas Nelson Publishers.

■ **Family meetings resolve disputes effectively.** Schedule council meetings regularly. Operate under rules agreed to in advance. All family members should help run meetings and contribute to them. *Meeting topics:* Solving problems, assigning chores, reviewing responsibilities—also, planning fun activities and expressing appreciation. *Important:* Avoid criticizing anyone's ideas—so everyone feels safe expressing thoughts and feelings.

Playful Parenting by Denise Chapman Weston, MSW, licensed play therapist, North Attleboro, MA. Jeremy P. Tarcher, Inc.

FAMILIES TALKING

Smarter Communication

Avoid statements that criticize him/her—they create anger, resentment and defensiveness. Do not lecture—give the teen time to express his point of view. Speak softly—yelling interferes with serious give-and-take. Work on your sense of timing—find a time that is convenient for both of you, not just for you.

Caring for Your Adolescent by Donald Greydanus M.D., FAAP, professor of pediatrics and human development, Michigan State University. Bantam Doubleday Dell Publishing Group.

SMARTER TEACHING

Teaching Your Kids to Drive Safely

Teach adolescents to drive safely by reinforcing the idea that driving is a privilege, not a right . . . letting them comment on your driving so they can learn about safe driving . . . asking them to point out when you fail to use a turn signal, come to a complete stop, etc. . . . focus on their driving behavior, not their personality traits . . . allow them lots of practice time behind the wheel.

E. Scott Geller, Ph.D., professor of psychology who studies driving safety and behavior, Virginia Polytechnic Institute and State University in Blacksburg, VA.

Kids and Questions

Treat all your child's questions as serious and important. This lets them know that who they are and what they have to say is important to you.

Raising Ethical Children: 10 Keys to Helping Your Children Become Moral and Caring by Steven Carr Reuben, Ph.D., Pacific Palisades, CA. Prima Publishing.

son who was supposed to cook the following night's dinner. Even more important than getting dinner on the table, he'll be motivated to take his commitments seriously.

All about the Oppositional Child

Wm. Lee Carter, Ed.D.

The oppositional child is a source of frustration and bewilderment to parents.

The oppositional child is consistently aggressive, argumentative, uncooperative, and in conflict with others—especially parents, teachers, and other authority figures . . .

- Yelling doesn't help.
- Reasoning doesn't help.
- Threats of punishment are ignored.
- Actual punishment doesn't seem to bother the child.

Parents may wind up feeling as though nothing they do will make a difference.

THE OPPOSITIONAL CHILD'S POINT OF VIEW

The key to dealing with the oppositional child is to see the world the way the child sees it.

People of any age want to have control over their lives. Control helps us feel that our lives are ordered, predictable, and secure.

While children feel that they have very little control in a world run by adults—some of them seize control aggressively . . . others by being overly dependent.

Oppositional children go after control assertively and forcefully, by manipulating the emotions of others.

Wm. Lee Carter, Ed.D., a psychologist at Child Psychiatry Associates in Waco, TX, and author of *Kidthink*. Word Publishing, Inc.

They may not be able to take away their parents' car keys or send them to their rooms—but they can enrage and frustrate them. That's why angry confrontation makes the problem worse—the child has won by causing parents to focus their emotional energy on him.

PARENTS, TOO, WANT TO BE IN CONTROL

Parents tend to try to control children by force—overpowering them, out-arguing them—or trying to reason them into seeing things the parent's way.

But using force with an oppositional child actually reinforces his/her behavior. You wind up with a noisy turf battle—and the child continues to control the emotional atmosphere of the home.

Trying to reason with the child is equally ineffective. Kids are smart—they can see when the parent is emotionally invested in bringing them around to the parent's point of view. This only reinforces the child's sense of control.

HANDLING THE OPPOSITIONAL CHILD

Paradoxically, we can actually have much more control by recognizing the child's need for control. When the child feels understood, he's more likely to come over to our side.

This does not mean stepping aside and letting kids "do their own thing." Children are inexperienced in the ways of the world and need our guidance.

By virtue of age, wisdom, and experience, parents are the natural leaders in the home. But leadership is demonstrated more effectively through communication than force. A wise leader solicits and takes into account the needs and desires of each family member . . . then makes the final decision.

Understanding is not the same as agreement. You don't have to approve of what your child is doing . . . but if you understand what motivates his behavior, you'll be less likely to act in ways that encourage it.

SMARTER TEACHING

Help Build Your Child's Self-Esteem

By not seeking help when it's needed, an otherwise easily surmounted difficulty can become a looming problem—and that crushes self-esteem. *Helpful:* Don't try to prevent children from making their own small mistakes—lose a game, spill the milk, step on a dance partner's toe. But always show that you love them. *Also:* Let them know when you make mistakes and that they can still love you. Teach children that all real learning comes from mistakes, whether they are Galileo's, Newton's, Salk's, or their own.

Save Our Schools: 66 Things You Can Do to Improve Your School Without Spending an Extra Penny by Mary Susan Miller, Ph.D., former schoolteacher and administrator who now teaches at William Paterson College, Wayne, NJ. HarperSan Francisco.

DID YOU KNOW THAT . . .

■ **Too much fluoride** can mottle a toddler's permanent teeth—years later. *Most at risk:* Young children who drink fluoridated water . . . and who use (and swallow) specially flavored fluoridated toothpastes.

Research at the University of Iowa College of Dentistry, reported in *The New York Times*.

■ **Girls participating in high school sports** are more likely to be injured than boys participating in the same sports. *Leading cause of injury:* Girls' high school cross-country—especially long-distance running. For every 100 girls who run, 61 are injured during the season. *Possible explanation:* Girls may be less well-conditioned—they may also get involved in sports later than boys. *Interesting:* Fall sports are far more danger-

DID YOU KNOW THAT . . .

ous for both boys and girls than spring sports. This may be the result of poor conditioning over the summer or of reinjury after summertime accidents and strains.

Stephen Rice, M.D., Ph.D., lecturer, division of sports medicine, University of Washington, Seattle, WA. His survey of almost 60,000 high school athletes was reported in the Medical Tribune, *257 Park Ave. South, New York, NY 10010. 24 issues. $75/yr.*

SAFER KIDS

■ **A child's breathing rate** can be an indication of a health problem. *Normal:* For a newborn—30 to 45 breaths per minute. For a toddler—20 to 30 breaths. For a school-age child—12 to 20 breaths. *Caution:* A child with abnormally slow breathing may be suffering from a head injury or a drug reaction. Breathing too fast may indicate pneumonia, fever, or blockage of the nose or throat.

Lawrence Mathers, M.D., director, pediatric intensive care unit, Lucile Salter Packard Children's Hospital, Stanford University, Palo Alto, CA.

■ **Bicycles injure more kids** than any consumer product except cars. About 400 children die in bike accidents every year. Another 400,000 kids need emergency room treatment. More than a third of those have head injuries and may become permanently disabled. *Self-defense:* Make sure your child always wears a bicycle helmet—even for short rides. New laws in many jurisdictions require the use of helmets.

Report: Maternal & Child Health, *Johnson & Johnson Publications, One Johnson & Johnson Plaza, New Brunswick, NJ 08933. Quarterly. Free.*

TACTICS THAT DON'T WORK
- Making threats that won't be carried out.
- Shouting to make a point.
- Making sweeping generalizations such as "You always" . . . "You never" . . . etc."
- Trying to reason with the child.
- Interrupting.
- Withholding affection.
- Trying to convince the child to agree with you.

WHAT PARENTS CAN DO
- **Control their own emotions.** The parent needs to develop a sense of detachment from the child's difficult behavior. That doesn't mean hiding your emotions—that would be impossible. It does mean allowing your child the room to make his own mistakes.

Trap: When a child does something we don't approve of, we tend not to stop at the behavior—we try to change the child's emotions and opinions as well.

The child's problem then becomes our problem . . . and he's once again in control.

Detachment isn't easy. Instead of thinking, "Well, 12-year-olds do that kind of thing," parents tend to think, "No 12-year-old girl is going to control me." But adults, too, are capable of maturing throughout life. We must be honest with ourselves and continually strive to develop insight into our thoughts and actions.

- **Set clear, consistent boundaries.** Rather than guiding by giving orders, offer choices that indicate the limits of behavior. Let the child know ahead of time which behaviors will result in punishment—and what those consequences will be. Avoid excessively harsh or aggressive punishment, particularly spanking. And don't ever punish when you're not in control of your emotions. Call a time-out first.

Example: Missing curfew results in loss of use of the car for a week. If the child exceeds the boundaries, impose the consequences—without lecturing or getting emotional about it. Parents don't have trouble getting the first part right. A teenager comes in at 3 A.M. and the parent says, "You know that you're supposed to be home by midnight. It's 3 A.M.—no more car this week."

The problem arises when the parent then starts to lecture or harangue the child: "I told you to be in by midnight! I tried to be fair! Now you've broken the rules again—I can't believe it! How do you expect me to trust you?"

Children may test the boundaries for a while to find out whether parents are serious. This is when it's especially important not to get emotional—just keep enforcing the rules.

• **Read between the lines.** Kids aren't skilled in verbal communication. It's often difficult for them to put what they feel into words. Often, it's through their behavior that they express what's going on inside.

With practice, parents can learn to cut through the offensive behavior and respond to the emotion beneath.

Example: A child who shouts "I hate you!" may mean, "I hate being told I can't do something!" or "I have no power in this family, and it's not fair!"

A parent's usual tendency is to tell the child why he shouldn't feel that way. A more effective response might be, "It feels pretty bad when I tell you what to do. I know you hate that." This allows the child a right to his feelings.

A nonopinionated, nonjudgmental response will encourage the child to reveal more layers of emotion until he feels understood . . . and once he feels understood, he's more apt to cooperate.

This response is difficult for parents. The parents who haven't mastered detachment fear that they are telling the child, "Go right ahead and hate us—we're rotten people." But when the child knows his feelings are accepted, the feelings will pass much more quickly.

• **Don't give advice unless the child asks for it.** You may have useful insights, but the child won't benefit from them unless he's interested. He can usually work out his own solutions if you listen in a nonjudgmental way.

• **Work on building a positive relationship with your children.** The oppositional child is crying out for attention, so make sure he's getting enough of the positive kind.

SAFER KIDS

■ **. . . preventable injuries** kill 8,000 kids under age 15 in the US every year—and disable 50,000. *Self-defense:* Think safety at all times. Keep harmful items out of children's reach. Use safety devices such as car safety seats, bicycle helmets, smoke detectors.

Report: Maternal & Child Health, Johnson & Johnson, One Johnson & Johnson Plaza, New Brunswick, NJ 08933.

■ **Overscheduled teenagers** often get too little sleep, placing themselves at risk. *Side effects of sleep deprivation:* Home and school problems . . . a higher accident rate . . . greater vulnerability to the effects of drugs and alcohol.

Mary A. Carskadon, Ph.D., a researcher at E. P. Bradley Hospital, East Providence, RI.

■ **Safety caps for drug containers** are only child-resistant—not child-proof. Toddlers can often open safety caps within 10 minutes. *Better:* Always, always, always keep all drugs—even those with safety caps—clearly out of reach of children.

University of California, Berkeley Wellness Letter, Box 412, New York, NY 10012. Monthly. $24/yr.

KIDS' NUTRITION

■ **Healthy snacks for latchkey kids.** Working parents should stock the kitchen with foods their children perceive as treats. *Examples:* Popcorn, pretzels, bagels, mixed fruit, vanilla wafers, trail mix, flavored rice cakes. Do not stock your kitchen with soft drinks or junk foods—especially those containing lots of fat. Agree on a specific snack time— at least two hours before dinner to prevent spoiled appetites.

Registered dietitian Brenda Gross, M.S., Sports Medicine Center, Emory University, Atlanta, GA.

KIDS' NUTRITION

■ **Fruit juice danger.** Children who drank fruit juice (12 to 30 ounces a day) as their primary beverage had unbalanced diets that were too low in calories and protein, which are necessary for growth. *Reason:* The juice was consumed instead of more nutrient-dense foods. Once fruit juice consumption was reduced, all the children resumed normal growth.

Melanie M. Smith, R.D., chief of pediatric nutrition, Maimonides Medical Center, Brooklyn, NY. Her study of eight children 14 to 27 months of age was published in *Pediatrics*, 141 NW Point Rd., Elk Grove Village, IL 60009. Monthly. $90/yr.

■ **To encourage kids to try new foods**—use praise, not bribery. Among children who sampled new foods, those praised for being "new-food tasters" were more likely to eat the foods later when no adult was around than were those rewarded with plastic dinosaurs, trucks, and other toys. Verbal praise may encourage children to view themselves as individuals willing to try unfamiliar foods—even when not influenced by adults.

Helen Hendy, Ph.D., assistant professor of psychology, Pennsylvania State University, Schuylkill, PA. Her study of eating habits among 49 preschool children was presented at a recent meeting of the American Psychological Association, 750 First St. NE, Washington, DC 20002.

HEALTHIER KIDS

Secondhand smoke and kids: Children whose parents smoke inhale the same amount of nicotine as people who smoke 150 cigarettes a year. The kids miss *one out of seven* school days due to illness caused by passive smoking . . . and are more likely to develop cancer and lung disease as adults than children of nonsmokers.

Report by the Royal College of Physicians, UK.

RECOMMENDED . . .

Spend time playing games and talking with your children.

Be generous with physical affection for your child.

Note: This is easier with pre-adolescents than with teenagers. Older children—who look to their peers, not their family, for support—may resist your attempts to enter their world. But it's important to show your willingness to build rapport.

Invite your child on outings—or to a one-on-one dinner. Don't give him a hard time if he turns you down. Even if he says no, continue to invite him to other activities in a no-big-deal way.

Or try a chat before bedtime. A child who's winding down at the end of the day may be more receptive to building rapport.

How to Help Your Child Overcome Childhood Fears

Marianne Daniels Garber, Ph.D.

While most childhood fears are a normal part of growing up, parents often worry that a particular fear or pattern of fears is abnormal. In such cases, a little information often helps.

COMMON QUESTIONS

• *Which fears are normal?* All children are born with innate fears of loud noises and of falling down. As they mature and come in contact with their environment, they typically begin to fear ma-

Marianne Daniels Garber, Ph.D., an educational consultant in private practice at the Behavioral Institute of Atlanta. She is the coauthor, with Stephen W. Garber, Ph.D., and Robyn Freedman Spizman, of *Monsters Under the Bed and Other Childhood Fears: Helping Your Child Overcome Anxieties, Fears and Phobias*. Villard Books.

chines, big objects, toilets, animals, strangers, leaving mom and dad.

As their imagination comes to life, children may fear the dark, sleeping alone, monsters, the supernatural, thunder, and lightning.

Still later, as children enter their pre-teen years, they'll encounter social fears—fear of looking foolish, speaking in public, doing poorly in school.

• *How should parents treat fears?* Never belittle a child's fear or say that the fear is silly. To the child, the fear is all too real. If you shame children for their fears, the fear may disappear for a brief time . . . only to explode later on. *Also important:*

• **Never force children to confront a fear**—for example, by throwing a child who's afraid of the water into a swimming pool. Doing so may intensify the fear.

• **Don't cater to a child's fear.** Some parents avoid the object of a child's fear altogether, keeping a child from ever having to confront a scary situation. On the other hand, some parents say, "Oh, don't worry about that doggie," but they send another message by holding the child close to them as the dog approaches.

• *How can parents keep a child's fears from snowballing?* Prepare your child for new experiences gradually.

Example I: Before the first day of school, take your child to visit the school and meet the other children. Read books about school and talk about things that children do at school.

Example II: A child who fears dogs may be thinking, "This dog is going to eat me!" Let the child stand back and watch the dog as it interacts with others. Talk about dogs. Explain that tail-wagging and jumping can be signs of friendliness. Pet the dog while your child watches.

• *What if a fear lingers . . . or becomes very intense?* Whether your child fears spending the night out, bees and wasps, bridges, germs, etc., do not ignore the fear and assume it will just go away.

Danger: Many full-blown adult phobias—including *agoraphobia* (fear of open spaces or leaving the home), *acrophobia* (fear of heights), and fear of ani-

HEALTHIER KIDS

■ **Childhood "sugar high" doesn't exist**—despite what many parents believe. In a recent study, children spent three weeks eating a high-sugar diet . . . then three weeks eating a diet low in sugar but high in aspartame (Nutra-Sweet) . . . and finally three weeks eating a diet low in sugar with saccharin as a placebo. Each week, the children were tested for memory, concentration, reading and math skills. *Result:* The kids—including some diagnosed as hyperactive—behaved the same way, regardless of what they ate. *However:* Some parents may continue to blame sugar for their children's unruly behavior. *Reason:* Children get the most sugary foods on Christmas, Halloween, and other special occasions. On such occasions, kids are worked up no matter what they eat, but parents blame the sugar.

Mark Wolraich, M.D., professor of pediatrics, Vanderbilt University, Nashville, TN.

■ **To avoid fractures later in life,** adolescent girls may need to consume more than the recommended dietary allowance (RDA) of calcium. The calcium RDA for ages 11 to 24 is 1,200 milligrams (mg). One cup of skim milk or nonfat yogurt contains 300 mg calcium. Other good sources of calcium include beans, broccoli and kale. Girls should take calcium supplements only under a doctor's supervision.

Tom Lloyd, Ph.D., professor of obstetrics and gynecology, College of Medicine, Pennsylvania State University, Hershey, PA.

■ **Better discipline.** Discipline is most effective when it is based on a mixture of love and authority. Even when you're angry, approach a child gently to help help him/her feel calm. Otherwise he will be too anxious to hear what you have to say. *More important:* A child must feel adequately loved even when being disciplined. He must not feel he is loved less when he makes a mistake or breaks a rule.

Parachutes for Parents: Learning to Parent from the Wisdom of Love by Bobbie Sandoz, MSW, Honolulu-based Family Works Publications.

■ **Don't use bed as a punishment.** Bedtime should be a pleasant time of stories, songs, or quiet conversation. If the bed is seen as a place to be sent when you're being punished, bedtime will become a struggle.

It Works for Us! Proven Child-Care Tips from Experienced Parents Across the Country by Tom McMahon, associate professor of counseling and psychology, Ohlone College, Fredmont, CA. Pocket Books

■ **Knowing the rules.** Be sure your child fully understands your rules . . . remember to "catch" him/her being good and compliment him for following your rule . . . choose your battles—if you're not selective, you're not effective . . . impose rules that are limited in number and clearly stated, such as, We hold hands when crossing streets.

Nancy Samalin, director, Parent Guidance Workshops, a parent education program in New York City, and author of *Love and Anger: The Parental Dilemma.* Penguin.

mals—have their roots in childhood fears that were never addressed.

TAKE DIRECT ACTION

There are several strategies for helping your child overcome his/her fear. *Most helpful:*

• **Explain that fear is a normal physiological condition.** Tell your child that it's part of the fight-or-flight response that arose to protect our ancestors from sabertooth tigers and other predators.

Assuming your child is in good health, the physical manifestations of fear are not dangerous . . . whether it's a rapidly pounding heart, "butterflies" in the stomach, fast breathing, lightheadedness or dizziness, trembling, clammy hands, sweating, tingling in hands or feet, etc. Make sure your child realizes this.

• **Work together.** Say, "We've got a problem, and we're going to solve it together. You've been waking up at night because you're afraid of the dark. Let's work on getting over this together. It's going to be fun."

• **Teach positive self-talk.** Explain to your child that it's possible to counter fearful thoughts by silently repeating positive ones based on real information. *Fear:* "That dog will bite me." *Positive self-talk:* "That dog is wagging his tail. He's friendly."

• **Give your child correct information** . . . what he needs to know to counteract the fear. *Problem:* Kids have gaps in their knowledge. A child who fears the dark may know something about darkness but may not understand why it gets dark or how long it takes the eyes to adjust. *Typical result:* Panic. As darkness falls, your child starts imagining monsters instead of thinking, "Wait a minute, I'm still in my room. That shape I see over there must be the lamp on my desk."

Educating your child about darkness and its effects on vision and the appearance of familiar objects may help him/her overcome fear.

Similarly, let your child know that not everything she sees or hears is true. If your daughter hears a noise and fears there is a monster under her bed, for example, explain to her, "That's not a monster, that's the water running."

• **Teach your child relaxation techniques.** Tension causes your child to take short, shallow breaths—and that intensifies the panic. *Fear reducers:* Deep muscle relaxation and "belly" breathing—deep, slow, rhythmic breathing from the diaphragm. Show your child how.

FOUR-STEP TECHNIQUE

In *Monsters Under the Bed*, we present a four-step desensitization process for extreme or persistent fears. Say your son is afraid of the dark . . .

• *Step one:* **Imagination.** Use picture books, videos, television programs, and "make-believe" games and stories to help your son create fear-reducing positive images. Tell a story in which he wakes up in the middle of the night, looks calmly around, and goes back to sleep.

• *Step two:* **Information.** Give your son helpful facts appropriate to his age and specific fear. Educate him about darkness. Watch sunrises and sunsets together. Use an encyclopedia to study the eye.

• *Step three:* **Observation.** Use modeling to help him safely come in contact with his fears. *What to do:* Without directly comparing your son to other children, let him observe a child who goes to bed easily in the dark. Say, "Look how the child falls asleep." Or, stand with your son in a darkened room so he experiences his eyes adjusting to the dark.

• *Step four:* **Exposure.** Slowly familiarize your son to the darkness using a set of graduated activities. First, have him walk into a dark room and stay for a few seconds. Slowly increase the time spent in the dark. Play hide and seek in the dark, follow the leader in and out of darkened spaces, eat dessert in the dark. Do as few or as many of these activities as your son needs to overcome the fear.

Crucial: Set a comfortable pace—don't try to do it all in one day. Have your child use a rating scale of 1 (no fear) to 10 (terrified). If your child signals five or greater, immediately stop what you're doing. Repeat the experience slowly until your child is more comfortable. This gives him/her a sense of control.

PETS . . . PETS . . . PETS

■ **Best time to bring home a new puppy.** Bring home a new puppy as early in the day as possible. This allows the pup several hours to adjust to the new surroundings before being left alone at night.

The Home & Family Protection Dog by Karen Freeman Duet, owner of K-9 Companions Dog Training Co., Lake Mathews, CA. Howell Books House.

■ **If you want a dog to help guard the house,** get one that's nervous and loud. Fox terriers are ideal. They'll deter burglars much more effectively than a quiet, 200-lb. mastiff. Forget beware-of-dog signs if you don't have a dog. While burglars usually aren't too bright, a sign still won't fool them. The same is true for phony burglar-alarm signs.

■ **Brush dogs before bathing them.** Wetting a matted coat tightens tangles, making them harder to remove. The best brushing gets down to the skin without brushing the skin itself. *Technique:* Push the dog's coat back with one hand and brush the hair down, a little at a time, with the other hand. Use quick, deep strokes. Brush one small area at a time.

Dog Fancy, Box 6050, Mission Viejo, CA 92690.

■ **Animals have trouble digesting** rich, fatty "people food." Feeding your pet table scraps can cause obesity, tooth decay and digestive problems. *Better treats:* Animal biscuits or other snacks that are made to meet your animal's dietary needs.

Linda K. King, DVM, writing in *McCall's,* 110 Fifth Ave., New York, NY 10011.

■ **Cat litter danger.** Cat litter often harbors *Toxoplasma gondii,* a microorganism that causes a potentially serious

PETS . . . PETS . . . PETS

human infection called toxoplasmosis. *Self-defense:*

• Feed cats dry, canned, or boiled foods—they acquire the parasite by eating rodents, birds, or undercooked beef or poultry.

• Use disposable plastic litter box liners. *If you do not use liners:* After each emptying, disinfect the box with scalding water. Leave the water in the box for at least five minutes.

• Change litter daily.

• Wash hands thoroughly after cleaning the box.

Important: Pregnant women and people with AIDS or other immune-deficiency disorders should avoid changing cat litter boxes, if possible. If not, they should wear disposable gloves.

FDA Consumer, U.S. Superintendent of Documents, Washington, DC 20402. 10 issues. $15/yr.

■ **Dogs and cats are good for your health.** A group of adults was monitored before they acquired a cat or dog—and then for 10 months afterward. *Result:* After getting a pet, most reported suffering fewer bouts of headaches, difficulty sleeping, nerves, colds and flu, general tiredness, indigestion, and sinus trouble. *Interesting:* For dog owners, improvements were still apparent 10 months later. In cat owners, they disappeared after six months. *Possible explanation:* Dog owners take more healthful walks.

Study by James Serpell, Ph.D., published in the *Journal of the Royal Society of Medicine* reported in *New Choices for Retirement Living,* 28 W. 23 St., New York, NY 10010. 10 issues. $16.97/yr.

■ **Cancer risk from pets:** Lung cancer risk doubles in people exposed to pet birds for up to 10 years . . . and triples in those exposed for more than 10 years.

WHEN TO SEEK HELP

If your child remains extremely fearful despite all your efforts, seek help from a psychotherapist specializing in fears and anxiety disorders. Before the initial visit, make sure the therapist has had previous success treating your child's specific fear.

For a list of specialists in your area, send a self-addressed, stamped, business-sized envelope to the Anxiety Disorders Association of America, 6000 Executive Blvd., Suite 200, Rockville, MD 20852.

No Summer Job?

Ralph Schulz

Summer jobs teach kids responsibility, provide them with spending money, and keep them busy while they're out of school.

More worthwhile: Businesses that kids start on their own—since a real business teaches them even more valuable lessons of all kinds.

BEFORE BEGINNING

A few hours of planning can mean the difference between the success and failure of your child's business.

Important: Help your child work out a business plan. This can simply be notes written on a sheet of paper.

The business plan can determine up-front costs . . . ongoing costs such as transportation, materials, and marketing . . . income potential . . . profits . . . and the competition.

Key: Don't be a know-it-all. Don't do all the planning and decision making for your child. Part of the value of this endeavor is for your child to get his/her first taste of running a business—that includes making mistakes. Also, contact the office of the secretary

Ralph Schulz, executive director of Junior Achievement Inc., a national organization that fosters entrepreneurship among young people, One Education Way, Colorado Springs, CO 80906.

of state, which will provide you with a list of legal and tax requirements.

To market the service, your child could place flyers under doors or on cars during the week and solicit neighbors in person on the weekends.

Here are the most popular jobs that kids are starting this summer . . .

• *Baking:* Opportunities vary according to the neighborhood. But there are probably more organized events in your area this summer than you are aware of—fairs, park gatherings, softball leagues, etc. Sales through local retailers are possible—but trickier.

Beginners' products: Cookies . . . muffins . . . and homemade breads. Cakes and pies are usually harder to make and harder to sell.

Requirements: A stove, recipes, and ingredients. If your child wants to bake bread, a $120 bread-making machine might be a good investment. Loaves can be made for as little as 15 cents to 30 cents each. If you set up your own selling stand, you may require a vendor license. Contact the event sponsor for information.

Income potential: $5 to $30 an hour. The profit margin on baked goods can be fantastic since they cost so little to make.

• *Car care:* Some kids just wash cars . . . others wax and clean the interiors.

Requirements: Bucket, sponges, towels, soaps, wax, and squeegee.

Income potential: $5 to $10 for washing a car. Add another $10 for cleaning the interior. Waxing will add another $15 to $20. Your child could charge $30 for all three services on a car . . . $60 to $70 on a van or truck.

Keep in mind: Much of this work has to be done in the evenings or on weekends since the clients use their vehicles during the weekdays. This schedule may inhibit a youngster's social life and cut into his income potential, since someone who starts working at 6 P.M. can't work an eight-hour shift.

• *Home-video cameraman:* Many adults would like to film a party or graduation but don't because then they can't enjoy their guests or the proceedings. That creates a business opportunity.

Theory: Airborne bacteria from bird waste or bird-feather particles, cause lung irritation that eventually develops into cancer. *Self-defense:* Keep birdcages clean and air out rooms frequently.

From a study of 239 lung cancer patients at Berlin's national institute of health led by Lenore Kohlmeier, M.S.C., Ph.D., professor of epidemiology and nutrition, University of NC, Chapel Hill.

■ **Pets really help sick people.** Pet owners have lower cholesterol and lower blood pressure than nonowners. They also report fewer minor health problems, such as headaches and gastrointestinal disturbances. Dog owners, in particular, feel increased well-being and higher self-esteem for at least 10 months after getting their pets—and have fewer complaints of nervousness and insomnia.

Study of more than 5,700 men and women by researchers at the Baker Medical Institute, Australia, and research at Cambridge University, England.

HOME ALONE

"Latchkey Kid" Basics

Have your child call you at work each day when he/she arrives home from school . . . let him know where you'll be and when you'll be home . . . rehearse with the child what to do should various problems arise.

Examples: An unexpected visitor . . . a power outage. Install an alarm system and a peephole in the door to help your child feel more secure . . . leave the radio or TV on to fill the house with music or talk and make it more comforting when he comes home alone.

Living with Teens and Enjoying Them Too by Blossom M. Turk, Ed.D,, Boise, ID counselor to schools and corporations. Legendary Publishing.

BETTER CHILD CARE

■ **Choosing child care.** Children cared for by family members are not necessarily better off than children in day care with unrelated adults. Since many relatives take care of kids out of a sense of obligation, a study found that children are no more likely to become attached to relatives than to nonfamily members.

Best caregivers: Those who truly want to care for children and who are willing to work in improving their own skills and knowledge.

Ellen Galinksy, Families and Work Institute, 330 Seventh Ave., New York, NY 10001

■ **Child-care placement agencies** can't do national criminal background checks on caregiver candidates . . . any such checks are limited in scope. *Reason:* Private citizens and businesses do not have access to national criminal records compiled by the Department of Justice. If an agency claims it conducted a criminal background check, ask how it was done. Be suspicious if the agency claims to have gotten into the national crime computer system. Only law-enforcement individuals have access to this system.

Joy Wayne, director, Nannies Plus, 615 W. Mount Pleasant Ave., Livingston, NJ 07039.

SMARTER PARENTING

Beyond Spanking

Jerry Wyckoff, Ph.D.

When it comes to disciplining children, shouting and spanking are counterproductive. Aside from sending them the message that it's okay to yell and hit to get what you want, these approaches drive bad behaviors underground—kids don't change behavior, they simply become expert at not getting caught.

Requirements: Camcorder, tapes. Also, a demonstration tape to show that your quality is acceptable.

Income potential: Typically $10 to $15 per hour . . . or a flat fee—sometimes as high as $50 or $75—for chronicling an event that is several hours long.

Important: Make sure that your child promises to deliver only unedited tapes. The venture will become too time-consuming and costly otherwise.

• *Lawn care:* Business potential is greatest if the child can use the client's lawn mower. This job can also include removing debris when trees are cut . . . trimming . . . and cleanup.

Income potential: $15 per hour, but not all is profit if your child has to supply gas and oil for the mower, which can cost up to $7.50 per job. *Aim:* 20 lawns per week.

Suggest that your child walk the property before agreeing to take the job. The size, roughness, and terrain or contour can make some lawns more difficult to mow than the client may think. The child should provide an estimate of the time it will take to complete the job.

If your child uses your mower: He shouldn't work on lawns in terrible condition. Rocks, roots, and thin grass can damage your equipment.

If your child needs to buy a mower: First determine the market potential. One young woman I know lined up 45 lawns to do each week before investing $800 in a self-propelling model.

• *Design shop:* With a computer, kids can design invitations, announcements, cards, flyers, etc. The market for this includes schools, small businesses and clubs. For example, a visit to the local Rotary Club may help drum up work. The promotion piece should be a great example of your child's work.

Requirements: Computer, a decent graphics program ($50 to $80), color printer. Make copies from your printer or through a local print shop.

Income potential: $5 to $30 an hour.

Questions to Ask When Choosing a Summer Camp for Your Child

Laurie Edelman

• *Is your child really ready for sleepaway camp?* Knowing your child's and your family's needs is the first step to finding the right camp. If your child can't handle being away from home overnight, a day camp is probably a better choice. You may want to have your child sleep overnight at a friend's home to make this determination.

• *Is the camp accredited?* The American Camping Association is the only organization in the U.S. that has a voluntary standards-and-accreditation program for all kinds of camps. These standards cover health and safety, camp management, personnel, programming facilities, and transportation. If a camp you're considering is not accredited, ask the camp director why not and then make your decision.

• *What is the camp's philosophy?* Does the camp have a religious background? Is the camp's philosophy one of sports and competition? Sports and instruction? Arts? How does the camp director describe the camp's philosophy? Is that what you want for your child?

• *Who is directly responsible for your child's supervision at the camp?* Find out the counselor/child ratio to determine whether supervision is adequate. This ratio differs by age group and between day and sleepaway camps. Some offer smaller ratios among younger children.

Ages six to eight: Day camp/one counselor to eight children . . . *sleepaway camp*/one to six children.

Laurie Edelman, executive director of the New York section of the American Camping Association, 12 W. 31 St., New York, NY 10001.

Alternatives:

• **Competition.** Children are competitive by nature and love to be "first." Exploit this natural tendency by playing "beat the clock" with your child.

Example: Set a timer for five minutes. Say, "You have to get in bed before the timer rings." Watch your child race to finish.

• **Praise.** Each time your child does something you approve of, let him/her know. *Key:* Be specific.

Example: Don't say, "You're a good girl for putting your crayons away." Say, "What a neat job you did putting away all your crayons."

• **Rehearsing appropriate behaviors.** A toddler who gets spanked for running into the street learns to avoid the parent—not the street. *Better:* Repeat lessons about looking both ways, avoiding cars, responding to traffic lights, etc. Once your child masters these skills, he/she will delight in showing them off—and getting your praise.

• **Contractual arrangements.** The basic principle is that, "When you have done A, then you may do B."

Example: Instead of shouting, "You're in big trouble if you don't do your homework," calmly say, "When you finish your homework, then you may call your friends." Never say, "If you do your homework." If you do, your child might ask, "What if I don't?"

• **"Time-out."** When your child is out of control, make him/her sit still in a chair for a prescribed period of time (one minute for each year of age is about right). Time-out helps your child cool off by preventing him from receiving any kind of attention (verbal or phys-

SMARTER PARENTING

ical) for an inappropriate behavior. Use a timer so that your child can anticipate when time-out is over.

Jerry Wyckoff, Ph.D., associate professor of human development, Ottawa University, Ottawa, KS. He is the author of *Discipline Without Shouting or Spanking.* Meadowbrook Press.

SETTING LIMITS

Saying "No" To Kids

Lawrence Kutner, Ph.D.

Parents can say "no" to their children even when the children complain that "all the other kids have it" . . . or "their parents say it's okay."

Important: Gear your explanation to your child's level of understanding. Preschoolers are prelogical, so avoid a lengthy discussion. For older kids, give your side . . . and then listen to their side. *Also helpful:* Talking to other parents.

If the disagreement is small, it may be worth giving in and saving your efforts for when it is important. Or negotiate.

Examples: Your son wants a $75 pair of sneakers and you'll spend up to $40—ask him what he is willing to do to earn the difference . . . your daughter wants to go to town with friends and you don't think she has the maturity—ask her how she'll show you can trust her.

If your answer is still "no," acknowledge their want but remind them that, after all, you are the parent.

Lawrence Kutner, Ph.D., is a child psychologist in Cambridge, MA. He is author of *Parent and Child: Getting Through to Each Other.* Avon Books.

■ **Children and praise.** Praise given to children should not make them feel pressured to do even better. Such praise can actually hinder children from further suc-

Ages nine to 14: Day camp/one counselor to 10 children . . . *sleepaway camp*/one to eight children.

Ages 15 to 17: Day camp/one counselor to 12 children . . . *sleepaway camp*/one to 10 children.

• **Who else besides the counselor can children go to with problems?** Make sure the camp offers a good support system (group or division leaders, counselors in charge of particular activities, head counselors, the director) so your child has more than one person to talk with if he/she is upset about something. Also find out what the camp's policy is on telephone calls home.

• **How are the counselors screened and trained?** If the camp is accredited, you can be assured that the staff is screened and trained. But get specifics on how the counselors are chosen . . . what the screening process involves . . . and what the training covers. Most important is that you feel comfortable that the camp director knows his/her business and is concerned enough to provide the best possible care and supervision.

• **How much instruction is provided during each activity period . . . and how long do activity periods last?** This will give you a good idea of whether the camp will suit your child's attention span and level of independence. Also find out which activities are required and how many electives your child can choose.

• **Are any trips offered as part of the camp . . . and what transportation arrangements are made for trips?** Accredited camps will have specific requirements for drivers, vehicles, and on-board safety equipment. If you choose a nonaccredited camp, make sure you're comfortable with these arrangements.

• **How does the camp integrate new campers into the group?** If your child is thrown into a group without being properly introduced and made to feel welcome, he won't enjoy himself, no matter how many exciting activities are offered.

• **What medical facilities are available on-site? Nearby?** Any time you have several children together in an active setting, you're bound to have a few injuries here and there. While the majority of these are minor scrapes and bruises, broken bones are not unheard-of.

Most camps have registered nurses or the equivalent on-site and doctors either on-site or nearby. You will want to know what the camp's policies are on medical insurance and notification of parents in the event of illness or injury. You should feel comfortable that the camp is prepared to deal with—and has the ability and experience to deal with—any eventuality.

• *What references can you give me?* Talking to the parents of children who have recently attended the camp can prove invaluable in your decision. Find out what the child and the parents liked best and least about the camp. Also find out whether the reference's child's temperament is similar to that of your child.

The Six Principles of Better Dog Training

Maureen Fredrickson

Adog is much happier and better behaved when he has a clear role in your family. Dogs must be taught to be followers and that every person in the household is a leader.

A well-trained dog eats after you eat . . . sleeps on your bed only when you grant approval . . . moves out of your way . . . follows you out the door . . . walks by your side with a slack leash. Lunging or straining at the leash should not be tolerated. *Six basic principles:*

Maureen Fredrickson, program director for Delta Society, a nonprofit organization that trains people-animal teams to visit patients in health-care facilities, Box 1080, Renton, WA 98057.

cess—because they may become afraid of failing . . . or afraid of letting down parents if they don't achieve as much as parents may expect.

Words like *brilliant, genius,* and *gorgeous* can be internalized by children as pressure.

Better: Words like *good thinking, hardworking, smart,* and *talented.*

Sylvia Rimm, Ph.D., director, Family Achievement Center, Metro-Health Medical Center, Cleveland, OH.

■ **Help your kids think creatively** by inventing a problem that has no apparent solution and asking them to solve it. They will probably come up with more than one approach.

Little Lessons for Teachers by Mary Kay Shanley, member of the board of the Gifted-and-Talented Association in W. Des Moines, IA. Sta-Kris, Inc.

Appreciative Kids Are Made—Not Born

Complaining is natural, but thankfulness requires the power of observation.

Helpful: Explain to children how even the poor today live better than the rich did 100 years ago . . . that until relatively recently, cars, telephones, and computers didn't exist . . . that not many years ago, millions of people died of pneumonia, infections, and other maladies that today are easily treated.

Aim: Contentment depends not so much on having more, as on appreciating what we already have. Always demanding more is a common trait among children. Parents should help by teaching them the inner joys of contentment.

Reuven Bar-Levav, M.D., a psychiatrist in private practice in Southfield, MI, and author of *Every Family Needs a CEO: What Mothers and Fathers Can Do About Our Deteriorating Families and Values.* Fathering Press.

SETTING LIMITS

■ **To teach your child values like caring and courtesy:** Be responsive to his/her requests when they come with words like *please* and *thank you* . . . hug him or pat his shoulder when you see him being nice to someone . . . ask before taking or using something that belongs to him . . . tell the truth—and admit it if you are caught in a lie . . . help him think of ways to be nice to other people.

Ann LaForge, contributing editor, Child, 110 Fifth Ave., New York, NY 10011. 10 issues. $9.98/yr.

Dust Allergy Self-Defense

Gerald L. Klein, M.D.

House dust is the most common irritant for allergy sufferers and asthmatics. *Self-defense:*

• **Dust and vacuum your home at least twice a week.** Conventional vacuum cleaners can blow dust back into the room. Use a vacuum fitted with a HEPA (High-Efficiency Particulate Actuation) filter, such as Nilfisk Model GS90. *Note:* The allergic person shouldn't perform these tasks. If no one else can do the cleaning, the allergic person should wear a face mask while doing the work.

• **Keep floors bare.** Dust mites, the main allergen in dust, thrive in carpets.

• **Cover pillows, mattresses, box springs, and furniture with plastic encasings.** Mites breed in furniture and bedding, but can't get through plastic encasings. The plastic should be vacuumed once a week when the linens are changed.

• **Choose a dog that matches your energy level.** All dogs can learn, but some are more active than others.

Example: Most terriers are very frisky, while hounds tend to be low-energy animals.

• **Give your dog specific verbal commands.** While most dogs can learn up to 30 words, eight commands are adequate for a well-trained house pet. These commands should be simple, concise—no more than three or four words per command—and consistent. If you order your dog to *sit down* while your spouse uses *sit here*, your pet may get confused. *The basic commands:*

• *Stay.* Keeps your dog from straying.

• *Come.* Releases your dog from a stationary position.

• *Down/sit.* Use this when your dog becomes overly playful.

• *Go to your bed/rug.* Tells your dog that it has its own place to sleep.

• *Leave it/don't touch it.* This will also keep your dog from confronting another dog.

• *Here.* A less-formal version of heel.

• *Take it.* This indicates your permission for the dog to take food from your hand.

• *Free.* This lets your dog know he can go play or relax.

• **When giving commands,** gear your expectations to the dog's age.

• **Build your pet's training around rewards.** When training is based on punishment, a dog may become too nervous to learn. Positive reinforcement is far more effective.

Is your dog motivated most by treats? By toys? By petting? Reward each successful performance with whatever makes your pet especially happy.

• **Stick to routines for the essentials.** Dogs are the most adaptable of all animals. They feel stress, however, when owners are erratic in meeting their basic needs, such as giving them food and water and providing opportunities to relieve themselves. To keep your pet relaxed and self-controlled, set regular convenient times for your dog's meals and outside excursions.

• **Review your command code with your pet every few months.** All of us—dogs and people alike—need refresher courses to reinforce what we've learned. Practice the commands to be sure the dog follows them each time. You should only have to say your command once.

Your Family History

G. G. Vandagriff

Start your search for your roots with a telephone call to the Family History Library of the Church of Jesus Christ of Latter-Day Saints in Salt Lake City, UT, 801-240-2331.

Ask for the address of its History Center nearest to you, and tap into the greatest genealogy collection in the world. Each of the 2,000 Family History Centers in the U.S. and Canada offers free access to its CD-ROM computer database program called FamilySearch.

• **Before you go, contact your oldest relatives** and get family names, dates of birth, countries and counties of origin, relationships and Social Security numbers . . . and design a family tree. Bring this, and a notebook filled with specific questions about relatives to the library so that you can use computer time in an organized fashion.

• **Put on your detective's hat.** There are five files available to you in FamilySearch. Each one holds family names . . . and maybe family secrets. The files: *Ancestral File, Family History Library Catalog, International Genealogical Index, Military Index, Social Security Death Index.*

G. G. Vandagriff, author of *Voices in Your Blood—Discovering Identity Through Family History,* Andrews and McMeel, 4900 Main St., Kansas City, MO 64112. $9.95.

• **Wash linens in hot water.** Warm or cold water doesn't kill mites.

• **Keep the windows in your house shut.** This helps to keep outdoor allergens outside. *Note:* Many trees pollinate between 2 A.M. and 4 A.M., so keep windows closed at night.

• **Don't use a humidifier.** It increases the mold content in the air. Use a dehumidifier for damp spaces.

• **Avoid heaters that release irritating particles,** such as wood-burning stoves, fireplaces.

• **Use the air conditioner in warm weather.** It filters out a lot of troublesome particles from the air. Clean or change the filter once a week.

• **Get an air filter.** Use it when it's too cool for the air conditioner. *Best:* A HEPA filter, which can remove particles that other filters can't. *Important:* When the filter is on, keep room doors and windows closed. *Cost:* About $150 and up.

• **Ask your allergist about injections.**

Gerald L. Klein, M.D., Allergy and Immunology Medical Group, 2067 W. Vista Way, Vista, CA 92083. Dr. Klein is an associate clinical professor at the University of California and a member of the Board of Regents of the American College of Allergy and Immunology.

■ **Make an ordinary home dinner special**—invite an unusual guest—someone outside your normal circle. *Examples:* A business associate you admire or someone you would like to get to know better, a neighbor or someone who has done you a favor. *Benefits:* You'll dramatically change your routine dinnertime interactions—and your relationship with your guest.

How to Be Happier Day by Day by Alan Epstein, Ph.D., California-based cofounder of True Partners, an introduction and relationship counseling service. Viking.

■ **Better buffet entertaining.** Set the buffet so guests will not have to balance too many items. *Example:* If guests will eat sitting at a dining table, set places with napkins, glassware and flatware so they don't have to carry all that along with their food. If they'll eat while standing or sitting but not at a table, roll up flatware in dinner napkins and place these at the end of the buffet table so guests can pick them up after filling their plates.

The Complete Party Book: How to Plan, Host and Enjoy Your Party from Conception to Conclusion by Don Ernstein, owner, Wonder Foods, California party-planning company. Viking Studio.

How to Throw a Very Successful Party

Penny Warner

A successful party isn't hard to put together once you get the formula down. Unforgettable parties are the result of this clever mix:

• **A legitimate reason** (or plausible excuse!) for a get-together.

• **A carefully orchestrated plan.**

• **Creativity.**

BE A DIRECTOR

Your party will be different if you direct it, rather than just invite folks and hope for the best. *Examples:*

• **If you host a baby shower**, make it a toys only or baby's bath only shower, and your guests will head eagerly to the stores now that you've eliminated guesswork.

• **Center a retirement party on the retiree's hobby**—say, golf and have guests wear golf clothes.

• **Turn a going-away party** into a movable feast where friends pick up and travel together from house to house for each course. Meet at the first house for drinks and hors d'oeuvres. Move on to the second for soup and salad. Travel to the third for the main course. Wind up at the fourth house for dessert and coffee and a fond farewell.

Penny Warner, author of *The Best Party Book—1001 Creative Ideas for Fun Parties*, Meadowbrook Press, 18318 Minnetonka Blvd., Deephaven, MN 55391.

PARTY CHECKLIST

Once you have chosen the reason for a party, you must get yourself organized.

You don't want to be expecting your first guest to come through the door, only suddenly to remember you forgot to buy ice. To avoid that kind of catastrophe, develop a "things to do and things to buy" checklist that is divided into four sections that help you organize your time and effort as the day of the party approaches:

Section 1: **Three weeks before the party.** Develop a guest list, create the invitations (and mail them), decide the menu, write a grocery list and hire any serving help you might need.

Section 2: **A week before the party.** Call guests who didn't RSVP, buy the food and drinks, prepare food and decide what you're wearing.

Section 3: **One day before the party.** Clean the house, arrange the party room, pull out the serving dishes and confirm deliveries and caterers.

Section 4: **The day of the party.** Decorate, finish cooking, set up everything, mentally "travel through" the party and get dressed.

INVITATIONS

Make your invitation a show stopper. *Best:* Homemade invitations. *Examples:*

• **For a birthday party**, go to your library and get a photocopy of the front page of a newspaper from the day and year your birthday guest was born. Design your invitation to the size of a column in the paper, paste your column over an old column and photocopy as many invitations as you need.

• **For a baby shower**, cut out small footprints on which you've written party details.

• **For a Christmas party**, make gingerbread people, each one decorated with a guest's name and a card tied around the neck.

THEME FOOD

Offer theme food—and serve it with flair. *Examples:*

• **For a graduation party**, serve high-quality food cafeteria-style—on trays.

GOLF

■ **Improved backswings for older golfers.** Backswings get shorter as golfers get older. When the swings get too short, you'll lose distance, accuracy and consistency. *Remedies:* Hold the club lightly. *Reason:* Too tight a grip tenses the arm and shoulder muscles and restricts the backswing. Put more weight on your right foot, especially on full swings with woods and longer irons. *Result:* A head start on your swing and less weight to shift. Turn your chin to the right (or to the left, if you're a southpaw) as you start your backswing. If it throws your timing off, cock your chin in the direction of the backswing before you swing.

■ **Best golf-instruction videos.** Filmed in 1930, the black-and-white videos feature Bobby Jones, the links legend of the 1920s and 1930s. He was the only U.S. golfer ever to win four major tournaments in one year. Jones was paid $101,000 at the time to narrate and demonstrate his skills in films that were then marketed to wealthy amateur golfers. Converted to video, *The Bobby Jones Instructional Series* includes *The Full Swing (Vol. 1)* and *From Tee to Green (Vol. 2)*. Sixty minutes/$33.95 each. *Source:* SyberVision Systems Inc., One Sansome St., Suite 1610, Department BJ01, San Francisco, CA 94104.

Keith Marks, director of the Royal Golf Academy, Port Royal Resort, Hilton Head, SC.

PICTURE PERFECT

■ **Videotaping basics.**
To hold the camera as
steady as possible,
keep your feet apart
with your weight evenly
distributed between
them . . . tuck elbows into
your body for
support . . . for a smooth,
side-to-side
pan, keep the bottom half
of your body still and pivot the upper
half, "rolling" your body over a solid
support, such as a wall . . . in windy conditions, find a firm support—wall, railing,
car trunk—to lean against.

John Hedgecoe's Complete Guide to Video by
John Hedgecoe, professor of photography, Royal
College of Art, London. Sterling Publishing Co.

■ **Beanbag camera support.** Fill a
small bag with any kind of dried
beans . . . set the bag on a steady surface . . . put the camera on the
bag . . . line up the shot and take the
photo—the camera stays still. Especially
useful for long-exposure shots.

Backpacker, 33 E. Minor St., Emmaus, PA
18098.

■ **Better fireworks photographs.** Use a
camera with adjustable shutter speed—
automatic cameras will not work. *Make
time exposures*—hold the shutter open
for several seconds to get the effect of
lights blooming in the air. *Use a tripod* to
keep the camera steady. *Shoot with print
film*—better for this purpose than slide
film. *Use a flash* for ground displays or
the faces of children watching—but remember that most camera flashes illumi-
nate only eight to ten feet.

*Photo experts at Eastman Kodak Co., quoted in
Woman's Day,* 1633 Broadway, New York, NY
10019.

• **For dessert at a family reunion**, have
each family contribute an eight-inch-square cake
decorated with the contributor's name on it, and
place the squares together to form a show-stopping
pièce de résistance.

• **Break out the wicker baskets**, old-fashioned tins and large seashells to serve food, rather
than using ordinary or dull serving dishes. Food
looks and tastes better when it is served creatively.

ACTIVITIES

Plan unusual activities. No charades. No board
games. Sustain the mood of the party. *Examples:*

• **For a baby shower**, buy eight jars of baby
food, remove the labels and have each guest taste
and write down the flavors she thinks she has just
tasted. The guest with the most correct answers
wins a prize—perhaps a home pregnancy kit or a
stuffed toy.

• **Create a great birthday videotape** by
having guests relate funny anecdotes about the hon-
oree. Play the tape during the party, and give the
tape to the birthday boy or girl as a souvenir.

• **For a family reunion** have the oldest
relatives tell their life stories.

DECORATIONS

A party without decorations is like a movie without a musical score—something is missing. Done
well, decorations add immeasurably to the atmosphere and to the enjoyment of the people at the
party.

And here's where the kids, a spouse, and friends
come in. Pass out assignments, for example, to cut
out legs and boots from felt and hang Santa's legs in
the fireplace at Christmas, to create a basket of honeymoon items (cologne, mints, body paint, silk
panties, videos) as a centerpiece at a bachelorette
party or to collect and hang photos of the guest of
honor from past to present (complete with captions)
at a birthday party.

UNUSUAL THEMES

Every month of the year, there is a ready-made
excuse to throw a party . . .

- **January 9**, Sherlock Holmes's Birthday.
- **March 24**, Harry Houdini's Birthday.
- **June 7**, Day of the Rice God.
- **July 14**, Bastille Day.
- **September 26**, Johnny Appleseed's birthday.

Any excuse can be the perfect excuse for a party. *Examples:*

- **An international evening** where the guests bring dishes from the old country.
- **A fashion-victim party** where guests wear the unwearable.
- **A ski party** far from the slopes where the guests dress in snow bunny or ski bum apparel.
- **An invite-a-friend party** where each guest brings someone new to the group.

PUT YOUR IMAGINATION TO WORK

Parties don't have to be held in someone's house or in a rented hall. You can also create your own car road rally or biking party by designing your own map and clues along the way with a favorite restaurant as the ultimate destination.

You might also consider having everyone meet at a bowling alley, espresso bar or at a nearby dance studio.

TRAVEL AND FAMILY

■ **Safer travel for children:** Tape the child's name, current hotel and phone number to the underside of an ID bracelet to help locate the child should he/she become lost. If traveling abroad, include the address and phone of the nearest U.S. embassy.

The Packing Book: Secrets of the Carry-On Traveler by Judith Gilford, Easy-Going Travel Shop and Bookstore, Berkeley, CA. Ten Speed Press.

■ **Easier car travel with babies.** For easier cleanups, hang a two-handled plastic grocery bag containing a roll of towels from the passenger door . . . carry a jug of water and plastic cups . . . pack the outfit the baby will wear on arrival—let him/her travel in anything comfortable . . . carry a medicine box containing bandages, antiseptic, syrup of ipecac and acetaminophen under the car seat.

Baby Tactics: Parenting Ideas That Really Work by parenting expert Barbara Albers Hill. Avery Publishing Group.

■ **Better flying with a pet.** Reserve a place for the pet in advance. Try to schedule a nonstop flight. Avoid the heavy air traffic on holidays and weekends. Put your name, address and phone number on the pet's carrier. For overseas travel—including Hawaii—find out about any special health requirements or quarantine procedures. Before traveling, get the pet used to the carrier. Avoid giving solid pet food for six hours before the flight, but give moderate drinks of water.

Consumer Affairs Division, U.S. Department of Transportation, 400 Seventh St. SW, Washington, DC 20590.

■ **Better outdoor trips.** Set aside an afternoon of rest for every morning of

TRAVEL AND FAMILY

travel, and a full day's rest for every full day's travel. *First-day rules:* Bicycle no more than 30 miles distance, to no higher than 750 feet elevation . . . canoe no longer than four hours . . . hike with a backpack no more than five miles distance, no higher than 1,500 feet elevation. On succeeding days, bike no more than 50 miles/1,000 feet elevation, canoe no more than five hours, hike no more than seven miles/2,000 feet elevation.

The Camper's Companion: The Pack-Along Guide for Better Outdoor Trips by outdoorsmen Rick Greenspan and Hal Kahn. Foghorn Press.

TRAVEL SAVVY

■ **Travel trap.** Business travelers gain weight while on the road. Traveling salespeople added an average of 15 pounds in three years—more than three times as much as blue-collar workers or leisure travelers.

Study comparing eating habits of 96 traveling salespeople from all over the country with those of other groups, by Maria Simonson, Ph.D., Sc.D., psychologist, Johns Hopkins Medical Institutions, Baltimore.

■ **Travel decisions.** Consider all costs when making travel decisions. *Example:* Should you rent a car or take taxis? Hidden expenses of renting a car include parking and gas, which may mean it will be cheaper to take a cab to your meetings and appointments—especially if your hotel offers free airport-van service. *On the other hand:* A rental car gives you the freedom to stay out of the downtown area where hotels are usually more expensive.

Rolfe Shellenberger, senior travel consultant, writing in *Runzheimer Reports on Travel Management*, Runzheimer Park, Rochester, WI 53167.

Rules to Keep a Friendly Poker Game Friendly

Stewart Wolpin

Neighborhood poker—exemplified by the guys on *The Odd Couple*—is more than just a game. It's a friendship around a table. And friendship thrives in a comfortable atmosphere where friends show each other consideration. *Bottom line:* Poker should be fun. *To set the scene . . .*

MAKE IT COMFORTABLE

• **The room.** It should be big enough for a table and at least seven chairs, with plenty of room to get up and leave the table without bumping other players. *Important:* A window that opens at the top . . . if there's cigarette and cigar smoke, it has to go somewhere. Provide large ashtrays or your floor will suffer.

• **TV.** Good for players who drop out of the game . . . and for everyone when there's a major sports event. It doesn't matter where the TV sits, but keep the sound low—it can be turned up for the exciting moments.

• **Music.** It's up to the individual group whether to have music . . . and what kind of music. Play the radio, so that no one has to hop up to change tapes, etc.

• **Table.** A round table is preferred, but any shape will do. Use a tablecloth to make a smooth, cushioned surface. Chips bounce when tossed on a bare table top.

• **Chairs.** Use strong, metal folding chairs . . . wood is not strong enough. Comfort is

Stewart Wolpin, author of *The Rules of Neighborhood Poker According to Hoyle*, New Chapter Press, 381 Park Ave. South, New York, NY 10016.

not a concern in poker games. If you're winning, you'll be very comfortable.

• **Cards.** Use high-quality cards. Cheap cards crease and bend easily—a card with a folded corner will be a marked card for the rest of evening.

Use two decks at a time, each with a different color backing. While one deck is being dealt, the other can be reshuffled by the player who dealt the previous hand. Hold on to decks from previous weeks in case you need an emergency replacement deck.

• **Chips.** Have at least three colors—one for each of the minimum and maximum bets, and one for double the maximum. Clay chips handle better than plastic. They're available from gambling supply houses—check your Yellow Pages.

• **Food.** Chips, pretzels, popcorn and nuts are the old standbys. Select food that can be eaten with one hand, leaving the other free to hold cards.

Later in the evening something more substantial will be necessary. Cold cuts or pizza work well. Both can sit for a while and remain edible, require few utensils and don't make a mess. Use paper plates, and keep plastic bags handy for garbage. *Mistake:* Chinese food. It's too messy.

Food should be supplied by the host . . . but paid for by all. Arrive at a set donation or take a cut from each pot.

• **Disaster control.** Keep plenty of paper towels and a portable vacuum cleaner handy.

• **Clean-up philosophy.** Nobody leaves until the garbage is bagged, ashtrays are emptied, and the immediate area is made neat.

PLAYING ETIQUETTE

• **Know what you are going to deal** when the deck comes to you. Poker has a rhythm. Being indecisive breaks it.

• **Turn all your cards face down** to indicate you're out of a hand. Or toss them to the dealer or into the pot so they're out of the way. Take care that no one sees your cards. What one player knows, all should know.

• **Clean up condensation** from beverage bottles and cans. Wet cards ruin the game.

■ **Better car renting in Europe.** Reserve the car through a U.S. travel agent, who can offer better rates than a European agent . . . ask for written confirmation of both the reservation and the rate in local currency . . . make sure that either your credit card or personal auto insurance provides accident and liability coverage in foreign countries . . . plan to pick up and return the car during business hours since European locations are likely to be closed at night and on weekends . . . confirm with the rental agent that the car you're returning is not damaged and request a final bill. *Reason:* Disputing charges can be difficult after you return home.

Roundup of car rental experts in *The Wall Street Journal.*

■ **Airplane headphone risk.** Airplane headphones increase risk of external ear infections. *Culprit:* The warm, moist environment created by the plastic earpieces—a perfect breeding ground for bacteria. *Self-defense:* Don't use the earphones for more than 30 minutes at a time . . . use only disinfected headphones—the ones in plastic bags passed out by flight attendants at the beginning of the flight, not those left behind by previous passengers.

Study by Itzhak Brook, M.D., Naval Medical Research Institute, Bethesda, M.D., and professor of pediatrics, Georgetown University, Washington, DC.

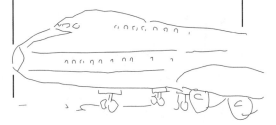

COLLECTING

■ **Collecting autographs.** You can often collect autographs from celebrities just by asking. *Best approach:* Writing a letter to create a conversation with the celebrity—and show a genuine interest in his/her work—in order to stimulate a reply. *Example:* Richard Berman got an autograph from astronaut Neil Armstrong by asking for his view on the theory that the world would be better if we blew up the moon. *To reach a celebrity:* Write in care of the institution with which he is affiliated (book publisher, movie studio, etc.) or join the Universal Autograph Collectors Club, P.O. Box 6181, Washington, DC 20044. It publishes a bimonthly magazine with the addresses of famous people. Include a large, self-addressed, stamped envelope with your letter.

Richard Berman, a media consultant in Chappaqua, NY, and an avid autograph collector.

FITNESS

■ **Crucial for better biking:** A comfortable fit between bike and rider. *Helpful:* Set seat height by placing one foot on the pedal in its lowest position so the heel is slightly off the top of the pedal. Make sure there's a slight bend in the knee to avoid complete extension. Adjust the handlebars so you can comfortably rest your hands on the handles. Handlebars should be as wide as your shoulders. Adjust the handlebars' stem height so it's two to five centimeters below the tip of the saddle.

Davis Phinney, 1991 U.S. pro champion from Santa Cruz, CA, quoted in Men's Fitness, 21100 Erwin St., Woodland Hills, CA 91367.

• **Be honest.** You only have to be caught once to be marked forever.

• **Bring enough money** to play for at least half the night. The worst thing you can do is quit early and leave only four players. *Rule of thumb:* Bring enough money to buy three full stacks of chips.

• **If you must leave early**, make it known in advance. This gives the other players a chance to find someone else.

• **If you drink beer . . . bring beer.** Once it comes into the house, though, it's community property. *Note:* If you want to drink or eat something different than what is being served, bring it.

• **Keep your up cards fully exposed** in a stud game so everyone can see them. Players who try to cover up their cards in a stud game are not trusted.

• **Announce your ante.** Say something like "I'm in" loud enough so that others hear you. Then, if the pot comes up short, you'll have witnesses.

Don't give another player advice on betting, even if asked. Your advice could sabotage a bluffer, or simply be bad advice.

• **Once you've dropped out**, don't look at another player's hand without permission. And don't react to what you've seen.

• **Don't look at another player's hand** if you've seen someone else's. Your expression could give something away. *Worse:* Giving advice to either of the player's whose cards you've seen. Your advice would be based on knowledge of two or three hands (including your own)—knowledge not available to other players.

• **Don't call out** what cards of possibilities another player has showing. Only the dealer has this right. This is all the more true when you've dropped out.

• **Never help another player** figure out what he/she has. A player must call his own hand.

• **Don't feel sorry for a loser** and hold the bet down. It's humiliating for the loser. Play to win big. It's not malicious—it's the game.

• **Don't feel sorry for a novice.** It's sink or swim. And you could find yourself in the position of carrying a bad player.

• **Don't show your complete winning hand** if you win the pot by default. You may have been bluffing and that's information no one paid to see . . . and you don't want anyone to know. Only by calling your final bet do players pay for the privilege of seeing your hand.

• **Never play poker with someone whose nickname is a city.** If he's good enough to be the best in town, he's good enough to beat anyone in your neighborhood.

Shrewder Lottery Playing

Alan J. Reiss

Most lottery players either choose their numbers at random or plug in family birth dates. *Their assumption:* Since winning numbers are chosen at random, there is no way to improve a player's chances. In fact, mathematical strategies can make a huge difference in playing the lottery.

Alan J. Reiss, president of U.S. Mathematical Labs, 18 Main St., Concord, MA 01742. His company sells two mathematical tools for lottery players...a computer software program available for IBM or MAC for $104 (please specify 3½" or 5¼" disk), and a mechanical "WinWheel" for $21.95...to help people to generate "original" sets of numbers unlikely to be selected by other players.

■ **New game of tennis.** Forget about the boundary lines . . . forget the number of bounces. Just keep hitting. It's much more aerobic, much less stressful. *Much more fun:* Start with at least a dozen balls—two dozen is better. Everybody wins.

Super Summer Drinks . . . without Liquor . . . Good Anytime

Jane Brandt

Teetotaler's wine can be made in any quantity and is best served in wine glasses. Mix equal parts chilled ginger ale and chilled, unsweetened grape juice. Serves 16.

Ellen's Energizer is a refreshing summer drink as well as a great stomach settler. Combine ½ cup of half-and-half with ½ cup ginger ale . . . or—if you're counting calories—½ cup skim milk with ½ cup diet ginger ale. Serve over crushed ice. Serves one.

Fast Fruit Punch is a great thirst-quencher and has a pretty purple color. In a punch bowl, combine 1 quart ginger ale, one 46-ounce can pineapple juice, one 32-ounce bottle grape juice, one 6-ounce can frozen orange juice (prepared) and one 6-ounce can frozen lemonade (prepared). Add ice and a fresh fruit garnish. Serves 40.

Festive Punch is a perfect beverage for summer barbecues, brunches or luncheons. You'll need three 6-ounce cans frozen lemonade concentrate (prepared), one 10-ounce package of frozen straw-

ENTERTAINING

berries (thawed), 1 quart chilled ginger ale, ice, one pint raspberry sherbet, and fresh whole raspberries.

Pour lemonade into the punch bowl and stir in strawberries. Just before serving add ginger ale and an ice ring, then stir in sherbet. Place a raspberry in each cup and serve. Serves 10.

Jane Brandt, author of *Drinks Without Liquor.* Workman Publishing.

FAMILY FUN

Wonderful Zoos

Anthony Marshall

• **Audubon Park and Zoological Garden**, run by the Audubon Institute, also includes a huge downtown aquarium.

The zoo's Louisiana Swamp exhibit has a population of alligators and migratory birds, nutria, cougars, muskrats and otters, and incorporates both natural and cultural history.

Other attractions: The South American pampas exhibit, Pathways to the Past museum, tropical bird house.

Audubon Park and Zoological Garden, 6500 Magazine St., New Orleans, LA 70118. 504-861-2537.

• **Bronx Zoo—International Wildlife Conservation Park** features an outstanding Jungle World exhibit that has set the standard for interior walk-through rain-forest exhibits in zoos throughout the country. The Jungle World building contains 530 animals of 87 species. There are waterfalls throughout, and a mist-maker recreates the humidity of a tropical rain forest.

Key: Choosing *unpopular* numbers that are unlikely to be selected by other players. *Result:* While your chance of winning the jackpot remains the same, the *amount* you stand to win is much larger . . . since you'll be splitting your prize with fewer (if any) other players.

In a "6/49" lottery (where the players choose six numbers between 1 and 49), there are about 14 million different combinations available. In a typical game, 20% of those combinations—2.8 million different plays—are selected by no one.

A shrewd lottery strategy will consistently land you within that 20% window . . . giving you a strong chance of pocketing the entire jackpot should you win.

Better: The larger the jackpot, the better your return on every dollar you wager. *Reason:* A disproportionate number of the extra bettors will be playing combinations that you'll be avoiding.

What are these unpopular numbers that you should be targeting?

• **All numbers over 31**, for the simple reason that they won't be chosen by anyone playing birth or anniversary dates. At least four of your six choices should be 32 or above.

• **Numbers ending in 1, 2, 8, 9 . . . and 0.** Most people tend to select numbers ending in 3 through 7. *Especially unpopular:* 10, 20, 30, and 40.

On the other hand, avoid playing the more popular numbers or combinations, including:

• **Multiples of 7**, which are favored by the superstitious.

• **Single-digit numbers (1 through 9).** Use no more than one of these among your six choices.

• **Numbers that form vertical, horizontal, or diagonal patterns** on your bet slip card. These are also quite popular.

• **The combination 1-2-3-4-5-6**, which may be the most popular of all.

Bottom line: By playing the least popular numbers, you can increase the amount of money you bring home by *more than 600%*.

What to Do When You Win The Lottery

Rob Sanford

Many people assume that winning the lottery would automatically solve all their problems.

In fact, winning the lottery creates a whole new set of problems. Steps to take if you're ever among the lucky ones:

• **Tell no one outside your immediate family that you've won.** Your silence—and the freedom from pressure that it buys you—will allow you to think about how to invest your windfall in privacy. If you are interviewed by the media, be an uninteresting, dull and boring interviewee. In the long run, that will discourage others from bothering you.

• **Don't assume that you've won.** Some people choose to buy a "quick pick" ticket, for which the numbers are chosen for you at random. If this was the case with your winning ticket, there is the possibility—although a slim one—that you may not have won at all.

Reason: Under the rules of most state lotteries, only a certain number of quick-pick tickets can hit the jackpot in a single game. If more than the intended number of big winners are mistakenly printed, all may be disqualified—leaving their owners with no more than a refund of the amount spent on the ticket.

Rob Sanford, certified financial planner based in Malibu, CA. He is the author of *Infinite Financial Freedom: What to Do Before and After You Win the Lottery*, Title-Waves Publishing.

FAMILY FUN

Other attractions: The World of Birds exhibit, Bengali Express monorail, African Plains exhibit.
Bronx Zoo, 185 St. and Southern Blvd., Bronx, NY 10460. 718-220-5100.

• **Caldwell Zoo** is fairly small (only 35 acres), but it has one of the best small African Plains zoo exhibit in the country. Giraffes, elephants, zebras and other Plains animals are separated by hidden moats, yet appear to roam together in harmony.

Other attractions: The Terrestrial exhibit, Flight Cage exhibit, cattle barn and petting zoo farm.
Caldwell Zoo, 2203 Martin Luther King Blvd., Tyler, TX 75710. 903-593-0121.

• **Fort Wayne Children's Zoo** has a one-of-a-kind, walk-through Australian exhibit that allows you to get extremely close to about 30 kangaroos.

The center of the exhibit is a clean, tidy plaza surrounded by buildings modeled after actual buildings in Australia. Open from the last Saturday of April until mid-October.
Fort Wayne Children's Zoo, 3411 Sherman Blvd., Fort Wayne, IN 46808. 219-427-6800.

• **Fort Worth Zoological Association** features a World of Primates exhibit that houses all the families of the great apes on 2.5 acres. This indoor, climate-controlled tropical rain forest is the only one of its kind in the U.S. and houses endangered lowland gorillas and more.
Fort Worth Zoological Park, 1989 Colonial Pkwy., Fort Worth, TX 76110. 817-871-7050.

Conservationist Anthony Marshall, author of *Zoo: Profiles of 102 Zoos, Aquariums, and Wildlife Parks in the United States.* Random House.

THE GREAT OUTDOORS

Alternative Vacations from Earthwatch

Earthwatch offers the public unique opportunities to work on important cultural and environmental research projects worldwide.

- **Helping scientists count whales** off the coast of western Australia.

- **Compiling videos and audiotapes** of songs, stories, dances, and costumes from ancient villages in southwest Russia.

- **Studying the environmental threats** to loons in northern Wisconsin, hawks in Michigan, or blue crabs in the Chesapeake Bay.

- **Helping archaeologists excavate** old settlements in the Scottish Hebrides, Moscow, the Pacific Spice Islands, or Easter Island.

Participants make tax-deductible contributions averaging $1,600, which cover food and lodging and support research. *More information:* 800-776-0188. On the Worldwide Web at http://www.earthwatch.org or E-mail info@earthwatch.org.

Earthwatch, 680 Mount Auburn St., Box 9104, Watertown, MA 02272.

- **Secure your winning ticket.** Start by signing the back of your ticket, which seals your right to the proceeds. Then photocopy both the front and back of the ticket to protect yourself. Type up a separate statement of authenticity with your signature, and, as an added precaution, have this statement notarized. You must surrender your lottery ticket to have it validated, and copying it will protect you in case the original is lost by the lottery bureaucracy. Keep the photocopies in a safe-deposit box until you are ready to turn in your ticket and claim your prize.

- **Claim your prize correctly.** If you neglect to mail in an official claim form (available from your lottery retailer) within a set number of days or fail to appear in person and have your winning ticket validated, you may be disqualified.

Deadline: Usually from 6 to 12 months after the winning drawing, depending on the state.

- **If you have indeed won big, get an unlisted phone number.** Database marketers, reporters, charities and curiosity-seekers obtain lists of lottery winners' names through the Freedom of Information Act. Though addresses and phone numbers are not so readily available, they may leak out eventually. Be prepared to change your phone number two to three times within the first nine months after you win—the period in which pressure to seek you out will be greatest.

- **Don't assume you've won the total jackpot.** Approximately one-third of the time, several winners share a prize.

- **If you've won as part of a group, set up a partnership** by drafting a simple agreement using one of the *Do-It-Yourself Fill-in-the-Blank* legal kits (available from TitleWaves and many bookstores). Call the IRS at 800-829-3676 and ask for the SS-4 Form to obtain a federal employer identification number. Validate your ticket under the name of the new entity. This will add another line of defense between you and the mail that is soon to come your way.

- **Get a post-office box**—preferably one from the U.S. Postal Service instead of a mail-service company—rather than receiving mail at home.

Winners often receive solicitations for business schemes, media deals, marriage proposals, etc.

• **Buy a home-security system.** It should include perimeter contacts on all doors and windows, interior infrared motion detectors, motion-sensitive lighting, audible on-site alarm *plus* a 24-hour monitoring service that connects your home to a central station alarm.

Consider: A drive-by armed-guard service. Request high-visibility protection for the first nine months after you win. Several lottery winners have had their homes burglarized even before they received any cash.

• **You may have to quit your salaried job.** It may not be practical for you to keep working at your company when you earn far more than your bosses. Resentment can arise, and bosses may assume that you will eventually quit, making promotions unlikely and limiting your responsibilities. In addition, many "jackpot chasers" will phone you at work, causing even further disruption of the workplace.

• **Be a little frivolous—and then a lot cautious.** Blow 10% of your first lottery check. Be mindless and irresponsible—and get it out of your system. Put the remaining 90% away for at least three months. Park it in a money-market mutual fund or a 90-day CD to avoid temptation. Few people are accustomed to dealing with large sums of money, and they need time to adjust. In either case, make sure your money is adequately insured by investing no more than $100,000 at a single bank.

• **Get out of town.** Take an inexpensive trip —and treat it like a business trip. Go where you will have the solitude you need to plan the next steps in your new life.

Little-Known Historic Towns in the Old West

Chuck and Rodica Woodbury

• *Bisbee, Arizona*, was a copper-mining town. Today, it is laid back and quietly becoming an artists' community with a handsome downtown area. There is a tour into the Queen Mine, an adventure replete with individual rain slicker, hard hat and flashlight.

Our favorite historic accommodations: The Copper Queen Hotel, 800-247-5829.

• *Nevada City, California*, was the state's third-largest city during the gold rush of the 1840s. Today, Nevada City is a quaint reminder of a brief era of gaslights and horse-drawn carriages . . . of gingerbread and coy pastels.

Our favorite historic accommodations: The Red Castle Inn, California's oldest bed and breakfast. 916-265-5135.

• *Ouray, Colorado*, is perched on a steep mountainside, accessible only by a single mountain road. Ouray is famous for hot mineral springs, making it one of the oldest spa towns in the country. Breathtaking Box Canyon Falls is a short walk from the town.

Our favorite historic accommodations: St. Elmo Hotel, 970-325-4951.

• *Silver City, New Mexico*, is where Billy the Kid grew up. There's a self-guided walking tour of his haunts, but the beauty of Silver City is really its out-of-the-way purity. The ancient Native American Gila Cliff Dwellings National Monument is nearby.

WILD WEST REVISITED

Our favorite historic accommodations: *The Palace Hotel*, 505-388-1811.

• **Silverton, Colorado**, is the terminus on the 45-mile-long Silverton-Durango Railroad, one of the slowest but most exciting train rides in the U.S. The steamer has been operating continuously since 1882. Silverton still has dirt streets, historic storefronts, and saloons.

Our favorite historic accommodations: *Alma House*, 970-387-5336, or 1-800-267-5336.

Chuck and Rodica Woodbury, editors and publishers of *Out West*, a travel newspaper that covers the back roads and small towns of the American West, 408 Broad St., Ste. 11, Nevada City, CA 95959.

FRESH AIR FUN

■ **Visit the great outdoors** through residential camp programs for people age 50 and older. Costs vary, depending on location and program. *More information—Voluntary Association for Senior Citizen Activities (VASCA)*, affiliated with 10 vacation centers in the Northeast, 275 Seventh Ave., New York 10001. 212-645-6590 (free guide available) . . . *YMCA*, which has special sessions for active people older than age 50 at some of its 250 camps. Call your local YMCA for information . . . *American Camping Association (ACA)*, 800-428-2267. ACA publishes a guide to accredited camps. *Cost:* $16.95.

■ **Learn from each round of golf you play** by keeping track of each shot you hit. Called *shot mapping*, the technique involves sketching all 18 holes (or using the diagram on the scorecard) and

How to Take Much Better Photos Outdoors

Susan McCartney

You don't need magical skills to be a nature photographer. Even without sophisticated equipment, you can come away with wonderful pictures of landscapes, plants or animals. *What you need to take great photos . . .*

PATIENCE

Nature photography is a contemplative activity. You cannot rush nature. You cannot make animals or a landscape do anything. For the best pictures, you must settle in and observe.

Types of questions to ask yourself: How is a flower affected by the play of sun and clouds or by passing breezes? How does a landscape change with the light from dawn to dusk?

Example: When I recently visited the Grand Canyon, I watched one person after another march up to the rim, stand with their backs to this marvel, have a friend take their picture and then move on. I sat on the rim of the canyon for the entire day, photographing at intervals and watching the play of light and clouds. I took the best pictures at sunset.

LOVE OF THE SUBJECT

The first challenge is to become familiar with your subject through repeated exposure. African safaris and trips to Yellowstone National Park are wonderful opportunities, but you can also profit from less expensive trips.

Susan McCartney, an international freelance photographer who conducts workshops at the School of Visual Arts in New York. She is the author of *Travel Photography: A Complete Guide to How to Shoot and Sell* and *Nature and Wildlife Photography: A Practical Guide to How to Shoot and Sell*. Allworth Press.

Where to start: A local park, zoo or woodland. For plants and flowers, a nearby botanical garden will do fine. Choose the subjects that most fascinate you, and "stalk" them like a hunter.

Caution: Avoid the woods during deer-hunting season. My own career was almost ended by a pot-shot in the Allegheny National Forest.

AWARENESS OF LIGHT

The best time to take photographs of nature is during the early- or late-day hours, when the low sun enhances the subject. *How to take advantage of the low-angle light:*

• **To produce dramatic pictures from even the simplest camera**—position yourself so that the light is coming diagonally over your shoulder onto the subject.

• **When shooting a landscape or the texture** of animal fur, bird feathers, fish scales or flower petals—position yourself so that the light is hitting the subject from the side. Side lighting reveals texture.

• **When you want to create a halo of light** around animals or flowers or show the translucency of insects and plants—position yourself so that the low sun is behind the subject. Be careful that the sun doesn't hit the camera lens directly.

Useful for all nature photos: Soft light that is diffused by thin clouds or light mist anytime of day.

To be avoided: "Top" light from overhead summer sun, which casts shadows that record almost black on film. As a rule, I will not shoot if my shadow is shorter than I am.

EQUIPMENT

You can take good nature pictures with virtually any camera as long as you know its limitations. In fact, I have seen very good shots from point-and-shoot and even disposable cameras.

For serious nature photographers, a good tripod is an important accessory. It is absolutely essential for use in low light with long exposures or for close-ups made with slow small apertures and shutter speeds for maximum depth of field. It will minimize blur caused by camera shake when shooting with telephotos and zoom lenses.

recording where each shot went and the club with which you hit. If you play the same course regularly, you can use these records to learn how best to play each hole.

Golf: Steps to Success by DeDe Owens, Ed.D., director of golf instruction, Cog Hill Golf & Country Club, Lemont, IL. Human Kinetics Publishers.

Camping with Kids

Roger Woodson

• **Start small.** Spend a night outdoors in a backyard tent.

• **Camp when you feel comfortable.** Young children, especially, will probably not enjoy a rugged hiking and camping trip. Wait until they're older—at least five or six years old.

• **See the experience through your child's eyes.**
Example: While you find the nighttime noises relaxing, they may terrify your child.

• **Acclimate your child to the wilderness.** Play tapes of outdoor sounds...take him/her to a petting zoo ... teach him about animals.
Example: Explain that wolves, while seemingly scary, prefer to eat mice, not people.

Roger Woodson, Maine-based writer and coauthor of *The Parents' Guide to Camping with Children.* Betterway Books.

EXPLORING

■ **EarthCorps volunteers** spend one to two weeks helping scientists on projects designed to protect threatened habitats, save endangered species and preserve cultural heritages. The research expeditions take place in 21 states of the United States and 54 countries. Participants make tax deductible contributions (about $1,600 for two weeks and as low as $600 for one week) that support research and cover food and lodging. Transportation is extra.

More information: Earthwatch, Box 9104, Watertown, MA 02272. 800-776-0188.

■ **Nature Conservancy tours** let travelers explore and learn about the ecology and wildlife of tropical areas. Some tours in 1997 will visit the Amazon River, a jaguar preserve in Central America and coral reefs in the Caribbean. *Cost:* $1,200 to $3,000.

More information: International Trips Program, The Nature Conservancy, 1815 N. Lynn St., Arlington, VA 22209.

■ **Become a volunteer Cruise Host** by contacting your local travel agent and asking for a letter of recommendation to a cruise line. Gentlemen Hosts—usually single men over age 50—receive free passage and sometimes airfare, but no salary. They dance with passengers, and otherwise make sure the people on the cruise are having fun. The usual required dances are the fox trot, rumba, cha-cha.

Lauretta Blake, Working Vacations, Inc., an agency that places Cruise Hosts with eight cruise lines for a fee of $175 per cruise week, 610 Pine Grove Court, New Lenox, IL 60451. For free literature and more information: 408-727-9665.

OVERCOME YOUR LIMITATIONS

It is valuable to look at nature photographs taken by the masters to see the elements of great pictures.

Even more important is experience. Like driving a car or playing the piano, nature photography requires physical skills and quick reflexes. As you practice and experiment, those skills will become second nature—allowing you to seize those magical photographic moments.

Most common error: Viewing a subject—such as a landscape—through your eyes, and then barely glancing through your viewfinder before taking the picture. The camera's translation from three to two dimensions will change the view.

Exercise: Train yourself to look at everything through your viewfinder, closing your other eye if necessary.

How to Start a Stamp Collection

Michael Laurence

S tamp collecting is often pursued primarily for pleasure. But the most satisfying stamp collections are those built with an eye toward value. *Chief considerations:*

• **Quality over quantity.** Beginners are often dazzled by the opportunity to buy a lot of cheap stamps to fill holes in an album. *Drawback:* Because these stamps are so common, they have no value to other collectors.

To put together a higher-quality collection, focus on *rarity* and stamp *condition*.

• **Used vs. unused.** This is strictly a matter of collector preference. Used stamps are generally

Michael Laurence, editor and publisher of *Linn's Stamp News*, the world's largest newspaper dedicated to stamp collecting, Box 29, Sidney, OH 45365.

cheaper and can be obtained from everyday mail. Simply cut off the corner of the envelope, soak in water and wait for the stamp to float to the surface after its gum dissolves. Hinges are perfectly acceptable for affixing used stamps.

Exceptions: If the piece of mail was sent before 1940, ask an expert to inspect the stamp before you soak it off. It may have far more value still on the envelope than it would by itself.

Warning: Some dealers defraud collectors by re-gumming uncanceled stamps. Collectors do not want regummed stamps. To be safe, purchase only from members of the American Stamp Dealers Association.

• **Centering.** Most stamps are printed off-center within their margins. Perfect (or superb) centering can make a ten-fold difference in value.

Example: The U.S. ten-cent stamp from 1869 is worth just $25 if the perforations are cut into the design on one or two sides. With superb centering, however, the same stamp is worth up to $400.

• **Cancellations.** A stamp's value drops if the black postal marks are heavy and deface or obscure the design.

• **Condition.** Over the years, many collectors have affixed stamps to albums with moistened hinges. When a hinge is removed, it leaves a mark on the stamp's gum—a flaw that reduces its value.

Alternative: Protect your unused stamps with mylar plastic mounts before placing them in an album.

• **Perforations.** One or two missing "teeth"—the notches along the edge—have only slight importance to U.S. collectors. But a stamp that is torn or missing a piece of its design is lower in value.

• **Specialty.** Collections are more satisfying—and valuable—when their focus is narrow. Follow your own interests.

Examples: A collector might begin with stamps of the world, then move to U.S. stamps, nineteenth-century U.S. stamps, U.S. stamps before 1870, stamps from 1869 and finally the ten-cent 1869 stamp. A doctor might collect medical stamps—pictures of famous physicians, medicinal herbs, or med-

GUEST GETAWAYS

■ **Classical Music Lovers' Exchange** will put you in touch with other classical-music lovers. The exchange has been in business for 15 years and has about 1,000 members. *Cost:* $65 for a six-month membership.

More information: 800-233-2657.

■ **Dude-Ranch vacations** offer easy riding and other outdoor programs—with special supervised rides, cookouts, and other activities for grandchildren. Most vacations last one week. *Cost:* $706 to $1,500 for adults, $500 to $1,000 for grandchildren.

More information: The Dude Ranchers' Association, Box 471G, LaPorte, CO 80535.

■ **Ballroom Dancers Without Partners** offers cruises for men and women who love ballroom dancing but find it hard to meet other singles who enjoy it. Dance instruction is provided at all levels.

More information: Ballroom Dancers Without Partners, 1449 NW 15 St., Miami, FL 33125.

■ **Stay with a host family** and share the everyday lives of people around the world by joining Servas, an international network of hosts and travelers. You do not need to be both a host and a traveler, although many are. The usual stay with a Servas host is two nights. Annual membership dues for Servas travelers is $55. No money is exchanged between hosts and travelers.

More information: Servas, 11 John St., Ste. 407, New York, NY 10038. 212-267-0252.

BETTER, FUN-ER GRILLING

Better Charcoal Cooking

Sandra Woodruff, R.D.

Stack coals in a pyramid in the center of the barbecue. Light the coals 45 minutes before cooking. The fire is ready when the coals are covered with light-gray ash. Spread them out all around the grill.

To judge how hot the fire is, carefully hold your hand, palm side down, four to six inches above the coals. Count how many seconds you can comfortably hold it there. The temperature is low if you can hold it for five seconds . . . medium, four seconds . . . medium-high, three seconds . . . high, two seconds.

Sandra Woodruff, R.D., a nutrition consultant in Tallahassee, FL, and author of several cookbooks, including Fat-Free Holiday Recipes. Avery Publishing.

■ **Better outdoor grilling:** If you grill more than just a few times each week, precook the meat by microwaving or parboiling so it is not on the grill very long. And raise the level of the grill so the food is farther from the heat. This will limit charring, which involves the formation of chemicals that some studies have linked to increased cancer risk.

Recommendations from the American Institute of Cancer Research, Washington, DC.

ical equipment. A car fancier might focus on race cars—or Volkswagens. A Philadelphian might look for stamps relating to that city.

First-day cover envelopes are colorful souvenirs. They are now produced in such volume that they are worth less than the stamp's face value.

All about the Trees and Shrubs That Attract Birds

Jeff Cox

BIRD-ATTRACTING TREES

• **Alder trees** attract chickadees, warblers, redpolls, and other small birds in the late fall and winter. These moisture-loving trees have smooth trunks and graceful foliage and must be watered regularly in areas that have dry summers.

Planting: Roots are shallow and invasive, so use these trees in backgrounds or grove plantings.

• **Ash trees** produce large quantities of aerodynamic, single-winged seeds in late summer that attract a variety of seed-eating birds, such as titmice and juncos. Ash trees are fast-growing, tough and undemanding. Most varieties turn bright yellow or purple in autumn.

Planting: Since most varieties grow big and round-headed, put them near plants that will benefit from the ash trees' shade. *Examples:* Joe-pye weed, American cranberries, elderberries, rhododendrons, and azaleas.

• **Beech trees** drop nutritious little nuts in the fall and winter that attract wood dwellers

Jeff Cox, host of PBS television's 26-part series Your Organic Garden. He is the author of nine books, including his latest, Landscaping with Nature: Using Nature's Designs to Plan Your Yard. Rodale Press.

(grouse, wood ducks, and wild turkeys) as well as seed lovers (evening grosbeaks). These majestic, imposing trees have ground-sweeping lower branches that provide heavy shade and rule out plantings beneath.

Planting: Set in the lawn or at the background of a garden.

• **Cherry trees** bear fruit that attract a variety of songbirds in summer. The deciduous varieties are known for their spring flowers on leafless limbs.

Planting: Use as accents to the patio or garden. But keep far enough away from the pavement to prevent the fruit from staining or making a mess.

• **Holly trees** provide wonderful nesting sites in the spring, berries in the winter and good, dense cover all year long.

Planting: Hollies make wonderful background screens or barriers and also work as accent trees for lawns, gardens, and patios.

• **Russian olive trees** are one of the best bird-attracting plants around, due to the abundant crops of olivelike berries they produce from fall well into winter. Narrow, willowlike, silvery-gray leaves cover an upright and angular branch structure that reaches no more than 25-feet high.

Planting: Use as a background tree or a windbreak hedge.

BIRD-ATTRACTING SHRUBS

• **Barberry bushes** produce hanging, reddish fruit that sustains birds throughout the winter. They also provide good, dense cover. Japanese barberry is a particularly pretty variety, with purple and yellow leaves and gorgeous scarlet fall color.

Planting: Use in sun or light shade for a screen, hedge, border, or barrier.

• **Viburnums** of many types produce lots of berries for a variety of songbirds. They are showy and fragrant when in bloom.

Planting: These medium to large plants are best when used for background, screen, and accent situations.

• **Woody vines** like climbing roses, honeysuckle and English ivy are also good choices for birds. Roses provide edible red fruit (hips), and hon-

■ **Videocassettes of silent movies** and tapes of old radio shows are available from Video Yesteryear and Radio Yesteryear. Video Yesteryear carries 1,700 films, Radio Yesteryear carries 60,000 hours of radio programs.

More information on both: 800-243-0987.

■ **Better video renting.** Rent early Friday morning, before the inventory of the most popular films is depleted . . . consider renting from a smaller store that will reserve a video days in advance... "rent" for free or for a modest fee at the local library.

John Ewold, editor, *Consumer's Best,* 4033 44th Ave. S., Minneapolis, MN 55406.

■ **When videotaping programs from your TV**, set the timer to start a few minutes before the program and end a few minutes after the program is over so you won't miss any part of the show. This allows for any difference between your VCR clock and the station from which you are taping.

John Coffey, video-game programmer in Salt Lake City, UT.

■ **Better home video.** Set the zoom lens *before* taping. Zoom lenses let you get close to an object, show detail of something small or take a wide shot that shows surroundings. But constant zooming in and out is distracting and makes the video look jerky. It is more effective to set the zoom before starting to tape. Then zoom in or out only when there is a specific reason to tighten the view of a subject or widen to show surroundings.

Basic Camcorder Guide: Everything You Need to Know to Get Started and Have Fun by Steve Bryant, consumer electronics expert, West Chester, PA. Amherst Media Inc.

Secrets of Quick Cooking

Linda Gassenheimer

Knowing your way around the kitchen will help you get your meals on the table in minutes. *Here are some hints to help you along the way:*

- **To use your food processor more efficiently,** first chop all dry ingredients, such as bread crumbs, in the processor, then wet ones, such as onions. This way it will not be necessary to stop in the middle of a recipe to wash the processor bowl.

- **To make ten-minute rice**, cook it like pasta. Place the rice in a large pot of rapidly boiling water for ten minutes, drain and add sauce, oil or butter. No need to cover it, but stir the rice once to ensure that it doesn't sit on the bottom of the pot.

- **If you make your own salad dressing**, mix it in the bottom of your salad bowl. Add salad and toss. You won't have to use extra mixing bowls.

- **Use a few small chopping boards.** They can be carried to the stove or pot with the ingredients — and you won't have to stop and wash boards while working.

- **To speed up stir-frying**, place each of the ingredients on a plate or chopping board in order of use so

eysuckle has masses of red or purple fruit. Both produce fragrant flowers for the yard and house. Sparrows, house finches and cardinals all love nesting in ivy and feasting on the insects it harbors.

Planting: Ask your local nursery, as each variety has different needs.

The Pleasures of Organic Gardening

Bonnie Wodin

There really is no need to use chemicals and gasoline-powered machines when gardening or tending to your lawn. Organic methods are just as successful and use only fertilizers and pest controls found in nature. *Advantages:*

- **Creates a healthier environment** by rebuilding the top soil, protecting ground water, and using less energy.

- **Produces homegrown, organic (chemical-free) vegetables**—fresher and cheaper than the ones you can buy in natural-foods stores or supermarkets.

ORGANIC FERTILIZERS

While synthetic fertilizers feed the crop, they deplete the soil, then make future crops dependent on continued applications. Organic fertilizers feed the plants and nourish the soil. *All plants need . . .*

- **Nitrogen** for lush foliage.

Best organic sources: Homemade or bagged compost —decomposed plants or animal wastes rich in nitrogen and other trace minerals. Add up to two inches to each garden bed yearly. *For fast results:* Use blood meal and dried blood (by-products of slaughterhouses), or cottonseed meal (ground from seeds of the cotton plant).

Bonnie Wodin, of Golden Yarrow Landscaping, Heath, MA 01346, designs custom gardens and landscapes. She also lectures frequently on horticulture and landscaping.

• **Phosphorus** for flower and seed production. *Best organic source:* Colloidal phosphate, a rock powder, also rich in lime and trace minerals. *For fast results:* Try bone meal—it's effective, but more expensive.

• **Potash (Potassium)** for strong roots and solid branches. *Best organic sources:* Granite dust (a rock powder) and greensand (a mineral-rich deep sea deposit). *For fast results:* Try wood ashes left from a wood stove or fireplace.

Important: Soil conditions in your garden—and the specific needs of plants you want to grow—should determine your choice of fertilizer. Your local garden center or the U.S. Department of Agriculture's cooperative extension service can test your soil and recommend the best organic fertilizer for your needs.

ORGANIC PEST AND WEED CONTROL

• *Insecticidal soaps:* Spray every three to five days for about three weeks to eliminate most pests on specific plants or plant groupings. *Cost:* $5 to $7 for 8 oz. of concentrate, which makes 4 gallons of spray covering 1,000 square feet. To deter pests, add onion, hot pepper and/or garlic blended to a pulp and squeezed through cotton cheesecloth.

• *Fabric coverings:* Sheets of very thin-woven polyester or thin-spun polypropylene, sold as "floating" row covers or super-light insect barriers. Use only for vegetable gardens—not for ornamental plants . . . make sure plants have enough water—high temperatures under the fabric can make them dry . . .and remove covers over squashes, melons and cucumbers when the flowers start to bloom—in time for pollination. *Cost:* Under $10, for a 10' x 10' sheet of polypropylene or an 8' x 20' sheet of polyester.

• *Beneficial insects:* Bugs that kill harmful insects that eat your vegetables or plants. They can be purchased at local garden centers or by mail order.*

Mail-order companies that sell these insects include: Gardens Alive!, 5100 Schenley Pl., Lawrenceburg, IN 47025. 812-537-8650 . . . Gardener's Supply Co., 128 Intervale Rd., Burlington, VT 05401. 800-863-1700.

COOKING ON THE RUN

you'll easily know which ingredient to add next.

• **To get a quick high- or low-heat response** from electric burners when sautéing or stir-frying, keep two burners going—one on high, one on low—and move your pot back and forth.

• **To help meat marinate quickly**, poke holes in it with a skewer or knife. Use high temperatures to brown, broil or stir-fry in order to seal in the juices.

• **To peel garlic quickly**, firmly press the clove with the side of a knife and the paper skin will fall off or peel away easily.

• **To wash watercress or fresh herbs quickly**, immerse the leaves in a bowl of water for several minutes. Lift them out of the bowl. Sand and dirt will be left behind. For quick, easy chopping, cut them with scissors.

Linda Gassenheimer, executive director of Gardner's Market, a chain of gourmet supermarkets in Miami. She is the author of *Dinner in Minutes: Memorable Meals for Busy Cooks*, Chapters Publishing, Ltd.

Prehistoric Creatures You Can See for Yourself

Richard Will

The dinosaurs brought to life in the blockbuster *Jurassic Park* have been a source of excitement for over 100 years. The best places in the U.S. to see and learn about them . . .

• **American Museum of Natural History** is redesigning its world-renowned dinosaur collection right now. It is the largest in the world. The collection includes one of the world's two mummified dinosaur fossils (with the skin dried over the bone) as well as mammoths, saber-toothed cats, and hundreds of fossil vertebrates. Visitors can enjoy several changing exhibits before the remodeling is completed.

American Museum of Natural History, Central Park West at 79 St., New York, NY 10024. 212-769-5100.

• **Carnegie Museum of Natural History** houses the third-largest dinosaur collection in the country. It gives free guided tours of its "Dinosaur Hall" every Saturday and Sunday. You can walk around and under the skeletons of 11 different species and examine about 500 fossil specimens. Most of the museum's dinosaur remains come from the Morrison Formation in Utah, where some of the best big dinosaur remains in the world were preserved.

Carnegie Museum of Natural History, 4400 Forbes Ave., Pittsburgh, PA 15213. 412-622-3131.

• **Cincinnati Museum of Natural History.** Walk into the ice-blue heart of a glacier and cross into a spring day 19,000 years ago. Meltwater runs over the sides of a simulated glacier into ponds and bogs. You can feel the

• *Mulching:* Cover the earth around each plant or row to deter weeds and conserve water with shredded bark mulch, wood chips, cocoa or buckwheat hulls. (Also use straw and shredded leaves for vegetable plants—but not for ornamentals.) Old mulch decomposes and can be worked into the soil. New mulch is spread after planting..

The Most Romantic Videos

Andrew Sarris

Although love is what is supposed to make the world and movies go round and round, remarkably few memorable love stories have materialized on the screen. Somehow we never lose our childhood giggles or embarrassment when the kissing scenes come on the screen. Hence, despite the omnipresence of "sex appeal" and "love interest" in the casting, writing, and directing of motion pictures, most movies pretend to be about something else.

Significantly, the two most famous love films, *Gone With the Wind* (1939) and *Casablanca* (1942) profess to be concerned with great wars rather than the chemistry between Vivien Leigh's Scarlett and Clark Gable's Rhett in the former, and Ingrid Bergman's Ilsa and Humphrey Bogart's Rick in the latter. In neither romance do the lovers live happily ever after. But that is consistent with most of the great love stories of literature and music.

Andrew Sarris, the noted film critic for the *New York Observer*, is professor of film at Columbia University and the author of 10 books on film, including *The American Cinema, Confessions of a Cultist* and the forthcoming *The American Sound Film.*

Most of my favorite love stories on film are somewhat more optimistic, though true love doesn't run smoothly in any of them, least of all in my all-time favorite, *That Hamilton Woman* (1941), in which Vivien Leigh's Emma Hamilton and Laurence Olivier's Horatio Nelson bring more passion and feeling to their ill-fated adulterous love affair than the historical originals ever did.

On a happier note, Wendy Hiller and Roger Livesey brought civilized grace and humor to a wartime romance in the Scottish Isles in the haunting *I Know Where I'm Going* (1945).

The great male lover of the 1930s and 1940s in Hollywood was, fittingly enough, a Frenchman, Charles Boyer. Three of his most charismatic partners in passion were Irene Dunne in *Love Affair* (1939), Margaret Sullavan in *Back Street* (1941), and Jean Arthur in *History Is Made at Night* (1937), one of the most adventurously romantic titles in the history of the cinema.

The lost art of letter-writing to one's beloved is preserved in the epistolary eloquence of *Shop Around the Corner* (1940) in which Margaret Sullavan and James Stewart carry on an anonymous romance by mail after placing ads in the personals columns . . . and *Love Letters* (1945) in which Jennifer Jones becomes victimized through a Cyrano-like imposture by which the Right Man writes love letters for the Wrong Man. A murder must intervene before a twentieth-century Roxanne finds happiness with Joseph Cotten's handsome Cyrano.

Life imitated art in *Woman of the Year* (1942) in which Katharine Hepburn and Spencer Tracy began their enduring love affair off-screen as they were making love on-screen in a movie ahead of its time in celebrating the emotional electricity generated by two highly competitive career people of opposite sexes. The picture was marred by a

MUSEUMS . . . MUSEUMS

damp wind on your face and listen to glacial creaks—and roaring Ice Age mammals. Fossils, sculptures, aromas and lighting complete the effect. Children love this simulated trip into the Ice Age.

Cincinnati Museum of Natural History, The Museum Center, 1301 Western Ave., Cincinnati, OH 45203. 513-287-7020.

• **Houston Museum of Natural Science** is the site of the largest specimen of a flying reptile found to date. The fossil remains of the Quetzalcoatlus northropi suggest a wingspan of nearly 50 feet (larger than that of an F-4 fighter jet). Other exhibits include a huge Diplodocus skeleton, a six-foot armadillo skeleton, saber-toothed cats, and early horses.

Houston Museum of Natural Science, 1 Hermann Circle Dr., Houston, TX 77030. 713-639-4600.

• **The Mammoth Site of Hot Springs**—a huge sinkhole of mammoth fossils preserved in layers of terraced sediments. The bones of an estimated 100 mammoths, a great short-faced bear, an extinct pronghorn, and a camel have been found at this site. You can view an assembled mammoth skeleton, life-sized silhouettes of 25 animals, and the excavation process.

Special opportunity: Hands-on experiences in the screening for fossils.

The Mammoth Site of Hot Springs, Box 606, Hot Springs, SD 57747. 605-745-6017.

• **National Museum of Natural History.** Part of the Smithsonian Institution, this museum warrants a full afternoon of your time with its skeletons of Albertosaurus, Tyrannosaurus Rex, Maiasaura, Stegosaurus, Triceratops, and other well-known dinosaurs.

MUSEUMS . . . MUSEUMS

You can run your fingers over mammoth and mastodon teeth—and then watch a slide program on glaciation.

National Museum of Natural History, Smithsonian Institution, 10 St. & Constitution Ave. NW, Washington, DC 20560. 202-357-2700.

• **Natural History Museum of Los Angeles County.** A three-toed dinosaur footprint, the largest catalogued vertebrate fossil collection in North America, a 72-foot Mamenchisaurus, a Tyrannosaur Rex skull, and a Pterosaur with a 23-foot wingspan are among the amazing things you'll see at this popular museum. This museum also operates the fascinating George C. Page Museum at the La Brea Tar Pits in Los Angeles. At the tar pits, you'll see skeletons of a saber-toothed cat and the La Brea Woman (the only human skeleton recovered from the pits). In the summer, you can watch the excavation of plants and animals from 10,000 to 40,000 years ago.

` Natural History Museum of Los Angeles County, 900 Exposition Blvd., Los Angeles, CA 90007. 213-744-3466.

• **Royal Tyrrell Museum of Palaeontology.** More than a half million visitors a year come to Alberta to visit this unique museum in the Red Deer River Valley. The museum has 35 complete dinosaur skeletons and a Palaeoconservatory with more than 110 species of plants. Its Nova Room enables you to examine fossilized insects through a microscope and touch original fossils and casts.

Tyrrell Museum of Paleontology, Box 7500, Drumheller, Alberta, Canada T0J 0Y0. 403-823-7707.

Richard Will, coauthor of *Dinosaur Digs: Places Where You Can Discover Prehistoric Creatures.* Country Roads Press.

studio-tacked-on ending in which Ms. Hepburn gets her comeuppance in a disastrous kitchen sequence. For the most part, however, Hepburn and Tracy's characters bickered in the exhilarating manner of Beatrice and Benedict in Shakespeare's *Much Ado About Nothing*.

Billy Wilder has given us two magical romances in two very different decades with *The Major and the Minor* (1942) in which Ginger Rogers plays a faux Lolita to Ray Milland's chivalrously susceptible Major Kirby—and *Love in the Afternoon* (1957) in which Audrey Hepburn as an impressionable virgin chooses as her first lover Gary Cooper's much older and disreputably promiscuous playboy-businessman. In one of the great endings in film history, the first love of her life almost miraculously becomes the last love of his.

You may have noticed that most of my favorites date back to the 1930s and 1940s, the most tightly censored period in Hollywood's history. There were no nude scenes back then, no rollicking between the bed sheets, but instead an eroticism of the heart, which is what Valentine's Day is all about, or at least should be.

The Best of Health for Only $1.83 a Year

Aspirin Miracle

Robert S. Persky

A remarkable, inexpensive key to better health is probably right in your medicine cabinet. It's called *acetylsalicylic acid*—better known as aspirin.

Research suggests that one aspirin tablet, taken every other day, helps reduce risk of heart attack, certain kinds of stroke, cancer of the gastrointestinal tract and possibly Alzheimer's disease, among other serious ailments. All this for $1.83 per year—less than a penny a day.

Caution: Aspirin is not a substitute for healthy habits like eating a balanced diet, exercising regularly, or not smoking, nor should it be taken regularly without your doctor's approval.

ABOUT ASPIRIN

Aspirin's active ingredient, salicin, occurs naturally in the willow tree. Willow leaves and bark have been used to relieve pain and inflammation at least since the time of Hippocrates.

Aspirin was first made commercially in Germany at the turn of the century. If it had first been synthesized today instead of a century ago, odds are it would be available only by prescription. *Reason:* As-

Robert S. Persky, coauthor of *Penny Wonder Drug: What the Label on Your Aspirin Bottle Doesn't Tell You.* The Consultant Press, Ltd.

VITAMIN HEALERS

Tim McAlindon, MD

Vitamin C vs. Arthritis

The progression of arthritis of the knee can be significantly slowed by vitamin C. An eight-year study of 640 people found that knee osteoarthritis progressed three times more slowly in those who consumed the most vitamin C than in those who ate the least.

Scientists offer two possible theories to explain this effect. One is that vitamin C's antioxidant properties mop up harmful free radicals that are released by the inflamed knee joint. The second theory is that vitamin C helps the body synthesize proteins that repair the arthritis-caused damage. But either way—you win.

Tim McAlindon, M.D., is an associate professor of medicine at Boston University School of Medicine.

■ **Vitamin E may help slow the effects of aging** on the brain and immune system. A recent study on mice found that when middle-aged and old mice were fed diets supplemented with vitamin E, normal age-related damage to vital proteins in their brain and immune system cells was delayed or prevented. Researchers believe that vitamin E, taken at the onset of middle age, will also slow damage due to aging in human brains and immune systems. The equivalent human dosage of vitamin E to that found effective in mice is about 400 IU a day. Caution: More than 1,000 IU a day of vitamin E may be dangerous.

Marguerite M.B. Kay, M.D., Regents Professor of Microbiology and Immunology and Medicine at the University of Arizona, Tuscon, AZ, and a geriatrician with the Veteran's Administration.

EASIER BREATHING

■ **Better breathing I.** *Bronchitis relief:* Blowing up a balloon, which exercises the lungs. After eight weeks of balloon blowing therapy, bronchitis patients were much less breathless, compared with members of a control group who showed no significant change.

Based on a study by researchers in Manchester, England.

■ **Better breathing II.** *To prevent asthma attacks:* Reduce pollutants in your home—especially dust mites. Mites are killed most effectively by very hot water (over 50° C). *Also helpful:* Avoid carpeting . . . use plastic mattress covers . . . keep pets—especially cats—out of the bedroom and off the bed (and bathe them at least once a week) . . . keep humidity levels at about 50% . . . don't allow smoking in your home. (Mothers or baby sitters who smoke pose the biggest risks)

Tom Wood, M.D., associate professor of medicine, University of Western Ontario.

■ **Adhesive nose strips really work.** Commonly used by athletes, they help hold nostrils open to make breathing easier. Now the strips are being bought by people for many purposes. The devices, sold without a prescription, can help some people who snore because of nasal blockages . . . have deviated septums . . . or have nostrils that do not stay open enough. But the devices may be only temporary solutions to conditions that require surgery for proper correction. *Self-defense:* See your doctor if breathing problems continue.

Jack Anon, M.D., otolaryngologist in Erie, Pennsylvania, and clinical assistant professor of otolaryngology, University of Pittsburgh School of Medicine.

pirin is far more complex and powerful than most people realize.

Inexpensive generic aspirin is just as effective as more costly brands. In fact, there's less difference than you might imagine. Although there are many brand names of aspirin for sale in the U.S., all the salicin found in these aspirin formulations is made by just six companies.

HOW ASPIRIN WORKS

No one knows exactly how aspirin works. It seems to interfere with the production of *prostaglandins*, hormones made by the body in response to injury. Aspirin seems to reduce the pain and swelling caused by prostaglandins.

Prostaglandins are also involved in blood-clotting. By blocking prostaglandin synthesis, aspirin acts as an anticoagulant. That probably accounts for its effectiveness against heart attack and stroke.

ASPIRIN AND ATHEROSCLEROSIS

Aspirin also seems to prevent atherosclerosis, the buildup of fatty deposits in the arteries. However, it cannot reverse atherosclerosis.

ASPIRIN AND HEART ATTACK

In the 1950s, doctors first observed that patients who took aspirin for pain while recovering from a heart attack were less likely to have a second attack.

Supporting data on aspirin's preventive value comes from the *Physicians' Health Study*, a five-year study of more than 22,000 male doctors between the ages of 40 and 84.

Half of the subjects took a standard five-grain aspirin tablet every other day. *Result:* Subjects older than 50 who took aspirin were 44% less likely to suffer a heart attack than were similar men given a placebo (sugar pill).

If the group who took aspirin had also been eating well and getting moderate exercise, even fewer might have had heart attacks.

Researchers looked only at men. However, a subsequent study of female nurses suggests that aspirin also helps prevent heart attacks in women.

Another study found that coronary care unit patients given aspirin immediately after a heart attack were about 25% more likely to survive the attack than patients who did not receive aspirin.

Evidence also suggests that an aspirin a day lowers the risk of a second attack.

ASPIRIN AND STROKE

Most strokes occur as a result of atherosclerosis. When arteries are narrowed, even a tiny blood clot can block blood flow to the brain, thereby depriving the tissue of oxygen.

Aspirin apparently fights stroke by preventing atherosclerosis and thinning the blood, which helps prevent blood clots.

One warning sign of impending stroke—sometimes the only warning—is a transient ischemic attack (TIA). This temporary deficiency of blood in the brain is caused by a blockage of blood flow or by a piece of arterial plaque or a blood clot that lodges in a blood vessel inside the brain. *Symptoms:* Weakness, numbness, dizziness, blurred vision, difficulty in speaking.

A study by Dr. James C. Grottar (published in the *New England Journal of Medicine*) showed that taking aspirin after a TIA cuts the risk of stroke by 25% to 30%. Although aspirin is often prescribed for TIA, it is not usually appropriate for anyone with high blood pressure or an increased risk of hemorrhage.

ASPIRIN AND COLON CANCER

Cancers of the colon and rectum account for roughly one out of five cancer deaths in the U.S.

The *Journal of the National Cancer Institute* reported that people who took aspirin or other nonsteroidal anti-inflammatory drugs at least four days a week for three months halved their risk of colorectal cancer. The results held for men and women across a broad range of ages.

An Emory University study suggested that taking one aspirin a week significantly reduces the risk of these cancers. Another study found a 50% reduction in the colon-cancer death rate among daily aspirin takers.

CANCER TREATMENT

■ **Skin cancer survival** is boosted by support groups. One group of melanoma patients attended six weekly meetings to learn about their disease and get emotional support. Another group did not attend meetings. After five years, only 9% of those in the support group had died of their disease—but 29% of the other group had died. Participants in the support group also had better immune function six months after the group sessions ended.

Fawzy I. Fawzy, M.D., professor and deputy chairman, department of psychiatry and biobehavioral sciences, University of California at Los Angeles Medical School. His study of melanoma patients was published in *Archives of General Psychiatry*, 515 N. State St., Chicago, IL 60610. Monthly. $90/yr.

■ **Nausea and vomiting** caused by cancer chemotherapy can often be controlled with medication. More than 70% of breast cancer patients undergoing chemo reported no nausea or vomiting when they took either the new drug ondansetron (Zofran) or a combination of two less costly older drugs, dexamethasone and metoclopramide. Chemo patients who aren't helped by one antinausea drug should ask their doctor about trying another drug—or a combination of drugs.

Martin Levitt, M.D., director of clinical investigation, Manitoba Cancer Treatment and Research Center, Winnipeg, Canada. His study of 165 breast cancer patients was published in the *New England Journal of Medicine*, 10 Shattuck St., Boston, MA 02115 Weekly. $96/yr.

■ **Cancer pain problem.** One-fourth of all cancer patients fail to get adequate pain relief. *Reason:* They assume that pain is inevitable . . . they don't complain because they want to be "good" patients . . . they fear addiction . . . and they are afraid that pain management will distract the doctor from treating the disease.

CANCER TREATMENT

Reality: Pain management is an integral part of cancer treatment. Patients should not hesitate to communicate their needs.

Jamie H. Von Roenn, M.D., associate professor of medicine, section of medical oncology, Northwestern University Medical School, Chicago. Her survey of 897 cancer doctors was published in *Annals of Internal Medicine,* Independence Mall West, Sixth Street at Race, Philadelphia, PA 19106. 24 issues. $92/yr.

HEALTHIER HEARTS

■ **Another benefit of vitamin E:** It seems to decrease the rate of progression of atherosclerosis—clogging of the arteries. *Study:* As part of the clinical trial, men who had had coronary bypass operations were given either cholesterol lowering diets and cholesterol lowering drugs or a placebo. Two years later, men who had also been taking at least 100 International Units of vitamin E a day had arteries that did not clog as rapidly as those in the group who took no vitamin supplements.

Study of 156 middle-aged men analyzed by Wendy Mack, Ph.D., University of Southern California School of Medicine, 1450 Alcazar St., Los Angeles, CA 90033.

■ **Soy protein cuts cholesterol**—perhaps better than other dietary factors, we hear from Dr. James Anderson. As little as 17 to 25 grams of soy protein cuts LDL ("bad") cholesterol without affecting HDL ("good") cholesterol. It may also limit postmenopausal symptoms and lower cancer risk. *Prime soy protein sources:* Soy milk (8 grams per serving) . . . tofu (15 to 20 grams) . . . soy flour (5 grams) . . . tempeh (16 grams) . . . nondairy frozen desserts (up to 12 grams).

James Anderson, M.D., is chief of the endocrine-metabolic section, Veterans Affairs Medical Center, Lexington, KY. His analysis of 38 studies, involving more than 700 people, was published in *The New England Journal of Medicine.*

But another study of older subjects (average age 73) showed that frequent aspirin users face a heightened risk of kidney and colon cancer, as well as of heart attack. More research is needed. But—at least for younger patients, the preliminary findings are promising.

ASPIRIN AND ALZHEIMER'S DISEASE

A University of British Columbia scientist observed during autopsies of arthritis patients—who tend to take a great deal of aspirin—that their brains showed fewer than expected signs of Alzheimer's disease.

This observation certainly doesn't prove that aspirin prevents Alzheimer's. However, it does suggest an important avenue for future research. *Also:*

Though aspirin isn't very helpful in relieving migraine pain, it may help prevent migraines. Preliminary research suggests that migraine sufferers who take aspirin regularly may be able to reduce their headaches by as much as 20%.

Aspirin seems to stimulate the production of interferon and interleukin-2—immunity-boosting proteins produced inside the body. This may explain why aspirin may prevent certain kinds of cancer . . . and suggests that it could be used in the fight against other immune disorders.

Finally, some evidence suggests that aspirin helps prevent cataracts, diabetes, and gallstones. As with other possible uses of aspirin, these potential uses of aspirin require further study.

ASPIRIN PRECAUTIONS

•**If you're thinking about starting an aspirin regimen,** check with your doctor first. This is especially important if you're taking anticoagulants . . . if you have diabetes, gout, or arthritis . . . or if you are taking any other over-the-counter or prescription drug.

Caution: Aspirin should generally be avoided by anyone with asthma . . . ulcers or other chronic stomach problems . . . or an allergy to aspirin.

•**If you're pregnant or nursing an infant**, take aspirin only with a doctor's consent. *Danger:* Aspirin taken during the last three months of pregnancy can injure the fetus or cause birth complications.

•**If regular aspirin irritates your stomach**, ask your doctor about buffered or coated aspirin. Also, tell your doctor if you experience ringing in the ears or hearing loss while taking aspirin.

•**Drink with caution when taking aspirin.** Aspirin boosts the concentration of alcohol in the blood. If you want to drive safely after a party, for instance, you may need to drink even less or wait longer than you normally would.

•**Children should not be given aspirin without a doctor's approval.** *Reason:* Aspirin has been linked to Reye's syndrome, a rare but potentially fatal brain disorder.

Proven New Nutritional Plan For Beating Arthritis

Dr. Stephen Sinatra

As a cardiologist, I've long used a natural, nutritional approach for prevention and treatment of heart disease.

To my surprise, many of my heart patients have found that my nutritional therapy also helps reduce pain and swelling in their arthritic hands, knees, and other joints. This observation led me to review the literature on nutrition and arthritis.

Ultimately, I developed a program of eating guidelines and nutritional supplementation designed specifically to ease the pain and inflammation of arthritic joints. (Of course, these same strategies help reduce the risk of heart disease.)

Stephen Sinatra, M.D., director of education at Manchester Hospital and a cardiologist in private practice in Manchester, Connecticut.

HEALTHIER HEARTS

■ **Best heart disease treatment:** Individually prescribed programs of exercise and diet and other risk-reduction programs reduce mortality rates among heart disease victims by 25%—but fewer than one-third of patients who could benefit from such programs are enrolled in them. *Why:* Many doctors fail to refer appropriate patients because they do not know of local programs, and many patients have inadequate insurance coverage. Exercise programs pose no health risk even for older patients. *Useful:* A free booklet, *Recovering from Heart Problems Through Cardiac Rehabilitation,* #96-0674 is available by calling 800-358-9295.

Nanette Kass Wenger, M.D., professor of medicine at Emory University School of Medicine, 69 Butler St. SE, Atlanta, GA 30303.

BREAKTHROUGHS

■ **New shingles treatment.** A new drug called *valacyclovir* relieves shingle pain far more effectively than the current treatment, *acyclovir* (Zovirax). Patients given the new drug got rid of their pain on average within 38 days. Patients given acyclovir took an average of 51 days to recover. *Important:* For maximum effectiveness, valacyclovir therapy must be initiated within 72 hours of the appearance of the first shingles blister. Pending FDA approval, valacyclovir should be available later this year.

Karl R. Beutner, M.D., Ph.D., clinical associate professor of dermatology, University of California, San Francisco Medical School.

■ **New migraine treatment:** The drug sumatriptan, made available in the U.S. 4 years ago. It quickly relieves pain for about 70% of migraine sufferers although it does not prevent future headache attacks. *Disadvantages:* Cost of $20 to $30 a dose . . . method of use—a prepackaged syringe for self-injection or 25 or 50 mg pills.

Roger Farber, M.D., director, Pennsylvania Headache and Pain Center, Bala Cynwyd, PA.

■ **Electroconvulsive therapy** has improved so much that it is often better than medication against severe depression. *New approach:* Reduced doses of electricity . . . changes in electrode placement. *Worst side effect:* Partial memory loss—though it's only temporary in most cases.

Matthew V. Rudorfer, M.D., assistant chief, clinical treatment research branch, National Institute of Mental Health, Rockville, MD.

■ **A caffeine pill** before surgery helps coffee drinkers recover faster. In a recent test, coffee drinkers were given either a caffeine pill (equivalent to one cup of coffee) or a placebo one hour before outpatient surgery. *Result:* Those who received caffeine were released from the recovery room 40 minutes earlier than those who received the placebo. *Theory:* The presurgical caffeine prevents symptoms of caffeine withdrawal—fatigue, muscle pain and clouded thinking—making patients more alert and aware.

Joseph Weber, M.D., fellow, department of anesthesiology, Mayo Clinic, Rochester, MN.

■ **Canker sore prevention.** Eat at least four tablespoons of plain yogurt a day . . . and avoid eating nuts, especially wal-

Follow these guidelines for at least eight weeks, and you'll see a significant reduction in pain and stiffness . . .

• **Raise your blood pH.** Each day, have a glass of carrot, apple or cherry juice. These juices have an "alkalyzing" effect on the blood.

Avoid orange juice, grapefruit juice and other citrus juices . . . as well as tomatoes, potatoes, eggplant and other foods from the nightshade family.

These "acidifying" foods lower blood pH. A lower pH promotes formation of crystals in your joints, which leads to arthritis.

• **Eat chlorophyll.** Be sure to drink a glass of green barley, chlorella or frozen wheat grass every day. Each of these is rich in this green pigment.

Chlorophyll helps remove excess heavy metals from the joints. Heavy metal atoms cause accumulation of free radicals, highly reactive compounds that damage the joints.

• **Eat cayenne and garlic.** Both herbs have an anti-inflammatory effect, helping to reduce swelling and pain.

I urge my patients to take a daily cayenne capsule. If it upsets your stomach, have it with bread or crackers. If stomach upset is severe, stop taking cayenne.

Garlic stimulates the immune system, which supports healing. Garlic also contains the antioxidant mineral selenium. It helps control free radical buildup.

• **Eat omega-3 oils.** Found primarily in flaxseed and fish oil, omega-3 oils stimulate the production of leukotrienes, natural compounds that inhibit inflammation.

I recommend taking one 1,000-mg flaxseed oil capsule after each meal. The capsules can be found in any health-food store.

Another way to boost your omega-3 intake is to eat at least one—and preferably two—helpings of fresh fish per week.

• **Drink ginger tea.** In addition to being soothing to the stomach, ginger is a potent anti-inflammatory agent. I recommend one cup a day.

• **Eat Certo.** This pectin-containing gelatin powder, available in any supermarket, is very effective at reducing swelling in the joints.

Each day, consume one tablespoon (mixed with apple juice or another alkalyzing fruit juice to form a soupy gelatin).

It's unclear why Certo relieves arthritis.

• **Take multivitamin supplements.** A combination of antioxidant nutrients is the best way to fight free radicals.

Although fresh fruit and vegetables are rich in antioxidants, the best way to be sure that you get enough is to supplement your diet with multi-vitamins.

Be sure to select an iron-free supplement. Too much iron has been linked to an elevated risk of heart disease.

The supplement you select should contain no more than 1 mg copper (half the government's recommended daily allowance).

It should also contain folic acid, vitamin B-6, vitamin D, zinc and calcium—deficiencies in any of these nutrients can cause arthritis.

The supplement should also contain selenium and vitamin E. Both nutrients are especially good for morning stiffness.

• **Take coenzyme Q-10 and quercetin.** I recommend 30 mg of coenzyme Q-10 after each meal . . . and 100 mg to 500 mg of quercetin once a day.

A remarkable substance, coenzyme Q-10 works to stabilize the membrane of every cell in your body. That prevents cell breakdown in your joints.

Quercetin blocks the release of histamines (inflammation-producing chemicals) into the bloodstream. Both supplements are available in health-food stores.

• **Avoid caffeinated beverages**—coffee, tea and soda—as well as chocolate. A diuretic, caffeine washes nutrients out of your body, thereby undermining your efforts to eat a healthful, nutrient-rich diet.

nuts. *To treat an existing sore:* Apply a warm, moist tea bag directly to the sore. The tannin in regular *black* tea acts as an astringent. *Ineffective:* Herbal or de-caffeinated tea. *Also:* Open and empty a 250-milligram capsule of tetracycline (available by prescription) into one and a half ounces of warm water. Shake very well—the tetracycline won't dissolve. Dip a cotton ball into the mixture. Apply it to the canker sore for three to four minutes. Repeat three to four times daily. *For multiple sores:* Gargle with the mixture.

Jerome Z. Litt, M.D., assistant clinical professor of dermatology, Case Western Reserve University School of Medicine, Cleveland, OH.

HEALTHIER SKIN

■ **Poison ivy self-defense.** Wipe your exposed skin with moist towelettes every half hour or so while in the woods. That will clear your skin of resins from poison ivy or poison oak, preventing irritation.

David Harris, M.D., clinical professor of dermatology, Stanford University School of Medicine, Palo Alto, CA.

■ **Treat psoriasis** consistently, even when no lesions are visible. *Reason:* The disease is there even when it does not produce symptoms. *Key:* Keep the skin moist and lubricated—mineral oil and petroleum jelly work well. *Also:* Avoid skin injury . . . practice stress-reduction at home and at work . . . and limit consumption of alcohol—it causes itching in persons with psoriasis. Expose skin regularly to moderate amounts of sunlight.

Anil Abraham, M.D., clinical research fellow, Psoriasis Research Institute, Stanford, CA.

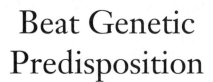

PAIN RELIEF

■ **Hypnosis can relieve pain** when opioid drugs (narcotics) fail. *Good news:* Hypnosis alleviates burn patients' pain, which is so intense during medical procedures that maximum dosages of medication are inadequate . . .

From a study led by David Patterson, Ph.D., staff psychologist, department of rehabilitation medicine, University of Washington Medical School, Seattle, WA.

■ **Recovery from tonsillectomy** is less painful when tonsils are removed with a scalpel ("sharp" surgery) instead of an electrically heated needle (electrocautery), we hear from Joseph Leach, M.D. In a recent study, patients undergoing tonsillectomy had one tonsil removed by a scalpel, the other via electrocautery. *Result:* The cauterized side was less prone to bleeding . . . but far more painful in the days following surgery. Electrocautery is good for persons with bleeding disorders and for children or others with limited blood volume. For others, "sharp" surgery is usually better.

Joseph Leach, M.D., assistant professor of otorhinolaryngology, University of Texas Southwestern Medical Center, Dallas, TX.

■ **Chronic abdominal pain** sometimes responds to low doses of psychotropic drugs—including the antidepressants *amitriptyline, desipramine, trazodone,*

Beat Genetic Predisposition

Raymond Kurzweil

If there is a history of heart disease or cancer in your family, there's a straightforward way to cut your risk by up to 90%, no matter how strong your genetic predisposition to these killers.

Like many American families, my family was hard hit by heart disease.

My father was just 12 years old when his father died of a heart attack . . . and I was only 22 when the same fate befell my dad. By the time I reached my mid-30s, I too seemed headed for an early death. I was overweight, I had Type II diabetes and my cholesterol level was elevated. According to the statistics of the Framingham heart study, my risk of a heart attack was 175% of normal. ("Normal" in our society is a 75% chance of having a heart attack in one's lifetime.)

I decided to try to cut my disease risk by adopting the 30%-fat diet recommended by the American Heart Association. *Problem:* The diet had little effect on my excess weight, diabetes, and cholesterol levels.

REVERSING THE INEVITABLE

At this point, I immersed myself in the scientific literature and developed an alternative approach to this problem. I cut my fat intake all the way down to 10% of calories and adopted a program of regular exercise and stress control. In a few months I lost 45 pounds, my diabetes vanished and my cholesterol level fell so low that my risk of heart attack wasn't just normal, it was way below that of someone with no family history of heart disease. My risk of heart disease fell 97%.

Raymond Kurzweil, chairman and CEO of Kurzweil Educational Systems Inc., a Waltham, MA–based software developer. He is author of The 10% Solution for a Healthy Life: How to Eliminate Virtually All Risk of Heart Disease and Cancer. Crown Publishers.

Bonus: I felt more relaxed and energetic than I had in years.

Here are the most common questions people ask me . . .

What exactly is involved with your "10% solution"?

Several things. First, regular aerobic exercise. I recommend working out at least four times a week, for at least 45 minutes each time. Next, stress control. Learn to strike a balance between self, friends, family, and work. Stop smoking. Get plenty of sleep.

Note: I don't mean to gloss over these nondietary recommendations because they're all-important. But the issue of fat intake is more critical—and more often misunderstood.

What's it like to eat a 10% calories-from-fat diet?

Most people think it must be terribly Spartan. In fact, while you will have to eliminate certain foods from your diet, you can continue to enjoy many of the foods you currently eat. The key is learning the subtle art of food substitution.

Illustration: A meal of broiled chicken, peas in a cream sauce, baked potato with sour cream, and a dish of ice cream contains a whopping 55 grams of fat. But a similar meal of baked skinless chicken, steamed peas, baked potato with nonfat sour cream, and a dish of nonfat frozen yogurt contains only nine grams. Once you get used to low-fat eating, this meal is just as satisfying—and much more healthful.

But I love fatty foods. I don't think I have the willpower to eat as you recommend. What can I do?

Oddly enough, while it's quite hard to eat a little less fat, it's actually quite easy to eat a lot less.

Reason: If you cut back only to, say, 20% or 30% fat, your appetite for rich, fatty foods never goes away. Consequently, every meal becomes a test of your willpower. But after five to six weeks on a 10%-fat diet, your taste buds actually begin to change. Fatty foods you once enjoyed will begin to taste too greasy while foods that once seemed impossibly bland will become tastier. *Bonus:* Because you'll be eating so little fat, you'll easily lose excess weight—while never feeling hungry or deprived.

and *fluoxetine.* This suggests that the pain may be at least partly neurophysiologic in origin. *Strategy:* If you're troubled by an irritable bowel or another type of abdominal pain, ask your doctor about psychotropic drugs or drug alternatives.

Martin Gelfand, M.D., associate clinical professor of gastroenterology, University of Washington School of Medicine, and staff gastroenterologist, Virginia Mason Clinic, Seattle, WA. His research was presented at the annual meeting of the American College of Gastroenterology, 4900B S. 31 St., Arlington, VA 22206.

■ **Emphysema patients** breathe much easier following a new surgical procedure that removes 20% to 30% of damaged lung tissue. Many patients who needed oxygen to climb stairs before surgery needed no oxygen to do so following surgery. Removing a portion of a patient's overly distended lungs seems to allow more room in the chest cavity for the remaining lung tissue to inflate more efficiently. Almost all cases of emphysema are caused by smoking.

Joel Cooper, M.D., professor of surgery, Washington University, St. Louis. His study of lung surgery in 20 patients with emphysema was reported at a recent meeting of the American Association for Thoracic Surgery, 13 Elm St., Manchester, MA 01944.

■ **Parkinson's patients** who take the drug *levodopa* may benefit from a high-carbohydrate, low-protein diet, we hear from Christopher O'Brien, M.D. In a recent study, patients who ate a seven-to-one carbohydrate-to-protein diet walked better and moved around better than those who ate high-protein meals. Such a diet ensures a consistent and predictable response to levodopa. Too much

REMEDY BREAKTHROUGHS

protein, and the drug does not work as reliably. Too little protein may cause malnutrition. *Helpful:* Calculate the carbohydrate-to-protein ratio by reading food labels and dividing the number of grams of protein into the number of grams of carbohydrates. The resulting number should be approximately seven.

Christopher O'Brien, M.D., medical director, Movement Disorders Clinic, Colorado Neurological Institute, Englewood, CO.

BEATING ARTHRITIS

■ **It is critical to describe arthritis symptoms** as precisely as possible. The more knowledge your doctor has of the details of your symptoms, the better he/she is able to diagnose them and prescribe the most appropriate medication to relieve the pain. Keep careful track of how often you suffer arthritic pain, which joints hurt and how long the pain lasts.

Lindsey Criswell, M.D., M.P.H., assistant adjunct professor of medicine at the University of California, San Francisco, CA.

■ **Knee pains suffered by arthritis patients** can often be improved by physical therapy rather than surgery. That treatment is effective when the pain stems from stress in the muscles or other biomechanical causes rather than from arthritis. Physicians can tell when that is the case by injecting the patient's calf with a small amount of lidocaine, a local anesthetic. If the anesthetic relieves the pain instantly, it shows that the problem is muscular. The doctor can then prescribe appropriate physical therapy, stretching exercises or orthotics.

Garry Sherman, D.P.M., is team physician for the New Jersey Stars of the World Teamtennis League.

Are any foods prohibited?

I divide foods into three categories—those to eat as often as you like, those to eat occasionally and those to avoid. *Emphasize:*

- Breads made without oils, butter, or margarine and any other whole grains or grain products.
- Pasta made without oil or eggs.
- Cereals free of fat, salt, or sugar.
- Fruits, fruit juices, and vegetables (except avocados and olives, which are too fatty).
- Peas, beans, lentils, and other legumes.
- Nonfat dairy products.
- Tofu and other soy products.
- Egg whites.
- Lean meats, preferably fish or fowl. Up to 4 ounces daily of fish, clams, oysters or mussels, or white meat of chicken or turkey (without skin). If you want red meat, choose round steak, flank steak, or other lean cuts.

EAT OCCASIONALLY

- Sugar, sucrose, molasses, and other sweeteners.
- Breads and cereals made with added fat.
- Pastas made with eggs.
- Low-sodium soy sauce.
- Low-fat dairy products (one-percent fat).
- Olive or canola oil . . . use very sparingly.
- Caffeinated drinks . . . no more than two cups daily.
- Lobster, crab, and shrimp. They contain too much cholesterol to be eaten regularly.
- Smoked or charbroiled foods. They contain a potent carcinogen.

NEVER EAT

- Fatty meats, including organs, cold cuts, and most cuts of beef and pork. Poultry skin is pure fat.
- Meat fat, butter, hydrogenated vegetable oils, lard, and margarine.
- Nondairy creamers and other sources of tropical oils like palm or coconut.
- Mayonnaise.

• Polyunsaturated fat, including corn oil and most vegetable oils.

• Whole dairy products, including cream, whole milk, and sour cream.

• Nuts (except chestnuts, which may be eaten regularly).

• Salt or salty foods.

• Egg yolks.

• Fried foods.

How can I tell how much fat I'm getting?

At first you'll need to keep a food diary. Jot down the calorie and fat content of each food you eat. At the end of each day, calculate the all-important fat percentage.

Procedure: Multiply your total daily intake of fat (in grams) by nine (the number of calories in each fat gram), then divide this number by your total daily calories. If this number is above 10%, you must find ways to cut out more fat. After several weeks, you'll be able to judge your fat intake without using the diary.

How about polyunsaturated fats?

Margarine, corn oil, and other sources of polyunsaturated fat have long been touted as safe alternatives to saturated fats. In fact, they are far less healthful than once thought—and may be more harmful than saturated fats.

Recent finding: Polyunsaturated fat not only raises levels of LDL (bad) cholesterol, but also reduces levels of HDL (good) cholesterol. And now it looks as if polyunsaturated fat promotes the growth of cancer cells.

Cancer rates in the U.S. began to rise just about the time polyunsaturated fats began to replace saturated fats in the American diet. *To be safe:* Limit your intake of all fats—saturated and polyunsaturated fats in particular.

Are there any immediate benefits to eating less fat?

Absolutely. Each time you eat a fatty meal, your red blood cells become "sticky." They clump together, moving slowly through the circulatory system and clogging up capillaries. This deprives your brain of oxygen, resulting in grogginess. But when you stop eating such meals, your red cells return to

BEATING ARTHRITIS

■ **Better arthritis pain relief.** Intra-articular morphine therapy, in which morphine is injected directly into the inflamed knee, hip or other painful joint tissue, provides much better pain relief than *systemic injection*—that's the current practice of injecting drugs into the bloodstream. *Safer:* The dosage needed is one-tenth of that necessary for systemic injection. And since very little of the morphine leaks into the bloodstream, patients do not suffer from drowsiness, nausea, and suppressed breathing commonly experienced with the other method.

Christoph Stein, M.D., assistant professor of anesthesiology and critical care medicine, Johns Hopkins Medical School, Baltimore, MD.

YOU AND YOUR DOCTOR

■ **Better help from the doctor.** Be specific when phoning your doctor about your medical problem. Nurses report that when patients are vague—saying they're just not feeling well or have a question—doctors are less likely to return their calls. *Helpful:* Describe the nature, duration and location of symptoms and any medication you have taken. This gives the doctor a "running start" in diagnosing the problem and an idea of how much time the return call will take.

Bruce Yaffe, M.D., in private practice, New York.

■ **Reasons to call a doctor** no matter what time it is: Severe headaches, vomiting, diarrhea, nausea, dizziness or sweating . . . chest pains or feelings of pressure or tightness in the chest . . . breathing difficulty . . . severe earaches or vision problems . . . high fever . . . difficulty urinating . . . any significant pain you can't explain.

Men's Health, 33 E. Minor St., Emmaus, PA 18098. 10 issues. $20/yr.

YOU AND YOUR DOCTOR

■ **Doctors often don't inform patients** about the side effects of prescribed drugs because they fear patients will imagine they suffer the side effects they are told of, we hear from Sidney Wolfe, director of the Health Research and Advocacy Group, Washington, DC. A patient who does suffer a side effect may mistakenly attribute it to the illness rather than the drug—a potentially dangerous mistake.

Sidney Wolfe is director of the Health Research and Advocacy Group, a branch of Public Citizen, 2000 P St. NW, Washington, DC 20036.

ASTHMA RELIEF

■ **Asthmatic bed danger**. To minimize the number of asthma attacks, keep your bed scrupulously clean. Wash sheets in hot water—at least 131°F—to kill the microscopic dust mites that can bring on asthma symptoms. *Also:* Don't use feather pillows . . . or allow pets on the bed.

Study of 49 asthma patients conducted at Royal Prince Alfred Hospital in Sydney, Australia, reported in The Medical Post, Maclean Hunter Bldg., 777 Bay St., Toronto, Ontario M5W 1A7. 42 issues. $105/yr.

■ **On-demand asthma therapy** works better than continuous treatment when sufferers use lung-opening medications called bronchodilators. Patients who used the medicines only during asthma attacks had better lung function than ones using the medications on a regular basis. Continuous use actually made some patients' conditions *worse*.

Commentary on a two-year study of more than 200 patients, written by James Li, M.D., Mayo Clinic, Rochester, MN.

normal, and your capillaries open up. *Result:* You feel calmer and more energetic, you sleep better and your complexion improves. And at the same time a subtler but even more important change is taking place within your body. The fatty plaques inside your arteries shrink and your immune system grows stronger.

Doesn't a vegetable-rich diet raise your intake of pesticide residues?

No. The pesticide content of fruits and vegetables is well below that of meat—which comes from animals raised on pesticide-sprayed crops. But to minimize your intake of potential toxins, buy organic produce.

Best Solutions to 10 of the Most Common Health Problems

Dr. Michael Oppenheim

Many common diseases can be treated quite easily. Others take more effort. There are some we can't do anything about—but that go away by themselves. Even though doctors can't cure every disease, there's no harm in seeing a doctor when you aren't feeling right. At the very least, your physician can help you understand what's going on in your body, and advise you on relieving the discomforts.

COLDS AND FLU

These are caused by viruses, and nothing a doctor gives you will cure them. The infection will run its

Family practitioner Michael Oppenheim, M.D., practices in Los Angeles, CA. He is author of A Doctor's Guide to the Best Medical Care *and* The Complete Book of Better Digestion. *Rodale Press.*

course by itself—usually within a few days, though sometimes it takes several weeks.

Cold clues: If you have congestion, a cough and/or a sore throat, you probably have a cold.

Flu clues: If you have a fever and your muscles feel weak and tired, it's probably flu.

Antibiotics are completely ineffective against viral infections—though patients continue to demand them.

The best we can do is treat the symptoms. Aspirin, acetaminophen, or ibuprofen can relieve pain and fever. *For cough medicines, decongestants, and throat treatments:* Those containing dextromethorphan are most effective.

Bed rest will not make the cold go away any faster, but it might make you feel better in the meantime.

BLADDER INFECTIONS

Bladder infections affect far more women than men. Because the urethra is shorter in women than in men, germs that live around the anus and vaginal area can travel up to the bladder fairly easily.

Antibiotics generally clear up most bladder infections within a week.

Some people believe baths encourage the spread of germs into the bladder. This has never been proven, but it can't hurt to take showers instead of baths until the infection clears up.

Cranberry juice is a popular folk remedy. It makes the urine more acidic—a hostile environment for germs. But, you have to drink a large amount of juice (a quart or two a day) for it to be effective.

It's hard to find pure cranberry juice—look for it in health food stores. The kind you buy at the supermarket is mostly water and sugar and won't do a thing.

IRRITABLE BOWEL SYNDROME

Irritable bowel syndrome (IBS) is considered the most common digestive complaint. When the intestinal muscles don't function as smoothly as they should, patients may experience constipation, diarrhea, cramps, and bloating, or some combination of the above.

ASTHMA RELIEF

■ **Asthma education saves lives.** Hospitalized patients who received asthma counseling stayed in the hospital for just about two days. Those receiving conventional care stayed almost twice as long. *Key:* Teaching self-management. *Important:* More use of inhaled corticosteroids—which *prevent* asthma attacks—and less use of bronchodilators and beta agonists.

Maureen George, R.N., clinical nurse specialist, and Reynold A. Panettieri, Jr., M.D., assistant professor of medicine, University of Pennsylvania, Philadelphia, PA. They led a study of 63 inner-city asthma patients receiving conventional care or special counseling

DID YOU KNOW THAT . . .

. . . Stress tests aren't always reliable? These tests, which are supposed to spot potential heart trouble before it occurs are routinely recommended for men older than 40 and women older than 50 who wish to start an aerobic exercise program. *Problem:* In a recent study, only 4% of exercise-related heart problems were predicted in a group of men with high cholesterol who took the tests. *More:* Misleading results can lead to costly, unnecessary medical procedures. A thorough physical exam and medical history may be all that's required for middle-aged people starting an exercise program. Ask your doctor.

Paul D. Thompson, M.D., director, Preventive Cardiology, University of Pittsburgh, PA.

. . . Alzheimer's disease is less common among individuals with high educational and occupational achievement? Those with less education may perform worse

on tests to detect the disorder. *Also:* Higher education and occupation may help create a "reserve" of brain power that delays the onset of Alzheimer's.

Yaakov Stern, Ph.D., associate professor of clinical neuropsychology, Columbia University College of Physicians & Surgeons, New York, NY. His study of 593 patients at risk of developing Alzheimer's was published in the *Journal of the American Medical Association*, 515 N. State St., Chicago, IL 60610. Weekly. $115/yr.

. . . diabetes is the leading cause of blindness in the U.S.? *Problem:* Glaucoma, retinal problems, lens abnormalities, and other diabetes-related eye disorders are often symptomless until it's too late to prevent blindness . . . and 26% of young diabetics and 36% of older diabetics have never been to an ophthalmologist. Essential: Annual eye exams for all diabetics—even those with good vision.

Matthew E. Farber, M.D., clinical instructor, Indiana University School of Medicine, Fort Wayne, writing in *The New England Journal of Medicine*, 10 Shattuck St., Boston, MA 02115. Weekly. $96/yr.

■ **Mail-order medication.** The AARP pharmacy is open to all. You do not have to be a senior citizen to use the mail-order pharmacy of the American Association of Retired Persons. The pharmacy is a full-line drugstore that carries both prescription medications and over-the-counter items. All orders are sent UPS or first-class mail. *Mailing fee:* One dollar per entire order. For more information or prescription price quotes: 800-456-2277.

Skinflint News, 1460 Noell Blvd., Palm Harbor, FL 34683.

No one really knows what causes IBS . . . and there's no sure cure. *Helpful:*

• **Adding fiber to the diet can be beneficial.** Eat lots of fruits and vegetables.

• **If you know you're sensitive to certain foods**—such as caffeine, other acidic foods, seeds—avoid them.

• **Get plenty of exercise.**

Also helpful: Low doses of antidepressants. We're not sure why—it may be that they alter nerves in the brain that regulate muscle function.

LOWER BACK PAIN

The back is very poorly designed for walking upright. The muscles are too small and weak to support the weight of the upper body, and the discs are easily injured. Ordinary wear-and-tear makes a certain amount of back pain almost inevitable with age.

If you experience acute pain, rest the back as you would any injured area. Applying heat and taking ibuprofen usually helps ease the pain. Most acute backaches subside within a few weeks.

If your problem is chronic, be aggressive. Most doctors don't know much about back pain, so look for one who specializes in backs —and who *doesn't* rush to recommend surgery. Minor complaints can often be helped by exercise programs and physical therapy to strengthen the back.

PSORIASIS

Psoriasis is a condition in which the skin grows more rapidly than normal, causing patches to turn red and flake off.

We don't know what causes psoriasis. Once the condition has erupted, however, any injury or irritation to the skin is likely to result in an outbreak. So psoriasis sufferers should avoid getting sunburned, and wear gloves when doing the dishes or if working with harsh chemicals.

Doctors commonly prescribe cortisone creams, which work by discouraging skin cells from multiplying. But long-term use of cortisone is a bad idea—it will make the skin thin and delicate.

Exposure to ultraviolet light is another fairly common treatment, but it increases the risk of skin cancer.

Best treatment: Tar, applied topically. Tar is a very old remedy. The current bottled solutions are not nearly as messy or smelly as the older kind of solutions. If the sufferer's doctor doesn't know about tar treatment, find a doctor who does.

PANIC ATTACKS

It's very common for patients to complain of pounding heart, dry mouth, sweating, difficulty breathing, and feelings of intense anxiety or fright—for no obvious reason.

Some people are awakened in the night by these attacks—others may experience them in the middle of a meeting. They seem to be most common among young adults.

We don't understand much about panic attacks, except that they're usually harmless. Symptoms are caused by the release of adrenaline, and they subside when the body runs out of adrenaline . . . usually after 20 or 30 minutes. They're generally not a sign of heart disease. And they don't usually occur often. If the attacks are chronic and interfere with everyday functioning, several medications can help. Check with your doctor.

IMPOTENCE

Not so long ago, impotence was thought to be a psychological problem, and patients were sent to psychiatrists for long, expensive treatments. Now we know that there are many physical causes as well—and that most cases respond to treatment fairly quickly.

Drugs are a common physical cause. Marijuana, alcohol, even smoking can interfere with sexual performance.

Impotence is also a frequent side effect of high blood pressure medication. If you take drugs for high blood pressure, ask your doctor about adjusting the dosage. There are so many different medications that you should be able to find one that doesn't cause this side effect.

Impotence is also associated with diabetes—but only as a long-term complication associated with damage to nerves or arteries.

MEDICATION SECRETS

■ **Aspirin** administered via a transdermal skin patch may help prevent heart attacks and strokes just the way aspirin tablets do. Bypassing the gastrointestinal tract may permit aspirin use for the 5% of the population whose stomachs cannot tolerate aspirin taken orally. Based on encouraging results of recent studies, an aspirin patch is now under development.

Rudolph M. Keimowitz, M.D., hematology section, Gundersen Clinic, LaCrosse, WI.

■ **Free prescription drugs** are available through most brand-name drug companies for those on limited incomes. Most free drug programs require the prescribing physician to make the request to the company. Medications are sent directly to that physician. *More information:* Ask your doctor to call the Pharmaceutical Manufacturers Association's number—800-762-4636.

DISEASE BUSTERS

■ ***Stomach gas self-defense.*** Avoid sugar substitutes. *Reason:* Up to half of all healthy people have trouble digesting the common sugar substitutes sorbitol and mannitol. Bacteria in the intestinal tract then ferment the undigested sugars, forming gas.

Gerard Guillory, M.D., chairman, Columbine Medical Group, Aurora, CO.

■ **Parkinson's disease treatment.** The monoamine oxidase inhibitor *deprenyl* delays the onset of disability in patients suffering from Parkinson's disease. Patients taking deprenyl were less likely to deteriorate to the point that they needed the Parkinson's drug levodopa. Those who did deteriorate did so almost nine months later than patients not taking deprenyl.

Ira Shoulson, M.D., professor of neurology, pharmacology and medicine, University of Rochester Medical Center, Rochester, NY. His study of 800 Parkinson's patients was published in the *New England Journal of Medicine,* 110 Shattuck Street, Boston, MA 02115

■ **Hypnosis boosts immunity.** People placed into a hypnotic state were told to imagine their white blood cells attacking germs in their body, then were asked to repeat this exercise using self-hypnosis twice daily. *Result:* After two weeks, there was a significant increase in the number of white blood cells in their bodies. Easily hypnotized people had a greater increase than those who had difficulty being hypnotized. Further research should indicate whether the immune-boosting power of hypnosis is effective against diseases like AIDS and cancer.

Patricia Ruzyla-Smith, Ph.D., A.R.N.P. (advanced registered nurse practitioner), assistant professor of nursing, Washington State University, Pulman, WA. Her study of 65 college students was reported in *Science News,* 1719

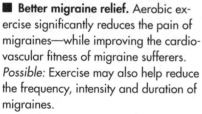

■ **Better migraine relief.** Aerobic exercise significantly reduces the pain of migraines—while improving the cardiovascular fitness of migraine sufferers. *Possible:* Exercise may also help reduce the frequency, intensity and duration of migraines.

Research led by Donna M. C. Lockett, department of psychology, Carleton University, Ottawa, Ontario, Canada, reported in *Headache,* Box 5136, San Clemente, CA 92672.

■ **Migraines** are far more common among women with low back pain than among the general female population? *Possible explanation:* Migraines are trig-

Psychological causes include boredom, depression and anxiety.

It's rarely necessary to embark on a long, involved course of psychotherapy in order to cure impotence. Often, just understanding that these emotions can contribute to the condition—and that it's temporary—is enough to provide relief. For stubborn cases, sex therapy may be helpful.

MIGRAINE HEADACHES

Unlike some other kinds of headaches, migraines are *vascular*. Blood vessels in the scalp become highly sensitive, and heartbeats stretch the arterial walls, creating a throbbing pain.

Migraine attacks tend to start during the teen years and decrease as a person gets older. They usually disappear by middle age.

Unless your symptoms are truly peculiar, don't invest a lot of time and money in tests—they probably won't show anything. Fortunately, migraines are treatable. Several drug families—including antidepressants and antihistamines—can be helpful.

Helpful: Standard pain medications, such as *acetaminophen* or Darvon, will relieve mild pain.

Better: Drugs that stiffen the arteries. Caffeine does this—a few cups of coffee for a minor attack may be effective.

For severe migraine, ergotamine is effective and prescribed by many doctors to be taken at the first sign of a migraine. It can be taken as a pill, suppository, or inhalant, and is sometimes combined with caffeine.

Nausea is a common side effect, so if the pill form makes you nauseous, ask your doctor about experimenting with the other forms.

INSOMNIA

The best treatment for insomnia may be to put it in perspective. Very few insomniacs spend a lot of time feeling sleepy during the day. They may be sluggish in the morning, but once they get going they don't feel too bad.

Upsetting: Lying awake in the middle of the night, trying to sleep and feeling frustrated because you can't.

Sleeping pills don't cure insomnia—they just induce poor-quality sleep. And they can be addictive.

Try to view insomnia as simply irritating—not dangerous. If you can't sleep, don't drive yourself crazy about it. Turn on the light and read.

Note: Insomnia can be a symptom of depression. If that's the case, then the underlying problem should be addressed.

WARTS

Warts are viral and contagious—you can catch them from going barefoot in a public place, using someone else's comb or from scratching and spreading your own warts. However, they may not appear until up to a year after exposure.

Though unattractive, warts are not dangerous. They're more common in children than adults—it's possible that we build up resistance as we age.

The vast majority of warts go away by themselves within a year or two. Treatments include freezing with liquid nitrogen, corroding with acid, and burning or electrocoagulation. I prefer liquid nitrogen—it's simple, effective and not very painful.

Why I Take Ginseng

Mark Blumenthal

While I often recommend herbs for the *treatment* of specific maladies, I believe herbs can also be used to *prevent* illness. One herb that I find especially useful is ginseng.

Mark Blumenthal, director of the American Botanical Council, a nonprofit organization that publishes the quarterly journal *HerbalGram*, Box 201660, Austin, TX 78720. Four issues. $25/yr. The Council is currently evaluating 500 ginseng products. It will publish its findings next spring.

HEADACHES, ETC. . . .

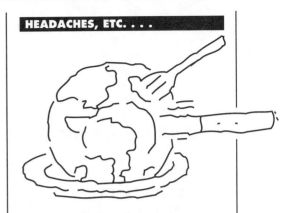

gered by back pain sufferers' incorrect use of their upper back and neck muscles . . . by psychological depression associated with long-term back pain . . . and by overuse of nonprescription painkillers against back pain.

Paul N. Duckro, Ph.D., professor of psychiatry and human behavior and director of the Chronic Headache Program, St. Louis University Health Sciences Center, St. Louis. He is the author of Optimum Health (Lincoln Bradley, $24.95).

■ **Cold sore relief.** The prescription drug *acyclovir* (Zovirax) helps prevent recurrent cold sores (oral herpes infections)—and speeds up healing of sores that do appear. Side effects, including headaches, nausea, and diarrhea, occur in about 5% of patients. *Caution:* Women who are pregnant or who plan to become pregnant should avoid using the drug except in extreme cases . . . under a doctor's supervision, of course.

Researchers at the National Institutes of Health, Bethesda, MD, cited in American Health, 28 W. 23 St., New York, NY 10001. 10 issues. $18.97/yr.

■ **Easier pill swallowing:** Take a swallow of fluid before putting the pill in your mouth. Advance lubrication makes pill swallowing easier. *Also:* Put the pill or capsule as far back on your tongue as possible.

University of California, Berkeley Wellness Letter, Box 412, New York, NY 10012. Monthly. $24/yr.

DIABETES

Eric B. Rimm, Sc.D.

How Not to Be at Risk for Diabetes

Obesity is the number–one risk factor, but smoking and drinking also play key roles. In a recent study, men who smoked 25 or more cigarettes a day were almost twice as likely as nonsmokers to develop noninsulin-dependent diabetes.

Reason: Smokers tend to have apple-shaped bodies, which are associated with poor glucose metabolism.

Moderate drinkers were 40% *less* likely to develop the disease than non-drinkers. Alcohol slows the body's absorption of glucose, putting less demand on the pancreas (which makes insulin).

There's no clear evidence that heavy drinking raises your risk of diabetes. However, heavy drinking is clearly linked to several potentially fatal ailments, including liver disease and cancer.

See your physician if you experience any of the early warning signs of diabetes. These include increased thirst, frequent urination, and unintentional weight loss.

Good news: Adult-onset diabetes can often be controlled with oral medications (sulfonylureas). In such cases, daily insulin injections are unnecessary.

Eric B. Rimm, Sc.D., assistant professor of epidemiology and nutrition, Harvard School of Public Health, Boston, MA.

I began taking ginseng more than 20 years ago. Back then, my goal was to increase my energy and enhance my overall wellness. In recent years, I've noticed that I never get sick. I don't even get colds. I suspect ginseng deserves at least some of the credit.

Recent studies in Europe and especially in Russia suggest that ginseng increases the body's resistance to stress and boosts immunity. The Chinese, who have been using the herb for more than 5,000 years, believe it increases energy levels.

Many convenience stores, grocery stores, drug-stores, and health food stores carry ginseng products. Ginseng is available in powdered, capsule or liquid form.

Good source of ginseng products: SDV Vitamins, Box 9215, Del Ray Beach, FL 33482. 800-738-8482.

Be sure to follow label directions. Taking too much may be overstimulating—particularly when combined with high levels of caffeine.

Price varies according to the type and quality of root, how much ginseng the product contains—and how it was processed.

Ginsana, the leading product, costs $13 to $16 for 30 capsules. This preparation has been clinically tested more than any other ginseng product on the U.S. market.

Best Ways to Protect Yourself from Hospitals

Walt Bogdanich

Not long ago, American hospitals were the envy of the world—proud institutions filled with high-tech equipment and staffed by dedicated and highly skilled workers.

But growing competition for a dwindling patient population, plus a decade of government-mandated cost-cutting measures, have transformed many once-outstanding facilities into dirty, dangerous places where care is haphazard—and overpriced, too.

CHECK THE STATISTICS

Until recently, there was no systematic method for comparing hospitals. Patients had to rely upon recommendations from friends and family members and from their doctors. Now, however, the federal government makes available detailed information concerning mortality rates at hospitals nationwide.

These statistics—known as Medicare mortality information—cover hospitals' overall mortality rates as well as their specific mortality for surgery performed. They give a good idea of the level of care the hospital offers. The higher the mortality rate, the lower the quality of care.

If your doctor recommends a particular hospital, ask about its mortality statistics. If your doctor

Walt Bogdanich, a Pulitzer prize–winning reporter with *The Wall Street Journal*. Bogdanich is the author of *The Great White Lie: How America's Hospitals Betray Our Trust and Endanger Our Lives*. Touchstone.

HOSPITAL SURVIVAL

■ **Hospital bill self-defense.** Over 90% of hospital bills contain errors—most of which are in the institution's favor. *Self-defense:* During your stay, keep a log of doctor visits and the medications, tests, and equipment you receive. When checking out, request a detailed bill listing these products and services. At home, compare the bill with your notes. Hospitals are usually quick to adjust or remove disputed charges.

Charles Inlander, president of the People's Medical Society in Allentown, PA, and author of *Take This Book to the Hospital with You*. Wings Books.

■ **Hospital food danger.** Many hospitals fail to make accommodations for patients with food allergies. *Illustration:* A hospitalized child almost died recently after being fed chicken broth containing the primary allergen in cow's milk—*sodium caseinate*. Although the boy's chart noted his life-threatening allergy to dairy products, hospital staff confused the condition with a different one—cow's milk *lactose intolerance. More:* Other children with lactose intolerance were served milk and ice cream . . . but alert parents intervened before any harm was done. *Self-defense:* If there's any doubt about the safety of your child's food, personally examine all of his/her meals during the hospital stay.

Robert H. Schwartz, M.D., director of pediatric allergy, University of Rochester Medical Center, Rochester, NY.

■ **Hospital comparison-shopping** is now possible in Pennsylvania, thanks to a state law that could become a national model. It requires each hospital to make public how many patients it treated for a specific illness . . . average length of stay . . . average charge . . . how sick patients were upon discharge . . . how many died while hospitalized. The information is available at local libraries. Legislators hope consumers will use this information to identify hospitals offering high quality and reasonably priced services.

Larry D. Gamm, Ph.D., associate professor of health policy and administration, College of Health and Human Development, Penn State University, University Park, PA.

ONE STEP AHEAD . . .

■ **There's more than one treatment** for virtually every medical condition, but a doctor will rarely inform a patient about a treatment other than the one he/she was prescribed. Studies show that when a second medical opinion is sought, a different diagnosis results in 14% of cases on average—and in up to 80% of cases concerning some procedures, such as arthroscopic knee surgery. *Self-defense:* Obtain a second opinion concerning all but the most routine medical procedures to be sure you're informed of all your options.

Charles B. Inlander, president, People's Medical Society, consumer health group, 462 Walnut St., Allentown, PA 18102.

■ **Your medical history** should be known by your dentist as well as your doctor. Without this knowledge, dentists may fail to take the precautions necessary to prevent complications in treating "medically compromised" persons—those with heart trouble, infectious disease, or certain other medical problems. *Also:* A dentist who knows your medical

doesn't know, check with a medical library or with the local chapter of the American Association of Retired Persons. If you have trouble interpreting the data, take a copy to your doctor and ask for help.

Of course, even superb hospitals occasionally provide substandard care. *Some of the risks faced by patients—and how to guard against them . . .*

• **Incompetent surgeons.** While no one would dispute that the majority of surgeons are competent, some are so deficient in their skills as to be downright dangerous. Yet because even a bad doctor has specialized knowledge, it's hard for a patient to evaluate the level of care he/she is providing.

Self-defense: Before engaging a surgeon, make sure he has performed the procedure in question at *least* several dozen times. Ask what percentage of these operations succeeded and what percentage failed. Finally, check up on your prospective surgeon with the state medical board. Ask for all pertinent information, including the details of any disciplinary actions filed.

• **Missing anesthesiologists.** Patients scheduled for surgery know the importance of a skilled surgeon, yet few recognize the key role played by the person responsible for administering the anesthetic. *Result:* Patients fail to pay attention to one of the most important details concerning surgery—the administration of anesthesia.

Self-defense: If your operation calls for general anesthesia, you may want to confirm that the anesthetic be administered by an anesthesiologist.

Important: That the anesthesiologist be present for the entire operation. In some cases the anesthesiologist leaves the room once the operation is under way, leaving the patient in the care of an anesthetist—who might not be equipped to handle an emergency.

• **Inexperienced or incompetent operating room staff.** Successful surgery depends not just upon a skilled surgeon and anesthesiologist, but also upon a skilled and experienced operating room staff.

Self-defense: Never submit to surgery until you know that the hospital staffers have done the procedure at least several dozen times previously . . . and make sure that mortality rates for both surgeon and hospital staff are low. If the surgeon or hospital lacks significant experience, or if the mortality rates are high, have your surgery performed elsewhere.

• **Part-time nurses.** In an effort to cut payroll costs, many hospitals have slashed the number of full-time nursing staff, relying instead upon "temps" whenever patient ranks swell. *Problem:* Even when they hold proper credentials, temp nurses often lack the specialized skills of full-time nurses. Those who are equally skilled may lack familiarity with the hospital's particular way of doing things. *Result:* Needless mistakes in patient care.

Self-defense: Before hospitalization, inform your primary physician that you prefer to be treated only by full-time personnel. If full-time nurses are unavailable, consider hiring your own. Most hospitals do allow the practice. *Note:* Temps are especially common in resort areas—places with unstable or seasonal populations.

•**Medication mistakes.** Getting one drug when you are prescribed another doesn't happen often, thanks to repeated checks by pharmacists, doctors, and nurses.

But mistakes do *sometimes* happen—often with catastrophic results.

Example: Two patients hospitalized for heart surgery died after receiving a glucose solution instead of the heart drug that doctors had prescribed.

Self-defense: Before allowing anyone to give you an injection or pill, ask the name of the medication, the reason it was ordered, and whether it is absolutely necessary for your health. If the answers you receive fail to make sense to you, ask your primary physician for a clarification.

•**Fatigued personnel.** Hospital personnel must be clear-headed and well-rested if they are to give patients quality care. Unfortunately, hospital rules and personnel shortages often conspire to force doctors and nurses to work long shifts, sometimes on little or no sleep. One hospital facing a severe shortage of nurses "solved" its problem by having its nurses work *24-hour shifts.* Under such conditions, mistakes are extremely likely.

history will be better able to treat and/or arrange for medical care in case of an emergency.

Barbara J. Steinberg, D.D.S., professor of medicine and assistant director of the division of dental medicine, Medical College of Pennsylvania, Philadelphia. Her recommendation appeared in the *Journal of the American Dental Association,* 211 E. Chicago Ave., Chicago, IL 60611.

■ **Bring medicines along** when visiting your doctors. Take all prescription and over-the-counter medications you use, put them in a bag and bring it to the doctor's office. The doctor can look for ones that may no longer be needed . . . can be safely taken in smaller doses . . . could interact hazardously with each other.

Bruce Yaffe, M.D., internist in private practice, 121 E. 84 St., New York, NY 10028.

■ **Falling self-defense.** More than 250,000 Americans—mostly elderly—suffer hip fractures each year. Most of these fractures are caused by falls. *Self-defense:* Exercise regularly to boost muscle strength . . . eat better . . . eliminate slippery throw rugs, poorly placed electrical cords, dimly lit stairs, and other hazards. Special undergarments that incorporate hip padding should be available within two years.

Susan L. Greenspan, M.D., director, osteoporosis center, Beth Israel Hospital, Boston, MA. Her study of falls among 149 elderly patients was published in the *Journal of the American Medical Association,* 515 N. State St., Chicago, IL 60610.

■ **Stationary bike danger.** More than 1,200 children in the United States have lost fingers in the last few years after catching them in the spinning wheels, chains, or sprocket assemblies of exercise

ACCIDENT SELF-DEFENSE

bikes. *Important:* All exercise bicycles should have a chain guard, and children should not be allowed to play near these bicycles during a parent's workout.

U.S. Consumer Product Safety Commission, Washington, DC 20207.

■ **America's other drug problem:** Most patients take medications incorrectly. This sometimes has dire results. Failure to follow instructions for taking cardio-vascular drugs alone kills 125,000 people a year—three times as many as the number who die in U.S. highway accidents. *Self-defense:* Ask questions about prescriptions—96% of patients don't. Write down and follow instructions precisely. Never adjust medications without consulting a doctor first.

National Council on Patient Information and Education, Washington, DC.

FAT BUSTERS

■ **Low-fat-baking basics:** Rely on high-flavor ingredients such as fruits, vanilla, rum, and lemon or orange extracts. Use low-fat or fat-free frostings. Add pureed fruit instead of the oil, butter, margarine, or shortening in the recipe. Bake a lower-fat apple crisp instead of an apple pie . . . a pumpkin *cake* rather than a pumpkin *pie* . . . mincemeat *bread pudding* in place of a traditional mincemeat *pie.* Use two egg whites for every one egg called for . . . or two to four tablespoons of water for every egg omitted.

The Low-Fat Epicure by Sallie Twentyman, R.D., a registered dietician and editor of *The Low-Fat Epicure* newsletter, Washington, DC. Berkley Books.

Self-defense: Whenever possible, schedule surgery and major diagnostic procedures for early in the day—and early in the week—when staff members are freshest.

INFLATED OR INACCURATE BILLS

• **Overcharging.** American hospitals are notorious for charging excessive prices—but that's not the half of it. At least half of all hospital bills in this country are wildly inaccurate—and the errors invariably favor the hospital.

To avoid being taken: Do not pay your bill unless you are certain all charges are legitimate. If you discover you have been charged for an item or a service you did not receive, or if you do not understand the bill, contact the hospital and demand a complete explanation.

• **Unnecessary diagnostic tests.** Beware of any doctor who recommends an expensive diagnostic test and then refers you to a specific testing facility. *Reason:* The doctor may have a financial stake in that facility—and may have found a sneaky way to pad his wallet.

Self-defense: If this situation arises, ask the doctor point-blank if he has a financial stake in the testing facility. If so, or if the doctor declines to answer your question, get another doctor. Such a relationship is unethical—and in several states, at least, is now illegal.

PASSIVE ATTITUDE

People who question everything else in life often are all too willing to blindly accept treatments ordered by medical personnel. Questioning your caregivers is essential, even if you cannot understand the answers. *Reason:* The very fact that you ask questions demonstrates that you expect quality care. *Bonus:* In some cases, a seemingly naive question may provoke a doctor to reconsider a particular course of action, thereby saving money, time, discomfort, or even a life.

BOTTOM LINE

Ask any questions that occur to you. Do not worry about alienating your caregivers. Odds are they will not be annoyed. Even if they are, you're still more likely to receive quality care than someone who silently accepts the hospital's course of action.

Choosing a Doctor Made Much Easier

Dr. Robert Arnot

If you think the smartest way to pick a family doctor is to obtain referrals from friends or coworkers, think again. No matter how good their intentions, your friends and coworkers are poorly equipped to evaluate a doctor's medical skills.

After all, a first-rate doctor might be poorly regarded by patients simply because he/she occasionally seems brusque or uncaring. Or a doctor with only marginal skills might come highly recommended just because he has a very pleasant waiting room or a genial bedside manner.

And—a doctor who is ideal for one patient might be wholly inappropriate for another. Doctors are "good" only if they meet your individual needs.

FIRST STEP

The most effective way to find a new internist or family doctor (as opposed to a specialist) is to work backward—that is, consider your own medical needs first.

• **Think about what particular area of expertise would be of greatest value.** This criterion should be based on your age, sex, medical risk factors, and medical history.

Example I: A generally healthy person might pick a doctor who is board-certified in one of the four key primary-care specialties: Internal medicine, family practice, pediatrics, or gynecology.

Example II: A person who has existing health problems or who is at risk for such problems might want to choose someone who specializes in treating those problems.

Robert Arnot, M.D., chief medical editor of the *CBS Evening News*, New York City. He is the author of *The Best Medicine: How to Choose the Top Doctors, the Top Hospitals and the Top Treatments*. Addison-Wesley.

FAT BUSTERS

■ **What's the best way to lose weight—*diet or exercise?*** Exercise is more important than calorie intake in keeping fat off. In a recent study, body-fat levels were *not* related to calorie intake in two groups of sedentary men. But in both groups, the men who exercised least had the most fat. *Note:* Physical activity throughout the day—walking, climbing stairs, etc.—burns more calories and body fat than a 30-minute aerobic workout with no other physical activity.

Physiologist Susan Roberts, Ph.D., Human Nutrition Center on Aging, Tufts University, Boston, MA.

■ **A round of golf burns 1,060 calories**—if you walk and pull the clubs on a wheeled cart for 18 holes. That's the equivalent of running six miles.

Darlene A. Sedlock, Ph.D., associate professor of kinesiology, Purdue University, West Lafayette, IN.

■ **Diet and exercise news . . . lifestyle and longevity**—*one more study:* Middle-aged and older men who took up regular, vigorous exercise—swimming, racket sports, running, and handball, etc.—who quit smoking . . . and who were not overweight had lower death rates than other men in their age group.

From researchers at the Stanford University School of Medicine.

EXERCISE VS. ILLNESS

■ *Moderate* **exercise can reduce high blood pressure.** In a study of 46 men with severe hypertension, researchers first used medication to bring down the whole group's blood pressure. Then half the men were put on an exercise program that eventually reached 45 minutes a day. After 16 weeks, the average blood pressure of the exercising group had fallen, while that of the non-exercising group went up slightly.

Peter F. Kokkinos, Ph.D., a researcher at the Veterans Administration Medical Center, Washington, DC.

■ **Exercise is beneficial** even to very elderly people. Two groups of volunteers (average age 81) met twice a week. One group participated in a 45-minute seated exercise program, the other listened to music and discussed their memories. After seven months, those in the exercise group were stronger, more agile, more flexible and less depressed than those in the social group.

M. E. McMurdo, M.D., senior lecturer, department of medicine, University of Dundee, Ninewells Hospital and Medical School, Dundee, Scotland.

■ **Which type of exercise is better, running or walking?** Both are equally effective forms of exercise. Both improve your muscle tone and cardiovascular system . . . and help you burn calories. *Advantages of walking:* Easier on joints . . . better for those starting a fitness program—especially older or overweight people. *Advantage of running:* Provides a better cardiovascular workout for those already fit. *Caution:* If you have a family history of heart disease or have been inactive, ask your doctor before starting to run.

Mark Anderson, Ph.D., P.T., A.T.C., professor of physical therapy at the University of Oklahoma Health Sciences Center.

• **Determine which hospital in your area is best suited to provide this care.** In most large communities, this will be a university-affiliated teaching hospital, one with hundreds of beds, sophisticated diagnostic equipment, and a large staff of doctors, nurses and medical specialists. Such hospitals are sometimes called "tertiary" hospitals because they accept referrals of difficult or unusual cases.

Even better: A "sentinel" hospital, such as Massachusetts General Hospital in Boston, the Mayo Clinic in Rochester, Minnesota, or Memorial Sloan-Kettering Cancer Center in New York City. These institutions have a range of top-notch doctors on staff and excellent facilities. They can provide you with superb medical care—or refer you to a top-quality doctor and/or hospital in your area.

Problem: Small hospitals with fewer than 100 beds, especially those in rural areas. These are often limited in the type of care they can provide.

• **Once you've chosen a hospital**, call the appropriate department there and ask to speak to the department chief or head nurse. Explain your situation, then request the names of several board-certified doctors who might be willing to take you on as a patient. Contact each doctor and set up a brief interview, by phone or in person.

SIZING UP A DOCTOR

Because the doctors whose names you've obtained were recommended by experts and are affiliated with a first-rate hospital, they've already been screened. So even the "worst" doctor on the list is no doubt perfectly competent. Nevertheless, the interview gives you a chance to find the best one for your needs. *Consider* . . .

• **Credentials.** Though a diploma from a prestigious medical school is no guarantee of stellar medical skills, it is reassuring. So is having completed a fellowship at a distinguished institution.

Note: If the doctor has been practicing for a decade or longer, find out whether he/she has been recertified. Seventeen of the 23 boards of internal medicine nationwide now periodically recertify their members. While recertification is not mandatory—nor is it a definitive indication of a doctor's ability or

quality one way or the other—it shows that he cared enough to have it done.

• **Professionalism.** In most states it's virtually impossible to find out if a particular doctor has ever been officially sanctioned for misconduct . . . but it doesn't hurt to call your state medical board to ask.

If the board declines to provide any information, contact the Public Citizen Health Research Group, 2000 P St. NW, Washington, DC 20036. It publishes "10,289 Questionable Doctors," a list of practitioners who have been disciplined by state medical boards.

• **Personality.** Some patients like a tough, authoritarian doctor who tells them what to do and makes sure they do it. Others prefer a doctor who makes decisions jointly with his patients.

Opportunity: Make sure the doctor is basically optimistic. Pessimism robs patients of hope—and hope is sometimes the only thing that pulls a person through a life-threatening illness or injury.

• **Humility.** No matter how vast his/her medical knowledge and experience, every doctor eventually confronts an ailment for which he has no solution. In such cases, the doctor should be humble enough to admit uncertainty . . . and should help "quarterback" patients' exploration of alternative treatments.

Tragic: I've seen too many patients get outdated or even dangerous care simply because their doctors had grown so accustomed to one particular form of treatment that they were unwilling even to consider newer, better forms. Find out what approach the doctor would take if you developed an incurable ailment.

• **Experience.** All other things being equal, the best doctors generally are those who have the most experience in treating the sorts of medical problems that you're most likely to develop. Ask the doctor if he treats many patients whose circumstances are similar to your own.

• **Clout.** A good doctor makes sure his patients get the treatment they need when they need it. If you have a heart attack, for instance, you need more than a good cardiologist. You need a good car-

---

NO MORE SMOKING

William J. McCarthy, Ph.D.

How to Quit Smoking

The most successful way to quit smoking is to use one of the national programs run by voluntary health organizations. These programs encourage people to make permanent lifestyle changes that make it difficult to smoke and provide motivation not to start again. *Recommended:**

• **American Cancer Society.** *The Fresh Start Stop Smoking Program* holds meetings focusing on group interaction and social support. Group leaders are ex-smokers trained by the American Cancer Society.

National Headquarters: 1599 Clifton Rd. NE, Atlanta, GA 30329. 404-320-3333. Five sessions/$40, nine sessions/$50.

• **American Lung Association.** *Freedom From Smoking* offers eight sessions over four weeks. Group leaders have been trained and may have a health-care background.

National Headquarters: 1740 Broadway, New York, NY 10019. 212-315-8700. $75.

• **Seventh-day Adventists.** *Breathe Free Plan to Stop Smoking* holds eight sessions over three weeks. Group support meetings are usually led by a pastor in addition to a health-care professional or an ex-smoker.

More information: Contact your local Seventh Day Adventist church or hospital. *Free.*

*Cost and length of each program may vary.

Research psychologist William J. McCarthy, Ph.D., adjunct assistant professor of psychology, Division of Cancer Control, University of California, 1100 Glendon Ave., Los Angeles, CA 90024. Dr. McCarthy has been evaluating smoking-cessation methods for more than 10 years.

NO MORE SMOKING

■ **Quitting smoking: Never too late.**
Lung cancer patients who kept smoking after diagnosis were three times more likely to get a second primary lung cancer than ones who quit after diagnosis. Stopping smoking benefits anyone, no matter how long he/she has smoked and no matter what the state of his/her health.

Bruce Johnson, M.D., chief of the lung cancer biology section, National Cancer Institute, Bethesda, MD. His study of more than 450 lung cancer patients was published in Annals of Internal Medicine, *Independence Mall West, Sixth Street at Race, Philadelphia, PA 19106.*

COLD-BUSTERS

■ **Cold weather wellness.** To get the vitamin C you need now, keep up your fruit and vegetable consumption—preferably at the same high level you achieved over the summer. Vitamin C, along with other vitamins, is necessary for optimal health . . . and studies show that it lowers the risk of heart disease and some types of cancer.
Best: A minimum of five servings—fresh or canned—per day.
Alternative: Two 250-mg tablets of vitamin C every day—one with a high-fiber breakfast and one at dinner. But these dietary supplements don't give you the extra nutrients or fiber that fruits and vegetables do.

John H. Weisburger, Ph.D., senior scientist at the American Health Foundation, Valhalla, NY.

■ **Best cold medicines** for teens/adults: Combination antihistamine decongestants. They reduce nasal congestion, post-nasal drip, coughing—and also reduce cold symptoms involving the ears.

diologist capable of immediately summoning the best cardiac surgeons and lining up a bed in a first-rate cardiac intensive care unit. Ask the doctor to describe what would happen if you had such a medical crisis.

Finally, if you belong to a health-maintenance organization (HMO) or managed health-care plan, your options will be more limited. But the same principles still apply. Choose an HMO on the strength of the doctors and hospitals it permits you to use—not because it's conveniently located or inexpensive or because it pays for comparative "frills" like eyeglasses or dental care.

Best Ways to Reduce Risk of Heart Disease

Dr. William Castelli

Designed to uncover the leading risk factors for heart disease in a typical American community, the Framingham Heart Study has been tracking the daily living and eating habits of thousands of residents of Framingham, Massachusetts since 1948.

Dr. William Castelli, director of the study for 15 years and a popular lecturer on heart disease, discusses the study's most recent findings.

How does the current generation of Americans compare with the original subjects of the Framingham Heart Study? Are we becoming healthier—or are we at greater risk?

William Castelli, M.D., director of the Framingham Heart Study, Five Thurber St., Framingham, MA 01701. Dr. Castelli is credited with coining the terms "good" cholesterol and "bad" cholesterol and is among the nation's preeminent experts on the heart and heart disease prevention.

While many of us are benefiting from lower-fat diets and the greater emphasis that is put on fitness, children today may actually be in worse shape than those of previous generations.

One surprise is that teenage boys and young men in Framingham today weigh more than their fathers did at the same ages and they are not as physically active. Therefore, they may be at higher risk for heart disease and diabetes.

The combination of TV and computer technology has made children more sedentary, and their diets are unacceptably high in saturated fat and cholesterol.

Girls in grammar and high school are now smoking at a much higher rate than ever before. If the present pattern continues, the rate of women's deaths from heart disease and diabetes will match or even exceed that of men. From other studies, we have learned that arterial disease can begin as early as the grade-school years.

What are the most recent findings regarding the links between diet and heart disease?

One of the latest discoveries in cardiology is that the newest fat deposit in your arteries—for example, the one that was placed there by the cheeseburger you ate yesterday—may be more likely to break loose, clog your arteries and kill you than the older deposits that have been partially blocking your arteries for years.

These "young" deposits from your most recent high-fat meal don't impede blood flow while attached to artery walls. But they are unstable and can easily snap off and block a coronary vessel.

An estimated 65% to 70% of acute heart attacks are now believed to come from these newer, barely detectable lesions, which are covered by only a thin layer of cells. The older, larger obstructions are covered by thick scar tissue and are rather resistant and stable.

But don't discount big blockages. They are, of course, still undesirable and an indication of widespread disease. In fact, if you have a coronary artery that is at least 50% blocked, the smaller arteries of your heart cannot possibly be free of disease. That would make you a "walking time bomb"—

COLD-BUSTERS

These medicines don't appear to be helpful for young children.

William Feldman, M.D., head of division of general pediatrics, Hospital for Sick Children, Toronto. His study, which reviewed 106 studies on colds, was published in the *Journal of the American Medical Association*, 515 N. State St., Chicago, IL 60610.

■ **I got my worst cold ever after a nasty fight with my husband. Could there be a connection?** Possibly. Marital spats sap the immunity of both spouses. A hostile argument temporarily reduces the number of disease-fighting white blood cells in the bloodstream—raising the vulnerability to disease. Couples who have the nastiest fights—marked by sarcasm, interruptions and criticism—experience the steepest decline in immunity. Wives experience greater drops than husbands, perhaps because women are better at detecting hostile emotions than men.

Janice K. Kiecolt-Glaser, Ph.D., professor of psychology and psychiatry, Ohio State University College of Medicine, Columbus, OH.

HEALTHFUL AGING

■ **People over age 65 who take multi-vitamins daily** were found to be sick with infection-related illnesses only *half* as often as people who did not take vitamins.

Study by National Research Foundations and Memorial University of Newfoundland, reported in Money, *1271 Avenue of the Americas, New York, NY 10020.*

■ **My elderly mother has been taking a lot of aspirin for her arthritis. Is this dangerous for her?** Possibly. In addition to stomach problems, overuse of aspirin can cause hallucinations, incoherent speech, and other mental problems. *Most vulnerable:* Elderly people who take aspirin *powders* for chronic pain. Each powder is the equivalent of two aspirin tablets. Some elderly patients take 20 or more powders a day. *Good news:* Once they limit their aspirin intake, patients usually return to normal within a few days.

David K. Gittelman, D.O., consultation liaison psychiatrist, Wake Area Health Education Center, Raleigh, NC.

■ **Despite arthritis and failing eyesight, my 80-year-old mother insists on living by herself in the same large house she has lived in for fifty years. What can I do to make the house safer for her?** *To elderproof a home, making it safer for aging residents:* Install extra lighting to make up for poor vision. Keep floors and pathways clear of cords, slippery rugs, and other obstacles. Install safety bars and/or a bench in the bathtub. Lower the hot-water temperature to avert accidental burns. Raise beds and toilet seats for greater ease of use.

Paula Bohr, associate professor of occupational therapy, University of Oklahoma Health Sciences Center.

and especially vulnerable to the effects of one fatty meal.

We have all heard that saturated fat is the chief culprit in heart disease. Where does cholesterol fit in? How much of each can we safely consume?

While fat is the primary villain in heart disease, cholesterol is definitely an accomplice.

As a nation, we would be better off if every day we each ate no more than 300 milligrams of cholesterol and 35 to 40 grams of total fat—of which 20 grams or less were in the form of saturated fat. This is the "bad" fat that contributes to heart disease.

Once you reach this goal, you can see whether making these changes gets your serum cholesterol down to a level of 200 or less. The closer you get to the 150-to-160 range, the less likely you are to have a heart attack.

If these adjustments don't "straighten out" your cholesterol, then you should aim for a daily quota of no more than 17 grams of saturated fat, 30 grams of total fat and 200 milligrams of cholesterol.

Example: A lunch of a four-ounce steak, coffee with low-fat milk, and a pat of butter on a roll is about 150 milligrams of cholesterol and 30 grams of fat—of which 18 grams are saturated.

Are triglycerides the same as "bad" cholesterol? How critical are they as risk factors for heart disease?

One of the by-products of the fatty foods we digest are substances called *triglycerides*. They are formed in the liver and are known as Very Low Density Lipoproteins (VLDLs). The familiar LDL, or "bad," cholesterol is not formed directly—it comes from VLDL.

We are now learning that there are four different types of triglycerides, two of which are damaging to arteries and two of which are not. The most dangerous ones are small and dense and associated with diets high in saturated fats. These VLDLs have been linked with very early heart attacks—striking victims in their 20s, 30s, and 40s.

Recently, we have discovered that these VLDLs enter the white blood cells in our artery walls even faster than LDLs. This makes them particularly destructive.

Genetic predispositions and unwise eating habits play roles in the formation of these dangerous fats, but the dangers can be curbed by maintaining a healthy lifestyle.

Other types of triglycerides can be raised by eating diets high in whole grains, vegetables and fruits, but these are not the kind that are harmful to our hearts or artery walls.

What are the best ways to raise levels of HDL, or "good," cholesterol?

When our Framingham data showed that the relative amount of HDL in our blood is even more important than total cholesterol and that exercise can have a favorable impact on HDL, I began jogging regularly. This raised my HDL level from 49 to 63. A regular routine of brisk walking or any other exercise is fine for most people—but talk with your doctor before beginning a new exercise regimen.

Losing weight also elevates HDLs, and certain foods and nutrients, such as brewer's yeast, garlic, onions, ginseng, and chromium, have been credited with boosting them as well.

My advice is to have a test done after eating such wholesome, harmless foods for about a month—as part of a low-fat diet—to see whether they have any measurable effect on your HDLs.

Aim: The ratio of your total cholesterol to HDL should be under 3.5.

How does the risk of heart attack in men compare with that of women?

One of the most shocking findings to emerge from the Framingham Heart Study is that one out of every five men has had a heart attack by the time he reaches age 60. The heart attack rate for women is only one in 17 by the same age.

Unless they have diabetes, smoke, or have familial hypercholesterolemia (inherited abnormally high serum cholesterol), women are relatively immune to heart disease before menopause because they produce high levels of estrogen, which apparently plays a protective role.

However, within six to 10 years after menopause—when estrogen levels drop off sharply—women's risk becomes similar to that of men. Unfortunately, women tend to have more advanced

TOOTH PROTECTION

■ **Does chewing gum really help prevent tooth decay?** Yes, although it's no substitute for regular brushing and flossing. Gum-chewing stimulates saliva flow and helps neutralize acids remaining in the mouth. *For maximum benefit:* Start chewing within five minutes of finishing a meal. Continue for at least 15 minutes. *Important:* Sugarless gum is more effective than gum containing sugar.

Kichuel K. Park, D.D.S., Ph.D., professor of preventive and community dentistry, Indiana University School of Dentistry, Indianapolis, IN.

■ **Dental cavities** are usually less common during midlife than in childhood, *but* can increase again in later life. For many, plaque accumulates around the edges of old fillings, bridgework, and crowns, causing decay. For those at risk for these or other reasons, such as gum recession and exposure of root surfaces, a new treatment applied by the dentist, *Durafluor*, with a fluoride toothpaste, is proving to be an efficient addition.

Irwin Mandel, D.D.S., professor emeritus, Columbia University School of Dental and Oral Surgery, New York, NY.

■ **Toothbrush germs** can be destroyed by storing the brush, bristles down, in a glass of mouthwash. *Problem:* A toothbrush stored in the open air is a magnet for airborne germs that can cause gum inflammation and possibly gum disease. *Important:* Replace the mouthwash every few days.

Warren Scherer, D.D.S., associate professor of restorative dentistry, New York University College of Dentistry, New York, NY.

POLLUTION DEFENSE

■ **Carbon monoxide exposure** can lead to long-term health problems. Initial symptoms—headaches and dizziness—may disappear after brief oxygen therapy. But some people exposed to the gas develop a severe, irreversible neuropsychiatric syndrome weeks or even months after exposure. *Symptoms:* Memory lapses, concentration problems, personality changes—even psychosis.

Donna Seger, M.D., assistant professor of emergency medicine, Vanderbilt University Medical Center, Nashville, TN.

■ **I live in a city where the air pollution levels are quite high. How dangerous is this?** Air pollution really does kill. Small increases in air pollution in specific areas are accompanied by small increases in percentage of deaths in those areas.

A study of particulate air pollution and death rates in Philadelphia over an eight-year period, led by Joel Schwartz, Ph.D., senior scientist, U.S. Environmental Protection Agency.

■ **Rug- and upholstery-cleaner danger.** These common cleaners sometimes contain toxic chemicals—naphthalene, perchloroethylene, oxalic acid, diethylene, glycol. *Safer:* Sweep and vacuum rugs and furniture regularly. *Helpful:* Sprinkle dry cornstarch, baking soda, borax, or cornmeal before beginning to vacuum.

The Solution to Pollution: 101 Things You Can Do to Clean Up Your Environment, by Laurence Sombke. MasterMedia Limited.

■ **The environment and the brain:** Certain environmental toxins—including those already thought to lead to cancer—may also contribute to degenerative neurological diseases, including Parkinson's, Alzheimer's, and Lou Gehrig's disease. But few of the 70,000 chemicals that are used commercially have been tested for neurotoxicity.

W. Kent Anger, Ph.D., behavior neurotoxicologist, Oregon Health Sciences University, Portland, OR.

heart disease by the time they are treated, since physicians still consider them to be less susceptible to coronary problems and often don't diagnose the condition early enough.

How many people survive heart attacks today? Can any of them ever return to "normal"?

As the Framingham data have shown, when people get heart attacks, about 85% of them survive.

With the new thrombolytic therapy, in which people having a heart attack are injected with a clot-dissolving drug, we can increase the percentage of survivors to about 93%. Even in the oldest age groups, 75% of first-time heart attack victims survive.

Of those who survive, about half lose the normal pumping ability of their hearts—when we put them on a treadmill, they "flunk." If we subsequently inject them with a radioisotope such as thallium, which allows us to scan the heart, we find that the heart muscle tissue in 30% of these people is "hibernating" but still very much alive—which means it can eventually be restored to normal function.

In the short run, we can't lower the cholesterol levels of these patients sufficiently or fast enough—either through dietary changes or drugs—to shrink the deposits inside their coronary arteries and get their hearts pumping at full capacity again.

Today's "high-tech" treatments, such as coronary bypass surgery, balloon angioplasty or atherectomy, can help restore cardiac function and allow these people to return to work. But in the long run, the only treatment that works is aggressively lowering blood cholesterol through diet and lifestyle changes. If blood cholesterol is lowered within three to five years of the first heart attack, we can markedly reduce the risk of a second heart attack.

What are your latest recommendations for a "healthy heart" diet?

When it comes to protecting yourself from heart disease, the best strategy is to become a vegetarian—eating primarily fresh vegetables, legumes, whole grains, fruits, and nonfat dairy products.

Vegetarians not only outlive the rest of us, they also aren't prey to other degenerative diseases, such as diabetes, strokes, etc., that slow us down and make us chronically ill.

If you can't *be* a vegetarian, the next best thing is to *eat* a vegetarian from the sea. One type of shellfish fits this description—mollusks (clams and oysters). They loll around on the ocean floor and are filter feeders, sucking in the phytoplankton (the vegetables of the sea). Mollusks have the lowest cholesterol levels of all seafood.

The second best choices are moving shellfish such as shrimp and lobster. While they contain more cholesterol than most meats and cheeses, they are so low in saturated fat that they are a much better bargain nutritionally—more desirable even than skinless white-meat chicken. Also good, of course, is to eat any fish—even fatty fishes. They are very low in saturated fat and contain fish oils, which also benefit your heart.

If you prefer a more standard American diet, recent changes at your supermarket allow you to have some beef, too. The newest grade of beef available—*select*—contains only 10% saturated fat by weight, or approximately four grams of fat in four ounces of precooked meat. And *ConAgra* now puts out a product called "Healthy Choice Extra Lean Ground Beef" that contains only 1.5 grams of saturated fat per four-ounce serving. That means you could have burgers for breakfast, lunch, and dinner and still have plenty of saturated fat to "spend" that day. Similarly, everything from ham to ice cream comes in a low-fat and delicious version at your local market today.

Does heart disease follow a predictable course—and is it ever too late to stop it?

Once it begins, atherosclerosis—the hardening and thickening of arteries because of fatty deposits—follows a fairly predictable course.

It starts in the abdominal aorta, spreads to the coronary arteries, the big artery in the chest, then down into the leg, up into the neck, and finally inside the head. This is why strokes generally occur later in life than heart attacks do.

BRAIN PROTECTION

■ **Stroke warning signs:** Sudden numbness or weakness in face, arm or leg on one side of the body . . . sudden loss or blurring of vision in one or both eyes . . . speech difficulty . . . sudden severe headache . . . unexplained dizziness, unsteadiness, or falling. *What to do if signs appear:* Call 911 or go right to a hospital.

James L. Weiss, M.D., editor, *The Johns Hopkins Medical Letter,* 550 N. Broadway, Baltimore, MD 21205.

■ **Alzheimer's disease update:** Separate studies have shown that use of nonsteroidal anti-inflammatory drugs and estrogen supplements seems to delay the onset of Alzheimer's symptoms. *Also:* Those who have higher levels of education and intellectually demanding jobs develop symptoms much later in life. *Smart for everyone:* Keep your mind sharp. Use it in new ways—solve puzzles, learn a foreign language, etc.—in order to increase the number of connections in the brain. These exercises can help you maintain brain function if you ever develop Alzheimer's disease.

Zaven Khachaturian, Ph.D., director, Office of Alzheimer's Disease Research, National Institutes of Health, Bethesda, MD.

■ **Prescription anticoagulants** work better than aspirin at preventing stroke in individuals who have already suffered one. In a recent study of 1,007 at-risk patients, the anticoagulant *warfarin* (Coumadin) cut stroke risk by 66%, as compared with 17% for aspirin. At-risk patients—those with *nonrheumatic atrial fibrillation,* high blood pressure, congestive heart failure, or a previous stroke or heart attack—should ask their doctors about taking warfarin to prevent a second stroke.

David Sherman, M.D., chief of neurology, University of Texas Heath Sciences Center, San Antonio, TX.

IMMUNITY MATTERS

■ **Zinc boosts immunity** in the elderly. The mineral is needed for synthesis of *thymic humoral factor,* a protein that aids in the production of white blood cells—the backbone of the immune system. After midlife, levels of this protein decline significantly, weakening the immune system. Zinc appears to replenish stores of the protein, thus boosting immune function. If you're 55 or older, ask your doctor about the benefits of zinc-rich foods, like seafood, liver, mushrooms, sunflower seeds, soybeans, and brewer's yeast—and zinc supplements.

Robert A. Good, M.D., Ph.D., D.Sc., head, division of allergy and clinical immunology, University of South Florida College of Medicine, St. Petersburg, FL.

■ **I know that vaccines are important for children. Are they of any use for adults?** Vaccinations for adults are the cheapest and most effective way to prevent disease, though most people—including doctors—think of vaccines as primarily for children. Review vaccination history with your doctor. *Recommended:* Measles, rubella, tetanus toxoid, influenza, and pneumococcal vaccines for adults—especially for the elderly. *Also advisable:* Polio vaccine for people traveling outside the United States.

F. Marc LaForce, M.D., professor of medicine, University of Rochester School of Medicine and Dentistry, Rochester, NY.

■ **The pneumonia vaccine** is often as important as the flu vaccine. Unlike the flu vaccine, which must be given annually, the pneumonia vaccine is usually given only once. *Important:* Anyone over age 65—or younger people with conditions such as diabetes, cancer, or kidney, heart or lung disease—should be vaccinated. *Urgent:* Increasing resistance of

Now that we have such diagnostic tools as echocardiography, which uses ultrasound, we can look inside the neck arteries of our Framingham subjects. By the time they are in their 60s, 76% of them have deposits or lesions in that area. This means that the disease is already well advanced elsewhere in their bodies and has been in their coronary arteries for at least ten years.

If these people continue on their present course, about half of them will end up dying from this arterial clogging.

While we can intervene and make a difference even at this point, the earlier one starts the better, so I don't want to exclude children or premenopausal women from good preventive programs.

Twenty-five years from now, when these children are adults and the women are past menopause, they and their families will have already acquired healthy eating habits to keep them well protected from heart disease.

I've yet to meet anyone whose genes are so good that they have license to eat whatever they want—or who can get away with being too sedentary. It's only by altering diet and exercise habits that I can change the destiny of 75% of the people who are headed for heart attacks. The remaining 25% will need lipid-lowering drugs in order to achieve the same result.

At age 62 and as the first man in my family to reach the age of 45 without any coronary symptoms, I'm living proof that a healthful change of lifestyle can definitely work.

Best New Solutions to Old Sleep Problems

Dr. James Perl

SLEEP WANTED

Two decades of research in the U.S., Europe, and Japan by hundreds of specialists in sleep disorders has paid off. There is now little reason for anyone—even executives or professionals in high-stress jobs who frequently travel—to suffer from insomnia, poor-quality sleep or sleep deprivation.

Proven techniques to get to sleep quickly and to get enough deep, refreshing sleep—without medications or alcohol—can be learned by everyone.

KNOW WHAT YOU NEED

About two-thirds of adults sleep between six and nine hours a night. That is a pretty wide range—but the remaining one-third sleep more or less than this amount.

Common mistake #1: People who think they need eight hours of sleep, but really need only seven often worry unnecessarily about their health when they get, say, only six-and-a-half hours of sleep.

Common mistake #2: Trying to force yourself to get more sleep than you need, simply because you think you need more. This often creates an insomnia problem. About one out of five adults is a short sleeper—someone who needs less than six hours of sleep. Thomas Edison slept four or five hours a night and a few people are fine with even less.

James Perl, Ph.D., a clinical psychologist in private practice, 4761 McKinley Dr., Boulder, CO 80303. Dr. Perl is author of *Sleep Right in Five Nights.* William Morrow.

pneumococcal bacteria to penicillin and other antibiotics makes this vaccine even more important.

Timothy McCall, M.D., an internist practicing in the Boston area. He is author of *Examining Your Doctor: A Patient's Guide to Avoiding Harmful Medical Care.* Birch Lane Press.

CANCER SELF-DEFENSE

■ **Surgery for ulcers** or other digestive disorders doubles or even triples a person's risk of stomach cancer. *Most vulnerable:* People who have had a gastrectomy (removal of the lower portion of the stomach) or any type of surgery to treat a gastric ulcer. *Theory:* Surgery reduces stomach acidity, which in turn encourages growth of stomach bacteria. These bacteria cause cancer-promoting biochemical changes in digestive juices. *Helpful:* Careful screening for all patients who have had ulcer surgery, including endoscopy for those with chronic indigestion, constipation, stomach irritation, change in bowel habits, or other stomach cancer symptoms.

Susan G. Fisher, Ph.D., assistant professor of epidemiology, Stritch School of Medicine, Loyola University, Chicago, IL.

CANCER SELF-DEFENSE

■ **Inhaling wood dust** increases wood-workers' risk of developing nasal cancer—a rare malignancy that is often advanced when detected and is very hard to treat. *To reduce inhalation of dust:* Wear a respirator-type filter mask.

Thomas Vaughan, M.D., associate member, Fred Hutchinson Cancer Research Center, and associate professor of epidemiology, University of Washington School of Public Health and Community Medicine, Seattle, WA.

■ **Melanoma may run in families.** If a person has this type of skin cancer, relatives should have careful, rigorous skin exams as well. Relatives should be especially watchful if they have moles that are irregular in shape, border, color or size. *Strongly recommended:* Regular skin exams—both professional and self-examinations—to detect melanoma early. The disease is curable more than 90% of the time if discovered when the melanoma is still less than one millimeter thick.

Arthur Sober, M.D., director, Pigmented Lesion Clinic, Massachusetts General Hospital, Boston, MA.

Your "normal" sleep need is largely programmed at birth by hereditary factors. It is possible to alter your sleep needs, but first you must know what those needs are.

If, however, your sleep pattern worsens to a bothersome degree as you get older, try to correct the problem by . . .

• **Keeping to a regular sleep-wake rhythm.** Don't linger in bed in the morning if work pressures ease up or when you retire.

• **Keeping busy during the day.**

• **Avoiding daytime naps.** If you do nap, however, do it before 3 P.M. and don't nap more than one hour.

• **Staying awake at least until 10 or 11 P.M.** If you get drowsy earlier, take a brisk walk, do some indoor exercise or listen to the radio or watch TV.

If you find you often don't get back to sleep during the night, develop some activities to do then—videos, craft projects, computer networking.

MEDICAL CONDITIONS

Many illnesses have symptoms that are hardly noticeable during the day but that interfere with sleep at night—such as pain, itching or shortness of breath. Identify and treat the symptoms of disease—rather than focusing on sleep. *Typical problems:*

• **Bladder problems.** Too-frequent urination during the night can be caused by excessive caffeine use. If avoiding caffeine doesn't help, try retraining your urinating reflexes by progressively delaying urination each time you feel the urge during the day and evening. Try to add fifteen minutes to the interval each week until you increase it to ninety minutes. To strengthen the reflex even further, start drinking more water (though not too close to bedtime).

• **Sunday night insomnia.** Some people have insomnia only on Sunday night. Or they say insomnia started on Sunday nights but now happens other nights as well. Worries about Sunday night insomnia may also be one of the major causes of the widespread Sunday afternoon blues.

The cause: Going to bed late Friday and Saturday nights and sleeping late Saturday and Sunday mornings—or napping Sunday afternoon—can put your internal clock two, three, or four hours behind the actual time you try to go to sleep Sunday night at your "regular" 11 P.M. bedtime. That's why you can't fall asleep. And because it's Sunday night, you begin to worry about work on Monday as you toss and turn. So you think work stress is causing your insomnia.

The cure: Get up at your regular weekday wakeup time on Saturday and Sunday mornings. If you absolutely must sleep later—make it no more than one hour later than your usual wakeup time. And expose yourself to daylight as soon as you wake up. Don't nap—especially not on Sunday afternoon. Get into the habit of exercising Sunday afternoon or early evening.

Best Immune System Boosters

Dr. David S. McKinsey

The immune system can be compromised by many things—from an ordinary cold to deadly cancers. That's the bad news.

The good news is that your immune defenses regularly repair themselves, and there are simple measures you can take to assist them when they have been breached.

Basically, your immune system is a thriving swarm of billions of white blood cells, all with just two goals . . .

- Recognize germ invaders.
- Respond to the threat.

David S. McKinsey, M.D., codirector of epidemiology and infectious diseases at the Research Medical Center, 2316 E. Meyer, Kansas City, MO 64132.

RX SELF-DEFENSE

■ **List all of the medications** you take when giving a doctor your medical history. *Problem:* Many people don't consider vitamin and mineral supplements and herbal preparations to be "drugs . . . but some of these remedies may be dangerous. *Examples:* The amino-acid supplement L-tryptophan has been linked to severe muscle pain . . . and the herb chaparral has been linked to hepatitis.

Stuart L. Nightingale, M.D., associate commissioner for health affairs, Food and Drug Administration, Rockville, M.D. His recommendation was published in the *Journal of the American Medical Association,* 515 N. State St., Chicago 60610.

■ **Medicine-bottle trap.** Cotton packed in bottles to keep pills from breaking during shipment can pass germs from one user to the next. This is one way that viruses and other illnesses are passed throughout a household. *Important:* Remove cotton when the medicine bottle is opened.

Bruce Yaffe, M.D., an internist in private practice, 121 E. 84 St., New York, NY 10028.

■ **Prescription trap.** Standard drug doses are often higher than necessary, especially for older patients with chronic illnesses. *Risks:* Side effects . . . and excessive costs. *Self-defense:* When starting to take a new drug, ask your doctor if it would be prudent to begin with less than the usual dosage. This dosage can then be gradually increased, as necessary, without crossing into the toxic range.

Marvin M. Lipman, M.D., a clinical professor of medicine at New York Medical College, writing in *Consumer Reports on Health,* 101 Truman Ave., Yonkers, NY 10703.

PREVENTION MAGIC

■ **Sunburn danger and drugs.** Some prescription medications make skin sensitive to sunlight. Severe sunburn may be sustained in minutes—or there may be a delayed reaction two to three days after exposure. *Examples:* Birth-control pills . . . the antinausea drug *phenothiazine* . . . arthritis drugs *piroxicam* and *naproxen* . . . acne drug *tretinoin* . . . allergy and cold medication *diphenhydramine* . . . and anti-infection drugs *tetracycline, griseofulvin, sulfonamides,* and *nalidixic acid. Self-defense:* Before using any prescription medicine, ask your doctor or druggist if it causes photosensitivity.

Madhukar A. Pathak, Ph.D., chairman, photobiology committee, The Skin Cancer Foundation, New York, NY.

When bacteria enter your body—for instance, through that razor nick you got yesterday—specialized cells called neutrophils rush to the scene to virtually devour the marauders. Other cells soon come by to clean up any bacterial fragments.

Against viruses—which are more insidious than bacterial infections because they sneak into our cells and commandeer them for their own evil purposes—your immune system dispatches antibodies to tackle the attacking aliens.

More important, your immune system has memory cells that look at the viral perpetrators and remember those particular villains for the rest of your life. When antibodies recognize and defeat a virus, your system has established an immunity.

Vaccines and medications may be thought of, in a sense, as backups that assist a person when the immune system is overloaded.

There are a lot of microscopic threats out there. But, don't worry. We have plenty of memory cells—enough to recall every virus, bacteria, or toxin that is in existence.

WHY IT FAILS

Without an immune system, even the mildest infection would be lethal. Under normal circumstances, our immune system serves us admirably. When it does malfunction, it is usually for one good reason or another . . .

• **Stress.** Chronic, unrelieved stress is probably the most severe threat to your immune system. Along with depression, grief, and anxiety, stress can trigger chemical changes, stimulating the release of neuropeptides, which adversely affect the operation of your immune system.

• **Exertion extremes.** Moderate exercise is necessary for basic health, of course, and that includes maintaining a healthy immune system. But, too much exertion—for instance, marathon running, mountain climbing in arctic conditions, or other such strenuous activities—has been shown to temporarily depress immune system functions.

• **Malnutrition.** The relationship between nutrition and the immune system is still a puzzle. We do know, though, that those with poor diets are

more susceptible to illness and infections, increasing the burden on their immune systems.

Beware: Rapid and excessive weight loss, through quirky diets or periods of starvation, also drastically reduces your immune system's effectiveness.

ROUTINE MAINTENANCE

- **Keep stress at a reasonable level.** Stress reduction is critical for your immune system to function well. If you're not addressing this common problem, make it a health-care priority.
- **Vaccinations.** These are key to preventing "sneak attacks" on your immune system. Follow the vaccination schedule your child's pediatrician recommends. You may be due for a tetanus booster yourself. When traveling internationally, seek medical advice on specific vaccinations you may need.
- **Follow a balanced diet.** Sustaining a fit immune system is another good reason for healthy eating. But, avoid the temptation to "boost" immunity defenses through fad diets or the currently popular vitamin or mineral therapy. Such self-treatment can have serious consequences. Large doses of iron, for example, can cause dangerous digestive tract problems. And, while vitamin A is crucial to combat infections, massive supplemental doses can actually suppress vital immune functions.
- **Follow your physician's advice exactly when you are ill.** Take all medication prescribed, especially antibiotics, which we tend to discontinue using immediately after symptoms disappear.

Give your immune system time to fight your illness and recover afterward. Finally, realize that we often have unrealistic expectations for our health. A few colds a year is not a sign that something is wrong with your lifestyle. Being sick occasionally is just a part of being alive. Thanks to your immune system, so is getting well.

- **Stay happy.** Just as depression and anxiety can adversely affect all aspects of your health, a happy and optimistic outlook will contribute to a healthier immune system. Recent studies show that this may not be entirely psychological, but may have a neurological basis as well.

VERY, VERY PERSONAL

■ **Antibiotic/diarrhea danger.** *Clostridium difficile*—a disease-causing bacterium carried by one person in 50—is usually held in check by "friendly" bacteria in the colon. *Problem:* Antibiotics can destroy these friendly bacteria, causing clostridium difficile to proliferate. *Result:* Diarrhea and stomach cramps. *Protection:* Never take antibiotics prescribed for someone else . . . never take them for colds or viral infections, for which there is no proven benefit. If you develop diarrhea while taking an antibiotic, notify your doctor. Tell him/her also if you get diarrhea within six weeks after taking antibiotics.

Lester Rosen, M.D., colon and rectal surgeon, Allentown, PA.

■ **Hookworm danger.** *A. caninum,* an intestinal parasite common in adult dogs, infects humans much more frequently than previously thought. *Symptom:* Mild to severe abdominal pain. To avoid hookworms, avoid contact with dog feces or soil contaminated with dog feces . . . have your dog dewormed regularly.

John Croese, M.B., gastroenterology department, Townsville General Hospital, Queensland, Australia. His study of nine patients infected with hookworms was published in *Annals of Internal Medicine,* Independence Mall West, Sixth St. at Race, Philadelphia, PA 19106.

HOME SWEET HOME

■ **You'll find that when applying for a home-equity loan,** home appraisals are almost always lower than the *market-value* appraisal of a home. The bank does this for protection in case of a default on the loan. If you want a larger loan than the original appraisal would allow, there is recourse. Have your home independently appraised—this can usually be done through a real estate agent. Ask for a *Comparative Market Analysis*, which reports on your home in relation to others in your area, and for an estimate of your home's fair market value. Then call the bank with the new information and ask it to reconsider. If the bank is still uncooperative, go to a new bank with your appraisal. The second bank will likely be more flexible than the first because its appraiser won't feel comfortable deviating greatly from the information you provided prior to his appraisal.

Edward F. Mrkvicka, Jr., president, Reliance Enterprises, a financial consulting firm in Marengo, IL, and author of The Bank Book. Harper-Collins.

■ **Home refinancing loans** that cover up to 95% of a home's value are now available from the Federal National Mortgage Association and the Federal Home Loan Mortgage Corporation. Formerly, these agencies would not provide money for refinancing in cases in which the home owner did not own at least a 10% equity interest in the home. The new policy opens a new refinancing opportunity to those who need it the most but were ineligible for refinancing under the old rule—persons who own homes that

What to Do If There's a Burglar in the House

Richard L. Bloom

Outdoor lighting, alarm systems, timers that automatically turn on and off household lights, and other precautions all help protect your home from burglary.

Just as important as taking steps to keep burglars outside is planning what to do if someone makes it inside. *Most important:*

• **Create a "safe haven."** Inside every home should be a specially equipped room where occupants can retreat in case of an attack or intrusion. This room—ideally a bathroom or bedroom—should have a window or some other means of escape . . . a solid-core door with a one-inch deadbolt that latches from the inside . . . a telephone . . . and a list of emergency phone numbers. If your home is equipped with an alarm system, install a panic button inside your safe room.

• **Develop an escape plan.** Know the fastest way out of your house from every room. Periodically rehearse your escape. Make sure windows, doors, and other escape routes can quickly be opened from the inside.

Richard L. Bloom, founder of the Crime Deterrent Institute, Houston, TX. A frequent lecturer on crime prevention and victims' rights, Bloom is the author of Victims: A Survival Guide for the Age of Crime. Guardian Press.

• **Don't go to investigate.** Confronting a burglar face-to-face can turn a simple burglary into an assault or even murder.

More prudent: Leave the investigation to the police. If you arrive home and find evidence of a break-in, *don't go inside.* The intruder might still be there. Leave the premises immediately and call the police.

If the burglary takes place while you're inside, lock a door between yourself and the intruder—ideally that of your safe haven—and telephone the police. If you cannot reach a phone, open a window and yell for help.

If it's possible to escape without risking an encounter with the burglar, then do so. Call the police from a neighbor's house.

• **Remain calm.** If you come face-to-face with an intruder inside your home, try not to panic. The more level-headed you are, the more likely you'll be able to think of a way to defuse the situation . . . and the less threatening you'll appear to the burglar.

If you don't provoke him, odds are he/she won't harm you. Most burglars just want to get out of the house once they've been detected. Don't attack or attempt to hold him until the police arrive. Just give him a wide berth so he can escape.

Most important: Fight only if attacked. Then use any weapon at hand—a knife, scissors, a heavy object, a canister of irritating chemical spray, etc. A gun is useful only if you know how—and are willing—to fire it at the intruder. If you wield a gun tentatively, he might take it away and use it against *you.*

have declined in value, reducing their equity/debt ratio to less than 10%.

US News & World Report, 2400 N St. NW, Washington, DC 20037.

HOME-REPAIR SECRETS

■ **Before storing,** take a plastic-coated twist tie, fold one end and push the folded end into the soft caulk at the tip. Leave an inch of twist tie exposed. Next time you need caulk, pull out the twist tie. The dried caulk will come with it, leaving the tip clean.

The Family Handyman, 7900 International Dr., Minneapolis, MN 55425.

■ **Always strike a hammer** with the face perpendicular to the surface being struck. Avoid "glancing" (off-center blows), which can cause metal chips to fly into the air.

• Use the striking face only—never the side of the hammerhead.

• The hammer face should always be at least ⅜" larger in diameter than the striking surface of a chisel, punch, wedge, etc.

• Never use a hammer with a loose or damaged handle. Periodically check to be sure the handle is seated tightly into the hammerhead.

• Pull nails or pry wood away from your face to prevent injury if loosened pieces fly.

• Never use one hammer to strike another hammer.

• Replace hammers with dents, cracks, chips, loose handles or any excessive wear.

• Always wear safety goggles.

Family Safety and Health, published by the National Safety Council, 1121 Spring Lake Dr., Itasca, IL 60143.

Cutting Utility Costs at Home

Susan Jaffe

Most of us turn out the lights when we want to save energy, but there are even smarter ways to reduce your bills this winter . . .

Refrigerators

The refrigerator represents about 30% of most electric bills. To find out how well yours operates, open the door and place a dollar bill against the seal. Then close the door. If you can remove the bill easily, the seal needs replacing. Vacuuming the coils behind or below the unit can improve efficiency as well, but be sure to first unplug the refrigerator.

Insulation

Up to 40% of home heating escapes outdoors unnecessarily because of inadequate insulation. A free energy audit by your local power company will show you how to improve insulation. *Opportunities:* Install more insulation under the roof and behind walls, and weather strip the windows or replace them entirely.

Lighting

Compact fluorescent bulbs last at least 10 times longer than regular bulbs and use one-fourth of the electricity while producing the same amount of light. Unlike the long fluorescent bulbs found in offices, these screw into ordinary sockets. Some utilities offer compact fluorescents at a discount. Some even give them away.

How to Work at Home Much More Effectively

Lisa Kanarek

More than 34 million Americans now work in their own kitchens, basements, spare rooms, and garages—doing work that used to be done in high-rise office buildings.

Computers, fax machines, new phone systems and personal organizers are making it possible to do almost anything that can be done in a corporate office from your home—or your car.

But running a home office is not like running a corporate office—or like running a home. It has its own unique challenges that you must recognize and address.

PICKING YOUR SPACE

Wherever possible, it's best to set up your office in a separate space, whether it's as small as a closet or as spacious as a spare room. While some people can work in the corner of their kitchens, there's no other place in the home that has more distractions.

Better: Carve out a space in the basement—or even the garage—that is away from household traffic.

When you go to your newly created office, you'll be ready for business. Keep all your supplies there . . . and keep track of them so that you won't run out of critical items while you're working.

Self-defense: Buy a second set of office supplies for the family (to be kept elsewhere) so they won't raid yours.

If children or pets will be coming into your office, arrange a comfortable area for them with their own playthings.

Lisa Kanarek, president of Everything's Organized, a consulting firm specializing in paper management, office organization, and productivity improvement, 660 Preston Forest Center, Suite 120, Dallas, TX 75230. She is author of *Organizing Your Home Office for Success*. Plume.

Trap: Nothing sounds more unprofessional while you're on the phone than a dog barking or a child crying in the background. Try to be alone when you make important calls. And never assume that because you're working at home you won't need child care. Until children are in school all day, you will almost certainly need backup during business hours.

SEPARATING YOUR TWO WORLDS

As a general rule, your business will be much more successful and your tax filing easier if you separate your business life from your personal life. That means having separate phone lines for home and office . . . using separate credit cards for business expenses . . . and keeping personal and business papers and records in two different places.

Exception: It's okay to have a column for personal activities in your daily or weekly planner. After all, one of the objectives of working at home is to see your family more often and to be able to fit in your kids' school activities, etc.

It's even a good idea to have your business mail sent to a post office box. This will protect your home address from unwanted commercial contacts. Also, you can leaf through your mail at the post office and discard material that doesn't need to come home.

TAKING CONTROL

When you work for a company, you get a day's pay, whether or not you accomplish a day's worth of work.

At home, however, your income is directly related to how productive you are. If you spend 30 minutes on the phone with a friend or 20 minutes looking for a misplaced piece of paper, that's time spent not earning money.

At home, you probably won't have a secretary or staff to help you with typing, filing, phone calls, and paperwork. You're on your own. Therefore, it is imperative to take control and get your office organized so that you can work efficiently.

Water

Once all leaks are fixed, the largest water-waster is the toilet. At about six gallons per flush, a lot of good water—and dollars—go down the drain. Low-flush toilets only use about 1.6 gallons, but there are other ways to save water without replacing the fixture. *Simple way:* Fill two or three slim plastic bottles with dirt or gravel and place them in the toilet's water tank. This will displace the tank water so that less is used with each flush. Flow-restricters for shower heads save water too.

Susan Jaffe, a writer who has been specializing in environmental issues for well over a decade.

■ **More than 40% of all previously owned homes** on the market will have at least one serious defect that is in need of repair or improvement. *Most common:* Cracked heat exchangers . . . failing air-conditioning compressors . . . environmental hazards (radon, asbestos) . . . wet basements . . . defective roofing and/or flashing . . . termites or other insect infestations . . . old galvanized piping . . . aluminum wiring . . . horizontal foundation cracks . . . major structural settlement . . . undesized electrical system . . . chimney settling/separation. *Self-defense:* A comprehensive inspection by a qualified inspector.

Kenneth Austin, chairman, HouseMaster, a national home-inspection franchise based in Bound Brook, NJ.

■ **Eliminate closing costs**—or shave one-quarter to one-half point off mortgage rates—by promising the lender that you will not refinance for a period of two

BETTER HOME BUYING

to five years. This strategy is especially beneficial for those who are now taking out fixed-rate mortgages and do not plan to move in the next five years.

Robert Van Order, chief economist at the Federal Home Loan Mortgage Corp., 8200 Jones Branch Dr., McLean, VA 22102.

DISASTER CONTROL

■ **When your property is hit by a major disaster,** document the damage *immediately. Reason:* Because of the growing number of overstated and fraudulent claims filed each year, the IRS is becoming more skeptical of those who deduct disaster losses. *Strategy:* Save a copy of the next day's local newspaper, along with pictures or videos of your damaged property, and a copy of your tax bill to prove you own the property . . . if you rent, get a letter from your landlord to prove you lived there at the time of the disaster.

Anna Maria Galdieri, certified public accountant and chairperson of the California Society of CPA's Fire Crisis Committee, which studies the tax implications of natural disasters, 275 Shoreline Dr., Redwood City, CA 94065.

TIME MANAGEMENT

Good time management is crucial for the home-office professional. Since no one is imposing a schedule on you, you need to discipline yourself. If you can't resist chatty neighbors, working at home may not be for you. Learn to ignore household tasks that need to be done. They can be done later.

• **Prioritize.** Determine your best time of day . . . and schedule important tasks for then.

Throughout the day (about every three hours), ask yourself if what you're doing at that moment is the best use of your time. I call this *structured flexibility*. You've made your to-do list and set your priorities, yet you're aware that your priorities could change at any moment.

Bonus: When you work at home, you have the freedom to work odd hours, nights, weekends, or early mornings, when there are fewer interruptions.

• **Be willing to change your schedule and focus on what seems more important.** The word "focus" is key, because you don't want to keep skipping from one thing to another. Then nothing gets finished.

Helpful: Make appointments with yourself to work on certain tasks. Block out time on your calendar to write a report, develop a marketing plan, etc. Turn on the answering machine during that time.

• **Set aside some time each week to read.** Even spending a half hour or an hour every morning makes a big difference when trying to get through all the newspapers, magazines, professional journals, sales brochures, and other material you need to review. Put those articles and brochures that you'll need to refer to again in a *reference* file (distinct from your *current* file).

• **Spend at least one full day a week in your office** to catch up on paperwork, make phone calls, etc. Choose a day that's most likely to be slow, and try to keep your schedule clear. This will make the rest of your week go more smoothly.

• **Learn to say "no"** not only to nonbusiness demands on your time but also to new business that you really can't handle. Clients are more understanding about being turned down than they are about missed deadlines. When you don't set limits on what you can accomplish, the quality of your work will suffer and you will lose business.

• **Hire outside help when necessary.** One of my clients had a beautifully organized home office but nearly failed because he couldn't type. We solved his problem with an outside secretarial service that picked up and typed drafts. Face the fact that you can't do everything yourself.

Example: If your time can be spent more profitably with a client, perhaps you should hire a high-school student to do some oft-postponed but necessary chore like entering 1,500 names into your computer.

• **Group similar tasks together.** Make all of your phone calls at once so you don't keep interrupting your work time all day. Write all of your letters during another block of time. Schedule all appointments on the same afternoon. Run several errands in one trip . . . perhaps at lunchtime when people are not likely to call you back.

• **Put everything in its place.** It's important to file related paperwork together so that you'll have fewer places to look for something. There are many different filing techniques. You can choose whichever one works for you.

I strongly recommend having at least one high-quality filing cabinet in which you can place hanging files. It is much more efficient to file papers rather than having them in piles that collect dust and are hard to sort through.

Telephone messages: If you're the only one taking messages from your answering machine, use either a telephone log or a plain spiral notebook to keep track of messages. You can write down the date, time, caller's name, company, and message. This will provide you with an orderly record instead of dozens of loose scraps of paper. It's also useful to keep a fax-activity logbook for tax and billing purposes.

Another key tool is your Rolodex. File things under the names by which you will refer to them in the future, and keep phone numbers up to date.

CLEAN . . . CLEANER . . . .

■ **Dangerous to kids**—*in descending order of accidental consumption:* Iron supplements . . . antidepressant and heart medications . . . methyl salicylate (wintergreen oil, perfumes) . . . alcohols (rubbing alcohol and liquor) . . . gun blueing . . . cleaning products . . . pesticides . . . ethylene glycol (antifreeze, brake fluids, solvents) . . . hydrocarbons (lamp oil, petroleum products, paint thinner, solvents, furniture polish).

Toby Litovitz, M.D., director, National Capital Poison Center, Georgetown University Hospital, Washington DC. Dr. Litovitz's study was published in Pediatrics, *141 NW Point Blvd., Elk Grove Village, IL 60009.*

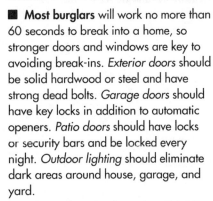

TIGHTER SECURITY

■ **Most burglars** will work no more than 60 seconds to break into a home, so stronger doors and windows are key to avoiding break-ins. *Exterior doors* should be solid hardwood or steel and have strong dead bolts. *Garage doors* should have key locks in addition to automatic openers. *Patio doors* should have locks or security bars and be locked every night. *Outdoor lighting* should eliminate dark areas around house, garage, and yard.

Home Mechanix, 2 Park Ave., New York, NY 10016.

■ **The siren box for a home burglar alarm** should be positioned far out of reach—or in the attic, where the sounds come through the vent. *Problem:* A burglar can prevent it from sounding by simply spraying foam insulation inside the alarm box. *Other ways to keep your home safe from burglars:* Use a post office box for your car registration, if possible, so that parking attendants, car

TIGHTER SECURITY

thieves, etc., can't get your address and burglarize your home—since they know you're not there . . . when selling an item through a newspaper ad, list your phone number but no address—arrange to meet in a public place or at the other person's home (and tell someone where you'll be) . . . install security bars over all skylights in your home.

CLEAN . . . CLEANER . . .

■ **Find out how long a cleaning company has been in business.** Check last year's phone directory to be sure it has been around for at least a year. Check the firm's complaint history with the Better Business Bureau. Pick a firm based on recommendations from people you trust. Find out from the maker or retailer of your carpet how it should be cleaned—do not leave it up to the service. Pay by credit card in case problems arise after the cleaning service leaves.

Carrie Getty, vice president, Better Business Bureau, New York.

■ **Establish a *halfway house*** for those items (clothing, books, papers, etc.) that you haven't used in years but can't bear to part with. *How it works:* Pack everything into cartons, marking the boxes with a date two years from now, and store it all away. After two years, review contents—and give away or throw away.

365 Ways to Save Time by time-management consultant Lucy H. Hedrick. Hearst Books, a division of William Morrow & Co.

■ **When using your garbage disposal,** flush refuse with *cold* water. *Reason:* Warm or hot water melts the fat . . . as it

INVEST IN TOMORROW

Just as it takes money to make money, it takes time to save time. Be willing to take a few minutes at the end of every day to clean up your desk, file important papers, and set up your schedule for the next day. This maintenance time will save you valuable hours in the long run. Think of it like laundry—if you do a little bit every day, it will never pile up and become a problem.

If your papers are already out of hand and your office mess has become embarrassing, resolve to take several interruption-free afternoons to straighten it out. You'll be much more productive afterward. *Important:* Every improvement will go right to your bottom line, so it's well worth the effort.

Too Many Dangerous Chemicals Are in Too Many of Our Homes

Karen Carroll, M.D.

According to the Environmental Protection Agency's estimates, the average household contains between three and 10 gallons of hazardous chemicals—and many of them are organic compounds that vaporize at room temperature.

In the effort to save money by sealing our homes to reduce heating and air-conditioning bills, and by becoming do-it-yourselfers for many tasks once left to professionals, we expose ourselves and our families to high levels of these toxic substances.

READ THE LABEL

"We are all guilty of not thoroughly reading labels," according to Charles Jacobson, compli-

Karen Carroll, M.D., departments of pathology and infectious diseases and Paul Summers, M.D., department of obstetrics and gynecology, both at the University of Utah Medical Center in Salt Lake City, UT.

ance officer, U.S. Consumer Products Safety Commission.

If vapors may be harmful, it doesn't do much good to read the label after you have used the product and inhaled the vapors.

Important: Read the labels before buying a product to select the safest in a category. If you find any of the 11 ingredients listed below on a container, avoid buying it. If you must buy it, use extreme caution when working with any of the following:

DANGEROUS CHEMICALS

1. Methylene chloride. A widely used solvent, it is in pesticide aerosols, refrigeration and air-conditioning equipment, cleansing creams, and in paint and varnish removers. Some paint strippers are 80% methylene chloride. Its toxic effects include damage to liver, kidneys, and central nervous system. It increases the carbon-monoxide level in the blood, and people with angina (chest pains) are extremely sensitive to the chemical. Methylene chloride has been linked to heart attacks and cancer.

2. Dichlorvos (DDVP). An investigation by the National Toxicology Program of the Department of Health and Human Services revealed a significant leukemia hazard from this common household pesticide. It's been widely used in pet, house, and yard aerosol products since the 1950s. The EPA has had DDVP in special review since February 1988 and it has been considering banning it from food packaging.

3. 2,4-D. A weed killer related to Agent Orange, which allegedly caused health problems in exposed Vietnam veterans, 2,4-D is widely used by home gardeners and farmers. It does not cause acute toxicity, but its long-term effects are scary—much higher incidence of cancer and non-Hodgkin's lymphoma has been associated with its use among farmers. The National Cancer Institute also reports that dogs whose owners use 2,4-D on their lawns have an increased rate of a type of cancer closely related to human non-Hodgkin's lymphoma.

4. Perchlorethylene. The main solvent employed in the dry-cleaning process, metal degreasing, and in some adhesives, aerosols, paints, and

CLEAN . . . CLEANER . . .

cools farther down in the pipes, fat can collect, causing a clog. *Best:* Remove grease and fat from dishes before washing.

The Complete Guide to Four Season Home Maintenance: How to Prevent Costly Problems Before They Occur by Richard M. Scutella, a home designer and builder, Erie, PA. Betterway Books.

■ **Smarter cleaning of a ceiling fan or chandelier.** Hang an open umbrella from the fixture to catch dirt when you are cleaning.

Family Circle, 110 Fifth Ave., New York, NY 10011.

. . . MORE HOME FINANCING

■ **By using a home loan** to pay off consumer borrowing, you can get a deduction for a larger portion of your total interest cost. *Reason:* Home-loan interest is deductible, while consumer interest is not. You can also reduce your total interest cost, since mortgage interest rates generally are far lower than the rates on consumer loans. *Opportunity:* Mortgage interest deduction is likely to be further restricted in coming years in an effort to cut the federal budget deficit. But, with outstanding loans "grandfathered" so they will continue to provide deductions under the old rules, now may be the best time ever to take out a home loan.

Paul Havemann, HSH Associates, 1200 Route 23, Butler, NJ 07405.

■ **Refinancing a mortgage** may reduce your monthly payment, but there's a catch—a large part of each payment on an old mortgage goes to building equity in your home. And almost all of each payment on a *new* 30-year mortgage is interest. *Solution:* Refinance with a shorter-term loan. You may be able to cut your monthly payment and keep building equity in your home. *Example:* Fifteen years ago you took out a 30-year $100,000 mortgage at 9% interest, with an $805 monthly payment. Today your balance is $79,331 and 26% of each payment goes to equity. By refinancing with a 15-year loan at a rate of 6.68% rate, you can cut your monthly payment to $698 and increase the equity portion of each payment to 37%.

David Seiders, chief economist, National Association of Home Builders, Washington, DC.

APPLIANCE SECRETS

■ **Just-washed dishes** streaked with black may have been rubbing against a dishwasher rack tine that is missing its vinyl coating. This is a common problem with older dishwashers. Repair exposed metal tines by covering them with either tine repair paint (about $5 for a one-ounce tube) or vinyl replacement tips (about $12 for a bag of 60 tips). Both are sold in most appliance parts stores.

The Family Handyman, 7900 International Dr., Minneapolis, MN 55425.

■ **Horizontal-axis clothes washer** uses half the water and one-fourth as much detergent as a conventional washer that churns clothes vertically with an agitator. In the System 2000, clothes tumble inside a six-sided tub perforated with holes and surrounded by an outer tub that increases force of water flow. *Manufacturer:* Staber Industries, Groveport, Ohio. *Price:* $800 to $900. *Coming next year:* A horizontal washer from Frigidaire. Maytag is also researching the technology.

Joe Gagnon, host of "The Appliance Doctor," a national radio talk-show on the TPT news network.

coatings, it can be absorbed through your lungs or your skin. The most common effects of overexposure are irritation of the eyes, nose, throat, or skin. Effects on the nervous system include dizziness, headache, nausea, fatigue, confusion, and loss of balance. At very high exposure it can cause death.

5. Formaldehyde. An inexpensive and effective preservative used in more than 3,000 household products. They include disinfectants, cosmetics, fungicides, preservatives, and adhesives. It is also used in pressed-wood products—wall paneling, fiberboard, furniture, and in some papers. There are serious questions about its safety. It is estimated that 4% to 8% of the population is sensitive to it. Vapors are intensely irritating to mucous membranes and can cause nasal, lung, and eye problems.

6. Benzene. Among the top five organic chemicals produced in the United States, this petroleum derivative's use in consumer products has, in recent years, been greatly reduced. However, it is still employed as a solvent for waxes, resins, and oils and is in varnish and lacquer. It is also an "antiknock" additive in gasoline—thus, make sure your house is well ventilated and insulated from vapors that arise from an attached garage.

Benzene is highly flammable, poisonous when ingested, and irritating to mucous membranes. Amounts that are harmful may be absorbed through the skin. *Possible results:* Blood, brain, and nerve damage.

7. Cyanide. One of the most rapid poisons known, it is used to kill fungus, insects, and rats. It is in metal polishes (especially silver), art materials, and photographic solutions.

8. Naphthalene. Derived from coal, it is used in solvents, fungicides, toilet bowl deodorizers, and as a moth repellent. It can be absorbed through the skin and eyes as well as through the lungs. It may damage the eyes, liver, kidneys, skin, red blood cells, and the central nervous system. It has reportedly caused anemia in infants exposed to clothing and blankets stored in naphthalene mothballs. This chemical can cause allergic skin rashes in adults and children.

9. Paradichlorobenzene (PDB). Made from chlorine and benzene, it is in metal polishes, moth repellents, general insecticides, germicides, spray deodorants, and fumigants. PDB is also commonly found in room deodorizers. Vapors may cause irritation to the skin, throat, and eyes. Prolonged exposure to high concentrations may cause weakness, dizziness, loss of weight, and liver damage. A well-known animal cancer-causing agent, the chemical can linger in the home for months or even years.

10. Trichloroethylene (TCE). A solvent used in waxes, paint thinners, fumigants, metal polishes, shoe polish, and rug cleaners. Tests conducted by the National Cancer Institute showed TCE caused cancer of the liver. A combination of alcohol ingestion with exposure to trichloroethylene can cause flushing of the skin, nausea, and vomiting.

11. Hydroxides/lye products. These include automatic dishwasher detergents, toilet bowl cleaners, fire proofing, paint remover, and drain cleaners. Ingestion causes vomiting, prostration, and collapse. Inhalation causes lung damage. Prolonged contact with dilute solutions can have a destructive effect upon tissue, leading to skin irritations and eruptions.

Poison-Free Pest Controls

Bernice Lifton

There are many alternatives to the dangerous chemical pesticides sold to control household pests.

Your first line of defense against indoor insects is to make your home as pest-tight as possible. *What to do:*

- **Caulk, paint, and patch all holes.**
- **Screen necessary openings**—attic air grilles, chimney caps, etc.
- **Cut back shrubs and plants** that hug outside walls.

Bernice Lifton, author of Bug Busters: Poison-Free Pest Controls for Your House and Garden. *Avery Publishing Group.*

APPLIANCE SECRETS

■ **Energy-saving compact fluorescent lights** can interfere with the signals from remote controls that are used to operate TVs, VCRs and stereos. *If you seem to have a problem:* Move the lamps away from where you use the remote . . . replace the remote's batteries so its signal is stronger.

Arnold Buddenberg, lighting-systems specialist at Rensselaer Polytechnic Institute, Troy, NY.

HOME COOKING

■ **Store food in shallow containers,** not deep ones, to prevent food-borne illness. Food in the center of a deep container may not cool down quickly enough to prevent bacterial growth. *Self-defense:* Divide large items, such as a big pot of soup, into several small containers, and refrigerate within two hours of cooking.

Tufts University Diet & Nutrition Letter, 203 Harrison Ave., Boston, MA 02111.

■ **Rid microwave ovens of unpleasant odors** by wiping the interior with a solution of four tablespoons of baking soda to one quart warm water. *Warning:* Never use a commercial oven cleaner in a microwave.

The Kitchen Survival Guide: A Hand-Holding Kitchen Primer with 130 Recipes to Get You Started by cookbook author Lora Brody. William Morrow & Company.

■ **Feel frozen food.** You should be able to feel the individual peas or the shape of the broccoli stalks through the package. If the package feels like a brick, it probably thawed and was refrozen—and that can destroy vitamins and minerals.

Earl Mindell's Food as Medicine by Earl Mindell, R.Ph., Ph.D., professor of nutrition, Pacific Western University, Los Angeles, CA. Fireside.

HOME COOKING

■ **To remove excess fat from stews, soups or gravy,** drop in several ice cubes, wait for the fat to congeal to them and remove . . . or wrap ice cubes in a paper towel and draw it slowly over the surface, allowing the fat to solidify and stick to the towel . . . or place a paper towel or a lettuce leaf lightly on the surface and allow it to absorb fat.

Substituting Ingredients: An A to Z Kitchen Reference by food writer Becky Sue Epstein. The Globe Pequot Press.

BETTER IMPROVEMENTS

■ **If you expect to sell your home** within the next few years, consider carefully any improvements you make. *Reason:* Some improvements add more to the value of your home than they cost, others add less. *Best values:* An off-white or neutral color paint job . . . landscaping and general exterior cosmetics . . . moderate kitchen and bathroom upgrades that don't involve unusual colors or deluxe appliances. *Worst values:* Swimming pools . . . hot tubs . . . outdoor spas . . . customized or built-in furnishings . . . expensive woodwork or cabinets . . . deluxe wall or floor coverings . . . bidets . . . tennis courts . . . central audio/video systems.

The Big Fix-Up: How to Renovate Your Home Without Losing Your Shirt by New York City CNBC personal finance commentator Stephen M. Pollan. Fireside Books.

■ **Renovations add more to home value** than changes that increase the house's size or modernize it. *Most important:* plumbing, electrical, heating, and cooling systems . . . roof, windows, and doors. *Key:* Renovations must improve comfort and convenience. *Big-ticket items that cost more than*

• **Install an 18-inch-wide strip of sand** circling the foundation to barricade against crawlers—cockroaches, earwigs, beetles.

Next, starve any indoor insects by keeping your home as clean and dry as possible.

WHAT TO DO

• **Vacuum** carpets, furniture, draperies, and shelves frequently.

• **Clean spills** immediately.

• **Store dry foods** in tightly closed metal, glass, or plastic containers.

Take specific steps to eliminate specific pests. *How to get rid of . . .*

• **Cockroaches.** There are many non-toxic ways to get rid of roaches. *Included:*

• **Fill a half-pint jar halfway with a beer,** a piece of banana peel, and some anise. Wrap the entire outside of the jar with masking tape to give the roaches footing and spread a thin layer of petroleum jelly along the inner upper inch of the jar so they cannot escape. Leave the jar out overnight where roaches have been seen. They will crawl in and die.

• **Freeze them out.** Roaches die at 23°F. If the weather permits, leave your windows open all day to wipe out roaches. This works for silverfish and clothes moths, too.

Warning: **Take steps to make sure your pipes don't freeze and burst.**

• **Use technical boric acid.** A least-toxic pesticide is good for bad infestations. Apply a light layer in out-of-the-way areas—under the stove and refrigerator, behind the bathroom vanity, etc.

Warning: **Boric acid is toxic.** Do not use it where children and pets can get at it. And do not use it where food is stored.

• **Ants.** Mix three cups of water with one cup of sugar and four teaspoons of boric acid. Pour half a cup of the mixture into three or four empty jam jars wrapped with masking tape and loosely packed half-full with absorbent cotton. Smear the bait along the outside of the jar and set along ant trail. The ants will swarm into the jar. Some will carry the mixture back to the colony, where it will kill other ants.

Warning: If you have small children or pets, screw the lids onto the jars, poke several small holes through the lid and smear some of the bait on the outside of the jar.

- **Mosquitoes.** Make your yard as dry as possible. *Suggested:*
- Drain all standing water.
- Change the water in birdbaths and wading pools every three days.
- Store wheelbarrows, plant tubs and other items so they can't catch water.
- Stock ornamental pools with mosquito fish—a type of minnow that eats mosquito larvae.
- **Rats and mice.** Repair cracks and holes in your foundation. Fit pipes and wires that enter the building with metal guards.

Don't use poison to kill rodents. Poisoned animals can crawl away and die in an inaccessible place. *Result:* Dead-rodent odors. *Better:*
- Use snap traps—make sure the trap is the right size for the rodent you are trying to catch.
- Use glue traps—open-ended boxes with glue on the bottom of the inside. Rodents can get in . . . but not out. Best for mice.
- **Garden pests.** Many successful gardeners control pests without poisons. *Techniques:*
- Pick off pests by hand. Best for small gardens. Put the insects into a glass jar with some water and let them drown and decompose. If the same species appears again, set the open jar under the plant they're invading—the smell will act as a repellent.
- Try natural controls. *Suggested:*
- Rotate crops so plant-specific pests will not have a chance to build up.
- Plant onions and garlic throughout the garden to repel insects.
- Make your own bug spray. Spray your plants with a mixture of one or two tablespoons of liquid soap (Ivory works well) dissolved in one gallon of water. These dislodge or smother mites, aphids, and thrips—tiny insects that destroy buds and blossoms. *Caution:* Rinse your plants with clear water after several hours to avoid leaf burn.

BETTER IMPROVEMENTS

they add to value: Swimming pools, hot tubs, outdoor spas, tennis courts, customized or built-in furnishings, deluxe wall and floor coverings.

The Big Fix-Up: How to Renovate Your Home Without Losing Your Shirt by Stephen M. Pollan, financial consultant and personal finance comentator for CNBC. Fireside.

■ **Have a landscape planner draw up a plan for your yard.** Then, spread out the project over several years and end up with a well-thought-out yard.

How to Be Your Own Contractor by do-it-yourselfers Gene and Katie Hamilton. Collier Books.

DID YOU KNOW THAT . . .

. . . **you should always clean your carpets before repainting or remodeling a room?** Cleaning will bring out the carpet's true color—setting up the color scheme for wall finishes and room furnishings.

Jack Luts, a professional painter in Madison, NJ, and coauthor of *The Complete Guide to Painting Your Home.* F&W Publications.

. . . **between 38% and 46% of all adjustable-rate mortgages are adjusted incorrectly**—usually in ways that favor the lender? *Other common mistakes made by banks and other mortgage-holders:* Improperly credited monthly payments . . . principal prepayments incorrectly credited to escrow accounts.

Contact the American Homeowners Foundation, a nonprofit organization in Arlington, VA, which audits ARMs and splits any refunds with the homeowner.

. . . **houseplants can serve as natural air filters**, removing indoor air pollutants such as carbon monoxide and formaldehyde? *Best:* Aloe vera, Chinese evergreen, elephant-ear philodendron,

English ivy, ficus, golden pothos, corn plant, peace lily and spider plant.

Bonnie Wodin, owner of Golden Yarrow Landscape Design, a garden consulting firm, Box 61, Heath, MA 01346.

. . . professionally mixed paint colors vary from can to can? *To avoid color inconsistencies:* When using more than one can of the same color paint, pour all the cans into a large bucket . . . stir well . . . then pour the paint back into the individual cans for easy use. The technique, called "boxing," assures consistent color throughout the job.

Jack Luts, a professional painter in Madison, NJ, and coauthor of *The Complete Guide to Painting Your Home.* F&W Publications.

■ **Designate a refrigerator shelf** for healthy treats. Allow kids to judiciously snack from it whenever hunger pangs strike. *Stock it with:* Cantaloupe cubes, orange sections, sticks of sweet red pepper and cucumber, mini-carrots, apples, non-fat yogurt, etc.

Bonnie Liebman, M.S., director of nutrition at the Center for Science in the Public Interest, 1875 Connecticut Ave. NW, Suite 300, Washington, DC 20009.

Environmentally Friendly Household Cleansers

Annie Berthold-Bond

Your favorite household cleansers may do a great job, but their contents are often toxic to breathe, hard on the hands and surfaces—and hazardous to the environment. In addition to being expensive, the containers in which they're sold add up to mountains of waste.

How to make environmentally friendly versions that are just as effective, but cost much less . . .

• **Air freshener.** Place a few slices of lemon, orange, or grapefruit in a pot of water. Let simmer gently for an hour or more. Your house will be filled with a citrus scent.

• **All-purpose liquid cleanser.** Cuts grease and cleans countertops, baseboards, refrigerators, and other appliances.

Combine in a plastic spray bottle: One teaspoon borax, one-half teaspoon washing soda (a stronger form of baking soda, available in supermarkets), two tablespoons white vinegar or lemon juice, one-half teaspoon vegetable-based detergent (i.e., Murphy's Oil Soap), two cups very hot water.

• **Floor cleaner.** Use on wood, tile, or linoleum for a long-lasting shine.

Mix one-eighth cup vegetable-based detergent, one-half cup white vinegar, and two gallons warm water in a plastic pail.

• **Oven cleaner.** Sprinkle water on the grimy spots, then cover with baking soda. Repeat the process, and let sit overnight. The grease will

Annie Berthold-Bond, editor, *Green Alternatives*, a magazine on environmentally friendly products and services, 38 Montgomery St., Rhinebeck, NY 12572. She is author of *Clean and Green: The Complete Guide to Nontoxic and Environmentally Safe Housekeeping.* Ceres Press.

wipe off the next day. Use liquid soap and water to sponge away any residue.

• **Overnight toilet-bowl cleaner.** Pour one cup borax into the toilet bowl. Let sit overnight. Flush in the morning. Stains and rings are lifted away.

• **Nonabrasive cleanser.** Scours sinks and bathtubs, and leaves no gritty residue.

Combine one-quarter cup baking soda and enough vegetable-based detergent to make a creamy paste.

• **Window cleaner.** Combine in a plastic spray bottle . . . one-half teaspoon vegetable-based detergent, three tablespoons white vinegar, two cups water.

• **Wood-furniture dusting and cleaning cloth.** Mix one-half teaspoon olive oil and one-quarter cup white vinegar or lemon juice in a bowl. Apply to a cotton cloth. Reapply as needed.

Secrets of Better Lawning And Gardening

Bonnie Wodin

Our front lawns and backyards have had a tough winter. Plants and shrubs damaged by severe storms must be removed or replanted properly, and debris must be carefully removed from under plants. *My spring strategies . . .*

LAWNS

• **Preparing your lawn.** First, clear all debris left behind from winter by using a wire or bamboo rake. Then test your soil's acidity, or pH.

Bonnie Wodin, owner of Golden Yarrow Landscape Design, a garden consulting firm, Box 61, Heath, MA 01346.

KITCHEN MANAGEMENT

■ **Freezers run most efficiently** when they're three-quarters—or more—full. When your provisions drop, fill milk cartons or jugs with water and put them in the freezer to take up empty space.

Dirt Cheap Gardening: Hundreds of Ways to Save Money in Your Garden by Rhonda Massingham Hart, gardening enthusiast in Chattaroy, WA. Storey Communications.

■ **Reorganize cupboards every six months.** Get rid of boxed foods that are past their expiration dates . . . throw out boxed foods that taste stale or soapy (a sign of rancid fats).

The Low-Fat Epicure by Sallie Twentyman, R.D., a registered dietician and editor of *The Low-Fat Epicure* newsletter based in Washington, DC. Berkley Books.

■ **Bacteria thrive in even the cleanest of kitchens.** *Self-defense:* Clean cutting boards thoroughly after each use with hot soapy water . . . sanitize sponges by running them through the washing machine frequently—and replace them every few weeks . . . wash manual can openers after each use . . . wipe counters and appliances often with a sanitizing solution of one quart water and one teaspoon chlorine bleach.

Bessie Berry, acting director of the Meat and Poultry Hotline, U.S. Department of Agriculture, Washington, DC.

AROUND THE HOUSE

■ **Water lawns more efficiently** by doing it early in the morning, when municipal water pressure is consistent . . . avoid watering in windy weather or in the heat of the day . . . water only when soil is dry . . . mulch all planters to lower surface evaporation . . . use a garden hose set at very slow drip to deep-water trees and shrubs . . . cut grass taller to keep soil shaded, reducing surface evaporation . . . give the lawn half the water it needs, then wait an hour to finish the job, to reduce runoff and deepen soil moisture.

The Budget Gardener by Maureen Gilmer, Dobbins, CA. Penguin.

■ **To maximize a "gardening" workout:** Heavy digging, raking, laying sod, turning compost and other garden chores burn 300 to 400 calories an hour. *To burn even more:* Use hand tools, such as an old-fashioned push mower instead of a power mower, a rake instead of a leaf blower . . . wear wrist and ankle weights to increase calories burned . . . split tasks into 30-minute segments so you'll get a good workout each day. *Caution:* Don't overdo it.

Jeffrey Restuccio, author of *Fitness the Dynamic Gardening Way.* Balance of Nature Publishing.

Procedure: Dig down four inches with a hand trowel in four random places across your lawn. Place small samples in a single jar and test them. Some garden centers will test your soil for free . . . or there are at-home soil testers available starting at approximately $10.

If the soil is highly acidic, it will have a low pH. Spread lime on your entire lawn by following the instructions on the package. Or if the soil has a high pH, spread sulfur over your lawn.

• **Reseed any problem patches.** Be sure to choose a grass-seed mix that contains the highest ratio of *annual* seed to *perennial* seed.

Reason: Annual seed grows rapidly but only lasts a year. It will make your lawn green quickly while allowing the perennial seed to establish itself.

If you recently moved into a newly built house or you are redoing your entire lawn, seed the new lawn as soon as the soil is no longer soggy from the winter thaw. Begin seeding right before another rain hits.

• **Fertilize lawns once** between mid-May and early June. Choose either a natural or synthetic fertilizer that is specifically formulated for lawns.

• **Cut your lawn** as soon as the new green grass has grown about two inches high. *First cut:* For a new lawn, wait until the grass blades are three inches high. *Yearly maintenance:* In the early spring, cut the grass very short, leaving grass blades ¾-inch to 1-inch high. Slowly raise the mower height throughout the spring to more than three inches by the time hot weather arrives.

Bonus: You don't have to bag the clippings. Leave them where they fall to compost. If you cut the top one-third of your grass, you won't even notice the clippings. Just be sure not to cut the grass less than 48 hours before having a party. Otherwise your guests will track the grass clippings into your house.

Important: Never cut your lawn when it is wet. This will damage the grass, ruin the look of the lawn, create messy clippings—and mess up your lawn mower's blades.

ORNAMENTAL GARDENS

• **Clear away winter mulches and garden debris.** For large areas, use a bamboo rake. For

smaller areas, you can use your hands. *Helpful:* Garden gloves.

Hint: Shred the leafy debris by running over it with the lawn mower several times. Use this material to start a new compost pile.

• **Cut off all dead plant material**—blackened tips of rose branches and dead wood from flowering shrubs. Lightly *cultivate* (by turning up the soil) around perennial plants with a *turning fork* or *hand cultivator*. Watch out for tender, new growing shoots.

• **Apply compost, bonemeal, and rock powders** or a light application of balanced synthetic fertilizer to all perennial beds and shrubs. The bag of fertilizer should read 10-10-10, which signifies the amount of nitrogen, phosphorus, and potash in it.

• **Separate any perennials that have become overgrown.** These plants grow rapidly and can overextend the area in which they were originally planted. They need to be cut or divided into smaller plants every three to four years.

To divide: Dig around the plant's root ball with a *garden fork* and/or *straight-edged shovel* until it can be pried loose. Be careful not to cut into any main roots. Some plants may need a lot of encouragement. Remove the plant from the hole and put it on the soil or a tarp. Study it to see where you can divide the plant. Look for areas where there are no branches coming up out of the soil. Then firmly insert two garden forks, back-to-back, tines intertwined. Using the forks as levers, pull the handles apart. New plants should measure four to six inches in diameter.

TO PREPARE OTHER PLANTS AND TREES

• **Roses.** Remove protective soil around plant stems. Watch for signs of new growth on bare branches and prune them back to give them space. Feed with high nitrogen and phosphorus fertilizer that includes some potassium. Ask the garden center for a recommendation when choosing the ideal fertilizer for your area.

• **New trees or shrubs.** Carefully decide where to put new trees, shrubs and garden beds in

AROUND THE HOUSE

■ **Prepare house plants to be moved indoors for the winter:** Remove each from its pot . . . shake off all old planting medium . . . rinse each plant in mild soapy water . . . trim the roots (about one-third of the feathery stuff—never the tap root) . . . repot using a clean planter and sterile potting soil. *Benefit:* This preparation rids the plants of any mites, ants, and other critters that may have taken up residence in the soil over the summer.

Reuse News, 609 Hobart Rd., Hanover, PA 17331.

■ **After a storm:** If your home has been damaged, videotape or photograph damage and do a complete inventory before cleaning up/ This documentation is critical for taxes as well as insurance. Your loss is deductible as an itemized deduction if it exceeds 10% of your Adjusted Gross Income after you have reduced the loss by any insurance reimbursement and $100. *More information:* Order the free IRS publication 584, *Nonbusiness Disaster Casualty and Theft Loss Workbook,* by calling 800-829-3676.

Carol Thompson, EA, chair, public disaster service committee, National Association of Enrolled Agents, Gaithersburg, Maryland.

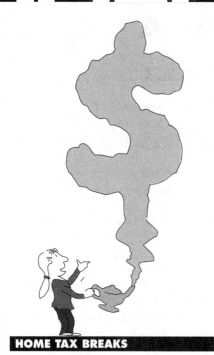

HOME TAX BREAKS

Home Tax Angle

Randy Bruce Blaustein, Esq.

Taxable gain on the sale of an old home can be deferred by making improvements to your new, replacement home within two years.

The cost of improvements increases your cost basis in the new home and can be used to offset gain on the sale of your old home.

Example: Your old home costs $60,000, you sell it for $110,000 and buy a replacement home for $100,000. You have a $50,000 gain on the sale of your old home—the amount by which its sale price exceeds its cost. But if you make at least $10,000 of capital improvements to the new home within two years, the gain on the old home can be deferred.

Randy Bruce Blaustein, Esq., a partner, Blaustein, Greenberg & Co., 155 E. 31 St., New York, NY 10016.

advance. Give them plenty of room to grow. Turn the soil deeply and fertilize well.

To plant a tree or shrub: Dig a hole twice as large as the root ball, and save the soil. Fill in one-third of the hole with compost and a handful each of bonemeal and rock phosphate. Mix in some soil. Fill the hole with water and wait until it is absorbed by the soil.

Place the tree in the hole. Remove the burlap covering immediately by jiggling the tree or shrub until you can pull the burlap loose and remove it. Then fill in around the sides of the root ball with soil taken from the hole, and firm it into place by grasping the base of the tree and moving it gently back and forth until it is solidly standing up straight.

Fill the hole to within one inch of its top with soil, leaving a saucer-shaped moat to catch water, which will slowly seep down to the roots. Water well. Water new trees daily for a week, weekly for a month, then only during periods of drought.

Old adage: A $5 tree will die in a 50-cent hole, but a 50-cent tree will thrive in a $5 hole. In other words, be sure to take great care when planting any tree.

VEGETABLE AND HERB GARDENS

• **Clear away garden refuse**—if you didn't last fall. Till or cultivate the soil as soon as it is dry, but not too dry. To determine when, take a handful of soil and make a fist. If the soil lightly flakes apart when you open your hand, it is ready to work. Add compost or synthetic fertilizer and cultivate deeply again.

• **Planting bedding plants.** These are those boxes of six to nine little plants. Plant or transplant them on a cloudy, drizzly day—in the early morning or evening—to minimize harm from the sun and maximize the amount of moisture. Water them well.

• **Never walk on wet or soggy ground** to avoid compacting soil.

• **Healthy soil grows healthy plants.** Feed your soil at least once a week by giving it lots of compost. You can't really overdo it.

Who Needs Life Insurance

Arthur Schechner

Anyone who has assets to protect or who will need to provide cash to family members in the event of his or her death needs life insurance.

REASONS TO BUY INSURANCE

The most common reasons for buying insurance . . .

• **Protecting a business.** If you have a family business, it's essential to have life insurance on key people in order to preserve the family assets and income stream. Insurance proceeds can be used to buy out partners if the business is to be reorganized on the death of a key person. And it can cushion the financial blow to the business that will result from the loss of a key manager.

• **Paying taxes.** Insurance proceeds can be used to pay estate taxes. *Trap:* A family that owns valuable assets that aren't readily convertible into cash (such as real estate or shares in a family business) may be forced to sell off assets to pay a large estate tax bill. A properly designed insurance arrangement can help avoid this problem.

• **Securing income.** If your family depends on your salary or other income that you generate, life insurance can meet their future income needs in the event of your death. Estimate how much income

Arthur Schechner, chairman of Schechner Lifson Ackerman Chodorcoff Inc., 225 Millburn Ave., Millburn, NJ 07041.

HEALTHIER HEALTH INSURANCE

■ **Health insurance trap.** Beware of opting out of your employer's health insurance plan because you're covered by your spouse's plan. While you may avoid paying premiums on a policy you think is unnecessary, there are risks. *Examples:* If your spouse loses his/her job you'll both be offered a COBRA plan, which only lasts 18 months. If your spouse's company goes under, both of you may have to pay higher fees for a conversion plan that may be more limited. And, if your spouse's employer downgrades its policy, you would be stuck with its coverage.

Howard Klein, partner with Klein, McGorry & Klein Ltd., an insurance broker and consultancy, 111 W. 57 St., New York, NY 10019.

■ **Don't delay filing your health insurance claims.** Delays can be costly in submitting health insurance claims. Most policies have a 90-day time limit—and claims will be rejected if filed after that point. Also, in most states, insurers must begin action on claims within a set period of time after submission. The sooner a claim is filed with the insurance company, the sooner it will be reviewed and paid.

Health Insurance: How to Get It, Keep It or Improve What You've Got by Robert Enteen, adviser on health-insurance policy issues. Paragon House.

■ **Faster filing of health insurance claims.** Prepare a master form for each of your policies. Use a blank insurance-company claims form and fill in the policy number . . . your name and address . . . insured's Social Security number . . . additional health coverage carried by the family . . . the signature of the insured. When you need to file a claim, simply

HEALTHIER HEALTH INSURANCE

photocopy the master form and add details on the bills you are submitting.

The Health Insurance Claims Kit by Carolyn F. Shear, MSW, medical claims agent, health insurance claims processor, Deerfield, IL. Dearborn Financial Publishing.

TRAPS TO AVOID

■ **The most serious insurance mistakes** made by retirees and near-retirees are not checking all of their retirement benefit options under company pension programs, not buying Medigap coverage and not taking *Part B* of Medicare. Approximately six months before turning 65, you must apply to get Social Security benefits. Medicare *Part A* (hospitals) is automatic. But you also need to buy *Part B* of Medicare (which covers doctors) . . . *and* one of the Medigap plans (to cover much of what Medicare doesn't) . . . *and* a long-term care policy (these are cheaper the younger you are when you first buy them).

Sam E. Beller, C.L.U., Ch.F.C., president of Diversified Programs, Inc., 450 Seventh Ave., New York, NY 10023.

■ **Don't buy long-term health care insurance** unless you really need it. Premium charges of up to $6,000 annually can add up to more than you risk losing if you do become sick. Because of this, 30% of people who buy such policies let them lapse within five years. *Guideline:* Buying such insurance is a good idea only if you and your spouse are older than 65, have

your family would need for how long, then buy a policy with a benefit sufficient, when invested, to meet those needs through interest and principal.

• **Pay off debts.** You may owe amounts on mortgages or other loan arrangements that couldn't be paid off if you died, leaving your family with debts. Life insurance can secure these amounts.

WHO DOESN'T NEED INSURANCE

Persons who have no assets or dependents that need protection (the house is paid off, the children are grown and earning good incomes for themselves, and your spouse has ample income of his/her own). Also, generally, there's no need to insure people who don't contribute to the financial support of the family. So you probably wouldn't insure the lives of minor children.

CHOOSING THE RIGHT POLICY

With some 1,600 insurance companies offering a total of about 40,000 life insurance choices, it's naive to think one can find the policy that best fits without expert assistance.

Don't try to make the choice by yourself, and don't be overwhelmed by a high-pressure salesperson. Find a broker you trust. Feel free to seek a second opinion.

WHAT NOT TO BUY

Don't buy policies pushed by credit card companies or banks. The rates on these policies are often higher because they're based on the companies' experience with high-risk policyholders. Also avoid trip life insurance, which is very expensive. You may pay nearly as much for a two-hour flight as around-the-clock protection for a year would cost.

TERM VS. WHOLE LIFE

Term insurance is least expensive because it is pure life insurance. You are left with nothing when the policy expires.

Whole life insurance, in contrast, accumulates cash value which you can borrow against, and pays dividends that can be applied against future premiums.

Some financial planners advise buying only term insurance, investing your premium savings elsewhere to earn more than the 6% or so that life insurance typically pays. *There's truth to this idea—and traps . . .*

    • **Term insurance gets much more expensive as you advance in age.** If you don't have the discipline to set aside and invest premium savings during early years, you may face much higher premiums later, without having available funds to pay them. (Premiums on a whole life policy are calculated to be level over the policy's life.)

    • **Investments that are more aggressive than life insurance** (such as the stock market or real estate) may earn more in some years, but can also go down in value. If you make a poor investment you may lose the premium savings earned from term insurance. Earnings on a whole life policy, in contrast, are conservative, but very secure.

If you do buy term insurance, be sure the policy is renewable and convertible into whole life later on.

PROBLEM CASES

If you're getting on in age or have any health problems, it's even more vital to put yourself in the hands of a good insurance broker. A good broker will know which companies are underwriting aggressively at any given time. Right now, for example, I'm aware of three companies that are underwriting coronary conditions that they would not have accepted two years ago. There are windows of opportunity when companies are willing to accept more risk to increase their business.

Caution: Always tell the truth about your condition. If you don't divulge your history, the insurance company can later claim fraud and refuse to pay off on the policy. Companies that don't investigate thoroughly when writing a policy are much more likely to before paying a benefit.

TERMINAL ILLNESS BENEFITS

Recently, one of the U.S.'s largest insurers announced a new plan to let the terminally ill collect life insurance benefits before they die. This is a very pro-

TRAPS TO AVOID

a net worth exceeding $100,000 excluding your home and have income over $50,000. Otherwise you probably don't have enough to lose to justify it.

Frank Lalli, managing editor, Money, 1271 Avenue of the Americas, New York, NY 10020.

■ **Check health insurance before traveling.** Some insurers and HMOs severely limit coverage outside specific areas. *Helpful:* If you frequently travel to one or two cities or areas, speak with your insurance carrier about a list of approved members or preferred providers in those locations.

Herbert Teison, editor, Travel Smart, 40 Beechdale Rd., Dobbs Ferry, NY 10522.

HEALTHIER INSURANCE II

■ **Hidden cash in health insurance:** If you and your spouse both receive family medical coverage through your employers, you should take advantage of each other's plans. *Reason:* Most insurance plans pay 80% of routine medical bills—but many partners forget they can file with their spouse's plan for whatever wasn't initially paid by their own insurer. *Big plus:* Many plans allow you to go back three years to file a spouse's unsubmitted claims. *Helpful:* Set up three folders—one for each spouse's medical claims and a third for those claims that are to be filed with the other spouse's plan.

Alexandra Armstrong, chairman of Armstrong Welch & MacIntyre Inc., financial advisers, 1155 Connecticut Ave. NW, Ste. 250, Washington, DC 20036.

163

HEALTHIER INSURANCE II

■ **Some health insurers** trick members into paying more of their hospital bills than they should. *How it works:* Though your insurer is supposed to pay 80%, some get *discounts* from hospitals—without passing on the savings to you. *Self-defense:* Pay the bill. Ask your insurer what *it* paid. If your share is more than 20%, it is likely that your insurer owes you money.

Robert Hunter, head of the insurance group at the Consumer Federation of America, 1424 16 St. NW, Washington, DC 20036.

■ **State-approved health insurance policies** are likely to be safer for you than those that are unapproved—especially if your state has a guaranty fund to protect you if the insurance company experiences any financial problems. Before buying a policy, make sure it is approved by your state's insurance regulators. *Caution:* Approval does not guarantee a good policy. Many shoddy policies are state-approved, either because they meet absolute minimum requirements or simply because the state insurance department is understaffed.

Money for Nothing, Tips for Free! Quick Advice on Saving, Making and Investing Money by Les Abromovitz, financial writer, Pittsburgh, PA. Great Quotations Publishing.

gressive idea intended to help patients who face the terrible costs of long-term care.

Catch: At present, many states forbid such accelerated death benefits on the basis that consumers may confuse life insurance and health insurance and that survivors may be left destitute. But the industry seems to be moving in this direction, and this may be one more benefit to purchasing whole life insurance.

Best Ways to Protect Yourself from Your Health Insurer

William M. Shernoff

Millions of Americans have no problems with their health insurance. They file the necessary forms . . . their claims are paid . . . and all parties are satisfied.

But thousands of Americans do have serious complaints regarding health claims. Frequently, policyholders are abandoned by their insurers when they most need the coverage. *Problem:* The higher the ultimate amount of your claim, the more likely you are to encounter a violation of your insurance contract by your insurer.

Due to the complexity of the laws governing insurance, what insurers can—and what they can't—do is often unclear. *Here are some of the most common questions policyholders must face . . .*

William M. Shernoff, a specialist in consumer claims against insurance companies, and author of *How to Make Insurance Companies Pay Your Claims.* Hastings House. His Claremont, CA, law firm, Shernoff, Bidart & Darras, has a staff of insurance analysts who will answer questions regarding insurance coverage, disputes and ERISA.

Can my insurer change or reduce my coverage? Unfortunately, yes. *Key:* The insurer must give policyholders early notice of the changes. *Recommended:* Read all mail from your insurer—*carefully*. Often, such notices are buried in communications that appear to be junk mail.

Self-defense: If the reduction in coverage is made before you have a health problem, complain to your employer or union or switch policies.

What if the coverage is reduced after I have filed a claim? It is unclear if insurers can legally reduce coverage once a policyholder is "on claim" for a particular accident or disease. However, insurance companies have recently been getting away with it in court.

Reason: Every state has consumer protection rules that limit an insurer's ability to change coverage in midstream. But for individuals insured through their employers, state laws are preempted by a federal law, ERISA (the Employee Retirement Income Security Act). ERISA makes *no* provisions for arbitrary reductions or changes in coverage.

Some courts are sympathetic to insurers rather than individual policyholders in the belief that premiums will rise if insurers are forced to pay all of the claims they have contracted to pay.

Example: Recently, a man who was insured under his employer's self-insurance plan had the $1 million AIDS coverage his policy promised reduced to a mere $5,000—*after* he became ill. The court allowed the reduced benefit to stand.

In this controversial area, trial attorneys take the position that this is a vesting issue . . . that once a person is "on claim," it is illegal to reduce benefits.

Self-defense: Seek legal advice if your benefits are reduced after you are on claim.

Can I be dropped from a group, or can my health insurance be cancelled? Generally, no. If you are insured as a member of a group, the insurer would have to cancel the entire group. It is illegal to single out just one person.

Exception: If you are insured through your employer and become so seriously injured or ill that you cannot work, your insurer may try to claim that

CONSUMER SAVVY

■ **When shopping for a life insurance policy**, be sure the premium costs quoted are guaranteed for as long as you think they are. *Trap:* States are raising the capital requirements on insurance policies with premiums guaranteed longer than five years. New York state has already done so, and residents there pay 20% more for long-term guarantees . . . other states are expected to follow. *Result:* Insurance companies are adding so-called five-year reentry clauses to their policies. These require policyholders to undergo another medical exam after five years if they want to avoid paying higher premiums.

Glenn Daily, a fee-only insurance consultant, 234 E. 84 St., New York, NY 10028. He is author of Life Insurance Sense and Nonsense.

■ **Avoid replacing one life insurance policy with another.** Agents often push policy replacement because they earn large commissions on the sale. But you'll pay high up-front costs—*especially* if you've accumulated a large cash value in your existing policy. *Self-defense:* Use caution when considering replacing a life insurance policy. Seek help from a fee-only financial planner or call the Consumer Federation of America (202-387-6121) for information on a low-cost service that can help you make this decision.

Robert Hunter, head of the Insurance Group, Consumer Federation of America, 1424 16 St. NW, Washington, DC 20036.

CONSUMER SAVVY

■ **Cheaper term-life insurance.** Look into switching underwriters every three to five years. *Reason:* Annually renewable term-policy premiums increase every year. But—a new insurance company will start your policy off at its low first rate. *Important:* This works only for those who are physically able to qualify for a new policy. If in doubt about health, stick to the old policy. *Caution:* Don't drop the old policy before the new one takes effect.

Jonathan Pond, president of Financial Planning Information, Inc., in Watertown, MA, is the author of The New Century Family Money Bank. *Dell Publishing.*

Complaint Letters That Get Results

• Keep your letter short.
• Type it instead of writing it by hand.
• Document your problem with names, dates and copies of receipts or bills.
• Ask for a specific amount of money or other compensation.

To get someone to accept responsibility: Address your letter to the chairman or a top executive—you can get a name by calling the company.

Follow-up: Call the recipient of the letter 10 days after you mail it.

Send This Jerk the Bedbug Letter by John Bear, PhD, educational consultant, El Cerrito, California (Ten Speed Press/$12.95).

your employment relationship has ended. Thus you are no longer part of the group—and can be cancelled in mid-claim.

Again, this is a gray area. Many states prohibit this type of cancellation, but the state laws are negated under ERISA. Trial attorneys say that a person is vested if he/she becomes injured or ill while employed. Case law precedent holds that the insurer must continue to cover claims resulting from that particular illness or injury. However, some courts have held otherwise.

Self-defense: Check your insurance contract for conditions under which you can be dropped. They are usually headed "Termination of Coverage." Don't automatically accept a cancellation if it occurs. This area of law is technical and esoteric. Insurance companies are making up the rules, generally to their advantage and policyholders' disadvantage, and thereby forcing policyholders to challenge them in court. Seek an attorney who is experienced in this area.

There are cases in which an insurer has dropped an entire group of policyholders, claiming it's discontinuing its group health coverage business. State laws that once required insurers to provide alternate coverage for such policyholders have been negated under ERISA, leaving large numbers of people uninsured, and uninsurable, in mid-claim.

When can my insurer decide that my *new* claim was a preexisting condition? This is an area where policyholders frequently fail to get the coverage they believe they are paying for. Carefully check your policy for conditions that are excluded for either a certain amount of time, or altogether.

General rule: For an insurer to deem a condition "preexisting," you must have seen a doctor for the condition, and had a symptom the doctor could diagnose as indicating that condition, previous to your insurance policy taking effect.

Everyone may have the symptomless beginnings of an undetected health problem. But some insurers stretch their definition of "preexisting."

Example: A man is denied coverage for his heart attack because his doctor told him he had high cholesterol three years earlier and recommended that he watch his diet.

Self-defense: Challenge the denial. Your condition must have been diagnosable to be considered preexisting. If it wasn't diagnosed, you have a strong case for coverage. Even if it was diagnosed, you may be able to prove it wasn't preexisting.

Can insurers apply exclusions in unfair or illegitimate ways? They can, and they do. Coverage exclusions are legal, and common for entire categories of treatment, such as alcoholism, drug dependence, and psychiatric care.

Caution: Insurers may try to "weasel out" of coverage *related* to these exclusions. *Example:* An insurer may deny coverage for a liver ailment, claiming it was a result of alcoholism and is therefore excluded.

Self-defense: Challenge the denial. It's the liver that's being treated, not the alcoholism.

Insurers also tend to deny coverage based on broad interpretation of legitimate exclusions.

Examples: Experimental treatment . . . medical versus "custodial" care . . . treatment or hospital days that are "not medically necessary."

Danger area: Policies that pay for accidents but not sickness. *Catch:* You file a claim for injuries resulting from a fall, the insurer says the fall was caused by dizziness resulting from a disease, so the fall was not accidental.

Can the insurance company's doctor's opinion overrule my doctor's judgment? Usually, yes. A number of insurance policies even state that the insurer reserves the right to have its own "medical director" make a final determination when benefits are being disputed.

Problem: As an employee of the insurer, this medical director almost always rules against the policyholder.

Self-defense: The best insurance contracts state that the deciding opinion in a claim will be by the policyholder's treating physician.

Reality: Most insurers will not put this issue in writing, and most insurance policies say *nothing* about who decides in the event of a dispute.

AUTO OWNERS ADVANTAGE

■ **Lower car insurance premiums** are easier to find as carriers face fewer losses and make lower payments to policyholders. Some insurers are even forgiving accidents and giving rebates to customers. *Important:* See if your insurer offers an accident-forgiveness program or other discounts . . . shop around for rates . . . and never drop an insurer until you have been approved by another.

Mary Griffin, insurance counsel at Consumers Union, a nonprofit consumer advocacy group in Washington, DC, and publisher of *Consumer Reports.*

■ **Some auto insurance companies** have stopped giving discounts for anti-lock brake systems. Recent studies have shown that anti-lock brakes do not increase car safety—possibly because people do not use them properly. Check to see if your insurance company still offers a discount for ABS-equipped cars.

David Solomon, editor, *Nutz & Boltz®,* Box 123, Butler, MD 21023.

■ **Count the cost of insurance** when buying a car. There are big differences in the cost of insuring different model vehicles. Differences in premiums reflect the cost of replacement parts and varying theft rates and safety records. The difference in insurance cost may tip your buying decision between two similarly priced vehicles.

Kent Moore, Ph.D., professor of management and information systems, Valdosta State College, Valdosta, GA, writing in *The Guide to Buying Insurance.* The Globe Pequot Press.

TRAVEL AND VACATION

■ **Cut insurance costs** for a vacation home. Many insurers offer premium reductions when you buy a home that's readily accessible to fire and emergency services . . . install fire and theft alarms hooked into a central monitoring location . . . install a temperature alarm that sounds off when it's almost cold enough for pipes to burst . . . have deadbolt locks, smoke alarms and a fire extinguisher . . . engage a caretaker or neighbor to watch your home when you are not there. *Also:* Some insurers offer vacation-home policies or other altered policies that provide lower-cost coverage of vacation homes, since people usually keep fewer valuables in their vacation homes than in their regular homes.

David L. Scott, Ph.D., professor of accounting and finance, Valdosta State University, Valdosta, GA, and author of *The Guide to Buying Insurance.* Globe Pequot Press.

■ **Travel insurance self-defense.** Buy trip cancellation/interruption insurance through your travel agent, not the tour operator. *Reason:* If the operator goes bankrupt, its insurance policies will be worthless. *Usual cost:* $5.50 per $100 in tour charges. *Caution:* Check exclusions and other limitations before buying a policy. *Also useful:* Book tours only with tour operators who belong to a national consumer-protection program, which can intervene in case of a dispute.

S. Burkett Milner, president, National Tour Association, Lexington, KY.

Exception: A union or large corporation may be able to negotiate an appropriate clause in its contract.

What can I do to protect myself? It's impossible to be totally secure, no matter what your insurance contract says. But there are ways to minimize risk. *Suggestions:*

• **If your employer offers a choice of insurers,** it's useful to investigate the claims records of each company.

Best source: Whoever handles claims for your employer. Inquire about each insurer's history of paying claims, delays versus timeliness, invoking exclusions and preexisting conditions, etc. *Reason:* There is no way to access an insurer's records on how well it pays claims. Your state department of insurance may keep records of complaints filed, but many don't keep records.

• **To ensure more clout when contesting a claim,** consider buying additional group insurance that is not provided through an employer and thus does not fall under the jurisdiction of ERISA. Such policies are regulated by state insurance law and are therefore easier to take recourse on if problems arise.

Examples: Plans offered through professional associations, organizations such as AARP, NOW, and many others.

How to Be Able to Afford to Get Sick

William M. Shernoff

Many employers are cutting back on health benefits—and some insurance companies have grown increasingly ruthless when it comes to paying their policyholders' claims. *What you should know to make sure you can afford to get sick . . .*

William M. Shernoff, a specialist in consumer claims against insurance companies and author of *How to Make Insurance Companies Pay Your Claims.* Hastings House. He is a partner in the law firm of Shernoff, Bidart & Darras in Claremont, CA.

• **Avoid switching health insurance plans** . . . if you're satisfied with your current coverage . . . if you have a chronic medical condition . . . or if you have had a recent health problem. *Reason:* A new insurer will exclude coverage for any "pre-existing" condition and may find you "uninsurable" if your medical problem is serious. Even if your health is good, many insurers impose waiting periods on new policyholders for certain procedures.

Exception: If your employer changes insurers, state law generally requires that the new insurer provide the same coverage without penalty to you.

• **Avoid temporarily dropping out of a health plan.** Many companies offer an annual "menu" of benefits to choose from—health and life insurance, paid vacation days, child care, retirement contributions, etc. Healthy employees or those who are included on a spouse's policy are often tempted to temporarily forgo the medical plan in favor of other choices.

Catch: Even if your company tells you otherwise, the insurance company is not obligated to take you back as an individual after you waive group benefits. Even if you provide evidence of your insurability, your coverage may be denied or restricted.

• **Don't drop family coverage either** . . . for the same reason. Many companies offer financial incentives to employees who waive family coverage. While at first it may not make sense to pay for double coverage when both spouses work, it is always a gamble to drop coverage. Should the insured spouse die, lose his/her job, or become divorced, the family could find itself uninsured. In cases of serious illness or injury, double coverage will be welcome.

• **Choose "household name" insurers.** Often, companies offer employees the choice of a traditional insurance plan, an HMO-type plan with a limited choice of participating doctors and hospitals and a self-insured trust. *Caution:* Beware of insurance companies you've never heard of. To check the financial status of an insurer, call your state's department of insurance.

• **Beware of policies that exclude coverage if you become eligible for Medicare.** Anyone

LIFE INSURANCE SECRETS

■ **To find how much life insurance you need:** Figure your monthly after-tax take-home pay. Then, determine how much of that your family will need to cover monthly expenses, should you die—a typical figure is 75%. Next, learn how much income your family will obtain from other sources—Social Security survivor's benefit, pension-plan survivor benefits, etc.—and subtract this number to find your monthly cash shortfall. Multiply that number by 12 to reach an annual figure. Decide for how many years you will have to cover monthly expenses—your future financial need may drop greatly after children graduate from college and move out, for instance. Buy enough insurance to provide that many years of income.

Life Insurance Handbook by Jersey Gilbert, financial reporter at *Money*. Consumer Report Books.

■ **Canceling your life insurance.** Most people who buy life insurance are not aware that they have up to ten days after the policy arrives in the mail to cancel it—and receive a full refund. *Problem:* Policies are often filed away as soon as they arrive. *Strategy:* Use the ten days to discuss with friends, experts and even other agents whether you've made the right decision.

James Hunt, a director of the National Insurance Consumer Organization, Box 15492, Alexandria, VA 22309.

Seven Ways to Cut Home Insurance Costs

Jonathan Pond

Premium savings are available from most major insurance carriers for policyholders who take the following steps . . .

1. **Protect your property.** Insurers give discounts for smoke detectors, alarm systems, and other security devices.

2. **Tell the insurance company when you retire.** If you are likely to spend more time at home during the day, the company may lower your premiums.

3. **Raise your deductibles.**

4. **Pay annually.** It's usually cheaper than paying semiannually or quarterly.

5. **Buy all your insurance from the same company.** You may be able to get a package deal.

6. **Quit smoking.** Many companies give nonsmokers discounts on homeowners' policies.

7. **Don't hire a public adjuster unless necessary.** This person's job is to help you evaluate your losses and settle with the insurance company. In exchange, the adjuster gets 10% to 15% of whatever you recover. To save money, try to settle with the insurance company by yourself first.

Jonathan Pond, a nationally recognized expert in financial planning. He is the author of The New Century Family Money Book. *Dell Publishing.*

disabled by a catastrophic illness or injury becomes eligible for Medicare. Insurers would like to shift the cost of catastrophic care to the taxpayer. But you are paying premiums to ensure better protection than Medicare can provide in case of crisis. Look for a policy that pays costs "over and above" what Medicare will pay.

• **Contact your federal representatives and ask them to close the ERISA loophole.** In 1984 the Supreme Court held that ERISA (Employee Retirement Income Security Act), a federal law, supersedes state consumer laws governing insurance. This created a loophole that gives health insurance companies immunity from damage suits filed by policyholders insured through their employers—85% of all insured Americans. *Result:* An explosion of bad-faith practices by health insurance companies—unconscionable refusals of claims and policy cancellations—against which insureds have no recourse.

When Both Spouses Have Health Insurance

Tom Beauregard

More employees are being asked to pay more of the cost of health-care coverage at work as health costs keep rising.

But working couples—where each spouse has health coverage—have options. While they can keep their separate health plans, they may save money if they opt for the spouse's plan that offers the most for the family.

Tom Beauregard, health-care consultant, Hewitt Associates, 40 Highland Ave., Rowayton, CT 06853.

DOING THE ARITHMETIC

How to do the economic analysis to determine if switching plans makes economic sense for you . . .

Using a legal pad, compare the four key costs of health coverage for each plan:

1. **Annual premium cost.** How much will it cost a year for everyone in the family to be covered?

2. **Maximum deductible.** How much must you pay before the plan starts to kick in?

3. **Co-insurance.** What percentage of each bill will the plan pay, and how much must you pay?

4. **Plan cap.** What's the most you will have to pay out-of-pocket for medical bills each year?

Example: It would cost $500 a year for the family to join John's health plan and $1,000 to join Jane's plan. But the out-of-pocket cap for Jane's plan is $1,000, while John's cap is $3,000.

Maximum possible total cost: $2,000 with Jane's plan, $3,500 with John's plan.

OTHER CONSIDERATIONS

• **Opt-out opportunities.** Many companies pay a cash payment if you drop your coverage and shift to your spouse's plan.

Example: Your employer will pay $500 if you don't join your company's medical plan. You can use the money to pay the higher premium required to get family coverage under the spouse's plan.

• **What is covered?** Money isn't always the only consideration. Consider switching if one plan offers considerably more liberal coverage for services important to your family, such as outpatient psychiatric or dental care, or chiropractic services.

Important: Paying extra to keep both plans seldom makes economic sense today. Working couples once could get 100% coverage for treatment by coordinating plans. Now most plans have a "non-duplication of benefits" provision that makes the employee's plan the primary provider.

Example: Before, your plan might have paid 80% of a $1,000 claim, while your spouse's plan would pay the remaining $200. That's rare today.

Key: Before you switch, determine if the family can rejoin your plan if your spouse is laid off or fired.

LONG-TERM PLANNING

Shrewder Long-Term Care Insurance Buying

Daniel Kehrer

Key features of a good long-term-care policy . . .

• **A prior stay in a hospital** is not required before you collect your benefits.

• **Coverage for Alzheimer's disease** or related illnesses or disorders is guaranteed.

• **Home care is included as a regular benefit** or available with an extra premium. *Best:* A policy that allows you to alternate between home and a nursing home.

• **Benefits are adjusted**, at least partially, for inflation.

• **The policy is guaranteed renewable** for life.

• **The policy has a "waiver of premium" clause** that allows you to make no payments if ill—and after receiving benefits for a specified period of time.

• **There's a "window"** that allows you to change your mind and cancel the policy at no cost within the first 30 days.

Daniel Kehrer, a Los Angeles–based business and finance writer and author of *Kiplinger's 12 Steps to a Worry-Free Retirement.* Kiplinger Books.

PROTECTING YOUR NEST

■ **Your home insurance policy** probably doesn't provide all the protection you need. Computers, fax machines, and other business assets receive very limited coverage under most home-owner policies. Such policies also are unlikely to cover liability to clients or business visitors who may be injured on your premises. And it's not enough if you *own valuable collectibles*. Policies usually impose sharp monetary or coverage limitations on items such as oriental rugs, artwork, antiques, silverware, and jewelry. *Safety:* Read the limitations in your policy. If you need extra coverage for a specific purpose, you can probably get it from your insurer at modest cost by obtaining a rider.

Rick Longueira, independent insurance agent, Petrocelli Group, 162-01 Sanford Ave., Flushing, NY 11358.

■ **Protect your homeowner's insurance** from big premium increases—or nonrenewal—by avoiding frequent claims. Submitting claims often—even for small amounts—marks you as a high risk. Your insurer may then drop you and force you into a high-risk pool at higher cost. *Self defense:* Consider raising your deductible—even as high as $1,000. This would reduce your premium and the number of claims you submit.

Jeanne Salvatore, director of public relations and consumer affairs, Insurance Information Institute, New York.

Most employers will count it as a "change in family status," and let you back in. But double-check, just to be certain.

What Should We Know About Life Insurance . . . Now??

Virginia Applegarth

Most people don't understand life insurance and don't want to understand it—and that's dangerous.

Here is useful information about the major categories of life insurance policies that will help you ask better insurance questions—and help you do what's best for you and your family.

GET AN AGENT

With almost 2,000 companies selling life insurance, choosing the best policy can be confusing. Your insurance agent is the key. Seek out someone with whom you feel comfortable, who has excellent credentials and who wants to have a long-term relationship with you.

THE BASICS

There are two basic classifications of life insurance—term and permanent. The most common types of permanent insurance are whole life . . . universal life . . . and variable life. For a first-time buyer, each classification has its own strengths and weaknesses to consider in light of your family and fi-

Virginia Applegarth, president of Applegarth Advisory Group Inc., a Boston-based fee-only financial insurance advisory firm. She is author of *How to Protect Your Family with Insurance*. Lee Simmons Associates, Inc.

nancial situations. Let's look at each of these categories, their drawbacks and ideal candidates . . .

TERM INSURANCE

A term insurance policy gives you protection for a specified time—usually up until age 70. The insurance premium is used to purchase risk coverage, after expenses are deducted from the premium.

Although premiums generally increase at stated intervals over time, the annual premium for term insurance has a much lower out-of-pocket cost initially than the premium for comparable whole life insurance purchased at the same age.

Term drawback I: Some term policies have re-entry provisions, whereby you have to requalify medically every four, five, or 10 years to keep your premiums at the lower term levels.

Term drawback II: Term insurance premiums increase periodically as you become older.

Term drawback III: Once you are over age 55, it can be quite expensive to acquire this kind of insurance.

Ideal candidates: People who require protection for specific purposes, such as mortgage payments or college tuition, and can't afford whole life insurance.

WHOLE LIFE INSURANCE

A typical whole life, or ordinary life, policy covers you for your entire life and offers a guaranteed death benefit—a fixed sum payable to your heirs when you die. Some whole life policies pay dividends, which can:

• Reduce your premiums.
• Buy paid-up additions to your life insurance policy to increase your death benefit.
• Be returned to you in cash.
• Be deposited with the insurance company, where it will earn interest and serve as an additional savings account.

When you purchase a whole life policy, part of the premium pays the actual cost of the insurance risk, part pays the insurer's expenses and part goes into a reserve fund known as *cash value.*

RENTERS' INSURANCE

Renters Insurance Is a Must

Jayna Neagle

Renters insurance protects your personal possessions in case of damage. It also covers your liability for damages that you, family members, and pets inflict on other people in your rented apartment.

Renters insurance is also important because the landlord's insurance will not likely cover the contents of your apartment.

Types of renters insurance: *Replacement value,* which will cover the full cost to replace a destroyed item . . . *actual cash value,* a less-costly policy that repays only the actual cost of a lost item minus depreciation.

Caution: Valuable items, such as heirloom jewelry, may need separate, additional coverage.

Jayna Neagle, Insurance Information Institute, 110 William St., New York, NY 10038.

Assessing Life Insurance Needs

Review insurance policies annually, and ask: *Do the insurance needs still exist?* As children become self-supporting and retirement accounts accumulate funds, your life insurance needs may decline.

• **Has the amount of needed coverage changed?** You may come to need more home-owners insurance as you accumulate belongings and inflation increases their replacement cost.

• **Are these policies the best available?** Insurance is a very competitive business with new products coming out all the time. Periodically look around to find the best deal.

How to Buy the Right Insurance at the Right Price, by Thomas E. Bailard, financial adviser, Bailard, Biehl and Kaiser, Inc., San Mateo, CA. Business One.

■ **Best time to buy life insurance** is when you are young. *Reason:* The younger you are, the cheaper the rates. And—many policies let young and presumably healthy buyers lock in the right to buy more insurance as they get older. Obtaining—and increasing—life insurance coverage can be difficult and even impossible should you develop health problems later in life.

Deborah Rankin, author of Investing on Your Own. *Consumer Reports Books.*

■ **Life insurance opportunity:** Consider buying a level-premium term policy now—or extending the term policy you own—if you'll need coverage for a 10-year period or longer. *Reason:* Guaranteed annual premiums for level-term

This cash value, which allows the premiums to remain level during your lifetime, builds up annually and grows in value on a tax-deferred basis. Insurance companies are not obligated to tell you how your premium dollar is divided.

Because of the conservative nature of life insurance, various state regulations and the desire of insurers to fulfill their obligations, these guarantees are very low. But your actual cash available is usually higher than that which is guaranteed in the policy, if your dividends are used to purchase more insurance or are left in savings accounts with the company.

The most widely used whole life contract insures one life and pays a death benefit to the beneficiary upon his/her death. A newer variation is called *second-to-die insurance,* which insures two lives and pays the death benefit when the second person dies. The cost of a second-to-die policy is lower than that of two individual policies.

Whole Life drawback I: The premiums for a whole life policy are higher than those for a term policy because some of the money goes toward cash value.

Whole Life drawback II: Not all whole life policies pay dividends. And even when dividends are paid, they are not guaranteed . . . but rather reflect the insurance company's earnings, net of expenses.

Ideal candidates: Individuals with estates of more than $600,000, or couples with a combined estate of more than $1.2 million, who will be hit with estate taxes upon the death of the surviving spouse.

UNIVERSAL LIFE INSURANCE

Universal Life insurance is a variation of whole life insurance. However, in a universal life plan, the cash value and actual insurance cost are unbundled.

Thus, the premium is used first to pay for insurance protection and expenses. Any excess amount is held by the insurance company at an annually predetermined rate of interest. The minimum rate—about 4% now—is guaranteed by the contract, but it is the current rate that is actually credited to your account.

Universal Life drawback I: Watch out for interest rates, since the investment return on your cash value is tied to them. When rates are high—as they were in the 1980s—universal life insurance looks more attractive than whole life insurance. When rates are low—as they are now—whole life insurance looks more attractive. This difference is most apparent in the first 10 years of the policy.

Universal Life drawback II: Unless you have a lot of self-discipline, you may not put aside enough each year in premium payments, which could mean that your death benefit won't be as high as you'd like it to be—or you have to come up with larger and larger premium payments to make up the difference and keep the same death benefit.

Ideal candidates: The same people who might buy whole life insurance but want premium flexibility and the ability to see how their premiums are used.

VARIABLE LIFE INSURANCE

Variable Life insurance is also a modification of the traditional whole life insurance concept. However, the rate of return on the cash value portion is not determined by the insurance company. Instead, it's dependent on earnings of "mutual funds" within the contract selected by the insured.

Companies selling variable life policies generally give you a choice of several such funds, ranging from the most conservative to the most aggressive.

Variable Life drawback: While there are fixed premium payments and a guaranteed death benefit, there is no minimum guaranteed cash value. That's because with variable life insurance, you assume the investment risk yourself and therefore could wind up with little or no cash value if the stock market should decline.

Ideal candidates: People who are risk-oriented and willing to participate in the sometimes fast-moving securities markets.

THE COST OF CONVERSION

Many term insurance policies can be converted to other types of insurance, regardless of your health at the time. But before you even consider a conversion, consider the following . . .

• The cost of a permanent contract is always greater than a term policy issued at the same age.

policies are expected to rise in January 1997. By buying now, you'll lock in a lower rate.

Glenn Daily, an independent, fee-only insurance consultant, 234 E. 84 St., New York, NY 10028.

COST-CUTTING

Buying Just Enough Home-Owner's Insurance

Robert Hunter

People often ask me how they can tell whether they have too much—or too little—homeowner's insurance. *Here's what I tell them . . .*

• **Don't buy more coverage than you need.** Some experts and insurance agents say you should insure your house for the amount you paid for it.

Problem: You only need coverage on the dwelling, not the land around it.

Strategy: Pay $200 to $300 to have your home appraised. Or call local developers and real estate agents and ask how much new houses, similar in quality to your house, would cost to build per square foot in your area.

Limit coverage to what it would cost to replace your dwelling if it is burned to the ground, not the cost of the dwelling *and* the land.

• **Lower your premium by raising your deductible.** It isn't economical to buy a policy that will cover your loss from the first penny. Instead, consider raising your deductible—meaning the amount you pay out of your pocket before coverage kicks in.

Example: Raising your deductible from $100 to $500 can cut your premium by 25%. Increasing it from $100 to $1,000 can cut the premium by 33%. Check with your company for exactly how much you might save.

• **Make sure you have replacement-cost coverage.** This will add approximately 15% more to your premium, but it's well worth it. Lost or damaged household items will be replaced at their current value—not what you paid for them originally.

Example: A living room couch may have cost you $1,500 five or 10 years ago but now may cost $2,000 or more to replace.

Robert Hunter, head of the insurance group, Consumer Federation of America, 1624 16 St. NW, Ste. 604, Washington, DC 20036.

Insurance Claim Self-Defense

Eric Tyson

To ensure that future insurance claims will be paid, document what you own *before* you have a claim.

Keep a detailed list of property—or make a videotape of what you own and keep it somewhere safe, like a safe-deposit box.

Buy the broadest policy you can, to make it less likely for a claim to be denied on grounds of noncoverage.

After starting the claims process, keep records of all conversations you have and copies of all documents you give to the insurer. Enlist the assistance of your agent, who can help you wade through the insurer's bureaucracy.

Eric Tyson, a personal finance counselor in San Francisco and author of *Personal Finance for Dummies.* IDG Books.

• You usually cannot convert a permanent policy to a term policy without a medical examination or questionnaire. On the other hand, the conversion from term to whole life insurance is normally guaranteed contractually without any medical requirements.

• The conversion to a permanent life insurance policy by the same company that issued the term policy may actually be more expensive than simply purchasing a new policy from a different company.

• Be sure that the new policy is in place before dropping coverage on the old one.

WHEN IT PAYS TO CONVERT

You should think about converting a term policy to a permanent one under two scenarios . . .

I. When you can afford a tax-sheltered savings account. Ask for a realistic comparison illustration for the new policy showing the current interest rate and one that is two percentage points less. This will help show what your return might be starting at that moment.

II. When you have a number of small policies. Exchanging them for a single large policy with equal or greater total death benefits may be financially advantageous—if you're in good physical condition.

BOTTOM LINE

Life insurance planning and purchasing should relate to your objectives at different points in your life cycle. That's why it is so important to deal with a professional insurance agent or financial adviser for guidance and advice.

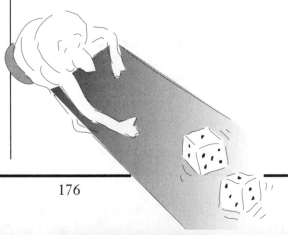

Secrets of Picking the Next Hot Stocks

Lee Kopp

L ee Kopp, who manages a small investment-management firm outside Minneapolis, has amassed an incredible performance record. For that, he has been called the next Peter Lynch—the legendary stock picker who recently rejoined Fidelity as a consultant.

Kopp's firm concentrates on small- and mid-cap companies. Below are some of Lee Kopp's suggestions on how individual investors can choose the next top stock performers.

• **Get informed—and stay informed.** Become a regular reader of your local paper's business section, read *The Wall Street Journal*, and, if you're analytically oriented, subscribe to specialized investment publications. If you have a full-service stockbroker, make maximum use of his/her research reports.

• **Look for stocks that are being ignored by Wall Street.** My firm concentrates on small- and mid-cap companies that are under-followed by pro-

Lee Kopp, head of Kopp Investment Advisors, an investment-management firm in Edina, MN. Total annual return for the typical emerging growth account averaged 48% for the three years ended June 30, 1993. That's more than four times the return of the S&P 500 . . . and three times that of small-company stocks. The firm's initial minimum required investment is $500,000.

Investment Risk

David Dreman
Dreman Value Management

Standard investment risk measures are flawed. The popular *beta* measure—designed to show whether a specific mutual fund is more or less volatile than the stock market as a whole—tells nothing about future *performance*.

A low-risk investment may perform very poorly, instead of shielding investors from market swings.

Example: Supposedly low-risk bond funds lost substantial value in 1994.

David Dreman, chairman, Dreman Value Management, Jersey City, NJ.

■ **When a mutual fund's assets grow too big . . .** its performance usually suffers, says Don Phillips of Morningstar.

Problems: Large-company funds that swell with assets are unable to do better than overall market performance because they *are* the market. Small-company funds that are flooded with cash often buy shares in larger companies to put cash to work. This can lead to a change in investment strategy.

Self-defense: Regularly monitor your funds' holdings. Consider reducing your position in funds that buy shares in companies that are different from those that led you to invest.

Don Phillips is president of Morningstar Inc., an independent research company that rates mutual funds. Morningstar is also the publisher of the newsletter *Morningstar Mutual Funds*, 800-876-5005. 26 issues. $425/yr.

■ **For safer investing.** Whenever you have an important discussion with a bro-

RICK REDUCTION

ker about your account, *put it in writing* . . . recommends Marshall Loeb.

Explain your goals by letter so the broker cannot later claim you wanted a more aggressive strategy. If the broker gives you verbal assurance, and you plan to make an investment on that basis, write down what you were told, and send it to the broker.

Also, don't automatically sign agreements giving your broker power to buy options or trade on margin . . . unless you are comfortable with significantly raising your risk.

Marshall Loeb is former managing editor of Money *and* Fortune, *and author of* Marshall Loeb's Lifetime Financial Strategies. *Little, Brown & Co., $27.95.*

INVESTING TRAPS

■ **Beware of bloated inventories** when investing in a company. High inventory levels may mean that the company's products are unattractive or growing obsolete . . . the company is wasting money on storage costs rather than investing in operations . . . prices will have to be cut to move stocks, reducing future earnings. *Key:* Look at the company's turnover ratio—its annual sales divided by the amount of inventory on hand. A high turnover ratio is a good sign that inventories are moving quickly. Compare the company's turnover ratio with those of its competitors and with its own turnover ratio in past years to get an idea of its competitive standing.

Blue Chips & Hot Tips: Identifying Emerging Growth Companies Most Likely to Succeed by W. Keith Schlitt, Ph.D., and Howard M. Schlitt, Ph.D. New York Institute of Finance.

fessional analysts. I think they are the most fertile area to find hot growth stocks—those whose prices will double within a three-year period and whose earnings are growing at a rate of at least 25% a year. Don't be afraid to look where others have not. It pays to be early.

• **Check what's going on in your own backyard.** This way, you're in a unique position to get in at the start of a big run-up in a relatively unknown company and can closely follow developments in its fortunes.

• **Attend annual meetings of nearby companies.** This will give you a chance to study the organization's players in action. Are they enthusiastic about new products in the pipeline? Overly optimistic about where the company stands in terms of meeting its objectives?

• **Scrutinize the company's balance sheet.** Look for such things as research-and-development spending and available cash. For technology stocks, my rule of thumb is that companies should be spending at least 10% to 15% of revenues on research and development to prepare for the future. If a high-tech company is skimping here, find out why. Sometimes a company can be criticized for sitting on too much cash, but the flip side is that a cash hoard can be a good tool for future acquisitions.

• **There's no such thing as a buy-and-forget investment.** We live in a rapidly changing world, and product obsolescence occurs more quickly than ever. It's vital to keep tabs on industry developments to make sure continued holdings are warranted, especially in the technology sector.

• **Keep portfolio turnover to a minimum.** My firm's portfolio turnover (annual changes in portfolio holdings) is about 30%. It's about 100% for the typical growth mutual fund. By being selective about our purchases in the first place and holding tight during the inevitable business cycle bumps, we not only keep transaction costs to a minimum but also save taxes for clients with taxable accounts.

• **Don't over-diversify.** I think you can get adequate diversification with between 15 and 20 holdings. That way, if you hit two or three major home runs, they can really have a big impact on your performance. But if you have a portfolio with between 100 and 200 holdings, it is very hard not to diversify into mediocrity.

• **Don't expect immediate gratification.** I am basically a buy-and-hold investor. My firm's holding period for most stocks is generally three to five years. But some investors want a stock to move two or three points in just a few months. Then they start looking for the next hot performer. That's simply not realistic. Really, really good new ideas simply don't come along that often.

Mistakes People Make Picking Mutual Funds Today

Sheldon Jacobs

Mutual funds are an easy way to invest in stocks and bonds, but watch out for these common mistakes:

1. **Paying a sales load to buy funds.** Investors don't need to pay up to 8½% of their investment—there are always excellent no-load funds to choose from.

2. **Failing to diversify a fund portfolio.** Diversification controls risk and boosts investment returns. Start with a core of conservative funds, then add stock funds that use a "growth" approach to picking stocks and some using a "value" approach. Growth managers look for companies with above-average earnings prospects—value managers look for bargain shares.

Sheldon Jacobs, editor and publisher, *The No-Load Fund Investor*, Box 318, Irvington, NY 10533.

INVESTING TRAPS

■ **Before buying high-yield bonds:** See if they are subject to a call provision that allows the issuer to pay them off before maturity. Call provisions reduce the potential for gain on any kind of bond by giving the issuer the power to redeem them if interest rates decline, which is just when a bond will go up in value. But they are especially onerous on high-yield "junk" bonds because of the greater risk investors incur with them. Investors have their potential gain limited by the call provision, while still incurring the full risk that if interest rates rise, their bonds will plummet in value.

Ben Weberman, financial columnist, *Forbes*, 60 Fifth Ave., New York, NY 10011.

MUTUAL FUNDS

■ **When to drop a mutual fund.** Major change in organization . . . turnover among key professionals . . . change in its investment philosophy . . . significant change in fund size—if it grows too much, it likely will not perform as well in the future . . . five to 10 years of under-performance compared with similar funds.

Get Rich Slowly by William Spitz, treasurer, Vanderbilt University. Macmillan.

■ **Mutual fund past performance.** Claims often are very misleading. Be especially wary of long-term claims stating that an amount invested in the fund 20, 30 or more years ago would be worth a huge amount today. *Reality:* A large portion of long-term gains expressed in dollar terms is due to inflation and the much reduced value of today's dollar. Also, if you really had invested all your money in one fund so long ago, by now you'd probably have spent much of it on chil-

MUTUAL FUNDS

dren's college costs, vacations, retirement costs, and other items.

Straight Talk About Mutual Funds by Dian Vujovich, former stockbroker. McGraw-Hill, Inc.

■ **Better mutual-fund prospectus reading.** To find the fees charged by the fund, turn to the section marked "Summary of Fees and Expenses" or "Expense Information." Then look for . . . *Shareholder Transaction Expenses:* Here you'll find the amount of any front-end load, back-end or deferred load, redemption fee, and transfer or exchange fee. *Annual Operating Expenses:* You'll find the management fee, 12b-1 fee and custodial, auditing, and shareholder service fees. These will be added up on a line labeled "Total Fund Operating Expenses." Remember that a fund with lower expenses than others has a head start on providing a higher return.

Jay Schabacker's Winning in Mutual Funds by Jay Schabacker, Schabacker Investment Management. American Management Association.

■ **Beware of fund descriptions.** So-called "balanced" and "equity income" funds are presumed to be less risky than growth funds but actually are often more risky than investors think. This is because many fund managers who wish to push their funds up in the performance rankings are tempted to invest in high-yield, high-risk investments that boost performance statistics—short-run. People who choose "balanced" funds on the basis of high returns may wind up buying more risk than they wanted to take.

Barron's Guide to Making Investment Decisions by John Prestbo, editor, *The Wall Street Journal.* Prentice Hall.

Finish up with funds that invest in large-capitalization stocks, small-capitalization stocks, and foreign issues.

3. **Buying tax-free funds without reviewing the tax implications.** While municipal bonds usually yield less than taxable bonds, the after-tax return is often higher because income earned by munis is tax-free. But not always. Figure taxable equivalent yield before buying shares by dividing the actual yield by 1 minus your tax rate.

Example: The taxable equivalent yield for a muni fund paying 4% for a 31% tax bracket taxpayer equals 5.8% [4 divided by (1–.31)].

4. **Paying too much attention to the headlines.** Most news has already been discounted by the market.

5. **Emphasizing too long-term performance figures.** By concentrating on 10- and 15-year track records, you miss too many good funds with shorter records. Five years is enough.

6. **Failing to set up a procedure to quickly redeem your shares.** Funds will not mail you a check or wire money to your bank unless authorized in advance.

What to do: Ask for and complete the application for wire privileges. Or open up a money-market account with the fund group and ask for a checkbook. You can sell shares, have the proceeds deposited in the money-market account and simply write yourself a check.

Lessons from One of America's Most Successful Investment Clubs

Shirley Gross

The Beardstown Ladies Investment Club in Illinois has averaged a 23.4% annual return since 1983 . . . and is the only club that has made the National Association of Investors Corp.'s All-Star team for six consecutive years. Charter member Shirley Gross shares the investing secrets of these 16 women, many of whom are in their sixties . . .

OUR STRATEGIES

• **Buy stocks that have had steady, predictable growth.** We choose companies with sales and earnings that have grown at 15% per year over a five- or 10-year period. We also make sure that this rate is projected to continue for the next five years. Investors can do this by consulting the *Value Line Investment Survey*, which is available at most libraries. It ranks more than 1,700 stocks on a 1-through-5 basis . . . 1 being the best in terms of performance over the next 12 months.

We avoid stocks with earnings that have grown well annually—while sales have grown much more slowly. Companies that fit this profile aren't real growth stocks.

• **Stalk a stock before buying it.** This strategy helps us avoid paying more for a stock than we should. Track a stock's price/earnings ratio for the preceding five years. We use the *National Association of Investors Corp.'s Stock Selection Guide*. It is an excellent tool to use when studying stocks to buy. The

Shirley Gross, charter member of the Beardstown Ladies Investment Club. A video on the club's methods, Cookin' Up Profits on Wall Street, is available from Central Picture, 2222 W. Diversey St. #310, Chicago, IL 60647.

Important Questions to Ask Your Stockbroker

John Markese

When your stockbroker recommends a stock, bond, mutual fund, or other investment, don't invest without first getting answers to these questions . . .

• How will this investment help me meet my investment goals?

• Is it the best course of action . . . or merely a suitable one?

• What are the worst, best and most-likely outcomes if I invest?

• Is the price negotiable?

• What is your commission on this sale? Will you receive any additional compensation from a third party?

• Can I buy this product on the open market . . . or can I purchase it only through your firm?

• Are you participating in a contest that rewards you for selling this product?

John Markese, president, American Association of Individual Investors, 625 N. Michigan Ave., Ste. 1900, Chicago, IL 60611.

■ **Open all statements from** your broker immediately. Check for discrepancies in your account. Be alert to indications of "churning"—repeated purchases and sales of securities undertaken by the broker to run up commissions. Remember that you must take responsibility for what occurs in your account.

Fire Your Broker, by Marvin B. Roffman, president, Roffman Miller and Associates, money managers, Philadelphia. Carol Publishing Group, 600 Madison Ave., New York, NY 10022. $18.95.

DID YOU KNOW . . .

■ **Up to 94% of investment returns** result from asset allocation, according to a study by Beinson, Hood and Beebower—the type of asset invested in, such as stocks, bonds, money funds, etc.—rather than the particular investments within the type. *Result:* Many investors would do better to spend more effort finding the right mix of investments for their needs, and less on seeking the "best" stock or bond funds among many high-quality candidates.

Alexandra Armstrong, CFP, chair, Armstrong, Welch & Macintyre, Inc., financial advisers, 1155 Connecticut Ave. NW, Ste. 250, Washington, DC 20036. She is coauthor of On Your Own: A Widow's Passage to Emotional and Financial Well-Being. *Dearborn Financial Publishing. $19.95.*

■ **A spun-off company** often does well, even when it performed poorly as part of a larger firm. *Reason:* Managers no longer take orders from higher executives who do not understand their business. This lets them cut costs, improve production and become more entrepreneurial. *Opportunity:* 14% of recent spinoffs became takeover targets. In a takeover, the stock price of a company is sure to rise. In general, the odds of a takeover of a company are only 3% to 4%.

Peter Lynch, vice chairman, Fidelity Management and Research, Boston, writing in Worth, *575 Lexington Ave., New York, NY 10022. 10 issues. $24/yr.*

■ **The daily grind of negative news** presents opportunities for investors. Effective investment is for the long term. If you allow frightening daily headlines to create indecision, you will not focus on a long-term investment strategy. The stock market often responds negatively to bad news for a time, but its long-term trend is up, and successful investors always look at the long term.

The Five Rituals of Wealth: Proven Strategies for Turning the Little You Have into More than Enough *by Tod Barnhart, financial adviser, Houston. HarperBusiness, $22.*

SSG is available through the NAIC or its regional councils.

Formula: Determine the stock's high p/e for each of the past five years. Add them up. Do the same for the stock's low p/e. Divide each sum by five to get the average high and low. Next, add these two figures and divide by two to get the average p/e for the last five years. Avoid the stock if its current p/e is higher than its average p/e.

• **Ignore most broker tips, but rely on research with proven value.** Don't listen to the so-called experts. Our club has an account at A. G. Edwards, a full-service brokerage firm. By going through a full-service broker, we're able to avoid having to get the signatures of 16 members every time we buy or sell. But we seldom look to the broker for advice. Instead, we swear by *Value Line*, relying on its research and rankings to lead us to potentially attractive stocks.

We almost always buy companies with *Value Line* timelines rankings of 1 or 2, and never those with a 4 or 5. We also use *Value Line*'s industry rankings as a sector screen, typically choosing companies in an industry in the top 25 (out of 98).

• **Avoid companies with substantial debt or unresolved problems.** Stocks in companies with comparatively low levels of debt traditionally do not drop dramatically in price. For almost all stocks purchased, the company's debt should not account for more than one-third of its capitalization. This information is also available through *Value Line* or the company's annual report.

• **Get paid for the risks you take.** Growth-stock investors can get clobbered if the company doesn't prosper, so make sure you invest in companies where the upside will be big.

Use the *Stock Selection Guide* and the data from *Value Line* to establish an upside/downside ratio for any stock being considered. It is the ratio used to evaluate the relative odds of potential gain versus our risk of loss for a given price per share. Look for ratios of at least 3 to 1.

Example: Determine the projected high price ($40). Subtract the present cost ($15). This leaves you with $25. Take the present cost ($15) and subtract the projected low ($10). This leaves you with $5. Divide the $25 by $5. This gives you a ratio of 5:1, a good buy.

• **Know when to sell.** When we buy a stock, we have a price in mind that we expect it to reach within five years. When it hits that price, we reevaluate the stock. If it's still strong, we hold onto it. If it's weak, we sell. If the stock price remains flat or drops, we also reevaluate. If the fundamentals are weak, we sell and take a loss.

• **Avoid any stock with a beta over 1.60.** A beta is the measure of a stock's volatility. A stock with a beta over 1.5 is more volatile than the market. Since our club meets only monthly, we prefer steadier stocks.

How to Look for Good-Quality Stock

David Dreman

1. **A price/earnings ratio that's lower than the market average.** I'm buying stocks with p/e's of no more than 14—and preferably no more than 12. When their p/e's rise to market levels, it's usually time to sell.

2. **A solid track record.** The growth of its earnings and dividends over the past five to 10 years should have outpaced the S&P 500.

3. **Above-average return on equity** compared with the S&P 500 for the past five to 10 years. This shows that the company really knows how to use capital intelligently to create higher profits.

4. **A strong balance sheet.** A good company can have long-term debt, but it should not exceed the company's equity. In recent years we've seen far too many companies struggling to get out from under debt that has prevented them from growing and prospering as they otherwise would have done.

David Dreman, chairman, Dreman Value Management, which manages $2.7 billion in stocks, bonds, and mutual funds for individual and institutional clients, 10 Exchange Place, Jersey City, NJ 07302.

How to Get a Better Rate on CDs

Before investing in a certificate of deposit, check the yields at out-of-state banks. They may be higher than at your local banks.

Major financial magazines and newspapers often list banks with the best nationwide rates. Their 800 numbers usually appear next to the rates.

Opportunity: Look for special CDs with unusual features, such as 10-month terms or the right to withdraw and reinvest at a higher rate if interest rates go up.

Or consider buying CDs through a stockbroker. Some brokerage firms negotiate higher interest rates with banks and pass them along to customers.

Lewis Altfest, L. J. Altfest & Co., 140 William St., New York, NY 10038. He is author of *Lew Altfest Answers Almost All Your Questions About Money.* McGraw-Hill, $11.95.

■ **Better CD-investment strategy:** Buy several smaller-denomination CDs instead of one large one—in case you need cash before maturity. *Example:* Buy five $1,000 CDs instead of one $5,000 CD. If you must cash in a $1,000 CD, you will pay an early-withdrawal penalty only on that CD. But if you need $1,000 and have only a $5,000 CD, you will pay the penalty on the entire amount when you cash it in.

Joel Lerner lectures on finance, and is based in Monticello, New York. He is author of *Financial Planning for the Utterly Confused.* McGraw-Hill, $9.95.

Mutual Fund Trap

Jonathan Pond, CPA

Don't pay taxes twice on the same mutual fund gains—it happens often. *How:* Say you buy shares in a mutual fund for $5,000 and some years later sell all your shares for $10,000. You have a $5,000 capital gain—*or maybe not.* The trap is that if you reinvested fund dividends or capital gains to buy extra shares, you've *already paid tax* on this income, which is represented by the shares you received. If you lump in these shares with your original shares when computing gain on the sale, you'll pay a double tax.

What to do: Keep precise records of all dividends and gains that are reinvested in the fund. Add these to the cost of your shares to reduce the gain on their sale.

Jonathan Pond, CPA, is president of Financial Planning Information Inc., 9 Galen St., Watertown, MA 02172.

Make the Most of Your IRA

Lewis J. Altfest
L. J. Altfest & Co.

All funds distributed from an IRA are taxed as ordinary income at rates up to 39.6%, even if they are derived from long-term capital gains that would be taxed at no more than 28%.

Tax planning: If you want a portfolio that contains both taxable bonds (or other income-producing securities) and appreciating stocks, buy the bonds for your IRA and keep the stocks in an account outside the IRA.

The Questions to Ask Before Investing in Rental Property

Jack Cummings

Now is still a great time to invest in a rental property. Though interest rates are rising, they are still low, housing prices are soft, and the rental market is strong. However, it is easy to make a mistake if you don't ask the right questions. Bad news doesn't have to scare you away, but you should know *all* the bad news before you buy.

• **What are the local real-estate market conditions?** How much are other property owners charging renters? How are the local water and school systems? What are the economic trends for the neighborhood?

Opportunity: Get to know real-estate brokers who have worked in the neighborhood for a long time. Ask them what they think will happen to the area. How are properties selling in this neighborhood compared with other properties nearby?

• **How much work does the property need?** Have an engineer inspect the property you are interested in. You need to know more about the condition of a rental property than the condition of your own home. *Reason:* With an investment property, you won't be able to put off making repairs just because you don't have the funds available immediately.

• **What are the local income and expense ratios?** What kind of rent can you command, and what vacancy level should you expect? The local tax assessor usually has such information.

Jack Cummings, a real-estate broker in Fort Lauderdale, FL. His most recent book is *The Real-Estate Investor's Answer Book: Hundreds of Money-Making Ideas for Today's Market.* McGraw-Hill Professional Book Group.

• **Can you make any cosmetic changes that will allow you to increase the rent?** Check with the local zoning board.

• **Are there any hidden "time bombs"?** These problems can include pending legal action against the property, bad title, existing code violations or contracts that would obligate you to pay for leased equipment, employment contracts, etc. Watch out for obsolete equipment, environmental problems, false income and expense statements from the previous owner, etc.

• **Do you know everything about existing leases and tenant records for the property?** Pay a certified property manager to research this for you. Watch out for leases that give tenants the option to renew in several years . . . allow them to paint the interior of an apartment without your approval . . . permit any kind and number of pets . . . allow them to have as many people as they like living in their apartments . . . or have no penalty for late payments.

What Everyone Should Know about Bonds

David L. Scott, Ph.D.

While most investors have a good understanding of how the stock market works, too few are even remotely familiar with bonds—or the bond market.

As a result, many individuals invest blindly and are unaware of the risks. That's unfortunate, because

David L. Scott, Ph.D., professor of accounting and finance at Valdosta State University in Valdosta, GA. He is author of *The Guide to Investing in Bonds*. Globe Pequot Press.

TAX-WISE INVESTING

The bond income that normally would be taxed at top rates will obtain tax deferral from the IRA . . . and the capital gain tax break will be preserved for the appreciating stocks.

Lewis J. Altfest, CFP, president of L. J. Altfest & Co., 140 William St., New York, NY 10038, and author of Lew Altfest Answers Almost All Your Questions About Money. *McGraw-Hill, 1221 Avenue of the Americas, New York, NY 10020. $11.95.*

STOCK-PICKING SECRETS

■ **Five signs of a good stock:** 1) Earnings per share show an upward trend over five years . . . 2) Increasing earnings are accompanied by increasing dividends . . . 3) A Standard & Poor's rating of A– or better for the firm's financial strength . . . 4) At least 10 million shares of stock outstanding, to assure liquidity if you decide to sell . . . 5) A price/earnings ratio that has not been bid up too much above market averages—which would indicate that investors have already discovered the stock and run up its price so that it is no bargain.

How to Invest $50–$5,000 by Nancy Dunnan, financial analyst. HarperPerennial.

■ **Don't pick a stock** just because an analyst forecasts strong earnings. One study shows that analysts typically get carried away with companies they follow . . . and overestimate earnings by as much as 40%. Use common sense. Ask yourself if such a company in such an industry could possibly post as big an earnings gain as the analyst is forecasting. Then . . . before you finally decide to buy . . . knock 15% to 20% off the analyst's earnings forecast.

Michelle R. Clayman, partner, and Robin A. Schwartz, portfolio manager, with New Amsterdam

STOCK-PICKING SECRETS

Partners, investment managers of corporate and public pension funds, 475 Park Ave. South, New York, NY 10016.

■ **Cash flow** is the life blood of a business. Before investing in a company's stock, check the firm's "Statement of Cash Flows," which is included in all annual and quarterly reports. Determine if the company is financing growth with internally generated cash or costly outside borrowing. *Will cash flow safely cover future debt payments? Is cash flow adequate to support a growing dividend? How does the firm's cash flow and level of outside financing compare with others in its industry?*

Stock Picking: The 11 Best Tactics for Beating the Market, by Richard J. Maturi, business and investment writer, McGraw-Hill, 11 W. 19 St., New York, NY 10011. $12.95.

INVESTING STRATEGY

■ **Define a mission before investing.** Too often investors chase investments that look good at the moment, making helter-skelter decisions. *Far better:* Have a specific investment objective, such as increasing personal net worth 15% a year, or creating enough wealth to retire, or start your own business by a specific date. A concrete goal lets you design a consistent investment program and monitor results to know if you are on track, making adjustments as needed. Having a target helps you avoid the twin errors of greed and fear to which many investors fall prey-taking too many risks . . . or being too timid.

High-Risk, High-Return Investing, by Lawrence W. Tuller, CPA and president of his own management consulting firm, Berwyn, PA. John Wiley & Sons, 605 Third Ave., New York, NY 10155. $27.95.

bonds deserve a place in every portfolio. Over time, they can produce higher returns than other fixed-income investments—if you understand what you are doing.

BOND BASICS

The face value of a bond is fixed at the time it is purchased. It is the amount a bondholder can count on getting in cash on the date the bond matures, which could be anywhere from one year to 100 years, depending on the particular bond.

The market value—the price at which you can sell a bond any time before maturity—is profoundly affected by changes in interest rates. These rates are driven by expectations about the course of inflation. The longer the amount of time until a bond comes due, the more vulnerable it is to these expectations on a day-to-day basis.

When interest rates go up, the prices of bonds held by investors go down. *Reason:* Newer issues offer higher yields. For example, investors won't pay the $1,000 you paid for a 7% bond if they can get 8% now.

A guess about the probable course of inflation is built into a bond's interest rate—or "coupon"—at the time it is issued. For example, a bond paying 7% may assume a 4% inflation rate, for a real return of 3%.

But if inflation turns out to be much higher, you will take a beating if you have to sell a bond before it reaches maturity. You can, of course, hold a bond to maturity and collect its face value—but the dollars you will get back may have a lot less purchasing power than they did when you invested them.

HOW TO PLAY INTEREST RATES

• **If you think interest rates will rise**—buy bonds with short or intermediate maturities, generally not more than eight to ten years. A spurt in interest rates after you buy the short or intermediate bond will not affect its price as much as it would a long-term bond because the substandard return lasts for a much shorter period. In other words, you will get back your principal sooner and be able to reinvest it at the new, higher interest rates.

• **If you think interest rates will fall further**—buy bonds with low coupons and long maturities (more than ten years) that are selling below their face values.

• **If you have no idea about which way interest rates are heading**—"ladder" your investments. Buy bonds of different maturities—short, intermediate, and long—to give you some protection against rate movements in either direction.

COMMON PROBLEMS
AND SOLUTIONS

• **Bonds can be difficult to buy at fair prices.** Bonds have always been a game for major players—commercial banks, insurance companies, pension funds, and mutual funds—which buy and sell them in huge quantities and pay less for them than you could. *Self-defense . . .*

1. **Buy new issues.** Initial offerings by governments, agencies, and corporations usually sell for set prices. Commissions are generally paid by the seller, not you.

2. **Buy U.S. Treasury securities directly from the government.** The Treasury "auctions" one-year bills every month. Other bonds and notes are auctioned at various times during the year.*

• **Bonds can be hard to sell at fair prices.** Many issues rarely trade in the secondary market. Dealers don't like to handle small numbers of bonds and often cut prices to move them quickly. If you have to sell, the bid price may shock you. *Self-defense . . .*

1. **Hold bonds to redemption.** This is almost always the best strategy for individuals. Invest in bonds with the intention of holding them to maturity.

2. **Buy bonds that are likely to have an active secondary market.** If you feel the yield on long-term bonds is too good to pass up, choose those that are part of large offerings from well-known issuers. Find out if they are actively traded by asking your broker.

INVESTING STRATEGY

■ **Adding international stocks to your portfolio reduces risk.** Every monitored investment newsletter that recommends a blend of U.S. and international investment has increased its return and lowered its risk by doing so. *Why:* International stock markets do not move in lockstep with U.S. markets, so when U.S. markets are down foreign ones are likely to be up and vice versa. Thus, buying international stocks reduces the risk that your whole portfolio will decline in value at one time. And international markets have equaled or surpassed the performance of the U.S. market in recent years. Investments in international stocks are easily made through high-quality mutual funds.

Mark Hulbert, editor, Hulbert Financial Digest, 316 Commerce St., Alexandria, VA 22314.

INVESTING STRATEGY

■ **Quick securities analysis.** You don't need an MBA to judge the financial health of a business in which you might invest. First get its latest financial statement. Then figure its quick ratio—cash and marketable securities divided by current liabilities. If this is more than 1.0, the company can pay its debts. If not, don't invest. Also figure its debt-to-capital ratio—total long-term debt divided by total capital, which consists of long-term debt plus the total value of all outstanding common stock. Long-term debt is part of the company's capital, so it is counted on both sides of the equation. Typical debt ratios vary by industry, but a ratio of more than 25% may be risky.

Barron's Guide to Making Investment Decisions by John Prestbo, markets editor, The Wall Street Journal. Prentice Hall.

INVESTING STRATEGY

■ **You are more likely to achieve your investment goals** if they are specific, not general.

Example: Instead of simply trying to do the best possible, choose an objective like paying off your mortgage within a specific number of years.

Calculate how much money you will need by a specific time . . . set your sights on that goal . . . and manage your investments with that in mind.

Ari Kiev, MD, president and medical director, Social Psychiatry Research Institute, New York, and author of A Strategy for Daily Living. (The Free Press/$12.95).

■ **To set up an investment club:** Have at least 15 members to share the work and create enough investment volume to obtain reduced commissions. Draw up a partnership agreement that specifies meeting schedules, required contributions, member duties, and how departing members are paid off. Draw up by-laws detailing investment philosophy, etiquette, and procedures for resolving disputes—and dismissing disruptive members. *Helpful:* Join the National Association of Investors (810-543-0612) to obtain practical advice on running the club as well as investor's manuals, stock analysts' charts and company reports. *Cost:* $35* per club—plus $11 per member annually.

*At time of printing. All prices are subject to change without prior notice.

Smart Money, 250 W. 55 St., New York, NY 10019.

• **Bonds can be retired early**—or "called"—years before their scheduled maturity. Issuers can call bonds when interest rates fall if a call feature is part of the original issue. Just as home owners rush to refinance mortgages, bond issuers reduce interest expenses by replacing old, high-interest bonds with new ones at much lower rates.

Even though the call price is usually slightly above a bond's face value, early redemption is almost always a blow to bondholders. They lose the high returns they've expected to earn for years and must then reinvest the principal at lower market rates.

Even worse: An investor may have paid a premium for a high-yielding bond and so will lose income when it's called. *Self-defense* . . .

Buy bonds that can't be called. Read the prospectus on a new issue carefully to check for call provisions. If a bond is already trading in the secondary market, ask your broker whether it is callable before you commit. If you decide to buy a callable bond for the increased yield, you should understand the call provisions and how they may affect your investment.

• **Interest and principal may not be paid.** Corporations and municipalities sometimes do go belly-up. When they do, you may lose most of your investment. *Self-defense* . . .

Look for quality. Unless you have good reason to think a company that is facing hard times is due for a comeback, forget it. Invest in conservatively managed companies that are leaders in growing industries.

• **Insist on collateral.** Don't rely on an issuer's revenue stream to service a bond. If the assets pledged to secure the debt are valuable, chances are you'll get most or all of your money back if disaster strikes. Bondholders can force the sale of these assets to pay their claims.

• **Invest in U.S. Treasury securities**—the ultimate security, since our government isn't going out of business.

A CASE FOR BOND FUNDS

Unless you have large amounts of money to invest in bonds (more than $100,000 for municipals, $50,000 for corporates), beware of buying individual issues. You are bound to sacrifice diversification—either in terms of issuers or maturities—and it is easy to get lost in the intricacies of some of the markets.

Generally, individuals are probably better off investing in bond funds.

Drawback: Mutual funds don't "mature," so there is no guarantee that you will get back your investment on any specified date.

Be sure to match a fund with your own investment standards and invest in at least two of the following types of bond funds:

- **Longer term**—13 years or more—for the higher yield.
- **Intermediate term**—from two to 12 years ––to reduce risk.

It's important to know a fund's fee structure before you invest, so read the prospectus carefully. *Look for:*

- **Low expense ratios.** This is critical. An expense ratio of more than 1% is a big drag on your yield.

Example: A bond fund with a gross return of 7.5% yields a net return of 7.2% if the annual expense ratio is 0.3% of assets, but yields only 6.5% if the ratio is 1.0%.

- **Loads.** Some funds charge a front-end load—or fee—when you invest. Others charge a back-end load when you sell. Back-end loads are generally reduced over time, for example, from 6% of net asset value on shares held less than a year to no fee at all on shares held five years or more. Clearly, it is more costly to sell before the fees phase out.

- **12b-1 fees.** Many bond—and stock—mutual funds charge 12b-1 annual fees to cover their distribution and marketing costs. The amount is small (0.25% to 0.50%), but over the long haul these charges mount up.

*For information on the direct purchase of Treasury securities, check with your local Federal Reserve Bank or write to the Bureau of the Public Debt, Division of Consumer Services, 300 13 St. NW, Washington, DC 20239; 202-879-4000.

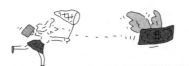

Tax-Exempt Municipal Bonds

Richard Shapiro

If I buy a tax-exempt municipal bond for less than face value, then hold it to maturity and redeem it at full face value, is my gain tax-free?

If you bought the bond at original issue for less than face value, then the gradual gain in its value until maturity is considered part of the interest paid on it and is tax-free.

Much more common, however, is the case where a previously issued bond, issued at face value, is purchased in the market at less than face value because it now pays a below-market rate of interest. In this case, any gain on the sale or redemption of the bond is a capital gain that is taxable. Any loss is a deductible capital loss, subject to the limitation on deductions for capital losses.

Richard Shapiro, partner and director of taxes, financial services industry, Grant Thornton, 7 World Trade Center, New York, NY 10048.

■ **Easy saving bond protection:** Photocopies. Make photocopies of your bonds and keep them somewhere safe—not the same place where you keep the bonds themselves. If the bonds are ever lost, stolen or destroyed, pick up Form PD1048 from your bank, fill it out, and send it with the photocopies to Bureau of the Public Debt, Third Street, Parkersburg, West Virginia 26106-1328.

Dan Pedersen, president, The Savings Bond Informer, a national fee-based service in Detroit that provides reports on the value and interest rates of savings bonds, 800-927-1901.

■ **Bank-failure loophole.** If your bank fails and your deposits exceed $100,000 (the maximum amount insured by the FDIC), you can still use the uninsured portion to pay off any outstanding debt to the bank you may have. Request a "voluntary offset" from the bank's claims agent. *Example:* Someone with $120,000 in deposits and a $50,000 bank loan can ask that the $20,000 not covered by the FDIC be used to pay down the loan. *Rationale:* You probably won't see the $20,000 for some time, and when you do, you aren't likely to receive the full amount. Meanwhile, your debt would be reduced by the amount offset, dollar for dollar.

Cody Buck, former senior executive of the FDIC's division of liquidation. He is author of *The ABCs of FDIC: How to Save Your Assets from Liquidation.* CoStarr Publications.

■ **Junk mail from banks** shouldn't be considered junk. Carefully read all the enclosures with your monthly statements. Notices of potentially significant problems are crafted very carefully. Banks use them to announce policy changes, mergers, and acquisitions . . . notify customers of new interest rates and fees . . . report earnings and compliance with federal regulations. If you don't understand a communication, call the bank and have an officer explain it.

Your Bank: How to Get Better Service by Jeff Davidson and the editors of *Consumer Reports Books*, 101 Truman Ave., Yonkers, NY 10703.

Best Money Strategies . . . for Your 20s, 30s, 40s . . . and Beyond

Jonathan D. Pond

When managing your money, you should learn to act your age. These are key strategies for investors in three different age groups—those in their 20s and 30s . . . those in their 40s and 50s . . . and those who are retired.

20s AND 30s

• **Buy a home.** It may turn out to be your single best investment, especially if you buy a single-family home rather than a condominium.

• **Invest for growth.** Those in their 20s and 30s should put 70% of their long-term investment money into stocks and/or stock mutual funds. The remainder should go into bonds or bond funds.

• **Plan now if you want to retire early.** Almost half of all working-age people hope to retire before age 65. Many of them do it—but they actually can't afford to. Successful early retirees typically established that goal in their 20s and 30s, when they still had plenty of time to accumulate wealth. They sacrificed early by saving 20% or 25% of their income and living in cheaper housing than they could afford.

Jonathan D. Pond, president of Financial Planning Information Inc., 9 Galen St., Watertown, MA 02172. He is author of numerous books on personal finance, including, *The New Century Family Money Book*. Dell Publishing.

40s AND 50s

• **Keep investing for growth.** You should have 50% to 60% of your investment portfolio in stocks and the remainder in bonds. When you're within 10 years of retirement, keep that same mix but change the types of securities you own to reduce your risk somewhat.

• **Avoid taxes.** Make full use of tax-deferred savings vehicles, including 401-k plans, Individual Retirement Accounts (IRAs) and variable annuities. Your 40s and 50s are your peak earning years and, hence, your peak tax years, so tax-favored savings are critical.

• **Project your retirement income and expenses.** Do this once a year, so you know how much you need to be saving and when you can retire.

• **Review estate plans every few years.**

• **Keep loved ones informed.**

The Most Common Mistakes in Financial Planning

James D. Schwartz

Mistake: Not knowing what is enough for your financial objectives. Too many investors are caught up in the cultural bias for *more* . . . more for more's sake. This is akin to putting the cart before the horse and then killing the horse. Too often, in investing, the push to make more requires overreaching—taking risks that can result, in the end, in *less* rather than more. Since more is by definition never enough, financial plan-

---

James D. Schwartz, a fee-only personal financial planner and president of ENOUGH, Inc., Englewood, CO. He is the author of ENOUGH, A Guide to Reclaiming Your American Dream. Re/Max International, Inc.

DEBT MANAGEMENT

■ **Figure how much debt you can carry** by making a list of all your monthly payments on debts that will take at least six months to pay off, excluding your mortgage. Then divide the result by your regular monthly gross income . . . this is your debt-to-income ratio. If monthly debt payments are 15% or less of income, you're doing fine . . . 15% to 20%, take steps to keep debts from accumulating . . . 20% to 35%, you're in a risky area and need to cut back . . . over 35%, you are in deep enough trouble to ask for help. Most people who hit 50% in debt payment are headed for bankruptcy.

Gerri Detweiler, author of The Ultimate Credit Handbook. Good Advice Press.

■ **You can't borrow your way out of debt.** *Lesson:* Don't enter a loan-consolidation agreement that stretches out the term of your borrowing, no matter how attractive its advertising sounds. *Catch:* Even if you obtain lower monthly payments, you'll pay much more interest over the long run. *Exception:* If you can obtain a reduction in the interest rate you're paying on your total borrowing, loan consolidation may make sense. This might be possible if you pay off high-rate, nondeductible credit-card interest with funds obtained through a home-equity loan carrying a lower rate of interest that is deductible.

Life After Debt: How to Repair Your Credit and Get Out of Debt Once and for All by Bob Hammond, retired credit-repair consultant. Career Press.

MONEY MATTERS

■ **Do you need a debit card?** *Pros:*
Using a debit card is safer than carrying
cash and handier than writing checks.
Fees are comparable to using a bank
Automated Teller Machine (ATM) card . . .
if you make many purchases, you can
get a card from an issuer that charges
only a flat annual fee—rarely more than
$24. *Cons:* Many merchants do not yet
accept debit cards. Some charge a fee
for doing so but since they get their
money instantly, this is an extraordinary
charge so be sure to ask about it before
using your card. If you already have a
bank ATM card that works like a debit
card in local stores, you won't need a
Visa or MasterCard debit card unless
you travel.

Gerri Detweiler, consumer credit consultant in
Herndon, VA, and author of *The Ultimate Credit
Handbook.* Good Advice Press.

■ **Beware of loans to family members.**
Fifty percent of loans to family members are never repaid. For loans to
friends, at least 75% are not repaid.
Self-defense: Before lending any money
to your family members or friends, think
the deal through carefully—as both a
business proposition and a personal
matter.

Andrew Feinberg, financial columnist and author of *Downsize Your Debt: How to Take Control of
Your Personal Finances.* Penguin.

■ **A dollar saved is worth more** than a
dollar added to current income. Reducing spending by a dollar lets you save
the full dollar. But in order to spend an
additional dollar, you have to make between $1.15 and $1.50 (the added
amount goes to taxes).

Make Your Paycheck Last by Harold Moe, Hol-
men, WI, airline captain who got himself out of
deep debt. Career Press.

ners are driven to accomplish the impossible. This
creates anxiety for both you and your planner.

What I advocate in my professional planning
practice is a radically different school of thought
that I call *Enough*.

This approach puts the client into personal financial planning. It recognizes the essential truth that
financial resources are only a means to achieve personal objectives. The goal is to look inward and
identify your life goals and then align those goals
with your personal resources.

If your retirement-income needs can be met, after
adjusting for inflation and tax increases, with an investment that is safely earning 6%, why take a big
risk to earn 20%?

When you have *enough* you can relax and be satisfied, or you can start a new fund. But you don't have
to push for more.

Mistake: **Abdicating responsibility.** Too many
people work for 40 years (that's about 80,000 hours
of making money)—but don't spend the relatively
few hours needed to protect their life's earnings.

You can't abdicate that responsibility. It's OK to let
a planner help you row the boat, but *you* must steer.

Once you have determined your objectives, you can
use a personal financial planner to provide technical
advice. Avoid planners who are transaction-oriented,
such as brokers and life insurance salespersons.
They're working for themselves, not you. *Fee-only*
planners are a better choice, *though they're not guaranteed to be competent.*

Beware: There are 250,000 people in the U.S.
who call themselves personal financial planners but
have virtually no expertise and are subject to no industry or government regulations.

Mistake: **Wanting results *now*.** Remember, anything worth doing is worth doing slowly. This is particularly true of investments. Going for a quick kill is
a sure way to get burned. Don't convey a sense of
impatience to your planner. Be satisfied to make
steady progress.

Mistake: **Piecemeal planning.** By doing piecemeal planning you may solve one problem, but you
can create two others. Planners are now pushing
what's called *modular planning*—e.g., how to finance

your child's education. But you can't plan that in isolation. What if you need to put aside $10,000 a year and you become disabled? *Comprehensive planning* is the only answer.

Mistake: **Concentrating on finances instead of on personal goals.** Much too much financial planning is based strictly on managing assets instead of on aligning your personal finances with your personal goals. Life planning must come before financial planning, not the other way around. *Enough* is a very personal thing.

Mistake: **Not asking what could go wrong.** Before making any investment, you should know about the downside. What could go wrong? What would be the cause of trouble? What's the probability? The seriousness? How can you prevent or minimize risk? The best surprise is no surprise.

Mistake: **Neglecting to ask to see the planner's own financial plan.** This should not be a secret. If he/ she is going to see your personal finances, you should be able to see his. If he doesn't have a plan or won't show you, go elsewhere. People who can't plan for their own lives certainly can't help you plan for yours.

Mistake: **Not distinguishing the "closer" from the "doer."** There are a lot of charming professionals out there who are very good at making the sale but don't actually do the work. It may be the partner of the CPA firm who signs you up, but your account is really handled by some clerk in a position that turns over every two years, meaning that you have to keep re-educating new people. Don't pay partner fees for a partner you never see. By the same token, an hour spent with a very good (but expensive) planner may be worth more than a month of someone else's time.

Mistake: **Not getting an estimate of fees and commissions up front.** Don't accept an answer of, *We won't know until we see how your account works out.* Any professional planner knows how to qualify prospects. At the very least, the planner can tell you what other investors of your general description are paying in average fees and commissions.

Note: Although there are only about 1,000 fee-only planners, you may be able to negotiate a fee-

CREDIT-CARD SAVVY

The Credit-Card Switch

Mary Beth Butler

Does it pay to switch credit cards every time you see a better deal on the annual fees? Does frequent switching affect your credit rating?

It pays to switch once—to a no-annual-fee card. There are many available, including some (like those from Texas-based USAA) that also offer low interest rates. Avoid cards that offer no fee for the first year only—after that, they have no advantages.

Officially, frequent switching does not hurt your credit rating, but why draw extra unwanted attention to your credit history with switches?

Important: Close accounts you no longer want by sending a certified letter to the issuer stating that you want the account closed—by customer request. This protects you against records saying your account was shut off. Accounts not formally closed may be carried in your credit history as still available for use, leading some issuers to reject you for new accounts because you have too much available credit already.

Mary Beth Butler, Bankcard Holders of America, 560 Herndon Pkwy., Suite 120, Herndon, VA 22070.

Correcting a Bad Credit Report

Thomas G. Collins, Jr.

What do you do if you are dissatisfied with a credit bureau's file and would like to contest the information contained in its credit report? Under the Fair Credit Reporting Act, you are allowed to dispute any item contained in your credit file. By law, the credit bureau is required to investigate and remove any information that is not correct.

What if you are still unhappy with the credit agency's resolution? Even if you can't change the actual information contained in the report, you always have the right to insert a statement of 100 words or less explaining why you feel the report is inaccurate.

Thomas G. Collins, Jr., director of planning for one of the five major credit reporting companies in the U.S., The Credit Bureau, Inc., 1600 Peachtree St. NW, Atlanta, GA 30309. His responsibilities are business, marketing, and strategic planning for the firm.

only relationship with a normally commissioned planner who's willing to strike a deal.

Mistake: **Believing that the specific investment is more important than asset allocation.** The term "financial planning" is used by insurance companies, brokers, investment companies, banks, partnership syndicators, and others who are trying to put an independent-looking mask on what is really just a delivery system for the sale of a product. Fully 93% of portfolio value is based on investment classifications (how assets are allocated between different types of investments), *not* on the specific investment or the timing of the purchase. If you tell a planner you have, say, $100,000 to invest and the planner tells you where it should go *before* finding out about your plans, goals, other assets, etc., the planner has failed.

The Secrets of Living on Just One Income

Amy Dacyczyn

It's not only possible for an American family to live on a single income—in some cases, it may actually be better for the family. While some families are forced to live on one income, others make that choice to improve their family life.

In fact, many families that have adjusted to a single income report that they have come out ahead financially as well. Most families with two incomes spend huge amounts on child care and conveniences—housecleaning, laundry, lawn care, restaurants, take-out food, etc. Single-income families may take home only one salary, but they manage far better since they spend their money much more conservatively.

Amy Dacyczyn, author of The Tightwad Gazette (Villard Books), a book of cost-cutting strategies that have appeared in her newsletter of the same name, Rural Route 1, Box 3570, Leeds, ME 04263.

WHAT'S IN IT FOR YOU?

A second income can be desirable for a couple when both spouses enjoy their jobs and dislike domestic work. But many people work at jobs they hate—and they overestimate the value of the second income.

Example: It may really take you 60 hours a week to work at a 40-hour-per-week job for $15 an hour. If you factor in the time to ferry the kids to the baby-sitter, a lost lunch hour and commuting time, you're really making $10 an hour. Add taxes and costs for child care, your wardrobe and transportation, and you're down to $3.33 an hour, or less than $7,000 a year.

How to calculate: Figure out the taxes on the two incomes combined, then the taxes on the larger income alone. Subtract the difference from the smaller income.

Example: Given equal benefits, a couple with annual incomes of $25,000 and $15,000 pays $8,638 in taxes—or about 22%. On an income of $25,000, they would pay $4,516, or about 18%. The second income incurs $4,122 in additional taxes, reducing its value to $10,878.

Next, subtract the costs of child care, wardrobe and transportation from the second income to arrive at its ultimate value. *Result:* The net income of the second salary is often less than $5,000.

Alternative: Reduce family expenses by $5,000 and improve home life at the same time. Some ways to live comfortably—and well—on a single, modest income . . .

- **Reduce the family food bill.** The average American family easily spends twice what it actually needs to on food.

Key: Comparison shop and keep track of prices. Eat at home more often. Pack school lunches. Prepare meals from scratch as often as possible. *Also . . .*

- **Eliminate convenience foods**—for example, single-serving sizes of "instant" soups, drinks, and oatmeal, microwave meals or popcorn, soda (no nutritional value), even cold cereals (substitute homemade pancakes, waffles, muffins, oatmeal, and granola).

- **Buy food on sale and in bulk.** Structure the weekly menu and snacks around foods that are on sale.

Checkbook Checklist

Heloise

Your check register is a good record of deposits and spending if you record all transactions in it. Be sure to include date, check number, name, and invoice number or date of invoice. *More ideas . . .*

- Keep a spare check or two in your wallet.

- Paperclip the checkbook on the page you are working.

- Write check numbers in the register ahead of time.

- Color code in the register. Use red for tax-deductible items.

- Round up check amounts to the nearest dollar.

- Cut addresses off extra deposit slips for address labels.

- Keep a small, thin calculator in your register.

- Use black or blue ink. Light-colored ink doesn't copy as well.

- Keep track of monthly expenses at the back of the book.

Heloise, whose syndicated column *Hints from Heloise* appears in more than 500 newspapers internationally. She is the author of a number of books, including *Heloise: Household Hints for Singles.* Perigee Books.

You and Your Money Month-by-Month

Kenny Luck

The wheels of commerce turn with predictable regularity. The key is timing your purchases.

- **January.** Traditional after-Christmas and New Year's bargains include suits, linens (white sales), appliances, and furniture.
- **February.** The season of love brings with it big reductions on china, glass, silver, mattresses, and bedding.
- **March.** Watch for special preseason promotions for spring clothing. Ski equipment is at an annual low as well.
- **April.** Sales begin again after the Easter holiday, especially on clothing.
- **May.** Spring cleaning means specials on household cleaning products. This also is a good month to shop for carpets and rugs.
- **June.** Shop for furniture. Semiannual inventory is on the way in, old items must go.
- **July.** Most stores liquidate their inventories to make room for fall goods during this month. Sportswear, sporting equipment, and garden tools and supplies take noticeable dips.
- **August.** If you are in the market for a car, August is clearance time on current models. Look for deals on equipment linked to the summer season, too—patio furniture, lawn mowers, yard tools and camping gear.
- **September.** The best deals on school clothes are at the *end* of the month. Hold off until then and you'll save big.

- **Buy generic brands.**
- **Make more soups, stews, and casseroles** rather than meat-and-potato meals.
- **Learn to make pizza from scratch,** plant a garden, make jams and preserves.
Savings: Cut a $500 monthly food bill in half, or $3,000 a year.
- **Economize on entertainment.** The average kid receives 250 toys by the age of five—yet he/she is often bored. *Better ways . . .*
- **Take kids to free events**, borrow videotapes from the library, and stop spending so much on toys and games.
- **Tolerate a period of complaining from your kids**, then be amazed when they find imaginative things to do by themselves.
- **Make kids responsible for buying their own extras.** When they have to work for what they want, kids want much less.
Savings: $60 to $100 a month, or more.
- **Buy secondhand clothing**, especially for kids. Children's clothing is outgrown before it's outworn or out-of-style.
Urban and suburban areas offer great deals at yard sales and thrift stores. Buy clothes on sale—never pay full retail price for anything.
Example: Buy end-of-summer clothes for next summer.
Avoid fads . . . stick with the classics.
Annual savings: Several hundred dollars.
- **Buy used furniture.** Watch for classic furnishings that, when repaired, refinished or reupholstered, become "antiques." *Savings:* Hundreds to thousands a year.
- **Practice small economics.** Watch the pennies, and the dollars will take care of themselves. Make your own birthday and holiday decorations, Halloween costumes, valentines, wrapping paper, greeting cards.
- **Change old habits.** Use the library instead of buying new books. Give up bad, costly habits—particularly smoking and drinking. Be vigilant about turning off your heat, air conditioning, and water heater when they are not in use. Buy generic prescription drugs. Water down your sham-

poo. Have a friend cut your hair. *Savings:* Hundreds to thousands of dollars a year.

MORE DRASTIC MEASURES

• **Drive cheaper cars.** Buy a used car, or a new car you can maintain for 10 years.

• **Move to a less-expensive neighborhood** or region of the country.

• **Instead of going on costly vacations,** take day trips to local lakes, museums, state fairs, historic sites, or hiking trails.

How to Get out of Debt and Stay out of Debt

Alexandra Armstrong

Millions of Americans are trying to reduce their credit-card debt. Faced with increasing financial responsibilities, many are looking for ways to eliminate the bills they receive each month and free up some of their income.

Fortunately, most debt is manageable—if it is addressed early enough. *Here's what I tell people who are overburdened with debt . . .*

ACKNOWLEDGE THE PROBLEM

Most people deny that they have debt problems. They refuse to admit that the problems exist or believe that they will go away by themselves.

The fact is that if you owe money on your credit cards and cannot pay the entire amount when the bill arrives, you have debt.

If your debt grows too large, you run the risk of being unable to meet your monthly payments and seriously damaging your credit rating.

Alexandra Armstrong, chairman of Armstrong, Welch & MacIntyre Inc., a Washington, D.C.-based financial advisory firm. She is coauthor of *On Your Own: A Widow's Passage to Emotional and Financial Well-Being.* Dearborn Financial Publishing.

• **October.** This is *the* month to do your Christmas shopping. Stores are postured to boost retail sales before the holiday season.

• **November.** Wool clothes, including women's coats and men's suits, come down significantly this month as store owners cut their inventories for their second shipment of the season.

• **December.** Next to August, this is the best time to buy a new car.

Kenny Luck, author of *52 Ways to Stretch a Buck.* Thomas Nelson Publishers.

Credit Cards Are Not All Alike to the IRS

The general rule is that you only get a tax deduction in the year you actually pay for a deductible expense. But there's an important exception when you pay with a credit card. For tax purposes, payment is considered made on the date of the transaction, not on the date you paid the credit card company. Expenditures charged at the end of this year can be deducted this year even though you don't pay for them until next year.

But if you charge a deductible expense on a credit card issued by the company supplying the deductible goods (or services), you can't take a deduction until the credit card bill is paid.

Example: If you have a prescription filled at a department store pharmacy and charge it on a credit card issued by the store, you can't deduct the cost of that medication until you get the bill and pay it. But if you charge the same prescription on a credit card issued by a third party, such as MasterCard or Visa, you can deduct it right away.

■ **Credit card mistake.** Increasing numbers of credit card owners are *not* signing their credit cards in the mistaken belief that this helps fight credit fraud. *Why:* They fear that if a signed card is stolen, the thief will be able to practice forging their signature before using it—and that the card issuer will then refuse to provide a refund for a charge made with a genuine-looking signature. *Reality:* It's much more dangerous to have an unsigned card—the thief can sign it himself/herself and use it as identification for all kinds of purposes, as well as making charges, since the signatures will obviously match. Forcing a thief to work to copy your signature is a deterrent to crime.

Ruth Susswein executive director, Bankcard Holders of America, 524 Branch Dr., Salem, VA 24153.

■ **New bank scam:** Safe-deposit box rental bills now arriving in the mail are likely to be about 80% higher than last year. *Reason:* Some banks are adding premiums for safe-deposit box insurance coverage. *Problem:* Tricky invoices hide the fact that the insurance policy and fee are optional—not mandatory. *Self-defense:* Pay only the rental fee and any tax. Include a note with your bill declining the insurance. *Important:* Insure your safe-deposit box valuables with a rider on your homeowner's insurance policy.

Edward Mrkvicka, Jr., a bank consultant in Marengo, IL, and author of *The Bank Book*. Harper-Collins.

The biggest drawback to debt is that it uses up income that could have been invested or spent elsewhere. You are also paying more for something over time than if you had paid for it in full right away.

Even if your debt situation is only temporary, immediate action must be taken to minimize interest payments.

PUT EVERYTHING IN WRITING

To determine how much debt you are carrying monthly, calculate how much you owe. Then determine your monthly income and expenses. If your debt is higher than your monthly income, you should take steps to reduce it.

Strategy: Make two lists—one for expenses that are essential and the other for those that are optional. Some expenses that seem essential may have to be reclassified as optional. Hold a family meeting to plan cutbacks.

While debt may be a difficult subject to discuss with your spouse and children, it is essential that all family members make sacrifices.

DON'T SLASH EXPENSES TOO DRAMATICALLY

Just as total deprivation diets do not help you lose weight permanently, budgets that completely eliminate anything that hints of fun do not permanently eliminate debt. Cutting back is better than cutting out.

Examples: Maybe you can no longer dine out twice a week. But you could go out once a month for special events. Your new budget should accommodate these occasional excursions.

WORK HARD TO STAY ON COURSE

Paying debt is an incremental process. Try not to take on new debt or go on a spending binge as a reward for being frugal.

If you're having trouble making payments, don't ignore the bills. That only gets you into deeper trouble.

Instead, contact all of your creditors to work out less onerous repayment plans or to assure them that you will keep making regular payments. That is what your creditors really want to hear from you, since regular lower payments are better than no payments at all.

How to Make the Most of Coupon Clipping

Sue Diffily

By clipping coupons and mailing in hundreds of rebates, Sue Diffily has saved $3,700 on her supermarket bill during the past three years. *Here are cost-cutting, income-stretching secrets . . .*

SETTING ASIDE TIME

At my clipping peak five years ago, when all of my three children were still at home and my food bill was $500 a month, I saved $75 every two weeks by using coupons and rebates. While today my food bill is lower, I still devote 17 hours each month to coupon clipping and rebates:

• Three hours for coupon clipping and sale hunting.

• Eight hours for filing the coupons.

• Four hours filling out paperwork on rebate offers.

• Two hours meeting with my coupon club, where I swap coupons and rebates.

This tally excludes the eight hours a month I spend shopping, since I would do that anyway.

Payoff: About $9 an hour in income, after taxes and expenses. It's a job for which I make my own hours and answer only to myself.

RATING THE SOURCES

• **Supermarket flyers** are a great source of store coupons and company rebate forms. They are distributed through the mail or at the stores themselves. You can also find valuable rebates in the flyers

Sue Diffily, a homemaker and former second-grade teacher who lives in Smithtown, NY. She lectures locally on coupon clipping.

HAPPIER RAINY DAYS

■ **How much money should you be saving?** Emergency funds need not cover three to six months of living expenses—the traditional amount of cash recommended.

If you can cover those costs with a combination of cash and credit, you need not keep all the money in cash. You can get by with less if you can easily borrow against assets—for instance, through a home-equity loan or against a retirement plan at work—or if you have multiple income sources. It's unlikely both spouses in a two-income family would lose their jobs at the same time.

Key: Keep more in reserve if your income fluctuates, your work is seasonal, you own a business, you rely on commissions, or the job of the sole wage earner may be in jeopardy.

Steven Camp, financial consultant based in Ft. Lauderdale, FL, and author of Money: 127 Answers to Your Most-Asked Financial Questions. *Trunkey Publishing.*

■ **Do not put *too much* money aside** for a rainy day. The common recommendation—to keep enough cash for six months' worth of living expenses—forces you to hold significant amounts of money in very-low-interest locations like savings accounts. *Better:* Keep enough cash to handle small-scale disasters such as the need for a new refrigerator or major car repairs. Put the rest of the rainy-day money into a good stock fund. *Reason:* The fund should provide good returns, eventually being worth far more than you need to

HAPPIER RAINY DAYS

live for six months. In case of personal disaster when stocks are down, tap home equity or get a credit card cash advance—then repay the loan by selling shares of the fund after the market recovers.

Jonathan Clements, financial writer for The Wall Street Journal *and author of* Funding Your Future: The Only Guide to Mutual Funds You'll Ever Need. *Warner Books.*

HMO'S AND YOUR MONEY

■ **Ask your HMO how your premiums are used.** *The medical-loss ratio* is the percentage of a premium that is spent on patient care—the rest goes for administrative costs and profits. It is an important indicator of an HMO's priorities. Good HMOs may pay as much as 90% of premiums to total medical care—85% is acceptable. If an HMO pays a lower percentage than that for medical care, avoid it—patient health isn't its top priority. *If your HMO will not tell you its ratio:* Consumer groups such as American Medical Consumers (818-957-3508) or other third parties track this information.

Vincent Riccardi, M.D., former professor of pediatrics and genetics at Baylor College of Medicine and now head of American Medical Consumers, a fee-based patients' rights group based in La Crescenta, CA.

■ **Before joining a Health Maintenance Organization (HMO)** check whether it has been accredited by the National Committee for Quality Assurance (NCQA)—an independent nonprofit organization now in the process of rating HMOs on their medical treatment, physicians' qualifications, preventative health

of supermarkets at which you don't ordinarily shop. Many contain rebate offers from national companies—such as Pillsbury or General Mills—which are valid regardless of where you purchase the items.

• **Daily newspapers**—especially Wednesday and Sunday supplements—and women's and parenting magazines, such as *Parents, Good Housekeeping, McCall's, Ladies' Home Journal*, etc., often have coupon sections.

• **Coupon club.** Although it's not essential to join a club to profit from coupon clipping, it can't hurt. I joined one about 10 years ago by responding to an ad in my local supermarket. Today, six of us meet for two hours once a month to pool nearly 1,000 unwanted coupons and rebate offers. Anyone in the club is welcome to take as many coupons as he/she would like. But a simple rule applies to the rebate forms—which may be worth several dollars apiece or much more—when you take one, you replace it with another.

• **Family and friends.** They can be a great resource. If you put the word out, you'll be deluged with coupons they've clipped for you.

ORGANIZING YOUR FILES

• **Coupons.** I keep my coupons in an expandable, accordion folder. Some people file them alphabetically by brand. This is great if you can keep track of every brand. However, I find this too difficult.

I prefer to organize my coupons by product category—breakfast products, meat and poultry, dairy and oils, beverages, desserts, cleaning products—which is how I shop.

Every two weeks, before I go shopping, I comb my file and pull out any coupons that are due to expire that month as well as any others I think I'll use. I also check the newspapers to see which products are on sale at my favorite supermarket. When I shop, I take along a shoe box filled with coupons.

• **Rebates.** Until recently, most rebate offers required that you mail a box top or side in with the rebate form. To save these items required a fair amount of space—for me, that meant three boxes, each of which were 1-foot-by-2-feet-by-1½-feet deep. But lately, companies ask only for the product's bar code or proof-of-purchase seal, which is much less bulky. For every product I buy, I simply tear off the front of the product package, put it in a large resealable bag, and slip in the proofs-of-purchase and bar codes as I accumulate them. This helps me know immediately which products they're for, in case a rebate is offered.

To keep track of my rebates, I keep a notebook. I divide the pages into columns for the company, the particular item, the date I mailed the form, the amount of the offer, and the date I received the rebate. It usually takes between one and three months to receive a rebate.

In the event of a long delay, I call the company's 800 number. In most cases, the rebate check arrives soon after my call—often with some free coupons thrown in.

Some people spend their rebates as soon as they get them. To stay motivated, I have set up a separate bank account. Whenever I've collected $10, I make a deposit.

SAVING MORE

I don't clip every coupon—and I don't use every coupon I clip. I only purchase items that I know my family will use. If I overbought just to cash in my coupons, I'd be losing money on the deal. *Other strategies that I use . . .*

• **Watch for sales.** By waiting until prices are marked down, you effectively increase the value of a coupon.

• **Don't get locked into brand loyalty.** I'll buy a store brand if the price is right and I have a good coupon. Often, one brand turns out to be just as good as any other brand, and if I don't like the store brand, I avoid it in the future.

• **When you find a good deal, stock up.** My family used to laugh when I'd come home with 20 bars of soap or a dozen bottles of cooking oil that I bought on sale with a coupon for each. But I knew we would use them eventually. In the long run, these big purchases make great financial sense.

• **Look for "double plays" and "triple plays."** These can save you two or three times what you would have saved with just a coupon.

HMO'S AND YOUR MONEY

services recordkeeping, and more. To date, HMOs covering 50% of all HMO enrollees have been rated. *Beware:* More than half have received less than a top grade because of various deficiencies. To see if a particular HMO has been reviewed and what the results were, call the NCQA at 202-955-3515 and request for its free Accreditation Status list, which is updated on the 15th of each month.

Barry Scholl, spokesperson for NCQA, 2000 L St. NW, Suite 500, Washington, DC 20036.

FAMILY FINANCES

■ **Don't own major assets jointly** with a *second* spouse if you wish to use assets to help provide for the children of a prior marriage. *Trap:* Assets that pass to your spouse may never reach your children—especially if that spouse remarries. *Better:* Establish a family trust to hold your assets after you die, pay income to your surviving spouse for life, then distribute its assets to your children. This way you provide for the future financial welfare of both your spouse and children—and eliminate the risk that a third party will gain control of your assets, either by marrying your surviving spouse or otherwise. Also, you should consider a prenuptial agreement prior to a second marriage.

Frederick Raffety, J.D., C.F.P., Robert Lawrenz Consulting Services, 5301 E. State St., Suite 302, Rockford, IL 61108.

FAMILY FINANCES

Teaching Kids About Money

Neale S. Godfrey

Divide young kids' responsibilities into three categories . . .

• **Citizen-of-the-household chores,** for which kids are never paid—things like cleaning their rooms and making their beds.

• **Work for pay**—taking out garbage or emptying the dishwasher—for which a child gets a weekly allowance.

• **Odd jobs,** such as weeding the garden. Let kids know that by performing such tasks, they can earn *extra* money.

Helpful: As allowances grow, give the amount in small bills, like 10 $1 bills instead of a $10 bill—so the amount can easily be divided into jars for immediate, short-term, and long-term use.

Neale S. Godfrey, a children's financial counselor in Mountain Lake, NJ, and author of Money Doesn't Grow on Trees: A Parent's Guide to Raising Financially Responsible Children. *Fireside.*

Double play: This purchase involves a combination of a sale and a coupon or rebate.

Example: While I like a particular brand of lipstick, it normally costs about $6, which I feel is a bit steep. But when the company ran a "buy-one-get-one-free" sale, I got four for a total of $12. With a rebate form I obtained at my local beauty aids store, I got back $2.50 per stick. *My net cost:* 50 cents per stick.

Triple play: This is a purchase involving a sale, a coupon and a rebate. By capitalizing on all three, you could wind up paying virtually nothing for an item.

Example: My favorite detergent normally costs $3.99 for a 64-ounce box. I'll accumulate a number of $1 coupons for that brand—and then use them all when it goes on sale for $1.99. *My net cost:* 99 cents per box. But if I then use a typical rebate—$2 back for two proofs-of-purchase—I get the detergent free.

Triple plays and organization are the keys to couponing and refunding.

What Credit-Card Companies Won't Tell You

Gerri Detweiler

As competition among credit-card issuers heats up, many people are being bombarded with a wide range of attractive offers from banks and other institutions.

While annual fees and percentage rates on outstanding balances are important, there are many other issues that you need to know about before you apply for a credit card.

Here are ten key points that rarely appear in

Gerri Detweiler, consumer credit consultant in Arlington, VA. She is the author of The Ultimate Credit Handbook. *Good Advice Press.*

credit-card issuers' promotional materials but usually turn up in the fine print on credit-card contracts . . .

• Check your statement carefully each month for error—and fraud. Most people know that if their credit cards are used fraudulently, they are liable only for the first $50 in charges.

But under the Federal Truth-in-Lending Act, if you do not report the disputed charges in *writing* within 60 days of the postmarked date on the bill, you may have to pay the fraudulent charges to avoid being reported to a credit bureau.

Important: Theft can occur without your wallet—or your credit card—ever being stolen. Increasingly, card numbers are being copied and sold to criminals or reproduced on counterfeit cards. Therefore, fraudulent charges can appear while you still have your card in your possession.

Check all your credit-card statements carefully. As soon as you realize that a statement lists questionable charges, call the issuer's 800 telephone number and report it.

Though most problem charges can be handled over the phone, protect yourself by sending a letter to the address that appears on the monthly statement and the credit-card agreement.

Use certified mail/return receipt requested. Then you will have evidence that the issuer received your letter. This precaution protects you in case the issuer fails to recall your original phone call . . . or denies your claim because you never informed them in writing.

• A credit card with a lower interest rate can save you a lot of money. Even if your card issuer offers a 25-day grace period—during which no interest is charged on new purchases—you will not be eligible for this benefit if you carry over a balance of even $1 from the previous month. Your new purchases will immediately incur interest charges.

Strategy: Carry two credit cards. Use one for purchases that you intend to pay in full each month . . . use the other—which should have a lower interest rate—for purchases you will repay over time.

If you carry large balances on several credit cards, consolidate debts on the lowest-interest card—pro-

DID YOU KNOW THAT . . .

. . . bank fees have risen as fast as medical expenses during the last five years? That's primarily because customers are reluctant to change banking relationships. Customers who are not "active shoppers" are subject to big fee increases. *Tactic:* If you are bothered by rising fees but don't want to break off a longstanding banking relationship that may provide useful references or help your credit rating, consider *splitting* your banking between institutions. Shop for a bank offering a better deal on specific services, and move part of your banking business there. *Attractive:* Credit unions, which often charge lower fees and pay higher rates than commercial banks, are growing rapidly.

Craig Shoemaker, assistant professor of economics and business administration, St. Ambrose University, Davenport, IA.

. . . you should always return unwanted credit cards after cutting them up? Don't throw them away. If you do, the issuer can carry your account as open. The account will appear in your credit file—and may cost you additional needed credit in the future, if a prospective lender decides you already have too much credit available.

Paul Richard, vice president, National Center for Financial Education (NCFE), San Diego, CA.

. . . the Federal Direct Loan Program allows all student loans to be consolidated into one simple payment? And—payments can be tied to the graduate's income level, so he/she pays less when entering the job market and more as his income rises and he can afford higher payments.

More information: Direct Loan Consolidation, 800-557-7392.

BETTER CREDIT-CARD CREDIT

■ **Big, bad, new credit-card traps.**
Beware of complicated interest-calculation methods that can wipe out the benefits of a credit card's grace period. With the *two-cycle billing method,* you'll need at least two back-to-back, no-balance months to avoid interest charges.

Also: Grace periods themselves are being shortened—some banks give only 20 days, down from 25 to 30.

Self-defense: When switching cards, avoid both traps.

Gerri Detweiler, a financial writer and credit card and debt-control consultant in Woodbridge, VA. She is author of *The Ultimate Credit Handbook.* Plume.

■ **Credit cards are being revoked** from customers with good credit standing but who do not use the cards to the issuer's satisfaction. One bank cancelled 100,000 no-fee credit cards it considered unprofitable because holders did not use them often enough. Another bank threatened to close some accounts that paid no interest. It said people who want to keep the cards would have to charge $2,500 within six months . . . transfer a $1,000 balance and pay interest . . . or have their accounts closed.

Ruth Susswein, executive director, Bankcard Holders of America, 524 Branch Dr., Salem, VA 24153.

vided you have the discipline to refrain from using the other cards and adding to a mountain of debt.

• **Pay more than the minimum amount required.** A typical credit-card bill of $2,500 can take longer to pay off than a 30-year mortgage. This is because most card issuers require a *minimum payment* of only 2% to 2.5% of the new balance.

Problem: The combination of interest and even a small additional purchase can stretch the debt out for decades if only the minimum is paid each month. Some 12 to 15 million Americans are deeply in debt because they habitually pay only the minimum amount required by the card issuer.

• **Not all credit-card issuers calculate interest the same way.** There are several methods to calculate interest. Almost 90% of card issuers use the *average daily balance* method, which charges interest on your average balance for the month.

Exceptions: The Discover Card, the Household Bank Card, and some cards issued by small banks use the *two-cycle* method. In some cases, this is calculated by adding the average daily balances for the current and previous months. This method can be costly.

Find out which method is used before you apply for a credit card. For those you already own, check the agreement or statement. If it's a two-cycle method, pay off your balance in full each month. Also carry a low-interest card that uses the average daily balance method for charges that you are going to pay over time.

• **Using a convenience check isn't the same as using a credit card.** Many credit-card issuers send convenience checks to cardholders. These look like personal checks and enable you to write checks against the line of credit on your card. *But there are two traps . . .*

• **You pay interest immediately** (no grace period) on the amount borrowed at the cash-advance rate, which may be higher than the interest rate on purchases.

• **Convenience checks are not covered by the Fair Credit Billing Act.** You do not receive the same protection you would if you had used a credit card and had a dispute over purchased goods.

Recent case: A man ordered a computer from an out-of-state retailer and paid with a convenience check. He never received the computer, and the credit-card company wouldn't help him get a refund.

Use convenience checks only for emergency expenses—paying off balances on cards with higher interest rates . . . or making a tax payment, if you must borrow to do so.

Important: If you do not need the convenience checks, tear them up. If you simply throw them away, someone may find them and forge your name.

• **Most credit cards offer 30-day grace periods for late payments**—before the debt is reported on your credit report. Most issuers do not mention this because they want you to pay quickly—and you should. But many people think that they are reported one day after missing the due date.

Important: Although a late payment may not be reported on your credit report, it will be on file with the card issuer. This could count against you if you request a higher credit limit in the future. Also, some issuers levy fees of $10 to $25 for even one day of lateness.

If it's the first time you were late and you're charged a late fee, call the issuer. You may be able to have it waived—if you prove there were extenuating circumstances, such as being away on a trip . . . health reasons . . . or the mail was lost.

If you have lost your job or have another financial crisis and cannot pay, call the issuer and work out an agreement for an extended payment plan. It's always best to discuss late payments with your credit-card issuer *before* you miss the deadline.

BETTER CREDIT-CARD CREDIT

■ **Credit cards aren't so fixed.** The rates on fixed-rate cards only stay the same until the issuer feels like changing them—which it can do at any time by giving 15 days' written notice to cardholders. *Also:* Fixed-rate cards may not even offer the best rates. If you carry a balance, pay your bills on time and if your credit record is good, you may qualify for a variable-rate card with a better rate.

Gerri Detweiler, a financial writer and credit card and debt-control consultant in Woodbridge, VA. She is author of The Ultimate Credit Handbook. *Plume.*

MONEY TRAPS

New Bank Trap

Edward F. Mrkvicka, Jr.

If your bank has recently been taken over and its fees raised, it's time to do some comparison shopping. Most banks have special fee structures for retirees or senior citizens, but don't advertise them. You have to ask. If it's too embarrassing in person, do it by phone.

Try several banks, savings and loans, and credit unions (which generally have the lowest fees and loan rates, as well as paying higher interest on savings). To locate a credit union you might be eligible to join, call 800-358-5710 to find the phone number of your state's credit union league.

Edward F. Mrkvicka, Jr., a former bank president who is now a financial consultant and president of Reliance Enterprises, Inc., Box 413, Marengo, IL 60152.

MONEY TRAPS

■ *Beware:* Buy-now/pay-later offers from retailers are only a good deal if you pay the bill within the allotted time. The offers typically promise no interest for three to six months. But if you do not pay in full on time, you will be charged interest all the way back to the original purchase date. Also—don't open new store charge accounts unless you will use them regularly. They add new charge cards to your credit report— which could lead to your being denied credit in the future. They also charge high interest rates.

Gerri Detweiler, a financial writer and credit card and debt-control consultant in Woodbridge, VA. She is author of *The Ultimate Credit Handbook*. Plume.

• **Your card can't be refused because you're not charging enough.** A merchant cannot impose a minimum amount of $10 or $25 for those who use American Express, MasterCard or Visa.

What to do: Tell the store clerk that a minimum is not allowed under the merchant's agreement with the issuer. Demand to see the manager if necessary.

Special strategy: If you feel strongly, find something more to buy so that you can charge it. Then write to MasterCard (888 Seventh Ave., New York 10106) and enclose a copy of the charge slip, which will help the credit-card company track down the merchant's bank. For Visa, you must report the merchant to the bank that issued your card. American Express prefers customers to call the 800 number on the back of its cards and discuss it with a representative.

You won't receive credit on your card for the additional items you charged—nor will you receive store credit—unless you return the merchandise. However, if you report the infraction to the issuer, the merchant may be fined up to $1,000 if similar complaints have been filed or are reported in the future.

• **Credit-card rates are flexible—if you're a good customer.** In this competitive market, a better deal may be yours for the asking. Issuers make money from the merchants as well as customers. If you charge several thousand dollars a year, the issuers don't want to lose you. If you pay in full each month, ask that the annual fee be waived. If you carry a balance and pay on time, call and request a lower interest rate. A reduction of at least two percentage points a year is reasonable to expect.

• **Turn down offers for higher credit limits.** Many issuers offer an initial waiver of fees or low interest rates as incentives. But by saying "yes" to too many offers, you will raise your outstanding credit limit. This can count against you on a credit report. That's because some lenders look not only at debt but also at available credit.

• **Do not change accounts frequently.** That looks bad on your report. But if you find a card with more favorable terms than you have now—cancel your present card and switch.

All about the Virtues of Being Open . . . Very Open

Sam Keen, Ph.D.

True intimacy is the key to personal, emotional, and physical health and interpersonal fulfillment.

True intimacy is achieved when two people travel beyond conventional romance and explore each other's emotions, experiencing the deepest level of trust, openness, and sharing. They feel a flame in their spirits, a celebration of self and each other, a movement toward wholeness, and a lust for life.

Genetic predisposition and cultural norms do play a role in how close we allow ourselves to get to others. It starts at the beginning of life, in the bond that unites mother and child, and serves as a model of giving and receiving care.

Everyone can experience true intimacy—if they're able to overcome the barriers that prevent them from freely expressing themselves.

THE BASICS OF INTIMACY

True intimacy is a two-way street. It requires that two people be able to express the following:

• **Trust.** You must be able to rely on the other person to live up to his/her word so you can be open without the fear of being betrayed.

Sam Keen, Ph.D., author and philosopher who practices in northern California. Keen is the author of several books, including the bestselling *Fire in the Belly* and *Inward Bound: Exploring the Geography of Your Emotions.* Bantam Books.

MENOPAUSE

■ **Japanese women** have fewer hot flashes and other menopausal symptoms than American women. *Possible reason:* They eat about two ounces a day of foods made from soybeans, such as tofu (bean curd) and miso (soybean paste). Soybeans are rich in isoflavinoids, which are converted during digestion to estrogen-like substances that can help prevent hot flashes.

Barry Goldin, Ph.D., and Sherwood Gorbach, M.D., Tufts University School of Medicine and Herman Adlercreutz, M.D., Helsinki University, Finland.

■ **Hot flashes** and other symptoms of menopause may be minimized by eating a diet rich in soybeans. Eating a soy-rich diet may also reduce the risk of breast cancer. Soy and other legumes (beans, yams, etc.) contain *phytoestrogens,* compounds that may mimic estrogens in older women and act as a natural estrogen-replacement therapy for menopausal symptoms. Phytoestrogens may also lower younger women's risk of breast cancer.

Barry R. Goldin, Ph.D., associate professor of community health, Tufts University School of Medicine, Boston, MA.

■ **For menopausal women,** "combined hormone therapy"—estrogen taken together with progestin—has several advantages. *Important:* It significantly reduces premature heart disease by dramatically lowering cholesterol levels. Combined therapy reduces LDL (bad) cholesterol by 30%. At the same time, hard-to-raise "good" cholesterol (HDL) goes up by 19%. *Helpful:* The important but less well-known risk factor Lipoprotein-a is reduced by as much as 50%.

MENOPAUSE

Overall cholesterol levels are reduced by 15%.

Joel Morrisett, Ph.D., professor of medicine and biochemistry, Baylor College of Medicine, Houston, TX.

PREGNANCY

■ **Early amniocentesis:** Miscarriage among women having amniocentesis as early as 12 weeks after conception—rather than the usual 16 to 18 weeks—is no more likely than miscarriage among women with normal pregnancies who have the procedure at the standard time.

From a study of more than 900 women who had early amniocentesis, led by Frederick Hanson, M.D., former director, prenatal diagnosis program, University of California, Davis, CA.

■ **Tubal pregnancies** caught early can now be ended without surgery—via injection of *methotrexate,* a drug commonly used to treat cancer. In a recent study, methotrexate successfully terminated 113 of 120 early-stage tubal pregnancies. Tubal pregnancy—in which an embryo develops in the fallopian tube instead of the uterus—can make the tube burst, causing life-threatening internal bleeding.

Thomas G. Stovall, M.D., associate professor of gynecology, Bowman Gray School of Medicine, Wake Forest University, Winston-Salem, NC.

■ **Menstrual cycles and fertility:** Menstrual irregularities could signal an ovulation disorder that makes it difficult, or impossible, to conceive. *At risk:* Women who began menstruating late . . . took a long time to begin having regular cycles . . . had irregular cycles as teenagers . . . or have cycle lengths longer than 31 days. *Helpful:* Women with

• **Empathy.** This requires putting yourself in someone else's shoes, to know and anticipate what the other person is feeling.

• **Enthusiasm and courage.** Both are needed to shatter illusions, strip defenses, break through stereotypes, confront fears, and explore emotional boundaries together until our insides "touch."

• **Sharing each other's worlds.** You must be able to maintain a solid sense of self. While you are fully engaged with the other person, you do not give up your separate life.

SEX AND INTIMACY

The spiritual connectedness and awakenings triggered by true intimacy can be achieved in a relationship without sex—between friends and family members. But sex within an intimate relationship can unite mind, spirit, and body to an explosive energy release. When no limits are placed on the physical interactions, touch and nonverbal communication can express deep levels of pleasure and intimacy.

The goal is to be with someone who expresses an equal interest and commitment to the journey toward true intimacy. Most people, however, are not so fortunate. Types of people who fight true intimacy . . .

• **The macho but insecure man** who tells a woman he loves her in order to seduce her into a sexual relationship.

• **The workaholic** who says he/she wants to be in love but constantly breaks dates to work.

• **The martyr** who appears to fall madly in love but constantly with "the wrong people." People who profess they want but cannot find anyone capable of true intimacy have an intimacy problem themselves.

• **The avoiders**, or those who engage in transitory relationships or make superficial commitments. They do not seek or encourage strong emotional ties. These include loners, control freaks, abusers, misanthropes, self-absorbed narcissists, and romanticists endlessly seeking the perfect romance.

• **Intimacy junkies**, who are so concerned about being emotionally close to others that it interferes with their ability to accomplish responsibilities.

When deprived of the "rush" of such closeness, they get depressed and are further unable to function.

This problem can lead to an endless cycle of starting and ending relationships, an inability to make commitments, chronic infidelity, and destructively inappropriate choices of partners.

FEARS . . . AND REALITIES

The goal to achieving true intimacy is to acknowledge your fears . . . and analyze your misperceptions. See your fears as repressed excitement, and mobilize this energy to be intimate. Make an effort to get over the most common fears . . .

- **Fear of being judged.**
- **Fear of abandonment, rejection, or loss.**
- **Fear of conflict.**
- **Fear of being hurt.**

At the same time, you must also move beyond the common misperceptions about intimacy . . .

- *Misperception:* **A long-term relationship with true intimacy gets boring.** *Truth:* It is quite the opposite. There is no limit to learning about oneself and each other. Face guilt, shame, laziness, and other feelings underlying boredom. Keep digging deeper into each other's archeology of self. See boredom as an opportunity into which risk, engagement, action, and communion can enter.

- *Misperception:* **Intimacy is a loss of freedom.** *Truth:* Fear of intimacy is a prison of the self where no one can touch you. More intense intimacy frees you to discover yourself.

- *Misperception:* **People who resist intimacy are tough.** *Truth:* These people are missing joy and deep down can be very lonely, disengaged, and alienated.

OVERCOMING THE HURDLES

- **Explore and self-analyze your feelings.** The deeper you know and feel for yourself, the deeper you are able to enter the lives of others. Understand the past that defines present patterns of intimacy.

Example: The woman who witnessed her father's constant betrayal of her mother grows up mistrusting all men.

PREGNANCY AND FERTILITY

these histories should seek medical care if unable to conceive after trying for six months.

From a preliminary study of data provided by more than 116,000 registered nurses, aged 25 to 42, led by Marlene Goldman, Sc.D., assistant professor in epidemiology, Harvard School of Public Health.

WOMEN'S CONFIDENTIAL

■ **Hidden danger for women:** Bacterial vaginosis (BV), which affects up to one in four women, raises a woman's risk for pelvic inflammatory disease and infertility. *Problem:* BV is frequently misdiagnosed as yeast infection—and the two conditions require different treatments. *BV symptoms:* A foul or "fishy" vaginal odor and a milky discharge that can stain undergarments. Your doctor can administer a vaginal pH test and a microscopic examination for "clue" cells.

From James McGregor, M.D., professor of obstetrics and gynecology at the University of Colorado.

■ **Between-period spotting** is not normal—even after strenuous exercise—and should be discussed with a gynecologist. Spotting could signal polyps, fibroids, infections, inflammations, hormonal problems or cancer. *Helpful:* Use a calendar to record every episode of spotting. This will help determine whether you are spotting at certain times during each of your menstrual cycles.

Mona Shangold, M.D., professor of obstetrics and gynecology at Hahnemann University, Philadelphia, PA, and coauthor of *The Complete Sports Medicine Book for Women.* Simon & Schuster.

■ **Frequently misdiagnosed:** *Vaginal infections.* Most women being treated for chronic yeast infections—either by their internists or by themselves with over-the-counter preparations—actually have a different condition. *Other causes of symptoms:* Bacterial vaginosis or herpes infections, which require different treatments than that for yeast infections. *Caution:* Never diagnose yourself. Over-the-counter treatments could make your symptoms worse. If you think you have a vaginal infection, ask your doctor to perform a complete physical examination and comprehensive medical history.

Karen Carroll, M.D., departments of pathology and infectious diseases and Paul Summers, M.D., department of obstetrics and gynecology, both at the University of Utah Medical Center in Salt Lake City, UT.

BABIES

■ **Breastfeeding** protects infants against certain chronic diseases, including adult-onset diabetes and some cancers. *Finding:* Breastfed babies are not only less vulnerable to *immediate* illness but are also less illness-prone throughout life. *Troubling:* Breastfeeding peaked in popularity in 1981 and has since steadily declined. Women say they're not sure it really makes a difference to their babies' health. It does.

Mary Frances Picciano, Ph.D., professor of nutrition, College of Health and Human Development, Pennsylvania State University, University Park, PA.

■ **C-sections** accounted for 23.5 of every 100 births in 1991 (the most recent year for which data are available). About 35% were repeat procedures, a rate relatively unchanged since 1985. Caesarian rates were significantly higher in the South (27.6%) than in the North-

• **Be open and honest.** Disappointment over past relationships and other issues cause you to close up emotionally.

Example: A 40-year-old man in danger of losing his job and being unable to send his child to college becomes fearful of sharing his concerns with his wife, so he shuts her out.

• **Develop self-esteem and independence.** In order to feel confident about sharing oneself, and prevent being either suffocating or suffocated in a relationship, one must develop a secure sense of self. Repeat affirmations and focus on successes.

• **Unfreeze your emotions.** The deeper you feel, the more you can enter another's life.

Exercise: Imagine lying on a rug before a fire with your partner. He/she whispers "I love you" in your ear. Feel the tenderness flowing.

• **Recover your "personal mythology."** Identify the negative stereotypes that you grew up with . . . and recognize the truth about who you are and what relationships and life are all about. Identify these stories so that you can recognize the difference between living a lie and experiencing a more honest and fulfilling relationship.

LIMITS TO INTIMACY

It's important to remember that in real life, the perfect balance needed for true intimacy is difficult to achieve—or sustain. Each person can be rocked anywhere along the way by insecurities, illness, distractions, stress, etc. In addition, people can naturally have different goals, careers, or levels of sophistication, maturity, or commitment. Frequently, there is discouragement or depression over these barriers to true intimacy.

Solution: Appreciate and adjust to differences as best as possible, but expect fluctuations in intimacy levels. Work toward the greatest potential of sharing, but allow for supplemental relationships with friends.

Impotence: What to Do Before You See the Doctor

Steven Morganstern, M.D.

Achieving an erection is nothing less than a feat of hydraulic engineering. Sexual arousal dilates blood vessels in the penis. The hydraulic fluid (blood) flows in, causing the penis to become engorged.

Anything that disrupts the flow of blood interferes with the process.

Result: Impotence. It's a problem that affects 30 million American men—one in five.

CAUSES OF IMPOTENCE

Until recently, impotence was considered primarily a *psychological* problem. Over the last two decades, however, we've learned that psychological factors—including, paradoxically, the fear of being unable to perform sexually—account for less than 25% of all cases of impotence. *Far more common is impotence caused by physical problems, including . . .*

• **Arteriosclerosis.** The same sorts of fatty deposits that build up in the coronary arteries build up in the arteries supplying blood to the penis. Instead of a heart attack, however, the result is impotence.

• **Smoking.** Toxins in smoke damage blood vessels in the penis, preventing the free flow of blood needed to produce an erection. Some have overcome impotence by giving up tobacco.

• **Prostate trouble.** Some cases of impotence are associated with an enlarged, inflamed, or infected prostate. *Symptoms:* Frequent urination, especially at night . . . burning or pain during urina-

Steven Morganstern, M.D., director of the Morganstern Urology Clinic, Atlanta, GA. He is coauthor of *Overcoming Impotence.* Prentice Hall.

BABIES

east (22.6%), Midwest (21.8%) or West (19.8%). *Encouraging:* In 1991, 24% of women who previously had a C-section gave birth vaginally—up from 20% in 1990 and 13% in 1989.

Morbidity and Mortality Weekly Report, Centers for Disease Control and Prevention, 1600 Clifton Rd. NE, Atlanta, GA 30333. Weekly. $79/yr.

■ **Can smoking during pregnancy hurt the baby?**

Yes. Data from almost 260,000 births show that besides low birth weight, babies born to smokers face a higher risk of premature birth . . . and have higher death rates, compared to other infants.

Allen Wilcox, M.D., Ph.D., chief, epidemiology branch, National Institute of Environmental Health Sciences, Bethesda, MD.

■ **Electric shock** can injure or kill a developing fetus—even if it has no apparent effect on the pregnant woman. *Reason:* Amniotic fluid surrounding the fetus is an excellent conductor of electricity. *Self-defense:* Pregnant women should be careful to avoid possible sources of shock. If a shock is sustained, seek immediate medical attention.

Robert L. Norris, M.D., assistant professor of surgery and emergency medicine, Stanford University Medical School, Palo Alto, CA.

CONFIDENTIAL FOR MEN

■ **Exercise versus prostate cancer:**
Physical activity may lower the risk of
developing this disease. Men who reported expending more than 4,000 kilocalories* a week through exercise had a
lower risk than those using up fewer
than 1,000 kilocalories.** *Possible explanation:* Increased physical activity
may lower testosterone levels—and
testosterone is thought to be involved
in the development of prostate cancer.

From a study of more than 17,000 Harvard
alumni, led by I-Min Lee, M.D., Sc.D., department of
epidemiology, Harvard University School of Public
Health, Boston, MA.

*The equivalent of jogging eight hours or walk-
ing 40 miles per week.
**The equivalent of jogging two hours or walk-
ing 10 miles per week.

■ **Prostate cancer kills** about 34,000
American men each year. *Risk factors:*
Aging—prostate cancer risk increases
faster with age than that for any other
major cancer . . . family history of the
disease . . . high-fat, low-fiber diets.
Helpful: All men older than 40—especially those with a family history of the
disease—should have yearly rectal examinations . . . and should increase consumption of high-fiber, low-fat foods
such as beans, lentils, peas, tomatoes,
and dried fruits.

Kenneth J. Pienta, M.D., assistant professor of
medicine, Wayne State University, Detroit, MI.

■ **Bicycle seats** can cause numbness,
temporary impotence, or even a painful
permanent erection (priapism) in men
who ride often or for long distances.
Reason: The traditional narrow, one-
piece design puts too much pressure on
the internal erectile chambers of the
penis. *Self-defense:* Pedal as smoothly as
possible to avoid bouncing . . . or fit

tion or ejaculation. If you experience any of these
symptoms, get a prostate exam.

• **Drug use.** Many cases of impotence are
caused by drug or alcohol abuse. Drinking can trigger impotence by raising blood levels of the hormone estrogen (produced by men as well as women)
and lowering testosterone levels. Testosterone levels
can also be lowered by marijuana. Cocaine, heroin,
and other illicit drugs can cause nerve damage.

Impotence can also be a side effect of tranquilizers, antidepressants, anti-anxiety drugs and diuretics
("water" pills) used to treat high blood pressure.

• **Nerve damage.** Getting an erection is
difficult or impossible without healthy nerves leading to and from the penis. These nerves can be damaged during surgery on the prostate, bladder,
rectum, or even on the aorta, the large artery leading
from the heart. The nerves can also be damaged by
injury.

• **Diabetes and kidney disease.** Roughly
half of all diabetic men become impotent within ten
years of the onset of the disease. Uncontrolled diabetes limits blood flow and causes nerve damage.

Hormonal disturbances caused by kidney disease
can lead to high blood pressure, which necessitates
use of medication that can cause impotence.

• **Obesity.** Being overweight is associated
with diabetes, hypertension, and high cholesterol—
all of which are factors in impotence.

SOLVING THE PROBLEM

Once you've considered the possible cause of
your problem, you can take steps on the road back to
full enjoyment of sex.

Here are some simple things you can do to determine what might be causing your impotence. Take
your findings to the doctor and you'll speed up the
return of your sex life.

• **Make sure you really are impotent.** If
you have trouble achieving or maintaining an erection less than 30% of the time, you're probably not
impotent. Occasional failure is perfectly normal.
More frequent problems, however, suggest that it's
time to check further.

• **Review your sexual history.** Jot down the specifics of your sex life during the past several months—when, where, and how often you had sex . . . how often you were impotent . . . what you had to eat and drink beforehand, etc. If you find a pattern to your impotence, you may be able to find a way to break it.

• **Keep a sex log.** Write down all the specifics of your *current* sex life. Such a log can help you pinpoint possible causes of impotence . . . and it can also be a big help to your doctor.

Caution: Some men find that keeping a written log makes them anxious—which, in turn, can make it even harder to get an erection. If this is the case, try making mental notes and reviewing them with a physician.

• **Test your "apparatus."** If you're impotent during sex but can achieve a full erection while masturbating, you're probably okay physically. Odds are it's a psychological problem.

If you cannot achieve a full erection during sex or while masturbating, try the "postage stamp" test. This is a crude but effective version of a common laboratory method.

Procedure: Before going to sleep, encircle your soft penis with a ring of postage stamps. Moisten one of the stamps on the end, then press it against the stamp on the other end until the ring is secure. It should be snug, but not tight.

During a normal night's sleep, you should have three to five erections. If any of the perforations is torn when you awaken, you've probably had at least one erection. Your impotence is probably psychological in origin. If the stamps are intact, your impotence probably stems from a physical cause.

• **Examine your relationship.** Be honest. Are you and your partner having problems? Have you stopped communicating? Are you depressed? Is your partner? Have you developed a bad case of "performance anxiety?"

If you answer "yes" to any of these questions, your impotence may stem from a psychological cause. In some cases, though, psychological problems are the *result* of an impotence problem—caused by a physical problem.

CONFIDENTIAL FOR MEN

your bike with a newer split seat that has one side to support the right buttock and another to support the left. Stationary exercise bicycles do not seem to pose a threat.

E. Douglas Whitehead, M.D, director, Association for Male Sexual Dysfunction, 520 E. 72 St., New York, NY 10021.

■ **PSA predictor:** *Bone scans for prostate cancer* are costly—about $650 each scan—and often unnecessary. *Better:* Blood tests for prostate-specific antigen (PSA) levels, which accurately predict bone scan findings in 40% of men with newly diagnosed prostate cancer. For these men, the more expensive bone scan can be eliminated . . .

From a research study of 2,064 men with prostate cancer led by Joseph Oesterling, M.D., Chairman of Urology and Director of the Michigan Prostate Institute at the University of Michigan, Ann Arbor, MI.

■ **Enlarged breasts in men.** The anti-ulcer drug *cimetidine* (Tagamet) can cause men to develop a benign but potentially embarrassing form of breast enlargement called gynecomastia. Other ulcer drugs, including *misoprostol* (Cytotec), *omeprazole* (Prilosec) and *ranitidine* (Zantac) do not seem to cause the problem. *Self-defense:* Any man who develops gynecomastia while taking cimetidine should notify his doctor.

■ **Men can get breast cancer**—although the disease is far more common in women. About one out of nine women develop breast cancer, compared with about one out of 1,000 men. *At highest risk:* Men who have male or female blood relatives with the disease.

A study led by Karin Rosenblatt, University of Washington School of Public Health and Community Medicine, Seattle, WA.

CONFIDENTIAL FOR MEN

■ **Exercises for sexual dysfunction in men:** Practicing pelvic muscle exercises (known as Kegel exercises) three to five times daily for 10–15 minutes may relieve premature ejaculation. The man needs to recognize his point of ejaculation inevitability. Prior to that point, he can delay ejaculation and orgasm and prolong the duration of his erection by performing the Kegel exercise.

E. Douglas Whitehead, M.D., F.A.C.S., urologist, director of the Association for Male Sexual Dysfunction in New York, 520 E. 72 St., New York, NY 10021.

■ **X-rated videos** help men with fertility problems produce better sperm for use in artificial insemination. In a recent study, those who masturbated while watching the videos produced semen with more than double the sperm counts—and with higher proportions of healthy sperm.
Theory: Sperm quality and fertilizing potential improve with increased sexual excitement.

Nikolaos Sofikitis, M.D., Ph.D., assistant lecturer in urology, Tottori University School of Medicine, Yonago, Japan.

■ **Impotence is caused in 10% to 15%** of all cases by injury during intercourse. Weight-induced pressure or abnormal bending of the erection can cause chronic impotence by damaging the lining of the erection chamber. The most common situation in which such injuries occur is when the female is on top.

Research led by Irwin Goldstein, M.D., Boston University Medical Center.

■ **Did you know that 82% of men with penile implants** are pleased with the devices? Each year, about 20,000 American men get penile implants.

Irwin Goldstein, M.D., professor of urology, Boston University School of Medicine. His survey of

The best way to deal with psychological impotence is to discuss the problem as candidly as possible with your partner, doctor—and possibly a psychotherapist. If talking about the problem fails to help, ask your doctor about self-injecting your penis with *papaverine* or *prostaglandin E,* prior to sex. In some cases—roughly 10%—the answer may lie in a surgically implanted prosthesis.

• **Take a "drug inventory."** Consider all the drugs you're taking. If you suspect that one might be causing your impotence, ask your doctor about alternatives. Another drug might be just as effective without causing impotence . . . or there might be a drug-free option.

Caution: Do not stop taking any prescription medication without first consulting your doctor.

Finally—relax. Your problem is probably not as hard to solve as you might think. In some cases, simply learning to adopt a more relaxed approach to life and sex is all it takes. Or take a relaxing vacation with your partner.

Enjoy the pleasures of intimacy. It's one thing to become a workaholic and throw oneself fully into a job. But to enjoy the pleasure of a loved one's company or the physical caring of sexuality is a very different thing.

If your problem persists, see a urologist who specializes in the treatment of impotence. The information you've already uncovered will speed the return of a fulfilling sex life.

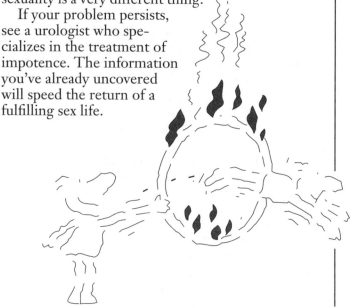

Lessons in Love . . . and Marriage

Helen E. Fisher, Ph.D.

The nature of love is one of the great mysteries of life. But after 10 years of researching what anthropologists know about the way men and women fall in and out of love in societies around the world, I am beginning to understand some of the many facets of love and marriage in America today.

STAGES OF LOVE

When a couple first falls in love during a courtship phase that establishes their mutual interest, they show the classic signs of infatuation . . . euphoria when together and constant thoughts about each other when apart.

But infatuation usually lasts no more than two or three years between adult lovers who see each other regularly. At that point, passion often gives way to attachment . . . a comfortable, secure feeling. That attachment is strong enough to keep many couples—half of all Americans, for example—married to each other for life.

But—for many married couples, attachment leads to boredom . . . and boredom leads to straying or divorce.

This same pattern occurs all over the world, with divorce occurring most often about four years after marriage. This "four-year itch" seems to be a part of human nature. We can explain it with the basic principles of biology.

HUMAN NATURE VS. MONOGAMY

A basic drive of every living creature is to perpetuate itself . . . and humans are no exception. The most successful mating strategies of our long-for-

Helen E. Fisher, Ph.D., research associate in the department of anthropology at the American Museum of Natural History in New York. Dr. Fisher has received the Distinguished Service Award of the American Anthropological Association and is the author of *Anatomy of Love: The Natural History of Monogamy, Adultery and Divorce.* W. W. Norton and Co.

CONFIDENTIAL FOR MEN

96 penile implant recipients was published in the *Journal of Urology,* 1120 N. Charles St., Baltimore, MD 21202. Monthly. $210/yr.

SELF-DEFENSE

The Questions to Ask . . . when choosing a gynecologist

Charles Inlander

A good gynecologist should be able to give preventive care and act as a woman's primary care physician. *Questions to ask when choosing a gynecologist:*

• **Are you board-certified in obstetrics and gynecology? When were you certified or recertified?** American Board of Medical Specialties certification is not a guarantee of competence or ethicality, but it can help a woman feel more confident in her choice.

• **When and where did you train, and how long have you been in practice?** Some physicians prefer other doctors to have at least five years of practice before they will refer patients to him/her.

• **What are your policies regarding billing, insurance, Medicare assignment? Will you negotiate fees?**

• **How long does it usually take to get an appointment?**

• **What percentage of your patients have hysterectomies?** Gynecology is a surgical specialty. It is not unusual for surgeons to be biased toward surgery as a treatment of choice. But if your interest is in preventing unnecessary surgery, you will want to find a doctor who will work with you.

Ask Yourself

• **Are you fully comfortable with your present doctor?** You wouldn't think twice about changing your auto mechanic if you weren't satisfied. Your comfort and security should be of utmost concern.

• **Am I more comfortable with a man or a woman? A younger or older physician? A more authoritarian or a more interactive practitioner?** Gynecologic care is a true partnership between patient and physician, because so much self-care is involved.

Charles B. Inlander, president of the People's Medical Society and coauthor, with Gale Maleskey, of Take This Book to the Gynecologist with You, *Addison-Wesley Publishing Co., Jacob Way, Reading, MA 01867. $9.95.*

■ **The best screening technique** for colon cancer is actually underused. *Barium enemas* are the most effective, most economical, and least risky method of detecting early colon cancer. But many doctors now rely on less efficient techniques—blood-in-stool testing . . . and colonoscopy and sigmoidoscopy, two forms of testing in which a telescope-like viewing instrument is inserted into the rectum. *Better:* Ask your doctor about

gotten ancestors are in the genes of every person alive today.

These biological drives urge men and women to pair off and stay together for three or four years . . . just long enough for them to cooperate in raising their infants until these children begin to join play groups and no longer need constant care.

Then these biological drives encourage both men and women to seek new partners with qualities that their first mates lack. That way of life probably suited an ancient hunter-gatherer society, but it conflicts with modern values.

Lesson: If you want to stay married, try to understand your needs and desires. They may cause destructive feelings that you have to anticipate and redirect.

HIDDEN BIOLOGICAL FORCES

• **Chemical basis of love.** Scientists have found that when a person falls in love, his/her brain produces large amounts of a natural amphetamine called *phenylethylamine*—or PEA—which causes the euphoric "high" of infatuation.

The brain eventually reacts to this overstimulation by producing *endorphins*—morphine-like drugs that produce the quiet, satisfied feeling of attachment. Sometimes, years later, the brain primes itself for a new round of excitement, spelling potential trouble for the relationship.

Lesson: If you want a long-term marriage, be prepared to provide the stimulation your partner needs . . . and work on avoiding your own "burnout" by appreciating what he/she is giving you.

• **Male-female differences.** Despite feminist rhetoric, men and women seem designed to play different roles and view the world in different ways. Men's genetic makeup—reflected in their hormones—prepares them to be strong protectors, while women excel as nurturers. Men are hunters by nature and often prefer to work side by side, with less verbal interaction. Women are mothers by nature and often like face-to-face contact, with more talk.

Lesson: To stay together, men and women must acknowledge their differences and appreciate the value of these differences. For example, men should try to talk more intimately and directly to their wives, while women should try more side-by-side activities with their husbands . . . leisurely drives, fishing, skating.

SOCIAL FACTORS THAT LEAD TO DIVORCE

• **Economic equality.** When men and women both work and are relatively economically independent, partners feel free to cut marital bonds.

• **Nomadism.** I use this term to describe people who have left their birthplaces and families and all the networking that often keeps spouses together. These people face fewer barriers to divorce. If they live apart, in a commuter marriage, divorce is even more likely.

• **Urbanism.** Away from the intimacies and social pressures of a small town, it's easier for couples to split up.

• **Secularism.** With less belief in religious objections to divorce, it becomes more prevalent.

SOLID FACTORS THAT DISCOURAGE DIVORCE

• **Age.** As couples age, they are less inclined to divorce. And if they are older when they marry, they are also more likely to stay married.

• **Children.** Childless couples divorce most frequently, and the rate decreases as the number of children increase—with three children, the rate drops to 7% . . . and then gets even lower.

HOW TO IMPROVE YOUR MARRIAGE

Armed with this knowledge of how biology, psychology, and society affect marriage, you can take some concrete steps to improve yours.

• **Avoid boredom.** Wives should try to stay as attractive as possible to their husbands . . . husbands should listen carefully and talk often with their wives.

• **Don't drive your partner away with threats of divorce** . . . and say no to adultery.

• **Increase commitment by responding to each other's interests.** That includes work and play . . . a shared sense of humor can be a great incentive to stay together through life's challenges.

combined barium enema-sigmoidoscopy testing every five years.

Joseph Ferrucci, M.D., professor and chairman, department of radiology, Boston University School of Medicine, and vice president, American College of Radiology, Reston, VA.

■ **Does smoking promote colon cancer?**

Yes. In a recent study of 51,529 men and 118,334 women, men who by age 30 had smoked one and a half packs of cigarettes a day for 10 years were *twice* as likely to develop colorectal cancer as nonsmoking men. Women age 30 who smoked a pack a day for 10 years had one and a half times the risk. *Theory:* Tobacco carcinogens reach the large bowel through the bloodstream or digestive tract.

Edward Giovannucci, M.D., instructor of medicine, Harvard Medical School, Boston, MA.

■ **Old condoms** rupture far more frequently than new ones. *Study:* 262 couples were asked to test about 5,000 condoms over a four-month period. *Result:* Less than 5% of brand-new condoms ruptured during intercourse. But condoms a year or two old broke about 10% of the time . . . and seven-year-old condoms broke about 19% of the time.

Research by Markus Steiner, B.A., contraceptive use and epidemiology division, Family Health International, Research Triangle Park, NC.

MANAGING YOUR 401(K)

■ **Better 401(k) investing.** It pays to know your options for investing your 401(k). Most company plans offer three to five choices. *Examples:* Company stock, equity mutual funds, money-market funds, and/or guaranteed investment contracts issued by insurance companies. *Helpful:* Request a prospectus from each company that manages one of these investment options and read it very carefully—with your accountant, if necessary. Contact your employer's retirement-plan manager for the name and address of each of these companies.

Legg Mason, president, Legg Mason Wood Walker, Inc., investment advisers and stockbrokers, 99 Summer St., Box 1, Boston, MA 02101.

■ **Pros and cons of borrowing against your retirement savings:** If you participate in an employer's 401(k) plan, you may be able to borrow half of your account value—up to $50,000—without incurring taxes. Borrowing is easy—nobody checks your creditworthiness and you pay interest on the loan to yourself. *Drawbacks:* You may end up with less money at retirement because the interest you pay yourself may be less than the earnings had you left the money in the account—and because you may be tempted to make loan repayments with amounts that you would otherwise use to make deductible plan contributions . . . if you leave the employer, you may have to repay the whole loan at once . . . and if you can't repay the loan, it will become a taxable distribution to you.

Neal J. Solomon, CFP, Solomon Associates, financial planners, 15 First Ave., Gloversville, NY 12078.

The Most Common Retirement Traps

Martin M. Shenkman

Because Americans are living longer—and are more active than ever before—much more planning is required these days to achieve a comfortable level of financial security in your retirement years. *The most common traps retirees should avoid . . .*

• *Trap:* **Relying solely on income-oriented assets.** A major error made by many retirees is sticking with only low-risk investments, such as municipal or Treasury bonds, bank certificates of deposit, and similar low-yield investments. However, this apparently conservative strategy is far riskier than you might imagine when you factor in the effects of inflation.

It makes more sense to diversify your assets and consider including some equities, mutual funds, mortgage-backed securities, or international holdings in your portfolio. Over and over again, studies have shown that the key to reducing risk over the long run is diversification. Your goal should be for your money to outlive you, rather than you outliving your money.

• *Trap:* **Investing a lump sum all at once.** A typical pattern at retirement is that you receive a big gain on the sale of a house or business, a large

Martin M. Shenkman, an estate attorney practicing in New York City and Teaneck, NJ. He is author of The Complete Book of Trusts. John Wiley & Sons, Inc.

lump-sum pension or insurance distribution, or other windfall. All too frequently, this money is invested immediately and with little diversification.

You would probably do better financially—and certainly sleep better—by carefully considering your options. Structure an investment ladder of different types, maturities, and issuers. Invest, say, 20% of your lump sum every three months or so. Your income-oriented investments should be spread out so they mature in different years. This way, you're "dollar-cost averaging."

By creating such flexibility, you can determine the best alternatives as each investment matures.

• *Trap:* **Engaging in investment clutter.** Most of my clients of retirement age have entirely too many different investments. Holding 40 or more separate stocks or bonds in your safe-deposit box can be extremely dangerous, since it is likely to become harder and harder to keep track of them—and certainly difficult to manage them well—with each passing year.

Ask yourself: If you were the person named as the agent under a durable power of attorney to take care of a person's finances when he/she was disabled, would you have the time and patience to deal with all of those securities?

If the answer is no, consolidate your holdings to a number you can manage. And think about placing your portfolio in an asset-management account at a brokerage firm, so that both safekeeping and record-keeping will be handled professionally, and you will get a single monthly statement.

• *Trap:* **Falling prey to a "snake oil" salesperson.** As soon as you retire, shady salespeople peddling investment, insurance, and real-estate products target you.

When a person with experience meets a person with money, the one with experience gets the money and the one with money gets the experience.

Most important: Retain your common sense and probe beneath the surface when so-called "one-time-only" deals are offered to you. What are said to be money-making investments might seem different if you insist on reading the prospectus or talking to

... AND YOUR IRA

■ **It pays to be an IRA early bird.** The earlier in the year you make your IRA contribution, the better. It gives you a head start on tax-deferred growth. Consider two savers, one who makes his IRA deposits as early as possible (January 1) and the other who waits until the last minute (April 15 of the following year). Assume each IRA earns at a pace of 10% a year. After 20 years, each will have contributed $40,000. But the early bird's IRA will be up over $125,000 while the procrastinator's will be about $110,000.

Daniel Kehrer is a Los Angeles–based business and finance writer and an executive with the publisher, Group IV Communications. He is the author of *Kiplinger's 12 Steps to a Worry-Free Retirement.* Kiplinger Books.

■ **Make IRA withdrawals** in years when your taxes are likely to be low, so the funds will be taxed at a lower rate. You may withdraw money at any time after the age of 59½. *If you don't need the money:* Keep your IRA intact until April 1 following the year you turn 70½. At that point you must begin withdrawals or face a stiff tax penalty.

Finances After 50: Financial Planning for the Rest of Your Life by United Seniors Health Cooperative, Washington, DC. HarperPerennial, 10 E. 53 St., New York, NY 10022. $13.

■ **Retirement fund withdrawal basics.** Most people incorrectly believe that they have to begin withdrawing from their retirement savings at age 70½. *Reality:* You're not legally required to make your first withdrawal until April 1 of the year *after* you reach 70½. Depending on your birth date, this may mean you can delay until you're almost 72. However, if you wait until April 1 of the year after you reach 70½, you must take the second distribution by December 31 of that same year.

Stephen Pennacchio, partner, KPMG Peat Marwick, 345 Park Ave., New York, NY 10154.

PENSION SELF-DEFENSE

Pension Knowledge

How can I tell if my pension is in trouble? Ask your pension-plan administrator—often in the employee-benefits office—for a copy of your plan's annual report (Form 5500) or an abbreviated version—the Summary Annual Report.

To see if your future benefits are fully funded, look for any "unfunded-benefit liability." If there is a dollar figure shown, your pension plan is not fully funded. Next, look for the plan's "funding ratio," which is expressed as a percentage of a plan's assets to a plan's liabilities. Any ratio below 100% means the plan is not fully funded. The lower the percentage, the more seriously underfunded the plan is.

What should I do if my plan is underfunded? First of all, don't panic. It may be a temporary blip, caused by falling interest rates coupled with increases in pension benefits. Second, let your employer (and your union, if it is a collectively bargained retirement plan) know that you are concerned that its promises of income in the future may not be kept.

Your company may respond that if it is forced to make larger contributions in order to fully fund its pension plan, it

former clients. There is no such thing as a free lunch.

• *Trap:* **Neglecting proper insurance coverage.** People who have given a lot of attention to accumulating a considerable estate during their working years—and have been diligent in purchasing sufficient life insurance for their heirs—can lose everything after retiring due to inadequate property and casualty insurance.

Yet a simple solution exists . . . buying an umbrella liability policy to supplement your homeowners and automobile insurance coverage.

Misconception: Long-term-care insurance to pay for nursing homes and home health services is an unnecessary luxury.

Since two out of every five people over age 65 will at some point enter a nursing home, and Medicare or Medicaid will not pay for everything, your long-term-care cost could be enormous if you are not properly insured.

Good policies, especially those with inflation riders, will ease the financial problem while you cope with the medical and emotional problems of long-term care.

• *Trap:* **Thinking that estate planning is no more than a will.** It's not unusual for recent retirees to ask me to draw up a will or review a will that was written years ago.

But when I tell them that even well-drawn wills do not address some of their critical estate, financial, and personal planning needs, more often than not they are quite surprised.

A will does not take effect until death . . . and does absolutely nothing to protect you and your family while you are alive.

At the very least, two other documents should be prepared even before you retire. One is a durable power of attorney, which provides for the management of assets in the event of temporary or permanent disability. The other is a living will or health-care proxy, which provides for health-care and medical decision-making when you are unable to do so.

A revocable living trust can also be an extremely effective tool. But while it can minimize many problems, it does not avoid them completely. This is why other documents and planning are necessary.

Whichever of these documents are right for you—and it may very well be all of them—don't procrastinate in gathering the essential material and consulting an adviser for implementation.

Answers to the Most-Asked Questions about Money and Retirement

Jonathan Pond

It's not easy building a strong, well-rounded retirement portfolio, given today's high stock prices and low bond yields. Each step of your planning raises questions about how and when to invest.

Here are answers to ten of the questions that retirees—and those saving for retirement—are asking most often today:

• *What's the best overall allocation of assets for a retirement portfolio—stocks vs. bonds vs. cash?* My rule of thumb is that your age equals the percentage of your portfolio you should be putting in bonds. Reasonably affluent people planning for retirement should have half to 60% of their assets in stocks, the rest in bonds. Whatever the split is, I recommend you further break down your retirement portfolio this way:

• *Stocks or stock mutual funds:*
• 30% income
• 20% growth
• 20% small cap
• 30% international.

Jonathan Pond, author of *The New Century Family Money Book* (Dell). He is president of Financial Planning Information, Inc., 9 Galen St., Watertown, MA 02172.

PENSION SELF-DEFENSE

may also be forced to resort to lay-offs . . . and your job may be among those eliminated. You might have to make a trade-off between having a job today or a pension tomorrow. So, you might also want to start looking for a job with another employer, or in another industry with a rosier economic future.

INVESTING FOR RETIREMENT

■ **Longer life expectancies**—and earlier retirement ages—mean that retirees must invest a larger portion of their savings in stocks. *Reason:* To get returns that will be needed to meet living expenses over 25 years or more. *Key:* Stocks are *less risky* as an investment when a retirement may last so many years. If the market drops in any one year, there's ample time for it to recover before the money invested in it is needed. *Strategy:* To figure out how much of your portfolio to keep in low-risk investments (such as bonds or money funds), multiply your age by 80%. Thus, a 60-year-old should be invested 48% in "safe" bonds or cash, and 52% in higher-yielding stocks.

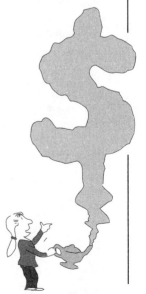

Value Line Mutual Fund Advisor, 220 E. 42 St., New York, NY 10017. 26 issues. $295.

INVESTING FOR RETIREMENT

■ **Save for retirement** by accumulating buying power through after-tax dollars. Before retirement, this may mean by-passing high-yield taxable investments for lower-yielding tax-exempt or tax-deferred ones. After retirement, when you fall into a lower tax bracket, the *reverse* strategy may be best—shifting out of tax-favored investments and *into* taxable ones.

99 Great Answers to Everyone's Investment Questions, by Linda Bryant of Moneywise, a St. Louis financial planning firm. Career Press, 180 Fifth Ave, Box 34, Hawthorne, NJ 07507. $10.95.

■ **Most common retirement planning mistakes:** Putting off planning until to-morrow . . . overestimating how much Social Security will pay . . . overestimating how much an employer's pension plan will pay . . . thinking you'll keep working and won't need retirement income . . . assuming that living expenses will drop after retirement . . . not considering personal matters such as *how* and *where* you'll live after retirement, so you can estimate future needs . . . not giving retirement funds time to grow safely—and instead chasing after high returns in risky investments that could cost you your savings.

Feathering Your Nest, the Retirement Planner, by Lisa Berger, financial writer, Workman Publishing, 708 Broadway, New York, NY 10003. $12.95.

- **Bonds or bond mutual funds:**
- 40% municipals
- 20% treasuries
- 20% corporate
- 20% mortgage-backed.

Obviously, keep the municipals outside the tax-sheltering of your retirement funds (they're already tax-free).

- **What's the best allocation of assets in a 401(k) plan for someone over 50?** Follow the same rule-of-thumb as above, your age equals the percentage of 401(k) assets that should be in bonds. Again, affluent people can put 50% to 60% of their 401(k) assets in stock.

But don't put any of your 401(k) money into the stock of your own company. I don't care how optimistic you are about that company's future; you never know what's going to happen to that stock. It's just too risky. I would also avoid money-market funds and Guaranteed Investment Contracts (GICs). Over time, bond funds will probably outperform GICs.

The range of choices in a 401(k) tends to be abysmally narrow. That's why it's important to coordinate your 401(k) plan with your other investments.

- **Are utility stocks still good retirement investments?** As a long-term investment, utilities do have a role in a portfolio. Just don't go too heavily into them. At current valuations they aren't providing a lot of income. Putting more than 20% of your wealth into utility stocks is placing too much of a bet on a sector that is reasonable but not spectacular.

- **Is it wise to invest in Real-Estate Investment Trusts (REITs) today?** REITs have been very hot lately, and arguably have better prospects at this point than do industrial stocks.

- **Is there one type of mutual fund that you particularly favor for retirement planning?** I refer to balanced funds as the one fund to own if you own only one fund. A balanced fund requires the manager more or less to stay within a fairly narrow parameter of stocks and bonds. Almost universally that is 60% stocks, 40% bonds.

Maintaining that balance forces the manager to do the right thing. If stock prices have risen, he/she is forced to sell stocks. If stock prices drop, he's forced to buy stocks. It's that enforced discipline that has given balanced funds, over the long term, just about as good a performance as the aggressive stock funds with considerably less risk.

• *How much of someone's retirement savings should be invested overseas?* I think 30% of the stock side of your portfolio could be invested overseas. I think there's an opportunity in the international bond market. I could see as much as 20% of the bond side of a portfolio going into the foreign-bond sector.

If you're going to invest in foreign stocks, invest in an international fund that only invests overseas, not in a global fund that can invest in the U.S. stock market as well. Avoid single-country or single-region funds. When you invest in an international fund, you're paying the manager not only to pick good stocks, but to decide in which countries those stocks should be.

• *What role should a variable annuity play in retirement planning?* It's certainly a vehicle to put money aside for retirement in a tax-advantaged form. But only buy a variable annuity after you've contributed the maximum to a 401(k) or 403(b) plan—and only after you've contributed the maximum to an IRA or to a Keogh plan if you have self-employment income.

The higher the fees on a variable annuity, the more your return will be reduced. You probably can save some money by going to one of three major no-load mutual-fund companies that offer variable annuities. In alphabetical order, they are Fidelity, Scudder, and Vanguard.

They have good underlying funds, and their fees aren't as onerous as the fees of many of the annuities that are sold by insurance salespeople. Weigh the allocations in favor of stocks, because you're going to need a big return to offset those annual fees you're paying.

• *How much of a retirement portfolio should be in bonds—and what are the rules for buying bonds today?* The way to play bonds is to "ladder" maturities—spreading your money over different maturities. That's easy to do with bond funds because you have short-term funds, intermediate-term funds and

CHOICES... CHOICES... CHOICES

■ **Ensuring retirement income.** Individuals have to take more responsibility to ensure retirement income than ever before. Many retirees are finding that their pensions amount to as little as 10% of their salaries. Companies that used to provide "defined-benefit" plans—guaranteeing a set payment amount after retirement—have been switching to nonguaranteed "defined-contribution" plans, or else requiring that employees invest on their own. This means they are likely to build up far smaller pensions than ever.

Arnold Brown is chairman of Weiner Edrich, Brown, Inc., trend analysts, 200 E. 33 St., New York, NY 10016.

■ **Early retirement choice.** Employees often are offered the choice of an enhanced pension or a lump-sum severance payment as an incentive to take early retirement. It can be difficult to decide which is most valuable. *Rule of thumb:* Multiply the increase in your pension by 100 and compare it with the cash payment. Thus, an extra $500 per month added to your pension would be the equivalent of a severance payment of $50,000. *Note:* The 100 multiplier is based on a series of complex calculations that take into account such factors as life expectancy, age of retirement and present value of the payment.

Bill Mischell, principal, Foster Higgins, benefits consultants, Princeton, NJ.

Exceptions to the 10% Early Distribution Penalty

Randy Bruce Blaustein, Esq.

Early distributions from retirement plans are subject to 10% additional tax. But there are exceptions to this penalty. The 10% penalty does not apply to distributions that are:

- **Made on or after the date the employee reaches age 59½.**

- **Made to a beneficiary** (or to the estate of the employee) on or after the death of the employee.

- **Attributable to the employee's being disabled.**

- **Part of a series of substantially equal periodic payments** (not less frequently than annually) made for the life (or the life expectancies) of the employee or the joint lives (or joint life expectancies) of such employee and his/her designated beneficiary.

- **Made to an employee after separation from service** after attainment of age 55.

These exceptions to the penalty are found in Section 72(t) of the Internal Revenue Code.

Randy Bruce Blaustein, Esq., partner, Blaustein, Greenberg & Co., 155 E. 31 St., New York, NY 10016.

long-term funds. Intermediate bonds, or intermediate-bond funds, give you 85% of the yield of a long-term bond with a lot less volatility.

Interest rates in real terms aren't that low because inflation is quite low.

But you can't let bonds play a major role in your retirement portfolio, even with low inflation, or you're going to run out of purchasing power before you die. Even in retirement, you need to keep investing for growth.

In lieu of bonds, I would look for stocks that have a good record of increasing their dividends over the years. There are plenty out there.

- ***Should you try to invest for life in your retirement portfolio—or should you actively manage this money?*** It's crucial to actively manage a portfolio, even when it's a retirement portfolio. After all, you're still a long-term investor when you're 65 or 75. The world changes and you have to be alert to that. In retirement you have the time to do it.

- ***What can help someone overcome inertia and fear—and start actively saving for retirement?*** You have to face reality, and the reality is that you've got to beat inflation by 3% after taxes to provide an income that's going to just keep up with inflation.

People have to realize how important this is—and that's the stick. The carrot is obviously that the more preparation you do for retirement, the more you are preparing a financially comfortable, worry-free retirement.

What to Do with Your Money Now to Enhance Your Retirement

Robert Bingham

While many people who are nearing retirement age are planning to take it easy, their money has to keep working. These are the steps to take before you quit the workforce to ensure that you are prepared financially. . . .

• **Review your debts.** If you're still paying off the mortgage on your home, see if it's worth refinancing at the current low-interest rates. Do it now, before you retire. Once you are no longer employed, you may find banks don't want to refinance your mortgage because your income will be lower than when you were still working.

When refinancing, don't extend the length of the loan and don't get an adjustable-rate mortgage. If anything, you want to shorten your mortgage and get a fixed-rate loan. Your mortgage payment is often your biggest expense, so be sure to determine how much you'll be paying each month. A fixed-rate mortgage will give you that peace of mind.

While you're at the bank, consider arranging a home-equity line of credit. Once again, it is better to do this while you're still working because you may have difficulty setting this up once you have retired. You can use this line of credit to pay off any consumer debt, especially high-interest credit-card debt.

Otherwise, don't plan on touching the money. This credit line is to provide emergency funds.

Robert Bingham, a partner at Bingham, Osborn & Scarborough, an investment advisory firm, 351 California St., Suite 1250, San Francisco, CA 94104.

YOUR MONEY

What Retirees Should Withdraw . . . and When

Jonathan Pond

People nearing retirement are often confused about which assets to tap first, which to leave alone, and how to avoid penalties and lessen taxes.

The basic rule: Avoid withdrawing tax-deferred money for as long as you can. This includes IRAs, 401(k) assets, deferred annuities, etc. *Strategy:* Tap your "life savings"—stocks, bonds, and other investments in taxable accounts—before invading tax-deferred retirement accounts.

The distribution rules and tax consequences for various retirement assets:

• **Annuities.** Payouts are subject to income tax—and there is generally a 10% penalty when they are withdrawn before you reach age 59½. Also, some annuities charge a surrender fee if you withdraw funds too early.

• **401(k) plans.** Withdrawals are usually subject to normal income tax, plus a 10% penalty for those under age 59½, although some exceptions apply.

Everyone *must* begin withdrawals by April 1 of the year after they turn 70½ or face a 50% penalty on the difference between what was paid out and what should have been paid out.

• **IRAs.** All deductible contributions and earnings are subject to regular income tax upon withdrawal, plus a possible 10% penalty if taken before age 59½. Withdrawals must begin by April 1 of the year after you turn 70½.

YOUR MONEY

• **Pension from current or former employers.** Your company may require you to begin taking payments at retirement, and you must always do so by April 1 of the year after you turn 70½. Regular income tax usually applies.

• **Social Security.** Payments can begin as early as age 62, but monthly checks will be greater the longer you wait—*until age 70*. Currently, there is no benefit to delaying Social Security payments past age 70.

Jonathan Pond, president of Financial Planning Information Inc., 9 Galen St., Watertown, MA 02172. He is the author of *The New Century Family Money Book*. Dell Publishing.

• **Update your pension benefits fully.** Write to the Social Security Administration to get an estimate of the benefits you are likely to receive.

You should also contact your company's personnel department to find out what you'll get from its defined-benefit pension plan. There aren't that many people who are covered by defined-benefit plans anymore. Unlike Social Security, most company pensions don't increase every year with inflation.

• **Simplify your finances.** Move all your individual retirement accounts to one brokerage firm or mutual-fund company. This will help simplify the paperwork and enable you to better track your investments.

My clients have found that a Charles Schwab brokerage account (800-435-4000) is very effective. Schwab makes it easy to build a well-diversified portfolio because it sells mutual funds managed by a host of different fund companies. And your Schwab account will allow you to buy individual securities as well.

When you retire, this new account will be the receptacle for the rollover money that you will receive from your company's defined-contribution plan. Similarly, you should try to consolidate your non-IRA money. Again, I favor a Charles Schwab account. I would also combine all bank accounts into one or two accounts at one bank—if the total will be less than the FDIC-insured limit.

• **Calculate how much income your portfolio will generate.** Once you've got all your assets consolidated, add them up. Then have a competent financial planner calculate how much income your assets will generate, taking inflation into account.

If you set up a portfolio with 60% stocks and 40% bonds, you will have only $5,000 a year to spend for every $100,000 in your portfolio. Your $100,000 should generate more than $5,000 in gains each year. But if you spent all your gains, your portfolio would stop growing and its real value would be badly eroded by inflation.

• **Figure out how much you currently spend, and how that's likely to change when you**

retire. It's important to know your annual expenses so you can see if your retirement plan is feasible.

If your lifestyle is too lavish to be sustained by the money you're likely to get from Social Security, your company pension and your portfolio, then you may have to delay retirement while you save more.

To calculate your current spending, total your canceled checks and ATM withdrawals for the past year. Then think about how that spending may change once you quit your job. A common rule of thumb is that retirees generally need 75% of their preretirement spending money.

• **Build a well-balanced portfolio.** Our grandparents bought bonds when they retired and lived off the income. Now, that doesn't work because we have higher inflation and are living longer. Plan to keep a hefty chunk of your portfolio in stocks, so that you can earn some capital gains. Once you have retired, stocks should comprise 40% to 60% of your portfolio.

Target 20% of your portfolio for foreign investments, including stocks and bonds. Foreign stocks and bonds perform similarly to U.S. stocks and bonds over long periods—more than seven years. But foreign securities often behave differently over the short term, so they smooth out performance if they're added to a U.S. stock and bond portfolio.

Small-company stocks can be 25% to 50% of your U.S. stock-market allocation. By including the small-capitalization stocks, you should be able to increase returns and reduce volatility.

Consider shifting out of long-term bonds. Intermediate-term bonds—those that mature in five to ten years—tend to perform as well as long-term bonds but don't fluctuate as much in price. With interest rates very low, this is no time to be in long bonds.

• **Use your tax shelters wisely.** Concentrate your stock-market investments in your IRA and other tax-sheltered accounts. Put bonds in your taxable accounts. Tax sheltering is more beneficial with stock-market investments because stocks tend to generate larger gains than bonds.

Retirement Havens

Laurence I. Foster
KPMG Peat Marwick LLP

If you have substantial retirement income, it makes sense to consider retiring to a state that has no personal income tax. Those states are Alaska, Florida, Nevada, South Dakota, Texas, Washington, and Wyoming.

New Hampshire and Tennessee don't have personal income tax, but they tax dividends and interest income. Florida has an intangibles tax—a tax on the value of your stocks and bonds—but it does not tax income of any kind.

Laurence I. Foster is a partner in the personal financial planning practice of KPMG Peat Marwick LLP, 345 Park Ave., New York, NY 10154.

■ **Tax reduction for retirees.** New federal law stops states from imposing income tax on the pension income of individuals who earned their pensions while working in one state—and then moved out of the state upon retiring. Until now, 14 states taxed the pensions of such out-of-state retirees. All these retirees get an effective tax cut in 1996 . . . *and beyond.*

Avery E. Neumark, Esq., is director of employee benefits and executive compensation, Rosen Seymour Shapss Martin & Co., 757 Third Ave., New York, NY 10017.

TAX-WISE RETIREMENT

■ **Custodian-to-custodian transfer** is a better way to move an IRA than an *indirect rollover*. Contact the new custodian and ask that your IRA be transferred from your old custodian—it will handle the paperwork and contact the old custodian. With an *indirect rollover*, the old custodian sends the money to you and you must then deposit it with a new firm *within 60 days*. After 60 days you incur a substantial IRS penalty.

Albert Fredman, Ph.D., professor of finance at California State University and author of *Building Your Mutual Fund Portfolio*. Dearborn Financial Publishing, $19.95.

PENSION MATTERS

■ **Minimizing taxes on pensions.** As important as putting money into retirement plans is having a strategy for taking it out. It's best to spend other moneys first, letting IRAs, Keogh plans, and 401(k) plans continue to build up on a tax-deferred basis until you reach age 70½. Then you must start taking minimum taxable distributions each year. Since there are various elections that can be made to minimize taxation, you need to discuss exact withdrawal strategy with your accountant, preferably as early as age 60. *Trap:* If all withdrawals from different pension accounts amount to more than $155,000 for 1996, the government levies a 15% excise tax in addition to federal and state income taxes.

Avery E. Neumark is a partner with the law firm, Rosen, Seymour, Shapss, Martin & Co., 757 Third Ave., New York, NY 10017.

■ **Retirement planning:** Make a list of all your past employers and the dates you worked for each one. Send each company a letter stating the dates of em-

Important: Once you have retired, plan to spend your non-IRA money first. Then your IRA savings can continue to enjoy tax-sheltered growth. Since you will be spending non-IRA money, which is allocated more toward bonds, you may need to rebalance your portfolio by gradually placing more bonds in your IRA.

• **Plan your medical insurance.** This is critical for people who retire before age 65 and need medical coverage before Medicare kicks in. Your employer may continue to provide your insurance. If that is not the case, consider your local health maintenance organizations or a Blue Cross and Blue Shield policy. Avoid smaller or lower-rated insurance companies, which sometimes cancel policies suddenly.

• **Consider canceling your life insurance.** In many cases, there's no longer any financial reason to protect a nonworking spouse from the death of the family's breadwinner. You'll need the premiums for other expenses.

How to Be Prepared When Your Spouse Retires

Gloria Bledsoe Goodman

One of the greatest mistakes a couple can make is to assume that retirement will simply be a continuation of married life as they have known it.

Retirement has its own rhythm, just as the honeymoon years, child-rearing years, and empty-nest years had theirs.

Most likely change: You will spend much more time together. *Result:* Trouble spots may arise in the

Gloria Bledsoe Goodman, author of *Keys to Living with a Retired Husband*. Barron's Educational Series, Inc.

smallest areas of daily life. Many newly retired couples, even those who agree on the major issues of their retirement—where to live, how to handle the finances—are surprised by how infuriating they may suddenly find their comfortable, cherished mate.

MOST COMMON TROUBLE SPOTS

• **Lack of retirement planning.** Many a husband has been shocked to learn that his wife has no desire to move to the fishing village he always pictured as a retirement home. Failure to communicate expectations about retirement, or to do the pre-planning necessary to make your plans a reality, can cause terrible conflict in retiring couples.

To offset clashes over major issues: Attend a retirement-planning workshop at your local chamber of commerce, community college, or senior center. Workshop leaders say that no session is conducted without each person making at least one amazing discovery about their spouse's retirement goals.

• **Failure to appreciate the psychological impact of retirement.** Couples must realize that retirement can be a traumatic passage, particularly for men. Even men who look forward to retirement may feel fearful and "lost" when they no longer have a routine and the familiar identity of their working selves. Concerns with mortality and self-worth may loom large for the first time.

Best course for women: Respect the grieving period. Don't crowd or smother your husband with suggestions, opinions, questions, or demands or push him into a full schedule before he is ready. But do let him know that you are there. This is a good time for extra cuddling, affection, and reassurance. Let him percolate a bit, and shift the focus to your own feelings.

Many women feel that they have spent their entire lives deferring to the needs of their husbands and families. They expect retirement to be "their turn" and fear being trapped again by their husbands' needs.

Best course: Have compassion for your husband's feelings, but be very firm regarding your own needs.

Once the transitional period passes, women can help their husbands back into active life. Men are

PENSION MATTERS

ployment and asking for forms to claim retirement benefits. Many people entitled to vested benefits never claim them.

Can You Afford to Grow Old? by James Addicott, Ph.D., business consultant, Monterey County, California. Probus Publishing, 1925 N. Clybourn St., Chicago, IL 60614. $21.95.

■ **Taking a pension in a lump sum**—rather than in monthly checks over a lifetime—makes more sense for most people. The media have recently implied that annuity checks are better now that a federal law prohibits states from taxing pension checks of former residents. Annuity checks make sense only if you are a poor manager of money . . . or if they will do a better job of satisfying your annual need for income than the interest on a lump sum when invested. *Helpful:* Talk with your accountant about the best option.

Anthony Gallea is senior vice president at one of the country's largest financial firms and author of *The Lump Sum Handbook: Investment and Tax Strategies for a Secure Retirement.* Prentice Hall, $14.95.

FUN TIME

■ **Join Elderhostel at age 55.** The nationwide education program has lowered its eligibility age. It used to be 60. Elderhostel offers educational seminars for retirees at 2,000 colleges and other institutions around the world. *Cost:* Usually about $300 for a week-long seminar within the U.S., including room and board. *More information:* 617-426-8056.

■ **Retirement moves.** Don't move to a new retirement home too quickly. Many people who retire move abruptly to a new location, only to find they don't like it as much as they thought they would.

FUN TIME

Better: Explore possible retirement locations several years *before* you retire. When you find an area you like, take an extended vacation there, then consider buying—or renting—a vacation home there that can serve as a base from which you can familiarize yourself with the entire region.

Robert C. Carlson, editor, *Bob Carlson's Retirement Watch*, 1420 Spring Hill Rd., Ste. 490, McLean, VA 22102. Monthly. $99/yr.

SENIOR ON-LINE

SeniorNet Online

Bradley Haas
SeniorNet

A computer network via America On-line links thousands of people age 55 and older. SeniorNet also has 70 Learning Centers throughout the U.S. where volunteers teach computer classes.

SeniorNet's Technology Leadership Corps counsels members about buying new equipment, going on-line or using specialized software. *More information:* 800-747-6848.

Bradley Haas is director of public relations, SeniorNet, One Kearney St., San Francisco, CA 94109.

■ **Seniors are buying PCs** at a faster rate than any other age group . . . and using them to connect electronically to local and national news, health care, and financial information, travel and other products. *Helpful:* SeniorCom, a free Internet on-line chat service offering coupons, video giveaways, trial offers and information on health care, housing and other topics. *More information:* 800-206-6989 or http://www. senior.com.

badly needed as community volunteers. Some may just want to "play" awhile, others may enjoy part-time work or a second career.

• **Alcoholism/clinical depression.** Alcoholism is under-recognized and badly under-treated in seniors, even though treatment has a high likelihood of success in this age group.

Depression, with or without alcohol, can afflict either sex, but is especially common among those forced to take "early retirement." Depression can also be triggered by many medications. If you suspect either problem in your family, don't hesitate to seek professional help.

SMALL STUFF—BUT MAJOR GRIPES

• **Grocery shopping.** It sounds hilarious—but this is a top area of conflict cited by retired couples. Often the wife has been shopping for years, and finds it insulting when her husband suddenly questions every choice and examines every tomato.

I have met many couples who have had bitter arguments over who gets to push the cart!

Solution: Decide that one of you will do all the shopping. Or shop with two lists. He can select the produce, while she does the rest.

• **Territorial strife.** With two people in one house, problems often arise over rooms and routines.

Examples: She wants the spare room as a sewing room, he wants a den. He used to leave for work, so she could drink coffee and watch *Good Morning, America* before starting her chores. Now he wants to watch CNN and complains when she starts the housework.

Solution: Communication, compassion, and compromise. It's your retirement as well as your spouse's. Wives must be willing to cede some domestic territory—it's his kitchen, too. Husbands must face the necessity to "get a life," and not expect their wives to provide one.

• **Comings and goings.** Insecurity often manifests as controlling behavior . . . *Where are you going? When will you be home? Who's on the phone?*

Solution: Stay calm and considerate. Reassure your mate, but don't be bullied. *Essential:* Keep your sense of humor.

• **Division of labor.** He expects her to perform the same chores she always has, even if she's still working part-time. She expects that now that he's retired, he'll take on some household chores.

Solution: It's time to be fair.

Men: You may have retired from work, but not from the partnership of a marriage. Offer to take on the vacuuming. Don't force her to ask.

Women: Acknowledge the work he does do—caring for the yard, garbage, car, etc. Then ask for the help you need from your spouse. But if you ask him to vacuum, let him do it his way. *Helpful:* List chores you each hate, and negotiate for the other to take them on. Hire help for chores you both hate.

• **Sex.** Many men find sex a means of self-proof as well as pleasure. So a pleasant side effect of the anxieties retirement can produce is that many men discover a renewed enthusiasm for sex. Older men often have a stronger sex drive in the morning—so don't be too quick to leap out of bed. You don't have to—you're retired!

Wives: Enjoy it, buy some new lingerie and be willing to try new things.

Caution: Some couples experience the opposite, and shy away from intimacy after retirement. If your sex life is unhealthy, this is a problem that needs to be resolved through frank discussion or counseling.

• **Television.** Get two!

SOCIAL SECURITY SECRETS

■ **Verify your earnings record** with the Social Security Administration every three years to be sure it doesn't contain errors. Call the Social Security Administration (800-772-1213) and ask for a free *Request for Earnings and Benefit Estimate.* Compare your listed earnings with your W-2s from the same years—you should have them attached to old tax forms. If you find errors, report them immediately and find out how to have them fixed. If you wait too long, they may not be correctable.

Joel Lerner, author of Financial *Planning for the Utterly Confused.* McGraw-Hill, $9.95.

Social Security Appeals

Ken Skala

Social Security benefits appeals are the right of any recipient after an unfavorable decision about benefits. *To appeal:*

• Ask for a reconsideration—an independent review of your case.

• If you disagree with the reconsideration, request a hearing before an Administrative Law Judge (ALJ).

• If that decision goes against you, ask for an Appeals Council review. The council may review, refuse to review or return the case to an ALJ for further consideration.

• If the Appeals Council refuses to review, or you disagree with its ruling, take civil action in U.S. District Court.

Caution: You have only 60 days to appeal after getting the notice of a decision.

Ken Skala is a consultant on public and private benefits for seniors, and author of *American Guidance for Seniors . . . and Their Caregivers.* Career Press. $17.95.

Better Furniture Cleaning

Carol Rees

You can get stains out better by using materials from around the house than with commercial preparations.

- **White rings left by drinking glasses on wood furniture.** This is the most commonly asked question about household stains. To remove, simply rub with plain white toothpaste (not a gel), then polish with floor wax—it's thicker and easier to work with than furniture wax. If the rings aren't too old, you can rub with cigarette ash—ask a friend to save some for you.

- **Cigarette burns on wood.** First, gently scrape away the black stain with a small knife. Then paint the cavity with clear nail polish. Allow to harden, then repeat . . . Apply as many coats as it takes to restore a level surface.

- **Scratches on wood furniture.** These will fill in if rubbed with camphor oil (you may have to go out to the drugstore to get some).

Some quick cures:

- **Adhesive furniture-delivery labels.** Rub with a washcloth dipped in cooking oil.

- **Candle wax on wood surfaces.** Harden with an ice cube then scrape away with a table knife.

- **Rust on chrome furniture.** Scrub with fine steel wool (#0000), then protect by applying sealer used to prevent copper or brass from pitting.

How to Save Money on Almost Everything

Linda Bowman

It's easy to cut costs by taking advantage of discounts and freebies. One woman we know saved enough in a few years to buy a new car!

Worthwhile: Keep track of your savings—and enjoy watching them grow.

UTILITIES/ENERGY

- **For free evaluation of your energy usage,** call your local utilities company. In addition, many utilities companies give away free energy-saving devices, such as low-flow shower heads, water-heater blankets and fluorescent bulbs.

- **Repair major appliances yourself** instead of paying for a costly service call. *How:* Call manufacturers' customer-service repair hotlines for instructions.

- **General Electric,** 800-626-2000.
- **Whirlpool,** 800-253-1301.
- **White-Westinghouse,** 800-245-0600.
- **Gather free firewood from any of our 155 national forests.** Contact your regional office of the U.S. Forest Service for a permit, which allows you up to six cords of downed or dead wood. At the going rate of about $150 a cord, this will save almost $1,000.

Linda Bowman, author of *The More for Your Money* series of guides, including *Free Food & More* and *Freebies (and More) for Folks Over 50.* COM-OP Publishing.

• **Install a water restrictor for your shower head.** That saves an average family thousands of gallons of water a year. Check with your local utility for a free water-restrictor head.

HOME- AND HEALTH-CARE PRODUCTS

• **Coupons are not just for food.** Some of the very best coupon savings are for cleaning supplies, tissues, toothpaste, shampoo, batteries and other home-care and health-care products. Keep an eye out for "Free with Purchase" offers . . . stores that pay double coupon values . . . coupons printed on product packaging.

• **Take advantage of refund/rebate offers.** You must take the time to save UPC symbols, labels and receipts, but the savings can easily reach hundreds of dollars a year. *Good source of offers:* Supermarket and drugstore bulletin boards.

Refund request forms are often mounted as tear-off pads where products are shelved. Don't overlook offers in hardware and home-building stores, pet stores and appliance stores.

• **Ask for free samples at department store cosmetics counters.** Just say you need to try products before you buy, and you'll walk away with handfuls of high-priced makeup, skin-care products and fragrances.

Watch for: Fine print in magazine ads offering free samples of perfume or moisturizer simply by writing or calling an 800 number.

• **Have your hair cut, colored, permed or styled at a cosmetology school.** Students have spent hundreds of hours working on mannequins and each other, and are closely supervised by expert instructors. Customers are usually pampered.

Savings: About 60% less than a salon. The average American woman spends $238 a year at hair salons, so expect to save $143.

• **Get routine dental care at a dental school.** Services at the country's 57 dental-school training clinics, including orthodontics, are high-quality and 60% less expensive than normal dentists' fees. To find one, check the phone book for your local dental society.

• **Picture frames scratched during moving.** Apply shoe polish.

• **Scratches on dark woods.** Tint with iodine.

Carol Rees, a home-care adviser, author of *Household Hints for Upstairs, Downstairs and All Around the House.* Henry Holt & Co.

■ **Moving and storage auctions** can be good sources of functional household and office items at low cost. Movers and mini-storage companies hold auctions whenever they have enough unclaimed inventory—often every two to three months. Cash is usually required for these purchases. Often items must be picked up within five days. Items are sometimes grouped by function—but more often, bidders pay for the entire contents of a storage compartment or container at the discretion of the auctioneer. *To find auctions:* Check listings in newspaper classified ads, or contact local storage or auction companies.

Jack Fuchs, owner, Whitehall Storage, New York., N.Y.

Supersavers

■ **Best ways to get senior discounts:** Always carry a photo identification that gives your birthday—such as a driver's license . . . always ask for a discount—they are widely available but often not given automatically . . . request the discount before you buy or make reservations—many merchants will not apply it after the bill has been drawn up . . . if no discount is available to you, mention in a friendly way to the manager that a discount would encourage your patronage.

American Guidance for Seniors by Ken Skala, advocate, lecturer and author. The Career Press.

SUPERSAVERS

■ **Don't buy a wedding dress.** Instead of buying—rent a wedding dress and save hundreds of dollars. Bridal apparel rental stores (listed in the yellow pages under Bridal Shops) typically rent designer gowns that cost $2,000 or more for under $400. *Important:* Gowns are professionally cleaned after each wearing. Most stores require deposits of $100 to $200.

Bridal Bargains: Secrets to Throwing a Fantastic Wedding on a Realistic Budget by wedding experts Denise & Alan Fields. Windsor Peak Press.

GROCERY SAVINGS

■ **Food-use patterns.** List the food items that you discard every time you clean out your refrigerator. If, after several cleanings, you see a pattern of underused items that often spoil, change your buying habits accordingly.

Lynn Parrinella, editor, *Dollar Wise*, Box 270924, Fort Collins, CO 80527.

■ **Better grocery shopping.** *Follow the MESS system:* Make a list before shopping to force yourself to decide in advance what you need and what you don't . . . Evaluate what are truly necessities and what you can live without . . . Shop the ads, which can alert you to where the best buys are . . . Stick to your agenda, and don't get distracted by impulse items.

Money Doesn't Grow on Trees: A Parent's Guide to Raising Financially Responsible Children by Neale S. Godfrey, chairman of the Children's Financial Network, Mountain Lakes, NJ. Fireside.

■ **Pay special attention at the check-out counter.** Group special sale items together when unloading the grocery cart, along with anything missing a price tag or a tag that may be wrong. Pay special attention when these items are rung up—they are

• **Ask your doctors for free samples of medications** whenever you are given a prescription. Most doctors have plenty to give away.

HOME ENTERTAINMENT

• **Take advantage of free magazine offers.** Don't throw away subscription invitations from periodicals. Most publications will send you a free issue, then begin your subscription unless you cancel.

Key: Remember to write "cancel" on the invoice they send, and mail it back to them. The postage is almost always paid, and you owe nothing.

• **Use your public library** to borrow books, records, audiotapes, videotapes, even posters and artwork.

• **Order free publications from your favorite manufacturers.** Almost every food product company offers a free cookbook, including Quaker Oats, Dannon, Kikkoman, Goya's Seasonings, and Nestlé... as does almost every trade organization, including the American Mushroom Institute in Kennett Square, Pennsylvania, the California Raisin Advisory Board in Fresno, and the Idaho Potato Commission in Boise.

Examples: Eastman Kodak of Rochester, New York, offers three free booklets on photography . . . the Chicago Roller Skate Co. has two free booklets on roller skating how-to's . . . United Van Lines of Fenton, Missouri, offers a free booklet called *How to Hold a Garage Sale.*

To find offers...check package labels for the location of company headquarters, or call 800-555-1212. Then contact the company's customer-service department.

Shopping Much Smarter Now

Brenda J. Cude

The old rules of shopping no longer apply. To spend wisely and get the best for the least, take heed of the following changes in shopping rules:

• *No longer true:* **Buy a known brand.** Once consumers find a brand name they believe delivers quality, they continue to select that brand with little comparison before purchasing. *Reality:* Our research has found that past performance of a brand is a poor predictor of future quality. *Better:* Check *Consumer Reports* for products that are regularly rated from year to year. There are often good reasons why a brand doesn't maintain the same quality.

• *No longer true:* **Look for a seal of approval.** It's fine to look for the seal of approval of Underwriters Laboratories, which assures the safety of electrical products—but some seals don't mean much. Good Housekeeping's seal, for example, only gives assurances of limited refund or replacement by Good Housekeeping.

• *No longer true:* **Buy the top of the line.** Many appliances and other durables are marketed in product lines, with a no-frills model at the bottom. Consumers assume that the top-of-the-line model not only has more features but is also of higher quality. *Reality:* People who buy top-of-the-line often pay for features they don't want or need. Many of the same features may be offered on lower-priced models of that manufacturer or a competitor. Check!

Brenda J. Cude, extension specialist and associate professor, family economics, Cooperative Extension Service, University of Illinois at Urbana-Champaign, 271 Bevier Hall, 905 S. Goodwin Ave., Urbana, IL 61801.

GROCERY SAVINGS

the most likely to be rung incorrectly, even in stores using scanners. *Self-defense:* Watch closely as all items are rung up— and check your receipt at home.

Money, Rockefeller Center, New York, NY 10020.

■ **Manufacturers' service contracts** are almost never a good buy. Salespeople push them because they carry high sales commissions. But the contracts very rarely pay back their costs—and are usually not renewable when a product has reached the end of its typical useful life—when it might start to need major repairs. *Better than a service contract:* Pre-purchase research to find reliable, high-quality products.

100 Ways to Avoid Common Legal Pitfalls Without a Lawyer by Stephen Christianson, Esq., a Virginia-based lawyer specializing in civil litigation. Citadel Press.

Bad Deals

■ **Hardware products cost more per item** when mounted on cardboard and encased in plastic than when they are sold loose. *Example:* 15 screws in a package may cost $1.29, while the same screws loose may cost 35¢. *Additional cost-cutting:* Buy full-sized sandpaper instead of precut sheets for pad sanders. Cut the larger sheets to size and save up to 50%. Buy wall-covering paste as powder instead of premixed. The powder just has to be mixed with water—and costs one-fifth as much as paste.

Michael Chotiner, editor-in-chief, *Home Mechanix*, 2 Park Ave., New York, NY 10016.

■ **Wrinkle-free shirts** are not wrinkle-free. Although they are advertised as never needing ironing, these shirts nonetheless carry additional care instructions.

Survey of menswear experts in *The Wall Street Journal*.

BETTER BUYING BASICS

■ **Better shopping.** Always buy two or more of nonperishable items—which include canned goods and cleaning supplies. Then, when there's one left in the cupboard, add the item to your grocery list. Running out wastes time—and money. It increases the likelihood of buying the one item at a smaller, more expensive store.

365 Ways to Save Time by time-management expert Lucy H. Hedrick. Hearst Books.

■ **Better clothes buying.** To gauge the true cost of a piece of clothing, calculate the price-per-wear. *Example:* A $200 pair of shoes, worn twice a week for a year, costs about $2 per wear. But a $25 pair, worn for only two special occasions, costs $12.50 per wear—not a bargain. An item's versatility and durability can be more important than its purchase price.

Out of the Rat Race, Gregory Communications Group, Box 95341, Seattle, WA 98145.

■ **Electrical cost of a refrigerator** for 15 to 20 years can be more than three times its original purchase price. *Best:* A top-freezer model. Side-by-side models let more cold air pour out when they are opened. Consider manual-defrost models—they cost less and use only half the energy of automatic defrosters.

The Earth and You: Eating for Two by April Moore, a Broadway, VA writer. Potomac Valley Press.

■ **Buy something of the highest quality** every once in a while. If you love to read—buy a beautifully embroidered bookmark . . . If you write a lot of letters buy some very handsome stationery that

• *No longer true:* **Price indicates quality.** Several studies have demonstrated a poor price-quality correlation and some have even shown a negative relationship—that is, higher prices associated with lower quality. But shoppers don't seem to learn this—even with frequently purchased or big ticket items where they should do more research before buying.

Exercise: Create a simple chart showing prices of all varieties of a product having the same level of quality. You'll quickly see which is the best buy. Of course it becomes more complex in comparing products with many features and product qualities, such as personal stereo systems. But even there, if you plot a chart with price on the vertical scale and quality features on the horizontal scale, you'll be able to quickly spot which models are way out of line.

• *No longer true:* **Larger sizes are better buys.** Don't assume that larger sizes of a packaged goods product are a better buy than smaller sizes. Much research has demonstrated that the larger size rule is frequently invalid. Sometimes there's actually a surcharge on the larger size. Quantity discounts, however, are more common than quantity surcharges—and are larger in amount. Consumers generally do get a good deal by buying larger sizes . . . but there are exceptions.

BOTTOM LINE

If you don't have the time or inclination to research every purchase, and some rules have worked for you, fine. Continue to use them. But pay attention to unit pricing labels in stores and, even with brands that have been satisfactory over time, occasionally check to make sure they're still competitive in quality and price.

Also read labels to make sure you're not getting something you don't want in terms of ingredients or environmental problems.

Helpful resources: The public library is the best place to start on consumer research. It has entire magazines devoted to product categories. People at the library will also know of local consumer-action groups.

Every state has a Cooperative Extension Service, funded partly by the U.S. Dept. of Agriculture and partly by the state and local counties. These are located at land-grant universities. They are a source of useful consumer-buying publications.

Also: Write the Consumer Information Center, Pueblo, Colorado 81009, for a free catalogue of U.S. government pamphlets, many of which are very useful for smart shopping.

How to Cut Your Family's Medical Bills . . . Now

Frederick Ruof

Here are ways that you can reduce out-of-pocket medical expenses right now . . .

HOSPITALS

• **Make sure your hospital stay is necessary.** Studies show that only one of every eight hospital admissions is medically necessary and only one of every five operations really makes sense. So when you're told you should have a certain procedure or test, be appropriately skeptical.

• **Ask the right questions.** The right questions concern both health and money. Often the answer that is best for your health is also best for your wallet. *Ask your doctor the following questions about any recommended procedure . . .*

• *What are the risks of the procedure?*

• *Which hospital do you suggest—and why?* Some are safer than others . . . some are cheaper . . . some are both.

Frederick Ruof, president of the National Emergency Medicine Alliance (NEMA), an organization that specializes in providing consumers with ways to reduce medical costs. NEMA publishes a booklet called *How to Cut Your Family's Medical Bills by $1,000.* 524 Branch Dr., Salem, VA 24135.

will make you feel like royalty when you sit down to write. Price doesn't always have to be your prime concern. Sometimes it's wise to treat yourself to something that's going to make you happy for years to come.

How to Be Happier Day by Day: A Year of Mindful Actions by Alan Epstein, Ph.D., California-based co-founder of True Partners, an introduction and relationship counseling firm. Viking.

■ **Three principles of saving money:** *Buy cheaper*—look for sales, rebates, generics, bonus sizes and discounts . . . *make it last longer*—take care of it, repair it instead of replacing it, use it longer . . . *use it less*—overusing almost anything limits its life span.

Dollar Wise Newsletter, Box 270924, Fort Collins, CO 80527.

■ **Better budgeting.** Track where your money goes by listing every penny your spend for two months. Afterward, review your list and mark each item with an "O" for optional or "E" for essential. *Aim:* Eliminate as many optional expenses as possible without budgeting out your fun.

Personal finance radio hosts Ken and Daria Dolan, writing in *Money,* Rockefeller Center, New York 10020.

■ **Beware of paying full price.** Never pay full price unless you are sure you have exhausted all other options. Decide if you must have something new, or can buy it used. If you need an item urgently, improvise—try borrowing it instead of rushing out to buy it.

The Tightwad Gazette: Promoting Thrift as a Viable Alternative Lifestyle by Amy Dacyczyn, founder, *The Tightwad Gazette* newsletter. Villard Books.

SMART MEDICAL CONSUMER

■ **Be a smart buyer of medical services.** *Before having a hospital procedure*—ask your doctor for a detailed estimate of likely hospital charges and doctor's fees. *In the hospital*—keep a log of services and procedures performed for you, visits from doctors and so on. *After being discharged*—ask for an itemized statement of your expenses—*not* the brief summary you'll probably be given if treatment is charged to an insurer or Medicare. Ask the hospital to explain obscure codes. If major discrepancies exist in the estimate, the log of services received and the final bill—*complain* to the hospital, your insurer and insurance regulators.

Charles B. Inlander, president, People's Medical Society, 462 Walnut St., Allentown, PA 18102.

■ **Cut prescription costs** by calling various pharmacies each time you need a new medication. Prices vary widely—and the pharmacy that charges the least for one drug may not charge the least for another. *Other medication cost-cutters:* Mail-order pharmacies . . . generic drugs.

Charles B. Inlander, president, People's Medical Society, 462 Walnut St., Allentown, PA 18102.

■ **Don't pay extra for vitamin supplements with herbal ingredients.** Herbal substances are of questionable value, and may interfere with vitamins in a manner that *blocks* your body from absorbing them. So you may wind up paying more for less.

David Roll, Ph.D., professor of medicinal chemistry, University of Utah, College of Pharmacy, 201 Skaggs Hall, Salt Lake City, UT 84112.

■ **To control your medical costs:** Negotiate with your doctor to keep charges in line. Find out what other doctors in your area charge for the same procedure.

• *Are there any less-invasive alternatives to this type of surgery? Examples:* Clot-dissolving drugs instead of heart bypass surgery . . . lumpectomy instead of total breast removal for a breast tumor.

• *Can I have this procedure done as an outpatient?*

• **Always get a second opinion.** An eight-year study by the Cornell Medical Center found that one out of four second opinions recommends against an operation. The long-term survival rate of people who take such advice is excellent. So even if your insurance company doesn't require a second opinion, get one. And be sure to ask a lot of questions of all doctors, since *you* must make the final decision regarding your treatment.

Studies show that the operations most often considered unnecessary are tonsillectomies, coronary bypasses, gall-bladder removals, cesarean sections, pacemaker surgeries and joint surgeries. Be particularly diligent about getting a second opinion in such cases.

• **Pick your hospital.** Don't let it pick you. Years ago, no one "shopped" for a hospital. Today, 35% of patients do. Clearly, this is the best option only if you have time before the surgery is necessary.

Opportunity: Community hospitals may be up to 25% cheaper than for-profit hospitals, which order more tests and have bigger markups on procedures and services.

Most doctors are affiliated with more than one hospital, so discuss your options, balancing cost against the success rate for your type of surgery.

• **Look for the least-expensive option.** Many procedures that traditionally required overnight hospital stays can now be done on an outpatient basis, which can be up to 50% cheaper than a regular hospital procedure. When you discuss outpatient alternatives with your doctor, ask about new "minimally invasive" surgical techniques, which can be considerably less expensive and less traumatic.

Trap: Never assume that your doctor or surgeon will automatically recommend the cheapest way of treating your medical problem. Ideally, you should go prepared to ask him/her about a variety of options that you've already researched.

• **Resist unnecessary tests.** Always ask your doctor why a hospital test must be given. The tests most frequently over-ordered are urinalyses, chest X rays, and two types of blood tests—one that measures white blood cell count and another that measures the amount of time it takes blood to clot. Once in the hospital, insist on advance approval of tests and procedures.

• **Save on "incidentals."** Check to see what the hospital charges for various services before you check in. The most frequently hidden hospital costs are the $50-to-$100 fees for providing routine information when filling out forms. These charges are levied by 25% to 30% of hospitals. If yours is one of them, ask to fill out the papers yourself—assuming, of course, that you are well enough to do so.

Another example: Fees for health and beauty aids. In some cases, you can save more than $100 by bringing your own toiletries and pills, if you are already on the appropriate medications before being admitted. You may also be able to fill new prescriptions outside the hospital when you are a patient.

• **Assume there is a problem with your bill.** A new General Accounting Office study found overcharges in 99% of all hospital bills. Why does this matter to someone who has health insurance? Because more and more plans are requiring patients to share hospital costs.

Strategy: Request a fully itemized bill. Then review it carefully. *Look for:*

• **Duplicate billings** (often for tests).

• **Shoddy testing** (don't pay for unreadable X rays).

• **Unauthorized tests** (if you previously specified that you wanted advance approval).

• **"Phantom" charges** (often for sedatives and other medications that may never have been given to you).

• **Bulk charges.** If you see a broad heading such as "radiology" or "pharmacy," you can't possibly know if the total is accurate. Ask for a more detailed breakdown of the charges incurred.

Make mention of your research to your doctor and ask him/her to accept the rate charged by his peers. *Also:* Work out fees for regular treatments—for instance, a charge only for a shot when you need one regularly, instead of an extra charge for an office visit each time. And—try to get flat rates for some procedures, such as being charged one price for having several moles removed instead of a rate per mole.

Charles B. Inlander, president, People's Medical Society, 462 Walnut St., Allentown, PA 18102.

How to Save on Your Medicines

Rick Doble

• **Buy double-strength pills** (if your doctor will prescribe this way) and cut them in half with a pill cutter. Pill cutters cost about $5.

• **Compare prices**—and include a discount mail-order pharmacy in comparison.

• **Always ask for generic medications.** When refilling a prescription, ask if a generic is now available. New ones come on the market regularly.

Rick Doble, editor, *Savvy Discounts Newsletter,* Box 96, Smyrna, NC 28579.

■ **For lower phone bills:** Gather your last three long-distance bills. Count the number of calls, calculate the average length and jot down the times of day you made them. Then call your long-distance company—and several others—and ask what discount plan will bring you the most savings. *Caution:* Do not let yourself be tricked into switching companies for a one-time rebate or savings offer. If

COST-CUTTING

a competing firm does make you a better offer, call your current long-distance service provider before switching and ask it to match the offer. Many firms will.

Neil Sachnoff, president of TeleCom Clinic, 4402 Stonehedge Rd., Edison, NJ 08820.

■ **Lower long-distance phone rates.** AT&T, MCI, and Sprint routinely match each other's offers. So when one carrier offers a bonus or special discount rate if you switch, call your current carrier and ask the company to match the offer. It usually will—and will sometimes throw in an additional bonus to retain you as a customer.

Neil Sachnoff, president of TeleCom Clinic, 4402 Stonehedge Rd., Edison, NJ 08820.

SMART MOVES

■ **Return unwanted merchandise** you receive in the mail by simply crossing out your address and writing *Return to sender—merchandise refused* on the box. This not only saves you from paying for the merchandise, but also saves return postage. *Caution:* This only works if you do not break the seal or open the box. If you break the seal, you need new postage to send the box back.

Rochelle LaMotte McDonald, a mother of three in Anchorage, AK, and author of How to Pinch a Penny Till It Screams. Avery Publishing Group.

■ **Always get a sales receipt**, even for small purchases. This will help you develop the habit of getting and keeping receipts—a key to resolving problems that may arise with larger purchases. *Warranties:* Register your warranties right away, and keep copies of them in a safe place, along with important receipts. This will make it easy to determine if a product that breaks or proves defective can be repaired under warranty.

DOCTORS

• **Get your money's worth.** Show up as prepared for each doctor's visit as you would for an important business meeting. Bring notes about your medical history, symptoms, medications and questions that you want the doctor to answer. Have your doctor explain what he is writing in your file.

Once you pay the bill, you're entitled to a copy of the lab report—*free*. Ask your doctor to explain it to you.

The more you know, the better able you will be to gauge what treatments are appropriate—and which expenses are worth questioning.

• **Phone it in.** Take advantage of a doctor's phone hours, which will save you time and money. A Dartmouth Medical School study found that this saved each patient an average of $1,656 over a two-year period.

Warning: There's a difference between avoiding unnecessary visits to specialists and forgoing important preventive measures. People who save money by avoiding flu shots or treatment for high blood pressure are making serious mistakes.

• **Avoid the annual physical.** Symptom-free adults under age 65 can save $200 to $500 a year by reconsidering whether they really need an annual physical. The American Medical Association's guidelines suggest a full checkup every five years for adults ages 21 to 40—and every few years thereafter, depending on your health. Doctors themselves get physicals much less often than do other professionals of the same age.

INSURANCE

• **Increase your deductible.** Talk with your insurance agent or with the benefits person at your company. The amount you save each year may be substantial, particularly if you are a healthy adult.

• **Avoid being overinsured.** Be prepared to absorb some occasional minor expenses rather than seeking a policy that covers every penny of your expenses all the time. This kind of insurance policy is never a bargain.

• **If your benefits are ever denied—fight back.** Some surveys show that policyholders who contest denials get partial or complete satisfaction 50% of the time.

DRUGS

- **Ask your doctor** to prescribe generic drugs when appropriate.
- **Ask your doctor** for free samples of prescribed medicines.
- **Cut back on over-the-counter (OTC) medicines.** Most OTC remedies for colds, pains and minor problems don't really do any good. In fact, only 30% of all OTC medications can prove their claims.

How to Take Back Anything You've Bought . . . or Been Given

Arlene Singer

Most shoppers would like to return many more purchases than they actually do—for many reasons.

The single biggest reason people avoid returning items they don't want is that they are afraid someone will say "no."

But why tie your money up in useless possessions?

Here's how to take back almost any unwanted purchase or gift—even when rude sales clerks insist you can't:

- **Have a valid reason for making the return.** There are many valid reasons for making returns, including "I just don't like it."

Arlene Singer, a professional buyer in the advertising field, and coauthor, with Karen Parmet, of *Take It Back! The Art of Returning Almost Anything.* National Press Books, Inc.

Rochelle LaMotte McDonald, a mother of three in Anchorage, AK, and author of *How to Pinch a Penny Till It Screams.* Avery Publishing Group.

■ **Examine hospital bills closely before paying.** Watch for phantom charges. *Examples:* Many hospitals have charged for tests that were not performed . . . drugs that were not administered . . . doctors' visits that didn't occur. Refuse to pay these charges, or notify your insurer if the bill will be sent to it directly. Also—ask your insurer about discounts it may have negotiated for hospital services. The amount shown on your bill may not be the true amount the insurance company pays—so your copayment should be lower as well.

Joe Altman, health care consultant, Towers-Perrin, 695 E. Main St., Stamford, CT 06901.

■ **Gold card scam.** A caller says you have been pre-approved for a gold card and he/she just needs a little information to send the card to you. He asks for Social Security, checking account and credit card numbers, and your mother's birth name. You never get the card. The caller gets information to tap into your bank accounts and credit lines. *Self-defense:* By law, credit card issuers must have your written approval to send you a card. Tell any caller to send you an application by mail. Or just hang up.

John Barker, National Consumers League, 815 15 St. NW, Washington, DC 20005.

■ **No-haggle trap.** Car buyers who shop at one-price "no-haggle" dealerships to avoid the discomfort of negotiating may pay as much as $1,000 more for the convenience. *Reason:* Prices at no-haggle dealerships are inflexible and typically higher than those that consumers could negotiate for themselves at traditional showrooms.

W. James Bragg, author of *In the Driver's Seat: The New Car Buyer's Negotiating Bible.* Random House.

■ **File all receipts** for returned merchandise with receipts. When you get your credit card statement, make sure you were credited for the returned item. *If no credit appears:* Contact your credit card company at the 800 number on your bill.

How to Return Just About Anything by Patricia Forst, Longwood, FL–based lecturer on consumer satisfaction. Thomas Nelson Publishers.

■ **Plan major purchases in advance.** This gives you time to look for sales on specific items you need—especially big-ticket ones. You will be less likely to shop for the best price after your present machine breaks down completely and perhaps causes household havoc.

Larry Roth, editor, *Living Cheap News*, Box 700058, San Jose, CA 95170.

■ **Limited-edition-collectibles trap.** Very few coins, plates, and artworks touted as rarities make good investments. They are manufactured on assembly lines and sold at high prices by professional direct-marketing firms. Within a couple of years, you can find these items at secondhand stores for a fraction of their original prices.

Scrooge Investing by Mark Skousen, Ph.D., adjunct professor of economics. Dearborn Financial Publishing, Inc.

■ **Department-store fluorescent lighting** often distorts colors. *Result:* You may not be able to tell the true color of clothing, lipstick, or other merchandise you've purchased until you get it home. *Self-defense:* If what you buy doesn't live

You do not need to invent a complicated story to return an item, nor must you justify yourself to a sales clerk. But for people who are uncomfortable making returns, it helps to be clear on your reason ahead of time. The clerk will probably ask for a reason to fill in on the store's return form. In most cases, this is not a challenge to your right to make the return. It is simply the clerk's job. *Common valid reasons for returns:*

- Item doesn't fit well.
- Item faded, bled, shrank.
- Color is wrong.
- Item is defective.
- Item does not perform as promised.
- Item arrived too late.
- Parts are missing.
- Item was an unwanted gift.
- Changed mind, don't like it.
- Ordered two, want to return one.
- Have one just like it.
- Found one for a lower price.
- No longer need it.
- Toy/item is dangerous.

• **Save proof of purchases.** It is always easier to make returns if you have the sales receipt. But a credit-card slip or statement is usually enough to prove where you bought an item and how much you paid for it. *Good policy:* Staple tags or credit-card slips to sales receipts and keep them for a while after making purchases.

• **Charge your major purchases.** Charging allows you more "return leverage" because you have a record of your purchase, even if you lose the receipt. If a store refuses to honor a reasonable return request, you can threaten to withhold payment. *Caution:* The store may use such action to file a negative credit report against you, so be sure to consult the credit-reporting company's rules before doing this.

• **Shop at stores that have favorable return policies.** Generally, large department stores are matter-of-fact about returns. Small shops and boutiques are likely to have more conservative return policies. We have found a wide disparity in store policies. *Common variable factors:* Window of time allowed for returns . . . whether cash refunds or store credits are issued.

Caution: Always ask about the return policies at small businesses.

• **Return merchandise promptly—in good condition.** If you know you want to return something, do it promptly, as some stores limit the amount of time from the date of purchase they will accept returns. Whenever possible, return merchandise in the original box or bag, clean, refolded or polished.

• **Deal with the person in charge.** Often, store clerks do not have the authority to accept a return. If you meet with a reluctant or rude store clerk, ask to speak with the manager. Most stores want their customers to be satisfied, and will try to please you—so don't take "no" for an answer.

• **Be prepared to compromise.** In the event you have exceeded a store's return policy, be flexible. You may not get exactly what you want—a cash refund—but you may be able to negotiate for a store credit, partial refund or exchange.

• **Don't feel—or act—guilty.** Returning merchandise is neither immoral nor illegal—so don't keep unwanted items.

Stores can resell merchandise returned in good condition . . . stores can usually return used or damaged merchandise to their suppliers for credit . . . losses incurred for merchandise that can't be returned are a legitimate cost of doing business that stores build into their prices.

You are already paying for your right to return—so use it!

• **Know your legal rights.** Manufacturer's warranties generally provide for repairs at no charge if an item doesn't work. Most merchants will exchange defective items for new ones. But even if an item you purchase has no warranty, all merchandise is sold by law under an "implied warranty."

This unwritten warranty provides that the product you buy will do what you bought it for, for a reasonable amount of time.

Example: A shirt is made to be washed or dry-cleaned. If it shreds, bleeds or shrinks, it is not performing as a shirt.

TRAPS TO AVOID

up to your expectations, take it back and demand a refund—the store's poor lighting isn't your fault.

Live Better for Less, 21 E. Chestnut St., Chicago 60611.

■ **Do not buy extended warranties.** They are high-cost insurance against small risks that you can cover out of your own pocket. *Beware:* Salespeople push the warranties hard—they are a major profit center for retailers. *Reality:* Only 10% of camcorders bought between 1987 and 1992 ever needed to be repaired.

Consumer Reports, 101 Truman Ave., Yonkers, NY 10703.

■ **Car-care traps.** Changing the oil is the most neglected routine car service. Car owners also often fail to take care of cooling and emissions systems and wheel alignment. Routine maintenance of these systems—including oil changes at intervals specified in the owner's manual—can make a car last longer, with far less chance of major repair bills for severe engine damage.

Donna Wagner, director of operations and spokesperson, Car Care Council, 1 Grande Lake Dr., Port Clinton, OH 43452.

■ **Avoid disputed hotel mini-bar charges** by keeping a list of what you take to eat and drink. *Even better:* Refuse to accept the mini-bar key, and insist that the hotel note this fact on your guest record.

Consumer Reports Travel Letter, 101 Truman Ave., Yonkers, NY 10703.

MONEY SAVERS

■ **Telephonic** Yellow Pages offers virtually all business information available in the Yellow Pages to people who have trouble reading the phone book. The free service, based in Lakewood, California, provides numbers and information on businesses anywhere in the U.S., and is available seven days a week, 24 hours a day. It will even give directions on how to get to an establishment. *More information:* 800-935-5672.

■ **Insulation cuts bills.** Heating and cooling can account for 60% of a home's energy use. Insulation can lower costs significantly. In cold climates, doubling the thickness of insulation on the attic floor can cut 40% of the heat seeping up through ceilings. In warm climates, the same insulation can prevent 40% of the heat trapped in the attic from coming into living areas.

Solving Your Financial Problems by Richard L. Strohm, attorney, Scottsdale, AZ. Career Press.

■ **Keep any utility bill** showing a deposit until the deposit is credited back to your account. This applies to bills from telephone and cable-TV companies and any other firms that require deposits when starting service.

Kiplinger's Personal Finance Magazine, 1729 H St. NW, Washington, DC 20006.

■ **Lightbulb savvy.** Compact fluorescent bulbs screw into standard lightbulb sockets and give off light that looks like that from incandescent bulbs . . . but last more than 10 times as long and use only one-quarter the energy. *Cost per 60-watt bulb:* About $20, plus $10 of electricity over its lifetime. Ten traditional bulbs would cost less (about $10) but use $45 of electricity. *Best places to use:* Where

• **Know your recourse.** Most problems with consumer products can be resolved by speaking to the store manager. When this approach fails, you should write a letter of complaint both to the retailer and to the manufacturer.

Helpful: Call the Better Business Bureau, a local action line, hot line or consumer action panel or your state consumer-protection agency.

If a substantial amount of money is at stake, you may wish to file a claim in small claims court. Finally, you may wish to complain to a federal agency, such as the Consumer Product Safety Commission.

DON'T FALL FOR THESE MYTHS

• *Myth: I've already worn it, so I can't return it.* While you can't return something because you ruined it yourself, you can certainly return any item that does not do what it is supposed to do.

Example: A popcorn maker that doesn't pop.

• *Myth: I can't return it—it was a gift.* Even if you don't have a receipt, most stores will accept returns of gifts that can be identified as theirs from a label or packaging.

• *Myth: The receipt says "All sales final."* Could be—but it's always worth a try. You may be able to exchange the item for store credit.

Exception: Personal items, such as bathing suits or underwear, are generally not returnable unless the original packaging is undisturbed.

• *Myth: I can't return it—I bought it months ago.* A defect may not appear for some time, but this doesn't mean that you can't ask to have it repaired or replaced at no charge.

Example: I bought a VCR which broke down after four months. Even though the 90-day warranty had expired, the store replaced it anyway, because it contained a defective part.

• *Myth: I can't return food.* Most supermarkets will gladly accept returns of unopened canned foods or foods that are spoiled or defective.

Example: After my cat went on a "diet," I returned several cans of a brand of cat food I no longer wanted.

• *Myth: It's my tough luck if I found one cheaper after I already bought this one.* If an item goes on sale soon after you bought it for the regular price, or if you find the same item elsewhere for a lower price, by all means, take it back! Many stores will refund the difference.

How to Solve Consumer Complaints

Shirley Rooker

To help you get the results you deserve when lodging a consumer complaint:

• **Evaluate the problem and decide what action you want taken**, whether it's repairing or replacing the faulty product, getting a full or partial refund, etc.

Cars: Get a receipt every time the car is serviced. Without a record of the car's problems, your complaint will be worthless.

• **Call the person you dealt with initially** and explain your problem and what you'd like done. If he/she is unable to help, proceed to the store manager. If he/she can't help, go to his/her boss, and so on.

Important: Be assertive, not aggressive. Aggressiveness puts the other person on the defensive and never helps your case in the long run.

• **Keep a detailed record of everything that transpires**, including the name, phone number, and title of each person you talk with, and the date and content of each conversation.

• **If your problem still isn't solved**, explain it in writing and include a summary of what you'd like to have happen and a record of all the steps you've taken so far. Send it to the person ranked above the last person you've talked with, and follow up by phone.

Shirley Rooker, president of Call For Action, a Washington, DC–based international consumer hot line.

lights are left on at least two hours per day. *Caution:* The fluorescent bulbs won't fit all lamps or covered fixtures.

You Can Change America by The Earth Works Group, dedicated to facilitating change at a grass-roots level. Earthworks Press.

■ **Kitchen energy-saver.** Avoid using your dishwasher's heated dry cycle. Most newer models have the option of drying dishes without heat. It may take longer but you'll save energy.

1001 Ways to Cut Your Expenses by Jonathan D. Pond, president, Financial Planning Information Inc. Dell.Inexpensive

Inexpensive Products to Make Your Home Safer

David Alexander

• **Carbon monoxide detector.** This smoke detector-like device warns you of high levels of carbon monoxide.

• **GFCI plugs in bathrooms and the kitchen.** A ground fault circuit interrupter instantly cuts off power when it surges or leaks—such as when a plugged-in hair dryer falls into a filled bathtub.

• **New extension cords.** Replace cords that are frayed or worn. Look for new cords rated "medium capacity" for household chores, "heavy capacity" for major appliances and power tools. *Test:* If a cord feels warm, it should be replaced by a heavier-duty cord.

• **Antiscald shower heads.** Shuts off the flow of water before it gets hot enough to cause first-degree burns.

MONEY SAVERS

- **Flashlight.** Keep one near your bed so you'll know where it is the next time disaster strikes.

David Alexander, spokesperson, National Safety Council, 1121 Spring Lake Dr., Itasca, IL 60143.

■ **Turn off the washing machine valve** when you are not doing laundry. Water hoses under pressure can burst at any time. Keeping the water turned off prevents *excessive* water damage if a hose bursts when you're out or asleep.

Stephen Gladstone, president of Stonehollow Inc. Fine Home Inspections in Stamford, CT.

■ **Buy gasoline early in the morning.** You'll get up to 5% more gas in the summer if you fill your tank before the hot sun has expanded the gas in the service station's fuel tanks.

Lee and Barbara Simmons, authors of *Penny Pinching: How to Lower Your Everyday Expenses Without Lowering Your Standard of Living.* Bantam Books.

■ **Keep fruit and vegetables fresh longer by putting a dry sponge in the crisper bin.** The sponge absorbs the excess moisture that causes spoilage—for about 39¢, as compared with more expensive "vegetable crisper bags."

Martha M. Bullen and Darcie Sanders, authors of *Never Throw Out a Banana Again.* Crown Trade Paperbacks.

■ **Low-cost pest control.** To eliminate ants, wash cabinets, floors, and counters with equal parts of vinegar and water. For mosquito repellant, rub your skin with apple cider vinegar or citronella oil, available in hardware stores. Leave an open bottle of pennyroyal or citronella oil in rooms that attract mosquitoes.

Dean King, coauthor of *The Penny Pincher's Almanac, Handbook for Modern Frugality.* Simon & Schuster.

- **If the company refuses to respond**, contact your local consumer hot line, the consumer protection office in your city or state, or small claims court.

FRAUDULENT COMPANIES

- **Ask for your money back** with the realization that you probably won't get it. Many of these companies operate for a short time in one area before moving on to another location and changing their name.
- **If they don't respond in a timely fashion** (in a few weeks), you should report them to the postal authorities, the Federal Bureau of Investigation, the Federal Trade Commission, or any other state or federal organization that can put them out of business.
- **Protect yourself from fraudulent companies** by avoiding prize offers with a price attached, offers that sound "too good to be true" and offers that are only good if you send your check or money order "today."

Secrets of Big-Time Food-Bill Savings

Linda Bowman

Most of us have had the thought, "I can't believe I'm paying this much for one bag of stuff," as the supermarket cashier finishes ringing up the "few things" we ran to the store for.

"Did I really buy that much?" we wonder. Usually, we haven't bought that much—just paid too much. Here are some ways to save big on the family food bill.

Linda Bowman, professional bargain hunter and author of the *More for Your Money* series of guides, including *Free Food & More* and *Freebies (and More) for Folks Over 50.* Probus Publishing Co.

SUPERMARKET SAVINGS

- **Shop with a list** . . . or you'll spend more than you save.
- **Clip coupons**—and keep them organized. Don't throw money away with the garbage. Coupons can easily save you $1,000 a year.

Be willing to give up brand loyalty in favor of a meaningful discount. One brand of tomato paste or dish detergent is much like another.

File coupons in envelopes by category—canned goods, cereals, pet foods, paper products, etc. Put coupons you plan to use right away and those with short expiration dates in the front. Take them with you to the store, along with an empty envelope to put coupons in for the items you select, so you don't have to sort them at the check-out counter.

Shop at a supermarket that honors double the value on the face of coupons. You can also increase your savings by combining in-store sales with coupons. Be sure to calculate the per-unit price of products when using coupons.

Example: A 6-ounce jar of instant coffee may cost $3.29, or 55¢ an ounce, and a 10-ounce jar $4.99, or 50¢ an ounce. Normally, the larger size is the better buy. But with a 75¢ coupon, at a double-coupon store, the 6-ounce jar costs $1.79, or 30¢ an ounce, while the 10-ounce jar is $3.49, or 35¢ an ounce.

- **Companion product offers.** Companies and supermarkets often issue coupons for a free item, with the purchase of a companion item.

Examples: A free gallon of milk with the purchase of a breakfast cereal . . . a free box of pasta with the purchase of spaghetti sauce.

- **Refund and rebate offers.** You may need to clip UPC symbols or save register receipts as "proof of purchase" to send for these offers. They are worth the trouble—and can be very lucrative, whether you get a cash rebate, additional coupons or free products.

- **Senior discounts.** Many large chain stores and some independent markets issue senior discount cards that allow cashiers to subtract as much as 5% to 10% off the final bill.

MONEY SAVERS

■ **Try out a new restaurant by visiting it for lunch** rather than for dinner. *Reasons:* Lunch prices are lower, and the food selection on a restaurant's lunch menu will usually be similar to that on its dinner menu. And—you can always return to a restaurant for a special dinner *after* you know for sure that the food and service are good.

Mary Hunt, publisher of *The Cheapskate Monthly*, Box 2135, Paramount, CA 90723.

GOOD DEALS

■ **Free books.** The Library of Congress gives away thousands of duplicate or unneeded books to nonprofit groups. *Important:* You will need to travel to the Library to select the books. *More information:* Exchange and Gift Division, Madison Building, 101 Independence Ave. SE, Room B-03, Washington, DC 20540.

■ **Free or low-cost information** on hundreds of health, family and consumer issues is available through the U.S. Consumer Information Center. The center's free catalog offers more than 200 publications. *Subjects:* Health and nutrition, cars, children, federal programs, money, small business, travel, and hobbies. *To request a catalog:* Send name and address to Consumer Information Catalog, Pueblo, Colorado 81009.

■ **Good buys on personal computers** can be obtained in this extremely competitive market. *Tactics:* Shop at the end of the quarter when hardware and software makers "stuff" retail channels to reduce inventory and retailers offer discounts to move the extra product . . . don't insist on advertised prices—in-store prices may be lower, so ask for the *best* price. Consider "old" models that may be available at a deep discount when the difference in performance compared with newer models is in fact minimal. Don't be seduced by a lot of preloaded software, most people never use most of it.

Lise Buyer, T. Rowe Price retailing analyst, in The Wall Street Journal.

■ **Super supermarketing.** Organize supermarket coupons in the same sequence as the products are arranged in the store. *Examples:* Pasta . . . canned goods . . . cleaning supplies . . . dairy. *Helpful:* Copy the store's aisle signs, and paste the list on your coupon envelope or folder.

Ed Ahrens, a Bottom Line/Personal *reader who lives in Miami.*

■ **Superstore limits.** Despite this growing trend in selling books, baby goods, sporting goods, pet supplies, clothing and more—*super* doesn't necessarily mean *better*. Smaller specialty stores tend to carry popular merchandise and offer the best sales support and service. Superstores may have wide selections . . . but they often don't have the best products and the salespeople tend to be less knowledgeable. Also, prices at superstores may not be the bargains many would expect.

Robert Kahn, president of Robert Kahn and Associates, a retailing consulting firm, and publisher of Retailing Today, *Box 249, Lafayette, CA 94549.*

■ **How to tell if that big holiday sale is really a bargain:** Go through your newspaper's Sunday circulars and make calls to several stores. Sales have become so common that it is impossible to tell if *50% off* is a real bargain or a cut in an artifi-

• **Generic brands.** Not only are they here to stay, they are growing and growing. Generics can provide substantial savings, especially on grooming products, cereals and canned goods.

• **Track savings.** Most supermarkets total the amount saved with coupons at the bottom of the register receipt. You can deposit monthly savings from coupons, refunds, etc., in an account earmarked toward a goal.

SUPERMARKET ALTERNATIVES

• **Join a wholesale or warehouse shopping club.** These huge operations are springing up in metropolitan areas nationwide. Shopping is a no-frills enterprise, and products must often be purchased in bulk or large sizes. Brand selection may be limited and may change at any given time. But savings can be excellent. *Key:* Know your prices. Some warehouse-club prices are not significantly better than prices at the discounters.

• **Shop at farmers' markets**, where vegetables and fruits are fresher, tastier, and cheaper. Buy in bulk in-season, then can or preserve.

• **Shop at bakery outlets and "thrift stores."** Thrift stores are one-brand outlets for companies such as Entenmann's, Pepperidge Farm, Arnold's Bakery, Sunbeam Bread, and Wonder-Bread/Hostess. Prices run 30% to 50% off retail for day-old goods.

• **Food co-ops and buying clubs.** Consumer cooperatives are run by members and usually buy food in bulk and then repackage it for buyers. Members can save 15% to 50% on most items, because brokers, middlemen, and costly packaging are eliminated from the exchange.

- **Do it yourself.** Grow a vegetable garden, make your own frozen dinners from leftovers.

RESTAURANT SAVINGS

- **Happy-hour buffets.** Between 4 P.M. and 6 P.M., for the price of a drink—not necessarily alcoholic—many restaurants provide free buffets. If you don't mind eating early, many people find these feasts to be filling, fun dinners and a change in daily routine.

- **Early-bird specials.** Many restaurants offer much lower prices for those who order dinner between 4 P.M. and 6 P.M. You get the same food as on the dinner menu, often with dessert and beverage included, for less than you'd pay for the entrée alone during peak hours. To find specials, check local newspapers or call the restaurants that you are interested in.

- **Senior menus.** Some restaurants, particularly large chains, have senior menus, which offer smaller portions at lower prices. Carry your identification.

- **Two-for-one or free item coupons.** Check newspapers and circulars for coupons from area restaurants for "buy one entrée, get the second of equal or lesser value free" or "free wine or dessert with entrée" offers.

- **Restaurant discount books.**
Examples: Entertainment Publications publishes regional guides for about $35, with about 200 coupons for 2-for-1 meals and discounts at restaurants, fast-food chains and specialty shops (2125 Butterfield Rd., Troy, MI 48084, 800-285-5525). The Premier Dining Club qualifies you for 2-for-1 or other discounts at member restaurants nationwide (831 Greencrest Dr., Westerville, Ohio 43081, 800-346-3241).

INVEST IN SAVINGS

Other companies publish local or regional discount books as well. These can be a wise investment if you like to dine out a lot—but shop around. Prices and services vary substantially.

Key: Make sure the book contains enough discounts you will really use to pay for itself.

GOOD DEALS

cially inflated list price. *Strategy:* Ignore promises of 30%, 40% or 50% off and focus on what you will actually pay for an item. A store advertising 20% may actually have a lower price than one claiming 50% off.

Barbara Berger Opotowsky, president of the Better Business Bureau, New York.

■ **Some generic supermarket items** are *exactly* the same as the more expensive brand-name items. Certain items are required by law to be exactly the same in content and composition, regardless of packaging or quantity gimmicks. *Examples:* Aspirin, baking soda, corn starch, honey, molasses, peanuts, pecans, salt, sugar, unbleached flour and walnuts. Always buy the lower-cost generic brands when purchasing these items.

Ted Carroll, author of *Live Debt-Free*. Bob Adams.

Better Budgeting

■ **Budgeting secret:** Carefully plan a major purchase. Break down the cost of the item into a monthly sum you can set aside over a period of time. *Example:* If you want to buy a new car, put pictures of the car you want on your refrigerator and in your checkbook. There is less of a sense of deprivation if your goal is firmly planted in your mind.

Eric Gelb, CPA, Woodmere, NY, and author of *Personal Budget Planner*. Career Advancement Center.

■ **Simple way to save $600 a year.** Save all your loose change in a can or jar. As the container fills, deposit the money in the bank. Saving a dollar day plus all your pocket change should give you savings of $50 a month—or a total of $600 a year. *Strategy:* Let your buying habits help you. *Example:* If you buy a newspaper every morning for 35 cents, make it a habit to pay with a dollar—and save the 65 cents in change.

Barbara O'Neill, CFP, author of Saving on a Shoestring: How to Cut Expenses, Reduce Debt, Stash More Cash. Dearborn Financial.

■ **Better money saving.** Break down your financial goals into manageable parts. *Example:* Instead of worrying about how long it will take to save $500 and then giving up in frustration, concentrate on saving $10 a week for a year.

Bill Staton, C.F.A., president of The Financial Training Group, which holds personal finance seminars nationwide. He is author of How to Become a Multimillionaire on Just $50 a Month. To order: 300 East Blvd., B-4, Charlotte, NC 28203.

■ **Know exactly what is in your wallet**—at all times—so you can report if something is lost or stolen. *Strategy:* Arrange your credit cards so you can immediately see if one is missing. *Best:* Carry no more than two or three cards at a time, and keep a photocopy of all your credit cards at home—along with a list of whom to call in case of a problem.

Christine Dugas, author of Fiscal Fitness—A Guide to Shaping Up Your Finances for the Rest of Your Life. Andrews and McMeel.

■ **Use appliances at night.** Most power companies charge lower electricity rates at night. Even if your power company doesn't do this, you'll still reduce air conditioning costs if you run your dishwasher, dryer, oven and other heat-generating appliances at night, when it's cooler.

Lucy H. Hendrick, time management consultant and author of 365 Ways to Save Money. Hearst Books.

How Amy Dacyczyn Avoids Overspending at the Supermarket

Amy Dacyczyn

Although most people go to the supermarket with a budget in mind, they usually spend much more money than they had planned to spend. But by using a variety of strategies, I spend only $180 a month to feed our family of eight.

The first step to saving money at the supermarket is to overcome your most common excuses for why your bill is so high . . .

THE BIG MYTHS

• *Myth:* **Never shop with your kids.** *Reality:* If you can't say no to your children, you have a parenting problem, not a shopping problem.

• *Myth:* **Shop the aisles in reverse order to avoid temptation.** *Reality:* If you can't resist temptation, you have a problem with self-discipline, not budgeting.

• *Myth:* **Menus must be planned in advance to save at the supermarket.** *Reality:* Don't plan meals more than one day in advance, or you're likely to spend more at the supermarket.

Example: If you scheduled pork chops and they're too expensive, you'll probably buy them anyway. *Better:* Stock up on foods that are purchased at a good price. Then prepare meals with the foods you have already bought. There should be pork chops that you bought on sale in your freezer.

SUPERMARKET STRATEGIES

Once you've overcome the myths, you're ready to put serious money-saving strategies into place. *My favorites . . .*

Amy Dacyczyn, author of *The Tightwad Gazette* (Villard Books), a book of cost-cutting strategies that have appeared in her newsletter of the same name. Rural Route 1, Box 3570, Leeds, ME 04263.

• **Work on your attitude.** Saving money on groceries depends on a consistent attitude toward shopping—every time you shop. It is essential that you enter the supermarket fully conscious and determined about what you will—or will not—buy.

If you are prone to impulse shopping, you must decide to take control of your shopping habits.

Helpful: Practice. Try the strategies listed below, and learn more about what it costs for your family to eat the food you normally buy. Before you know it, nothing on earth could induce you to spend your hard-earned cash on a hamburger mix or sugarcoated cereal.

• **Shop with a list.** Make a list of specific groceries that you will buy at certain prices . . . but be flexible. What's on your list may not be on sale, but you may find a great deal on something that's not on your list.

Key: Be steadfast about what you will not buy. Certain products, such as toaster pastries, are too expensive at any price.

• **Keep a price book.** This strategy helps to save me more time and money than anything else I do.

In fact, comparison shopping is essential, since most people's memory for prices is not as good as they think it is. It's easy to figure out the cheapest can of green beans in one store, but most of us shop at more than one location—supermarkets, wholesale clubs, farmers' markets, natural food stores, discount stores—and foods come in different-sized packages.

To keep track of prices, I carry a small loose-leaf notebook that fits in my purse. On each page, I have listed the prices I've encountered for a specific product, with abbreviations for the store name, brand, item size, price and unit price. The pages are arranged alphabetically by product for easy reference.

Try shopping at a different good value store each week, so that you visit them all within a month. You will soon find patterns emerging.

Example: Cheese is usually a good buy at the wholesale club and seldom on sale at the supermarket.

■ **Reduce air conditioner use** by preparing oven-cooked meals during the coolest part of the day. When you're ready to eat, reheat the meal in a microwave or toaster oven.

Rochelle LaMotte McDonald, author of *How to Pinch a Penny Till It Screams*. Avery Publishing Group.

■ **Planting trees around your house** can save up to 25% on home energy bills. They block the wind in winter, and keep the house shaded in summer. Next to good insulation, energy-conscious landscaping is the best way to cut cooling and heating costs.

Marc Schiler, associate professor of architecture, University of Southern California, and coauthor of *Energy-Efficient and Environmental Landscaping*. Appropriate Solutions Press.

Rug-Care Regimen

Sara Wolf

To keep rugs in good shape, vacuum the *underside* at least twice a year. Rotate rugs to prevent fading and limit their attraction to insects. The insects that are attracted to rugs prefer quiet, static situations.

If you rotate rugs, you disturb insects and you also have the opportunity to examine the rugs for problems. If you have a rug with chemical dyes, use window treatments and screens or shades to keep the sun away from it or it will probably fade.

Do not mothproof—the chemicals can damage rug dyes. If a rug becomes damaged, have it repaired quickly—when damaged areas expand, they can be costly to fix.

Sara Wolf, director of conservation and collections management, The Textile Museum, Washington, DC.

SECRETS OF SUPER SAVINGS

Supersavers

Jackie Iglehart

When food shopping, weigh produce priced by the bunch, such as carrots, celery, broccoli, onions, and fruit. Buy the heaviest and get extra pounds free.

■ **Drink water.** It takes 15,000 eight-ounce glasses of tap water to equal the cost of a six-pack of soda.

■ **Freeze your credit card—literally.** Freeze in a plastic bag partially filled with water (it will not damage the magnetic strip). In an emergency, thaw.

■ **Furnish a college student's dorm or apartment** with "finds" from garage sales.

■ **If you have a chronic illness,** schedule telephone home visits with your doctor in place of regular office visits. This is a new option you should explore with your doctor.

■ **Veterans and senior citizens** can qualify for an exemption on property taxes. Your local tax office has information on the amount to which you are entitled.

■ **Make your own stationery.** Press small flowers and leaves in a thick phone book. Later glue the dried flowers on paper for an elegant look.

■ **Enlist your children's help to lower the utility bill.** Post last month's bill and let them share any money saved in the future.

Added benefit: You'll soon find that not every advertised sale is really a sale. Prices at the same store for the same item may vary from week to week by as much as a third.

Rule of thumb: The items at the front and back of the sale flyers are usually the best deals, though there may be a few on the inside pages.

• **Buy groceries in bulk.** This does not necessarily mean you have to buy huge quantities. It simply means you must buy enough of each item at its lowest price to provide for your family from sale to sale—or to last until your next trip to the wholesale club. Buying in bulk can save the average family at least $50 a month.

Helpful: Not all food has to be stored in the kitchen. If you were offered $50 a month to rent the space under your bed, would you do it? Use a closet or a shelf in the garage for that bargain case of peanut butter.

For maximum savings: Invest in an extra freezer. For example, the largest Sears model costs less than $6 a month to run. Even apartment dwellers can often arrange to keep locked freezers in the basements of their buildings.

• **Determine which products are the least expensive,** and how to buy them as inexpensively as possible.

Examples: I calculate which meats are the least expensive based on portion size, and I watch for sales. I generally choose from the lower end of cuts—with occasional treats. I also calculate the cost per gallon of fruit juice, whether it is frozen, bottled, or canned.

My family drinks apple, orange or grape juice . . . or lemonade made from sugar, water and lemon juice concentrate. We don't buy processed blends of fruit juices, which are always more expensive than other juices. We do buy store brands.

Stay away from: Single serving packages, snack packs, lunch sizes . . . almost anything disposable, except toilet paper and tissues.

Examples: Diapers, paper plates, napkins, tablecloths.

• **Set limits on what you are willing to pay for staple food items.** Gradually, you will determine realistic upper limits for the items you routinely buy. Stick to your limits.

Example: In my area of the country, I will pay no more than 69 cents a pound for meat on the bone—or $1.20 a pound or less for boneless.

• **Buy food in its "original" form.** Avoid convenience and processed foods. Pop your own popcorn. Make your own breading for chicken and pork. Buy regular oatmeal rather than processed cereal or "instant" oatmeal.

SECRETS OF SUPER SAVINGS

■ **Put summer grass clippings, autumn leaves, and vegetable scraps in a "compost pile."** Next spring there will be free mulch and fertilizer for the garden.

■ **Get a shoe "tune-up."** Have the uppers conditioned, attach neoprene protective soles, and apply a sealant to uppers that allows wear in any kind of weather with minimum damage.

■ **When the supermarket sells out of the loss-leader items,** always ask for rain checks and buy at rock-bottom prices when items are back in stock.

■ **Do your own wallpapering after viewing a do-it-yourself video.** Purchase wallpaper at a discount store for additional savings.

■ **Save on your food budget.** Contact the County Cooperative Extension Agent and receive information on gardening in your locale.

Jackie Iglehart, editor of The Penny Pincher *newsletter, 2 Hilltop Rd., Mendham, NJ 07945.*

ORIGINAL PARTY INVITATIONS

 Make original party invitations instead of buying cards at the store. Making them as a craft project helps your child become involved in planning his/her party. And it can be as much fun to make invitations by hand as to receive them.

Examples: Fold a paper, draw a design on it, cut around the design, then open the paper to create accordion-fold invitations. Cut out shapes of toys or animals from colored paper, then decorate each cutout with paper in a contrasting color—on which you can write the details of the invitation.

Child Magazine's Book of Children's Parties by Angela Wilkes, author of more than 30 children's books, London, England (Dorling Kindersley / $18.95).

CHEMICAL SELF-DEFENSE

■ **Ammonia and chlorine bleach danger.** Never mix these two common household cleaners. Many people do, thinking they will get a more powerful cleaning agent. *Truth:* When mixed, bleach and ammonia produce a noxious—and potentially deadly—gas. Ironically, the combination has virtually no cleaning power compared with the separate liquids.

Complete Trash: The Best Way to Get Rid of Practically Everything Around the House by Norm Crampton, secretary, Institute for Solid Wastes of the American Public Works Association. M. Evans and Co.

■ **Mothball danger:** Some moth repellents, particularly camphor balls, contain *naphthalene* and can be fatal if swallowed by children. Some infant deaths have occurred when babies were merely exposed to clothing and blankets stored with mothballs. *Also dangerous:* Mothballs containing *paradichlorobenzene.* They're less toxic but may be carcinogenic.

University of California Berkeley Wellness Letter, 5 Water Oak, Fernandina Beach, FL 32034.

■ **Fabric danger:** Formaldehyde resin used to keep no-iron linens, permanent-press clothing, and polyester/cotton fabrics wrinkle-free emits formaldehyde fumes for the life of the fabric—which could be years. *Symptoms of formaldehyde vapor inhalation:* Tiredness, headaches, coughing, watery eyes, respiratory problems. *Self-defense:* Buy only natural fibers, which are generally not treated with formaldehyde. *Also:* Avoid fabrics with labels reading "easy care 100% cotton" or "no-iron cotton,"

How to Avoid Becoming a Victim of a Violent Crime

Patricia Harman

From purse-snatching and car-jacking to assaults, rapes, and kidnappings, violent crime has become a frightening fact of everyday life. While there's little you can do to control the rise of these crimes, there are ways to limit your chances of becoming a victim.

IN YOUR CAR

• **Car-jacking self-defense.** Unlike professional car thieves, who have no wish to encounter car owners, car-jackers are out for a thrill—and violence for them is thrilling. Tell yourself *now* that if someone tries to pull you from your car or demands your keys, you will behave passively and give them the car. When the event occurs, you should instinctively give up the vehicle rather than panic and fight back.

• **Keep doors locked while driving.** Close windows in slow traffic and at red lights. When coming to a stop, leave enough room between you and the car in front. This will allow you to maneuver around the vehicle if necessary.

• **Pay attention to your surroundings.** Car-jackers almost always approach on foot. Avoid

Patricia Harman, a crime-prevention officer with the Prince William County, VA, police force. Harman, who conducts lectures nationally on personal safety, is the author of *The Danger Zone: How You Can Protect Yourself from Rape, Robbery, and Assault.* Parkside Publishing.

self-absorbed distractions, such as combing your hair, fumbling with cassette tapes, etc.

• **Park under a streetlight or as close as possible to the mall or well-lit buildings and stores.** Avoid parking next to potential hiding places, such as dumpsters, woods, etc.

• **Scan parking lots before approaching your car.** Try to walk with other people, or ask a doorman or security guard for an escort.

• **Have your key ready in your hand as you approach your vehicle.** Look inside the car and around the outside before getting in. *Caution:* On some new cars, all doors will unlock when the driver's door is unlocked—a dangerous feature if someone is hiding outside the passenger door. If you do sense danger, retreat to a place of safety and call the police immediately. Do not confront an intruder.

ON THE STREET

• **Carry purses and briefcases close to the body**—but be able to release them if necessary. *Avoid:* Shoulder straps across the body, straps wrapped around the wrist. People have been dragged by the straps and injured in purse-snatchings. If someone tries to take your wallet or purse, let it go. *Useful:* "Fanny pack" belts and pouches seem to be an unattractive target for street thieves.

• **On the bus or subway**, do not sit next to an exit door or place briefcases or purchases on an empty seat. Robbers tend to grab valuables as they are leaving and while doors are closing.

• **If you are held up, do not resist.** Most armed robbers only want your money. *Problem:* Many will turn to violence if they are alarmed or disobeyed. Surrender your valuables quickly.

AT HOME

• **Keep doors and windows locked**, especially after you turn in for the night. Keep curtains drawn after dark. Most home intruders are opportunists.

• **Install deadbolt locks with reinforced strike plates** on front and back doors. A few dollars will purchase a reinforced strike plate that secures

which could mean formaldehyde finishes.

The Nontoxic Home and Office: Protecting Yourself and Your Family from Everyday Toxics and Health Hazards by consumer advocate Debra Lynn Dadd. Jeremy P. Tarcher.

Scam Avoidance Checklist

Jonathan Pond

Don't be a participant in your own financial downfall. *Avoid* . . .

• Anything that requires up-front cash to get rich quick.

• Anything that requires you to pay for the secrets of someone else's success.

• Anything that promises to make you or your house the envy of your neighbors.

• Anything that costs you money in order to save you money.

• Anyone who tells you that rather than working for your money, you should let your money work for you.

• Anyone who doesn't tell you in plain English what it is you're putting your money into.

• Anyone who doesn't have the time, inclination, or willingness to let you get a second opinion about the proposed investment idea.

Jonathan Pond, president of Financial Planning Information, 9 Galen St., Watertown, MA 02172. He is a nationally recognized expert on financial planning. Mr. Pond has written many books, including *The New Century Family Money Book.* Bantam Doubleday Dell Publishing Group, Inc.

YOU AND YOUR HOME

■ **Tap water** can cause illness or even be fatal to people born with weakened immune systems, or who have immune systems that are weakened as a result of disease or drug treatment. *Problem:* The water-borne parasite, *Cryptosporidium,* is not eliminated by typical municipal water-treatment systems, and can cause serious digestive-tract illness in persons with weakened resistance. *Defenses:* If you are at risk, boil tap water at least one minute before using it . . . buy a water filter specifically designed to remove the bug . . . buy bottled water certified as bug-free. For more information, call the International Bottled Water Association at 800-928-3711 for brand names of bottled waters available in your area. ⋙

The Electricity/Health Connection

Robert O. Becker, M.D.

Electric razors may heighten leukemia risk, according to a scary new study—but they aren't the only electrical appliances that could cause cancer. Details of study by the authoritative Batelle Institute show that men who used electric shavers more than 2½ minutes a day were twice as likely to get leukemia as those who didn't.

Probable cause: Electrical fields from plug-in razors disrupt cell division controlled by the pineal gland. This study shows an effect from intermittent electromagnetic fields. Previous studies found higher cancer risk only in people exposed continuously to such fields—

the door frame to the first wall stud. Locks like these are also deterrents.

• **Secure sliding glass doors** by placing a broomstick or piece of wood along the interior track and by blocking the dead space in the upper channel that allows the door to be lifted off the track.

• **Consider installing an alarm system.** Ground-floor windows can be equipped with an alarmed jamming stick for $30 to $40.

• **Never confront a burglar.** If you come home to a door that's ajar or has been tampered with, leave the scene immediately and call the police. If you wake up to find an intruder in your bedroom, pretend to be asleep until he leaves.

• **Don't depend on your dog to alert you.** Most people command their dogs to stop barking when a stranger arrives. Many a dog has slept through a burglary or been seduced by a doggie treat.

• **Do not open the door to strangers.** If you have to hire an unfamiliar repairman, ask someone to be with you at home or plan to be on the phone when he arrives . . . or pretend there is someone else at home. If a repairman or stranger arrives at your door unannounced, do not let him/her in. Lock the door and call his office for verification.

• **If you think you hear a prowler, call the police.** Don't assume it's just the wind, that the police are too busy, or that they might get mad if no one is there. It is always better to feel foolish than to be a victim.

• **Unless you are well-trained, do not keep a gun in the house.** People who are untrained with firearms are more likely to have them stolen or taken away from them by intruders, who may have arrived unarmed. If you do keep a gun in the house, the gun and ammunition should be stored separately.

Caution: According to law, in order to shoot an intruder on your property, you must be "in fear for your life." This does not mean in fear of losing your TV and jewelry.

• **Know your neighbors.** Neighborhood watch programs and "telephone trees" to alert neighbors of strangers in the area are very effective.

AT WORK

• **Know your neighbors.** Set up a building-wide security policy to identify visitors. "Business watch" programs for merchants in shopping areas are highly effective, too.

• **Team up in pairs** to use public rest rooms or locked rest rooms located in public hallways. Avoid using remote stairwells alone.

• **Keep the office's doors locked** when working late, on weekends, or early in the morning.

• **Do not get on an elevator** with someone who makes you feel uncomfortable or unsafe.

• **When traveling on business**, ask a bellhop to accompany you to your hotel room and to check it before you enter. Avoid ground-floor rooms. Make sure that the phone is working and that security numbers are provided. Never open the door to someone you're not expecting. If someone knocks unannounced, call the lobby for verification.

AT PLAY

• **Exercise with a partner**, or take along a dog or stick while jogging. Avoid isolated parks and paths. Wear glasses if you normally need them, and do not use a stereo headset. Avoid loose clothes that are easy to grab.

• **At parks, beaches, or other recreation areas**, know where the ranger or lifeguard stations are located. Leave expensive cameras, jewelry, and credit cards at home or locked in the trunk of the car. Do not use recreation areas after hours.

IN ALL SITUATIONS

• **Make direct eye contact with people around you.** This sends a message of confidence, an effective deterrent to violent crime. Criminals seek passive, distracted victims, who make easy targets.

• **Trust your instincts.** Humans are extremely instinctive. *Important:* Tune into the messages. Some of the most common statements police officers hear following a crime are, "I had a feeling I shouldn't have walked to my car," "The guy gave me the creeps, but . . ."

Bottom line: If a situation makes you nervous, avoid it. Learn to respect your instincts and act on them.

YOU AND YOUR HOME

at work or at home (power lines, computer terminals, electric blankets, etc.).

Self-defense:

Limit exposure time—or maintain a safe distance from the following sources of electromagnetic fields . . .

• **Electric shavers.** Use only if in a rush or away from home.

• **Hair dryers.** Minimize home use—professional users should avoid holding at chest height.

• **Massagers/vibrators.** Minimize use.

• **Microwave ovens.** Pregnant women should avoid standing in front of these during use . . . all users should stand at least three feet away. Have technician check oven-door seal periodically for radiation leakage.

• **TV.** To find a safe distance for any set, use a portable AM radio: Tune to a spot between stations to get static . . . turn up volume . . . turn on TV and—holding the radio two to three feet away—back up until static starts to fade.

• **Laser printers, fax machines, and photocopiers.** Should be at least four to six feet from the nearest worker's desk—pregnant women should avoid use entirely.

• **Electric blankets.** Discard those made before early 1990 . . . look for new models that emit no electromagnetic radiation . . . or—turn on blanket an hour before bedtime to warm bed, then turn off and unplug the blanket before getting in.

Robert O. Becker, M.D., Lowville, NY. He is the author of Cross Currents. *Jeremy Tarcher, Inc. The book is about electromagnetic radiation and your health.*

YOU AND YOUR HOME

■ **Avoid packing valuables** in checked baggage—carry them on the plane. Some travel-insurance policies exclude cameras, jewelry, and other valuables from theft coverage. If you must carry expensive items in checked baggage, before you leave home buy an insurance policy that specifically covers those items.

Ed Perkins, editor, Consumer Reports Travel Letter, 101 Truman Ave., Yonkers, NY 10703. Monthly. $39/yr.

Where to Hide Your Valuables

Bill Phillips

To decide where to hide valuables, you need to understand exactly how burglars operate. The worst room to use is the master bedroom—the place where most people like to hide things. Thieves are likely to start right there. Burglars usually know just where to search both in the master bedroom and in other rooms—including the kitchen, where they are almost sure to check the cookie jar.

But thieves are in a hurry. They rarely spend more than 20 minutes in a house. You can take advantage of a burglar's haste to get away before he is detected by storing valuables in stealth devices. These hiding places take a thief a long time to locate.

• **The Wall Outlet Safe** has a tiny compartment, and it requires installation. But if you choose a color and style indistinguishable from your real outlets, there's little likelihood of its being detected. The sockets accept plugs, so you can plug in a combination

The Most Commonly Asked Legal Questions

Thomas Hauser

Sooner or later, you'll probably need the advice of a lawyer. What are you most likely to ask about and how can these legal problems be resolved? *Here are the top eight . . .*

When and how can I use small claims court? This is a quick, inexpensive way to solve minor legal problems (typically around $1,000). You don't even need a lawyer.

Step 1: Look in your local telephone directory under "Courts," "City of . . ." for Small Claims Court, Justice Court, Magistrates Court, or Court of Common Appeals. You must sue in the county where the defendant lives or conducts business. Check the county clerk to make sure it's the right court, and to get the proper legal name for the company you're suing.

Step 2: When you arrive at court for the first time, a clerk will give you a complaint form to fill out. *Cost:* Between $2 and $10. It asks for your name and address, the defendant's name and address, a brief description of why you're suing, and the damages claimed. *Note:* Small claims courts only award money. They cannot order actions.

Step 3: The clerk will assign you a hearing date (usually in about two weeks) and notify the defendant by mail. Often the sessions are held in the early evening.

Step 4: Before your hearing, gather evidence—contracts, photographs, accident reports, witnesses—and organize how you will present your case. A written outline helps. Be sure to get to court on time.

Step 5: If the judge is overloaded, you may be asked to submit your dispute to arbitration—to an

Thomas Hauser, lawyer and author of The Family Legal Companion. Allworth Press.

impartial third party . . . often an attorney. That may make sense, but you should know that an arbitrator's decision is final. You won't be able to appeal it to a judge or a higher court. If the defendant fails to appear, you will be sent before an arbitrator who will listen to your testimony and award you appropriate damages (usually including repayment of your filing fee and interest). If the defendant, after being notified by mail, fails to pay up, call the court clerk and ask how to use law-enforcement personnel to collect your judgment.

Is there a statute of limitations on medical malpractice? Yes. As with other causes of action, claims of medical malpractice must be initiated within a given period of time, which differs from state to state. In New York, in the absence of qualifying circumstances, a medical malpractice suit must be initiated within 30 months of the act. However, New York and most other states grant children under age 18 who are the victims of malpractice an extension of time within which to sue. Ask your local bar association for the name of an attorney who can tell you exactly what the law is in your state given your particular circumstances.

What can I do if my landlord refuses to make repairs . . . or paint? A lease is a contract entitling the landlord to receive rent if he/she provides you with certain guarantees, including a "warranty of habitability" that the place is safe and livable. This means the plumbing should work, etc. Repairs must be made within a "reasonable" period of time, which, of course, varies depending on whether it's a dangerous gas leak or merely a broken dishwasher.

Recourse: Most towns have special housing courts where tenants can file complaints without a lawyer. You could also send the landlord a letter by certified mail warning him that if repairs are not made immediately you will hire a contractor yourself and deduct the cost from your monthly rent.

Under very damning circumstances—if, for example, he has a policy of refusing repairs in order to drive tenants out—you could withhold rent. However, this carries with it the risk of eviction. Don't do it without first consulting a lawyer.

YOU AND YOUR HOME

battery/outlet clock radio with a light-up dial and actually run it on batteries. Or, you can install the outlet safe in a child's room. This is usually the last place thieves look, but also the place people don't like to hide valuables lest children get at them. They won't, though, if the fake outlet is behind a piece of furniture. And a thief probably won't, either—especially if you insert convincing child safety clips in the sockets.

• **The Flower Pot Safe.** A real, plastic flower pot with a hollowed out hidden compartment within. The compartment is no larger than a small juice glass, but it makes a pretty safe place to keep a necklace and earrings or other valuables, as well as a few large bills.

• **Book Safe.** Especially effective if you have lots of real books to hide it among. *Helpful:* Models hollowed out from actual books. You can't order these by title, but unlike a wooden fake book this model will age exactly like a real book.

• **Safe Cans.** These are facsimiles of popular canned products: Shaving creams, cleansers, spray cans, etc. As stealth devices they are well-known to thieves. But they come in a wide variety of designs, and new ones appear all the time. *Best:* Spend extra money for a weighted model, since one that feels too light could betray its real use.

Bill Phillips, a lock expert who writes on security and safety issues. He is the author of *Home Mechanix Guide to Security: Protecting Your Home, Car and Family.* John Wiley & Sons.

ONE STEP AHEAD

■ **Always carry adhesive bandage strips** when going hiking, in-line skating, biking, running, etc. Sports and walking sometimes cause blisters that can ruin an outing . . . spoil a workout . . . and make it tough to get home. Simply using a little bandage can make a big difference in comfort.

Fitness Hollywood by Keli Roberts, personal trainer, Los Angeles, CA. Summit Group, $19.95.

■ **Get a tetanus booster shot** every 10 years. The protection generated by the shot deteriorates over time. Older people, in particular, who have not had a booster shot in decades lose immunity to this completely preventable but potentially fatal disease.

Timothy McCall, M.D., internist practicing in the Boston area and author of *Examining Your Doctor: A Patient's Guide to Avoiding Harmful Medical Care.* Birch Lane Press, $22.50.

■ **Carry baby wipes** to use on public toilet seats to remove dirt and germs. The wipes clean quickly and are better than toilet paper for getting rid of germs. Choose a flushable wipe so you can dispose of it easily.

Bruce Yaffe, M.D., gastroenterologist and internist in private practice, 121 E. 84 St., New York, NY 10028.

■ *Reminder:* **Safest way to lift objects**—bend knees and squat down to the object's level. Bring it close to you, then stand up slowly. This lets your leg muscles do the work of lifting, reducing the chance of back injury. *When lifting objects out of a car trunk or rear seat:* Since you must bend at the waist, put a knee on the bumper or a foot inside the car—to reduce back-muscle stress.

Stephen Hochschuler, M.D., cofounder, Texas Back Institute, Plano, TX.

The terms for painting are usually specified in the lease. If the landlord stalls, you can go to the special housing court or to small claims court to have your rent reduced or to get the money needed to hire a painter yourself.

Do I need a lawyer when I'm buying a house? Yes. Buying a house is an extremely complex undertaking and you should be represented by counsel who will look out for your best interests. Is the title good? Does the seller have a faulty deed? Are there any outstanding claims against the property? Does the house satisfy zoning ordinances? Many of these questions are matters of subtle legal interpretation, and you will want written guarantees that fully protect you.

What happens if my credit card or ATM card is stolen? Under the Consumer Credit Protection Act consumers are liable for only $50 if a credit card is stolen, and even that may be waived under some circumstances. However, a different standard applies to automated teller machine cards. Under the federal Electronic Fund Transfer Act, your liability is limited to $50 if you notify the bank within two business days. Thereafter, your liability jumps to $500.

If an unauthorized transfer appears on your bank statement and you don't report it within 60 days of the mailing date you risk losing everything in your account plus any credit line. Report any lost or stolen card to the bank immediately by phone and in writing.

Protection: Don't carry your ATM password in your wallet, and avoid obvious numbers like your birth date and the first four digits of your Social Security number.

Am I legally entitled to see my personnel file at work? You might be, depending on the kind of job you have and the state in which you work. Virtually all employees of the federal government have access, and union contracts provide this same privilege to many workers in the private sector.

Otherwise, your rights depend on the laws of the state where you work. California's Labor Code mandates access to all records "which are used or have been used to determine that employee's qualifications for employment, promotion, additional compensation, termination, or other disciplinary action." Letters of reference and records relating to the investigation of possible criminal offenses are exempt.

Many states have similar statutes, and Oregon requires employers to keep personnel records available to employees for at least 60 days after termination of employment. Contact your State Department of Labor to find out what the law allows.

What can I do about a noisy neighbor? Depending on the specific complaint, your neighbor's actions may constitute a violation of civil or criminal law. Playing loud music late at night amounts to disorderly conduct, for which you can call the police. Civil steps can also be taken under the "nuisance" law, which provides that people have the right to reasonable comfort in their homes. Acts that might be perfectly proper under some circumstances become unlawful if they interfere with your enjoyment of this right.

Example: Your neighbor can use a chain saw, but not at midnight. He has the right to mow his lawn, but maybe not at 6 A.M. on a Sunday morning since he could do it at another time that wouldn't interfere with others' one day to sleep in late.

Do I have a case when I wait for a delivery person who never comes? Yes. This is a breach of contract. If you take a half day off work, for example, and the couch isn't delivered as promised, the store has violated its part of the contract. Call and ask for a new delivery time at your convenience. Most stores can deliver at night, for example, although they don't advertise that. Failing satisfaction, demand that the cost of additional time off from work be deducted from your bill. If all else fails, take the case to small claims court.

ONE STEP AHEAD

■ **Sitting on a cushion while driving** is safer. Many drivers need to sit high so their seat belts cannot slip across their necks. Pressure on the neck can stimulate points along the carotid artery that send messages to the heart and peripheral blood vessels, causing blood pressure to lower—resulting in dizziness or fainting.

Padmanabhan Iyer, M.D., is an internist at Lenox & Addington Hospital, Napanee, Ontario.

MEDICATION SAFETY

■ **Prescription drug scare** resulted from news reports that 25% of older Americans are taking drugs that could hurt rather than help them. *Reality:* The risk is exaggerated—most problems with prescription drugs result from failing to follow doctor's instructions. In a small number of cases, drugs also may have adverse effects when taken in combination with over-the-counter remedies or other drugs that your doctor does not know you are taking. *Important:* Always consult your doctor or pharmacist before combining any medicines.

Ralph E. Small, M.D., professor of pharmacy and medicine, Medical College of Virginia Hospital, Box 980533 MCV, Richmond, VA 23298.

How to Keep Your Neighborhood Safe from Crime

Stephanie Mann

The key to making any neighborhood safe from crime is the willingness of its residents to play a role in crime prevention.

Most people believe that this task should be accomplished by law-enforcement officers. Unfortunately, the criminal justice system—police, courts, jails, etc.—is designed to deal with crime only after it has taken place.

Though the police are better able to root out criminal activity, neighbors have far more power to stop crime from happening in the first place.

In my experience as a crime-prevention consultant, the best way to reduce crime is to form a Neighborhood Watch-type of group. These groups—also known as Block Watch, Home Alert, or Neighborhood Alert—now protect more than 20,000 neighborhoods in the U.S.

Neighborhood Watch groups are most effective in stable neighborhoods where most residents own their homes. But with enough persistence, they can also work in apartment buildings.

HOW TO START A GROUP

• **Ask your police department for pamphlets and other instructional materials.** In neighborhoods with significant gang or drug activity, a strong relationship with the police is important.

• **Start small.** Find one neighbor who shares your concern about crime and wants to do something about it. See if each of you can bring another neighbor to a preliminary meeting to discuss the Neighborhood Watch concept.

Stephanie Mann, who helped start the Neighborhood Watch concept in 1969 in Orinda, CA. A crime-prevention consultant to police departments and businesses nationwide, she is coauthor, with M.C. Blakeman, of *Safe Homes, Safe Neighborhoods: Stopping Crime Where You Live*. Nolo Press.

• **Define your neighborhood boundaries.** It is generally best to cast a small net at the start, then expand as membership grows. My watch group covers a cul-de-sac with 20 homes.

• **Conduct a door-to-door neighborhood concerns survey.** This written survey serves several purposes—it brings the neighborhood's crime problem into focus . . . it is a key step in enlisting help from the police . . . and it recruits new members. *Basic survey questions:*

• *What do you consider to be our neighborhood's biggest crime problems now?*

• *What are our neighborhood's biggest potential problems?*

• *How do you feel the police are handling these problems?*

• *What do you think the police should be doing?*

• *Do you have any ideas about what we could do to prevent crime?*

• **Make it clear that a Neighborhood Watch group is not a vigilante organization.** Though some neighbors will quickly rally to support a watch group, others may be reluctant to commit themselves because of apathy, fear, or a misunderstanding of the concept.

Key selling point: Neighborhood Watch groups look for suspicious activities, compile data and report information to the police. They do not intercede in potentially dangerous situations.

• **Return to the police department** to share your surveys and obtain further crime data. Check statistics for neighborhood crime rates—and see what times and days of the week crimes are most likely to occur. Ask about police patrol patterns, duties, response time . . . and how your group can be of assistance.

TO REDUCE CRIME

• **Target the criminal population.** One myth about crime is that most of it is committed at night by strangers to the neighborhood.

Facts: The typical burglary occurs between 10 A.M. and 2 P.M., when most people are out of their homes. Most crimes are committed by males between the ages

---

Self-Defense for a Child Who Is Being Followed

Susan K. Golant

• Safely cross the street.

• Walk or run to the nearest well-lit public facility—restaurant, store, or gas station. Go to a trusted neighbor's house and wait there.

• Call or wave to an imaginary friend.

• If caught, scream, "Help". . . "Fire" . . . "He's not my father"—or anything else to attract the attention of passersby.

• Report any unusual situation to parents, teachers, a neighbor, or the police by dialing 911 or the operator.

Fifty Ways to Keep Your Child Safe by Susan K. Golant, Los Angeles–based parenting author. Lowell House.

■ **To ensure your children's safety while on-line**—and protect your own budget—do not allow them to log on unless an adult is present to supervise. Get to know your children's on-line friends by reading the messages they send them—and letting them know you are watching. Set time limits for on-line use, and cancel the service immediately if you get a large bill or see things on screen that you do not like.

John Edwards, a computer industry analyst in Mount Laurel, NJ.

HEALTH HAZARDS

■ **Food poisoning can turn deadly** if one of four symptoms appears: *Bloody diarrhea,* which could mean a dangerous type of *E. coli* infection . . . *stiff neck, severe headache and fever at the same time,* which could indicate meningitis . . . *excessive diarrhea or vomiting,* which could lead to life-threatening dehydration . . . *any symptom lasting more than three days.* Most food poisoning lasts a day or two and disappears by itself. See a doctor if it lasts longer.

Bruce Yaffe, M.D., an internist and gastroenterologist in private practice, 121 E. 84 St., New York, NY 10028.

■ **Magnesium poisoning from antacids** can occur in people who take large doses for a long time. Magnesium is also found in many laxatives and some pain relievers. People most at risk: Those with improperly functioning kidneys . . . older people, since kidney function generally declines with age . . . people who have had intestinal surgery . . . those taking medicines that slow intestinal transit . . . anyone with longtime diabetes. *Self-defense:* Use only the recommended amount of medicines that contain magnesium. If those doses do not help, do not increase them—see your doctor.

Bruce Yaffe, M.D., an internist and gastroenterologist in private practice, 121 E. 84 St, New York, NY 10028.

of 13 and 22. Quite often, neighbors observe these youths getting into trouble—committing vandalism, writing graffiti—as young as ages seven or eight. They often receive inadequate parental supervision.

These young people can be helped to change—but only if the community takes collective responsibility for them. *How a watch group can intercede . . .*

• **Truancy can be reported to the school** when the youth is of school age.

• **One or two delegates from the watch group** can approach the youth's parents and ask how they might help to resolve this problem together. A group is more likely to be taken seriously than a single irate individual. Be sure the group representatives express a positive attitude and do not blame the parents.

• **Train group members to recognize and report suspicious activity.** Criminals are more likely to be stopped and apprehended when neighbors trust their instincts and call the police.

Many people are reluctant to make that phone call, fearing they might appear foolish. Most crimes, in fact, are not reported.

"Safe" strategy: Next-door neighbors could agree to call each other first if they see something suspicious around the other person's home. If they find no one at home, they would then call the police.

• **Distribute crime-report forms.** These forms are to be sent to the police when a group member observes possible criminal activity. Members would describe the suspect and any weapon or vehicle.

In addition to heightening awareness, a watch group can help reduce crime by:

• **Distributing decals or window signs to members for their homes.** *Note:* To be truly effective, the signs must be backed up by alarms, lights and other security measures.

• **Conduct a neighborhood security survey** to identify physical features that make the community vulnerable to crime. Again, local law-enforcement agencies may be of aid. *Most helpful:* An officer trained in Crime Prevention Through Environmental Design (CPTED), the concept of manipulating building design, landscaping, and traffic flow to fight crime.

Best Ways to Avoid IRS Problems . . . without Paying Too Much in Taxes

Paul W. Eldridge, KPMG Peat Marwick LLP

A mistake in your tax paperwork need not lead to an encounter with the IRS—which could escalate into an audit, tax assessment, and costly court fight.

Preparation can help head off most paperwork problems with the IRS. Understanding how the bureaucracy works will enable you to efficiently resolve those problems that do arise.

PREVENTION

Begin by minimizing those risk factors that can lead to unwanted inquiries from the IRS in the first place. *Advice:*

• **File all required forms**—and answer *all* questions on the tax return—even if they don't seem to apply to you.

Examples: Answer the question about whether you have a foreign bank account. If you made a non-cash gift to charity, file Form 8283. Work through

Paul W. Eldridge, partner, KPMG Peat Marwick LLP, 599 Lexington Ave., New York, NY 10022.

■ **IRS loses. Deduct rent paid to your spouse.** An attorney who used a property that he owned with his wife as an office paid himself an annual rent of $18,000. He deducted the rent as a business expense on his tax return's Schedule C and reported it as rental income on his Schedule E, which produced a net tax benefit on his return (because the rental income let him claim other real estate-related deductions). But the IRS disallowed the transaction saying one can't pay rent to oneself. *Court:* Half the rent paid became the legal property of the attorney's wife, so he could claim rental treatment for the $9,000 that accrued to her—even though she filed a joint tax return with him.

D. Sherman Cox, TC Memo 1993–326.

■ **IRS loses. Spouses' worth computed separately.** A married couple defeated the IRS in a court case and then argued that the IRS should be required to pay their attorney fees. The IRS responded that the law allows fee awards only to taxpayers with a net worth not exceeding $2 million and that the couple exceeded the limit. *Court:* The couple had filed a joint tax return on which each spouse could be held separately liable for the full tax due, so the income limit should be applied to each spouse separately. The husband's net worth was over the limit but the wife's was not—so the wife was entitled to collect her share of the legal fees.

Deiter Christoph, S.D. Ga., No. CV495–88.

HOME-LOAN SECRETS

■ **IRS loses. Auction on house voided.** Joseph Marshall and his former wife owned a house as joint tenants. The IRS levied on Mr. Marshall's interest in the house and auctioned it off to settle a back tax bill. *Court:* Under state law, a joint tenant cannot sell an interest in a property without the consent of the other owner. While the IRS could levy ??????????????????????.

Carole Marshall, D. Minn., No. 3-95-554.

Retirement Savings Can Be a Tax Trap

Irving Blackman
Blackman Kalick Bartelstein, LLP

Most people think of their retirement plans as tax shelters. But for many they may prove to be costly tax traps. *Why:* If you die with a large balance in a retirement plan, it will be subject to estate tax at rates of up to 55% plus income tax of 39.6% when it is distributed to heirs.

The top total tax rate on your retirement savings can reach over 79% when your plans hold more than $750,000—a 15% excise tax is imposed on the excess, in addition to estate tax and income tax. And this doesn't consider state taxes!

Planning: If you plan to leave savings to heirs rather than consume the money in your retirement years, you may do much better to fund bequests through life insurance that is placed in an irrevocable life insurance trust.

• Insurance placed in an irrevocable life insurance trust is not subject to estate tax.

the Alternative Minimum Tax computation on Form 6251, even if it shows you do not owe the tax.

• **Avoid claiming large refunds.** A return requesting a large refund is likely to draw extra scrutiny from the IRS. Also, a request that a refund be applied to the next year's taxes gives the IRS a chance to misapply the refund.

Best: Adjust wage withholding and estimated tax payments to balance out your final tax liability for the year, so you neither owe tax nor get a large refund. Remember, being entitled to a large tax refund simply means that you've made an interest-free loan to the government.

• **Report all income.** Check all the 1099 returns issued to you by payers of income during the past year. Be sure they are accurate and that you include all of them on your return. Copies of these forms have been supplied to the IRS, and any discrepancy will likely draw a query from the agency.

• **Act on inaccuracies.** If you find that a 1099 is inaccurate, ask the issuer to send a new, corrected one.

• **Report rollovers.** If you received a Form 1099-R reporting a rollover of retirement-plan proceeds into an IRA, remember that you do have to report the amount shown on your tax return even though the rollover is tax-free. These amounts and the taxable portions are reported on page one of Form 1040.

Remember that any IRS inquiry about your return will likely occur 18 months to two years after you file. Make sure that you keep your tax files in good order so you can quickly respond to any question that arises at a later date, and provide necessary documentation.

SOLUTION

An IRS notice concerning a filing or payment problem will most likely be sent to you from the IRS Service Center where you filed your tax return. Service centers are not well equipped to handle telephone inquiries. *Best:* Resolve the problem by mail.

When corresponding with the IRS, make it *easy* for the agent who opens your letter to handle your problem. That agent initially is unlikely to know anything about the matter except what you relate, so try to present him with the letter. Include copies of canceled checks, tax forms, and any other documents that relate to the matter. Remember, if the agent finds it necessary to go back through the IRS's own files to find any documents, it will only delay your case.

Do not send originals of important documents to the IRS—only copies. Correspond with the IRS by certified mail with a return receipt requested. Your mailing receipt proves that your letter was sent before any applicable deadline, and the delivery receipt proves the IRS actually received it.

After you mail your explanation to the IRS, you are likely to continue receiving computer-generated notices concerning the problem. This may be because the computer simply hasn't been updated—but don't assume it. Never ignore an IRS notice. Answer it with a letter referring to your previous reply, and include a copy of your earlier response.

If the notices keep coming, make contact by phone with an individual in the branch of the agency that sends the notices—for example, the collection division if you are receiving collection notices.

Phone numbers for IRS offices can be found among the government listings in the phone book, and a detailed IRS phone directory may be available in the office of your tax adviser, or among the tax reference services in the public library.

Although it can be difficult to find an individual within the IRS who is willing to take responsibility for handling your file—including the documentation you have already provided to them—doing so can be the key to solving a recalcitrant problem.

Again, keep full records concerning all phone conversations with IRS personnel, including the name and title of any agent you talk to.

INSIDE HELP

If in spite of all your efforts you find yourself with a problem that just won't go away, you can contact the IRS's *Problem Resolution Office (PRO)*. The PRO is the taxpayer's advocate *within* the IRS.

Generally, you must be able to show that you have made at least two attempts to solve your problem on

HOME-LOAN SECRETS

• Insurance proceeds are received by policy beneficiaries income tax free.

The result can be a far higher after-tax return on your investment than is obtained through a retirement plan. Consult an experienced estate-planning expert for details.

Irving Blackman is a partner, Blackman Kallick Bartelstein, LLP, CPAs, 300 S. Riverside Plaza, Chicago, IL 60606.

FILING BASICS

■ **Last-minute tax-filing exam**: Before you sign and mail out your tax return, compare this year's return to last year's *line by line,* we hear from tax expert Edward Mendlowitz. Look for differences between the two returns. If you don't know why there is a difference, there may be an error. *Example:* If your income was about the same both years, but taxes owed this year are significantly different. *Important:* The IRS holds the *taxpayer* responsible for any errors—whether you prepare the return yourself, use tax-preparation software or hire, someone. So . . . the added caution definitely pays.

Edward Mendlowitz is a partner in the accounting firm of Mendlowitz Weitsen, LLP, CPAs, 2 Pennsylvania Plaza, New York, NY 10121.

FAMILY PLANNING

■ **A couple's full pension can be attached** by the IRS to pay off *one* spouse's tax debt. The IRS levied a taxpayer's pension to collect a tax debt, but his wife argued that it couldn't take her half. *Court:* The pension was the husband's, who had earned it. (The wife would obtain a survivorship interest if he died.) So the IRS could levy on the whole pension amount.

Travelers Insurance Co. v. John J. Rattermann, S.D. Ohio, No. C-1-94-466.

■ **Must put alimony agreements in writing.** For alimony to be deductible, an agreement to make payments to support one's former spouse must be in writing. When a husband orally agreed to make support payments to his wife while the terms of their divorce were being negotiated, he received no deduction for the amounts paid.

Anthony Albert Mercurio, TC Memo 1995-312.

■ **Divorce planning.** When a divorce decree requires one spouse to make payments to the other, but does not state how much of each payment is allocated to alimony and how much to child support, the entire amount may be deemed to be alimony, deductible by the spouse who pays it, taxable to the one who receives it.

Beverly Roosevelt, TC Memo 1995-430.

■ **Children's Social Security numbers** must be correct on tax forms to avoid inquiries from the IRS. This year, the IRS is trying to match every dependent's name with his/her Social Security number. It will hold up refunds or send requests for detailed information if a deduction is claimed and the child's name and Social Security number do not match exactly.

John Stevens, EA, tax adviser in Sebastopol, CA.

your own before turning to the PRO—an important reason to keep good records of all correspondence with the agency.

Also, the PRO handles only administrative problems. It won't get involved in a dispute involving interpretation of the tax law, such as whether or not a deduction is proper. However, the PRO *will* handle such matters as lost refunds, miscredited tax payments, unexplained tax bills or penalties, the loss of documents from IRS files, or the refusal of an IRS office to answer taxpayer queries or provide tax account information.

There is a PRO in every IRS Service Center and District Office. The phone number for the PRO can be found in the phone book under United States Government Offices/Treasury Department.

Specific conditions must be met before you can get help from the PRO concerning these common problems:

• **Missing refunds.** You must have made at least two inquiries about the refund, the last one being made at least 90 days after the refund claim was initially filed.

• **Notices.** After responding to two IRS notices, you can go to the PRO if you receive a third notice on the same issue that does not acknowledge your earlier replies.

• **Questions.** After asking the IRS a question, you must wait at least 45 days for a response before you ask again. You can go to the PRO if you receive no reply to the second inquiry or if you fail to receive an answer promised by a specific date.

While you can contact the PRO by phone, you may have to follow up with correspondence containing a detailed explanation of your problem, copies of relevant tax forms and documents, and a record of the previous attempts you have made to resolve the problem.

Cases accepted by the PRO are assigned to individual case officers, so you'll no longer be dealing with the nameless IRS bureaucracy. And you should at least receive an explanation of the status of your problem fairly quickly, even if the resolution of the problem takes longer.

EMERGENCY HELP

In an *emergency* situation—if you're informed of a levy or property seizure and you received no prior notice—the PRO can provide *immediate* help. File IRS Form 911, *Taxpayer Assistance Order*, with the PRO. Mail the form to the Internal Revenue Service Problem Resolution Office in the IRS district where you live. These requests get top priority.

To get a copy: Call the IRS at 800-829-3676. It's a good idea to have a 911 form handy in case you're ever stymied by IRS bureaucracy, especially since it may take a week or two to get the form. *Alternative:* The PRO will fill out a Form 911 for you over the phone.

What to Do If You're Audited

Edward Mendlowitz, Mendlowitz Weitsen

Fear of being audited by the IRS is one of the biggest fears people have. But audits are very straightforward and nothing to be afraid of. *Specifics:*

CORRESPONDENCE AUDITS

Correspondence audits are conducted by mail. The IRS has information about something that should have been on your income tax return but wasn't. The IRS writes you, saying it is going to adjust your return unless you can prove otherwise.

• *Loophole:* **Respond immediately.** If you don't, the proposal will become an assessment and you'll owe the IRS extra tax plus penalties and interest. If you made an inadvertent error on your return, you may be able to avoid penalties by responding to

Edward Mendlowitz, partner, Mendlowitz Weitsen, CPAs, Two Pennsylvania Plaza, New York, NY 10121. He is the author of New Tax Traps, New Opportunities. Boardroom Special Reports.

FAMILY PLANNING

■ **Did you know that summer camp has tax benefits?** If you send your child to day camp (but not to an overnight camp) during his/her summer vacation, camp costs can qualify for the child-care credit. *More information:* Consult your tax adviser.

James Glass, Esq., 402 W. 20 St., New York, NY 10011.

Best to Get an Early Start on Your Return . . . It Pays

Randy Bruce Blaustein, Esq., Blaustein, Greenberg & Co.

Don't wait until April to start putting together what you'll need for your return. *Start now . . .*

• **Forms and publications.** If the IRS hasn't already sent you everything you need, pick up the forms at your local IRS office or order them by phone (800-829-FORM). Don't overlook any new forms you'll need that you didn't use last year.

• **W-2s.** Your employer must mail W-2s by January 31. If you don't get one, contact your employer. When you receive your W-2, check it for accuracy. If it's wrong, get it corrected immediately.

• **1099 information returns.** These, too, should be mailed to you by January 31. You should get 1099s from any persons, companies, banks, financial institutions, etc., that have paid you interest, dividends, freelance income, etc., during the year.

Again, check for accuracy and get any mistakes corrected.

• **Deduction data.** Sort out your checks, credit-card statements, paid invoices, bills, etc., by category—medical expenses, charitable donations, travel and entertainment, and any other items you need for your tax return.

Randy Bruce Blaustein, Esq., partner, Blaustein, Greenberg & Co., 155 E. 31 St., New York, NY 10016.

Homeowners' Tax Breaks

Ivan Faggen, Arthur Andersen & Co.

For the alert taxpayer, the family home can be a major source of tax savings. Federal tax law is studded with provisions that encourage and enhance home ownership, as opposed to other forms of investment.

Breaks when you buy:

Mortgage points: For borrowers other than homeowners, mortgage points (a prepayment of interest represented by a percentage of the loan) have to be capitalized and deducted over the life of the loan. But points charged on money borrowed to buy a principal residence are fully deductible by homeowners in the year they're paid.

Deductions for interest paid on personal debts have been eliminated. But interest paid on mortgages on your primary residence and on one second residence are fully deductible up to a total of $1 million in acquisition debt (to acquire, construct, or improve a residence) plus $100,000 in home-equity loans (for any purpose). *Note:* The dollar limits

the notice promptly and explaining the circumstances of the error. If the mistake was reasonably beyond your control, the IRS may excuse any penalties it has charged.

OFFICE AUDITS

Office audits are conducted at IRS offices. They are initiated by a letter from the IRS that usually tells the taxpayer the items on his/her return that are being questioned.

• *Loophole:* **Try to resolve the issue by mail.** You may be able to wrap up an audit without ever setting foot in an IRS office. Write to the IRS explaining that you can't attend in person but you are enclosing copies of all your substantiation for the deductions it has questioned. Time the letter so it arrives at the IRS at least two weeks before your appointment date. Give a telephone number where you can be contacted during the day. It has been my experience that the IRS accepts this method of proving deductions. If your proof is sufficient, you'll get a letter back from the agent telling you that your return has been accepted as filed—examination closed.

• *Loophole:* **Limit your exposure.** Take only the information the IRS asked to see to the audit. While office audits don't generally go beyond the items checked off on the audit notification letter, the IRS isn't precluded from digging into other areas on your return. If you take only the information requested, the agent will have to go to the trouble of scheduling another appointment to dig deeper into your return.

Caution: Don't volunteer information. Answer only the questions that are asked by the agent.

• *Loophole:* **If you're missing some proof for your deductions** . . . prepare a detailed schedule for the audit showing how you arrived at the figure shown on your return. Be as detailed as possible. The IRS is not obliged to accept this, but the agent will usually go along with some or all of it if your explanation makes sense and is reasonable.

Trap: Don't ignore the IRS's request for an office audit. This can get you in very deep trouble with the service. The IRS will disallow every single item on your return, not just the items it says it is auditing, and send you a bill. Then you will have to substantiate everything on your return.

FIELD AUDITS

Field audits are conducted on the taxpayer's premises, usually his/her place of business.

• *Loophole:* **Avoid having the audit at your home.** Have it at your accountant's office instead. If you allow the agent to come to your home, he/she may very well form opinions about your standard of living. This could lead to questions about unreported income. Another reason to avoid having the audit at your home is that people tend to be more relaxed when audits are held in familiar surroundings. They may very well let down their guard and say something they shouldn't to the agent.

Reminder: You can never tell the auditor too little.

BUSINESS AUDITS

The best place to have the audit of a business is at your accountant's office—it's neutral ground. The agent, however, may try to have the audit at your place of business. Don't go along with this. The agent may form opinions about the company's deductions if the audit is held at the business. He may overhear damaging conversations about the company.

Self-defense: Insist that the audit be held at the agent's office at the IRS. You have a right to have the audit there.

If the audit does not take place at your business, the agent will still want to see the premises. Arrange this for a time when you, the owner, are not present. Having the agent meet you there can't help your case. The agent may get ideas about your life style if he meets you at your place of business. He may feel jealous. He may decide that your deductions are extravagant.

APPEALS WITHIN THE IRS

If you don't agree with an auditor's findings, you can take your case to the appeals division of the IRS. The purpose of the appeals division is to settle cases without going to court.

VERY, VERY PERSONAL

don't apply to mortgages taken out before October 14, 1987.

Ivan Faggen, tax partner with Arthur Andersen & Co. in charge of the Tax Division for the South Florida offices, 1 Biscayne Tower, Suite 2100, Miami, FL 33131. Mr. Faggen is coauthor of *Federal Taxes Affecting Real Estate.* Matthew Bender.

DEALING WITH THE IRS

■ **You cannot rely on oral advice from the IRS.** If the advice conflicts with the law, the law governs. *Example:* An IRS employee advised a taxpayer not to file a court motion to recover seized property until after the IRS issued a final administrative determination on his earlier request to have the property returned. The taxpayer waited. The deadline for filing the motion expired. The taxpayer then went to court and said he had been misled: *Ruling:* The IRS keeps the property.

Pete J. Medina is a principal and tax consultant on practice and procedure before the IRS, Ernst & Young, LLP, 787 Seventh Ave., New York, NY 10019.

■ **When writing to the IRS to dispute a tax ruling,** keep your letter simple—and short. One page is good—a half page, better. *Include:* Your name, address, Social Security number and the year of the disputed tax return . . . the document locator number (DLN) appearing on the IRS notice, the type of tax owed, and a copy of the notice itself . . . what type of mistake the IRS made . . . the action you'd like taken . . . *copies* of all documents needed to prove your case—canceled checks, corrected 1099s, mailing receipts. *Important:* Never send originals.

Eric Tyson, a personal finance counselor and coauthor of *Taxe$ for Dummie$* (IDG Books, $14.99).

BEAT THE IRS

■ **Better Record-Keeping.** Keep all tax records forever, including gift and estate tax returns. The normal statute of limitations on a tax return is three years. But it can be extended to six years if income was underreported by 25% or more. No limit applies when fraud is committed. If the IRS makes such allegations, you'll need your returns to rebut them. *Also:* You need old returns to prove your "tax basis" in property you own—its cost for tax purposes, which is used when computing gain or loss on a subsequent sale.

William G. Brennan, tax and financial adviser, Washington, DC, writing in *Financial World,* 1328 Broadway, New York, NY 10001. 26 issues. $37.50/yr.

SHREWDER FILING

■ **Electronic filing** of your tax return speeds your refund, delivering it within three weeks instead of the usual 12. *Also:* Mathematical errors and other simple mistakes that can delay processing are detected immediately, so your return preparer is notified of them within 48 hours, instead of the usual five to six weeks. *Added plus:* Your tax preparer receives notice within 24 hours that the return has been properly filed and accepted.

Charles Peoples, IRS assistant commissioner for returns processing, quoted in *Financial World,* 1328 Broadway, New York, NY 10001. 26 issues. $37.50/yr.

■ **Free tax-return help** is available to persons age 60 and over who need last-minute assistance in preparing their returns but can't afford professional advice. The Tax-Aide program, sponsored by the American Association of Retired Persons, provides assistance at more than 10,000

• *Loophole:* **You get a fair hearing at an appeals conference.** It's not a kangaroo court. An appeals officer will be more inclined than an auditor to settle a case that appears to be reasonable.

• *Loophole:* **Appeals officers can take into account the hazards of litigation** in deciding whether to settle. The hazards of litigation are the chances the government might lose the case if it goes to court. If the appeals officer thinks the IRS has only a 50% chance of winning in court, he may settle for half of the disputed amount.

TAX COURT

If all else fails, you can take your case to tax court. You can go either to regular tax court . . . or to the small case division if the amount of tax in dispute is less than $10,000—whichever is appropriate.

• *Loophole:* **You have a second chance to settle the case** in discussions with an IRS attorney before it is set for court. Like the appeals officer, the attorney will take into account the hazards of litigation, *but these carry more weight here.* You may have a better chance of settling the case with an IRS lawyer than with an appeals officer.

AVOIDING AN AUDIT

• *Loophole:* **File your returns on time.** There's a high audit rate among individuals who have not filed returns for many years. Eventually these people are picked out by the IRS and made to file their delinquent returns.

• *Loophole:* **Attach detailed proof of items** for which you're filing an amended return. Amended returns for large refunds are more likely to be audited than original returns. You can reduce the audit risk by attaching complete, detailed proof of the items that prompted the amendment.

• *Loophole:* **Avoid repetitive audits.** The *Internal Revenue Manual* says that taxpayers shall not be subjected to needless and repetitive examinations. If you've been audited in either of the past two years on a particular issue, and the audit resulted in no change in your tax bill, you can request not to be audited on that same issue again.

Procedure: As soon as you receive your audit notice, write to the IRS to claim an exemption under the Repetitive Audit Program. Enclose a copy of your previous audit notice and report. *Important:* You must request the procedure before your first appointment with the agent.

IMPORTANT

Good records. If you can document your deductions with the proof the IRS requires, you'll have no trouble at an audit.

Compensation Loopholes: Deferring Pay

Edward Mendlowitz, Mendlowitz Weitsen

The compensation package you get from your employer probably includes some form of deferred compensation whereby money is put away for you but is not available until some time in the future. This form of compensation boosts your pay and offers significant tax advantages.

LOOPHOLES

• **Pension and profit-sharing plans.** Your employer contributes money to a retirement plan on your behalf and the money accumulates on a tax-deferred basis. You don't pay a current tax on the contribution or on the interest the money earns. No tax is due until you receive a distribution of money from the plan. *More:*

Loophole: **Take a tax-free *loan* from the pension or profit-sharing plan.** Borrowing is *not* a taxable transaction. You can only do this *if* the plan

Edward Mendlowitz, partner, Mendlowitz Weitsen, CPAs, Two Pennsylvania Plaza, New York, NY 10121. He is the author of *New Tax Traps, New Opportunities.* Boardroom Special Reports.

SHREWDER FILING

sites throughout the U.S. For the site nearest you, call 800-TAX-1040.

Margaret Drescher, Northwest area coordinator of the American Association of Retired Persons, quoted in *The New York Times.*

■ **Prescription eyeglasses** are tax-deductible as a business expense if you need them to do your job. To qualify for the deduction, the glasses must have been customized for the workplace and unsuitable for general use. *Helpful:* Have the optometrist write "occupational use only" on the lens prescription. The deduction is taken as a miscellaneous expense and is subject to the 2% of miscellaneous itemization deduction limit on Schedule A of Form 1040.

American Optometric Association, 243 N. Lindbergh Blvd., St. Louis, MO 63141.

How to Talk Your Way out of IRS Penalties for Late Filing

Randy Bruce Blaustein, Esq., Blaustein, Greenberg & Co.

Showing the IRS that you had a good reason for filing your tax return late may get you off the hook for penalties even if you didn't file an extension form. You must convince the IRS that it wasn't your fault that you filed late, and your excuse must be reasonable. *Excuses that have worked:*

• **Your return was mailed on time** but was not received by the IRS until after the filing date.

• **The return was filed on time** but was sent to the wrong IRS office or district.

SHREWDER FILING

• **You relied on erroneous written information** provided by an IRS officer or employee.

• **You or a member of your family** was seriously ill.

• **Your business, residence or records** were destroyed by a fire or other casualty.

• **Tax forms that you requested** in time from the IRS were never received.

• **You were unable**, for reasons beyond your control, to obtain the records necessary to determine the amount of tax due.

Important: The IRS is not required to accept any of these excuses.

Randy Bruce Blaustein, Esq., partner, Blaustein, Esq., Greenberg & Co., accountants and auditors, 155 E. 31 St., New York, NY 10016.

KIDS AND TAXES

■ **College-aid strategy.** Deductible retirement-plan contributions made by parents can increase the amount of college financial aid offered to their children. *How:* The amount of aid offered to a child depends in part upon the value of the parent's assets. For financial aid purposes, however, the amount of money accumulated in retirement plans —such as IRAs, Keoghs, and 401(k)s—is not considered an asset in determining eligibility for assistance. Therefore, by putting assets in retirement accounts before a child goes to college, and by making plan contributions while the child is in college, you may increase aid significantly.

Kalman A. Chany, president, Campus Consultants Inc., 338 E. 67 St., New York, NY 10021. Mr. Chany is author of *The Princeton Review/The Student Access Guide to Paying for College.* Villard Books.

permits borrowing—not all do. Plans that allow borrowing usually make it easy on the participant—there's no need to justify why the loan is needed.

Tax law limits: The amount you can borrow is limited to your vested balance in the plan up to the greater of $10,000 or one-half of your vested balance, with a maximum of $50,000.

Loophole: **Put some of your own money into the plan**—many plans allow employees to make voluntary contributions. Such contributions are not tax-deductible, but the money accumulates on a tax-deferred basis.

Loophole: **If your company's plan is inactive**—no additions are being made and no benefits are accruing on your behalf—you are eligible to contribute to an IRA.

• **401(k) plans.** You contribute part of your salary to a company-sponsored savings program. You pay no income tax on the money you contribute until you make withdrawals. Interest, dividends and other earnings accumulate tax-deferred until you take them out.

Many companies "match" employees' contributions by putting additional money into the plan for the employee.

Loophole: **Though the amount you can contribute each year is limited by the tax law**, it's far more than you can put into an IRA. It's nearly $10,000 as opposed to $2,000.

• **Company-paid term life insurance.** As long as the coverage doesn't exceed $50,000 worth of insurance, you are not taxed on the premiums the employer pays. But if it is more than $50,000, you are taxed on part of the premiums.

Loophole: **The taxable amount is figured from IRS tables and is less than the actual premiums the employer pays.** You pay some tax for the extra coverage, but it is far less than it would cost you to buy similar life insurance coverage outside the company.

• *Stock options.* When a company gives an employee an option to purchase stock that does not qualify as an *incentive stock option* (more relevant information below), the employee must pay tax when the option is exercised. The taxed amount is the difference between the option price and the fair market value of the stock at the time the option is exercised.

Loophole: **There is no tax paid when the option is granted.** Stock options are a form of deferred compensation. The employee benefits on a tax-deferred basis from the growth in value of the company stock.

• **Incentive stock options.** These are options that qualify under the Tax Code for special treatment. No tax is levied when the options are issued to the employee.

Loophole: **No tax is levied when the options are exercised.** Tax isn't payable until the options are sold.

Trap: The difference between the option price and the fair market value at the time the option is exercised is a "preference item" that is subject to the Alternative Minimum Tax (AMT). Employees should be careful not to exercise so many incentive stock options that they fall into the AMT. The exercise of these options must be carefully timed.

• **Restricted stock.** Sometimes an employer issues stock to an employee that is subject to a "substantial risk of forfeiture." *The most common situation:* The employee will have to give up the stock if he/she doesn't continue working for the company for a specified number of years.

When the restriction lapses, the employee is taxed on the difference between the fair market value at that time and the price paid for the stock.

Loophole: **The employee can make an election under Section 83(b) of the Internal Revenue Code** to pay tax on the value of the stock when it is originally issued. Then, there is no tax when the restriction lapses. (Tax on any gain is payable when the employee ultimately disposes of the stock.) Employees should make the Section 83(b) election in instances where they expect the company's stock to appreciate considerably.

• **Phantom stock**, also called *stock appreciation rights*, is sometimes issued to employees. No actual stock is given, but payments are made as if actual stock had been issued. If any dividends are paid to stockholders, they are also paid to the phantom stockholders. And when the employee leaves

KIDS AND TAXES

■ **Help a child buy a house** and help yourself in the process by entering a "shared-equity" financing arrangement that includes a formal contract. *Example:* You might pay the down payment and closing costs to obtain a 25% interest in the house. Your child would then pay the mortgage interest, 75% of other expenses, plus rent to you for your portion of the house. As part owner, you can deduct depreciation on your share of the house—a non-cash expense that helps turn it into a tax shelter. This will shelter some or all of your rent income from tax. Plus, you'll earn capital gains if the house is sold for a profit in the future.

Don Battle, editor, Research Recommendations, 1101 King St., Alexandria, VA 22314. Weekly. $125/yr.

SECRETS OF WINNING

Hide Assets from the IRS—Legally

Edward Mendlowitz

Many people keep assets in a safe-deposit box thinking that no one will ever find out about it. But the name of the renter of a safe-deposit box isn't kept secret. It doesn't help to rent a box in your own name. There's an organization called the American Safe Deposit Association (330 West Main St., Greenwood, IN 46142. 317-888-1118) that for less than $100 will run a search of their member banks (approximately 3,500 nationwide) for an estate, family of a deceased individual, or for a person appointed as a guardian over an individual. And the IRS, if it's looking for

SECRETS OF WINNING

assets of yours, will do a bank search for safe-deposit boxes held in your name. (It's especially easy for the IRS to track down boxes that you pay for with a personal check . . . it simply goes through your canceled checks.)

To conceal the existence of a safe-deposit box:

• **Ask your lawyer to set up a nominee corporation**—a corporation that has no other function but to stand in your place for the purposes you designate, such as to rent a safe-deposit box.

• **Rent a box in the name of the corporation and pay for it in cash.** Your name and signature will be on the bank signature card, but the corporation, not you, will be listed as the box's owner on the bank's records. And because you paid cash, there will be nothing in your records to connect the box with you.

• **You can, if you wish, name another person as signatory in addition to yourself.** Then, if something happens to you, that person will be able to get into the box.

Additional protection: Having a safe-deposit box in a corporation's name permits the box to be opened by your survivors without the state or the bank being notified of your death and having the box sealed. Otherwise, the survivor must get to the box before the funeral to look for a will and to find whatever else may be there.

Fees are subject to change without prior notice.

Edward Mendlowitz, partner, Mendlowitz Weitsen, CPAs, New York, NY 10121.

the company he/she is compensated for his/her phantom shares. Payments to the employee are taxed as compensation, rather than tax-favored capital gains.

Loophole: **The employee doesn't pay tax until there is an actual payment** to him as a phantom stockholder. No tax is payable when he first receives the phantom stock. So phantom stock is another form of deferred compensation.

Medical Deduction Loophole

Vincent D. Vaccaro

Special medical deductions can help raise unreimbursed medical expenses to 7.5% of your Adjusted Gross Income (AGI)—at which point they become deductible.

Included: Home improvements for medical reasons—to the extent their costs exceeds any increased value to your home . . . costs of trips needed for health reasons ($50 limit per night for lodging) . . . a special diet prescribed by a doctor, to the extent it costs more than a regular diet . . . eye glasses, contact lenses and contact lens insurance.

Vincent D. Vaccaro, partner, Personal Finance Services, Coopers & Lybrand LLP, New York.

How to Stay Healthy While Traveling

Karl Neumann, M.D.

No matter what your destination or reason for traveling, staying healthy is a prime concern whenever you're far from home.

Fatigue, stress, an upset stomach or worse can spell disaster for your vacation—or sap your business productivity. Fortunately, the wear and tear of travel can be kept to a minimum with some simple advance planning.

Here are some easy ways to make your travel more comfortable—and healthful.

SELF-CARE CHECKLIST

Your chief consideration when packing for a trip will be where you're going, how long you'll be away and what the climate is like at your destination. But no matter what sort of trip you're planning, bring along a well-stocked self-care kit. It should be easily reachable in your carry-on luggage and should contain . . .

    • **Antacid.** Familiar store-bought remedies such as Maalox, Mylanta, Gelusil, Tums, or Rolaids combat stomach upset, heartburn, and abdominal cramping sometimes caused by unfamiliar food or drink—or overindulgence in either.

    • **Diarrhea remedy.** Over-the-counter preparations like Imodium AD, Kaopectate, or Pepto-Bismol are all effective at stopping diarrhea.

Karl Neumann, M.D., editor and publisher of *Traveling Healthy*, 108-48 70 Rd., Forest Hills, NY 11375. He is also coeditor of *The Business Traveler's Guide to Good Health While Traveling*. Chronimed Publishing.

FLYING SAVVY

■ **Better flying.** Avoid the sun's glare when flying by reserving a seat on the right side (facing the cockpit) of the plane when traveling east to west . . . and on the left side when traveling west to east. This keeps you on the plane's shady side. For morning north-south travel—in either direction—book the west side of the plane. For afternoon north-south travel, book the east side.

Men's Health, 33 E. Minor St., Emmaus, PA 18098.

■ **Aisle seats are safest in plane crashes.** Rear seats are best for surviving initial impact. But after the crash, the key to survival is fast escape from smoke and fire—the worst killers in plane crashes. Fire usually blocks exits on one side of the plane and quickly fills the cabin with smoke. *Self-defense:* An aisle seat that gives quick access to exits on both sides and the rear of the plane.

National Transportation Safety Board specialists, reported in The Safe Travel Book by Peter Savage. Lexington Books.

■ **Better airfare basics:** Buy tickets at least 14 days in advance . . . book flights on Tuesdays or Wednesdays (and Saturdays to some destinations) when fares are lowest . . . check fares with your travel agent on Tuesdays or Wednesdays. *Reason:* Most fare wars start on Sundays, Wednesdays or Thursdays, so put your bid in with your agent in advance . . . always charge your trip on a credit card so you have recourse if there's a problem with the ticket or the airline goes under.

Straight Talk on Your Money, 7811 Montrose Rd., Potomac, MD 20854. Monthly. $39.50/yr.

RENTAL-CAR SAVVY

■ **To avoid rental-car penalties** and higher charges, ask the time at which you must return the car. Some companies give a one-hour grace period, some charge an hourly rate for late returns and some charge for an additional full day even if you are only an hour late. Also, if you return a weekly rental early, you may be charged the higher day rate instead. When renting at a weekend or weekly rate, find out the earliest and latest times you can return the car.

Consumer Reports Travel Letter, 101 Truman Ave., Yonkers, NY 10703.

■ **Better car-rental rates.** Quote the advertised discount directly from the company's ad when calling the reservation number. *Problem:* Reservation agents often will not volunteer the best available price up front. *Helpful:* Mention the promotion's discount code, usually listed in small print beneath the boldly displayed rate, or in the description of the terms and conditions of the rental.

Ed Perkins, editor, *Consumer Reports Travel Letter,* 101 Truman Ave., Yonkers, NY 10703.

■ **If a rental car breaks down,** the renter is usually not financially responsible. Most rental companies pay for towing and mechanical repairs. *Exception:* Any breakdown caused by off-road or other prohibited use of a vehicle. *What to do:* Follow the company's guidelines from the agreement jacket or glove compartment. Notify the rental location as soon as possible. *Overseas:* In remote locations, you may need to have the car repaired yourself. Save receipts for reimbursement.

Condé Nast Traveler, 360 Madison Ave., New York 10017.

Tablets are easier to take along on a trip, although the liquid forms of these medications usually offer faster relief.

• **Laxative.** On the road, constipation is often more of a problem than diarrhea.

Reason: Your diet while traveling is apt to lack high-fiber foods. Also, it may be difficult while traveling to maintain a regular exercise routine. Take along some Metamucil or Senokot just in case.

• **Antihistamine.** The over-the-counter medication Benadryl is effective against a host of potential allergens and irritants and is well-tolerated by most people. If you have to stay alert, ask your doctor to prescribe Seldane. It causes little or no drowsiness.

• **Antibiotic.** For tooth abscesses, severe bronchitis, festering skin wounds or other stubborn bacterial infections, ask your doctor to prescribe an antibiotic in advance.

Caution: Antibiotics should be used only under a doctor's supervision. Call your doctor at home for instructions.

• **Motion-sickness remedy.** Dramamine or Bonine tablets and scopolamine skin patches (Transderm Scop) are all effective. The patches are especially useful if you'll be spending long periods of time at sea, although they can cause dry mouth and, in the elderly, confusion.

Caution: Dramamine and Bonine can cause drowsiness. Avoid them if you have to stay alert.

• **Athlete's foot remedy.** Include antifungal foot powder or solutions like Lotrimin, Micatin or Tinactin in your travel kit since showers in hotel rooms and fitness centers aren't always fungus-free. *Also helpful:* Rubber thongs to wear in the shower.

• **Sunscreen, sunglasses, and hat.** These are a must for travel to sunny places or if you intend to be outdoors for extended periods of time. Your sunscreen should have an SPF of at least 15 and should guard against both UVB and UVA rays.

• **Insect repellent.** Look for one that contains 20% to 30% DEET.

• **Aspirin, acetaminophen, or ibuprofen.**
• **Decongestant and facial tissues.**

You might also want to bring along a basic first-aid kit containing an antibacterial cream or ointment, bandages, gauze, thermometer, scissors, tweezers, and a pocketknife.

If you wear corrective lenses, pack a spare pair of contacts or eyeglasses—plus your prescription.

If you intend to swim in unchlorinated water, take along a remedy for swimmer's ear, an infection marked by redness, itching, and pain of the outer ear canal. I recommend an over-the-counter preparation called Vosol.

FIGHTING JET LAG

Anytime you fly across several different time zones, you disrupt the body's circadian rhythms. The resulting jet lag should be thought of not as a special problem, but as another form of manageable stress. *Ways to control it:*

• **Avoid alcohol during your flight.** Alcohol, a depressant, can aggravate lethargy and fatigue, two classic symptoms of jet lag. It can also cause restlessness, which can disturb your sleep or keep you from sleeping altogether. And because it acts as a diuretic, alcohol can leave you feeling dehydrated.

• **Limit your consumption of caffeine.** Like alcohol, caffeine is a diuretic that can leave you feeling dehydrated and out of sorts. Too much caffeine can also cause nervousness, anxiety, tremors, and insomnia.

• **Drink plenty of water.** Recent studies have shown that even slight dehydration can cause listlessness and fatigue and can even make you more prone to mental errors—symptoms similar to those of jet lag.

Bear in mind that you may be dehydrated even before departure. *Reason:* Your eating and drinking patterns may be erratic in the hours before your flight. Breathing dry cabin air only increases this dehydration and all its enervating effects.

To stay hydrated, drink plenty of water or other nonalcoholic beverages before and during your flight—one eight-ounce glass every two to three hours. Don't wait until you feel thirsty—by then you may already be dehydrated.

How to cut hotel costs

To gain big savings in the company's travel costs . . .

• Initiate pre-trip authorizations and/or video teleconferencing to eliminate unnecessary trips.

• Trade down from first class to moderate—or from moderate to economy—facilities.

• Match hotel to business needs (limited amenities for travelers who arrive late and leave early).

• Negotiate guaranteed lowest rates—to control lodging expenses.

• Reclaim value-added taxes (VATs) on international hotel expenses.

Important: It is still a buyer's market, and that enhances the likelihood of discounts, complimentary meals and other amenities.

American Express Business Travel Review, free to American Express corporate cardholders.

Hotel help

Don't neglect to ask hotel staff for extra pillows, stronger light bulbs, extra blankets or any other amenities you may need or desire.

Customer satisfaction is vital to hotels and service staffs exist to answer such requests. For best response, call the housekeeping department as soon as you become aware of your need.

Service is likely to be quickest early in the day—and slowest after normal work hours. A tip of a couple of dollars works wonders.

Ed Perkins, editor, Consumer Reports Travel Letter, 101 Truman Ave., Yonkers, NY 10703. Monthly. $39/yr.

HOTEL SAVVY

■ **Hotel rooms designed for older travelers** have brighter lights, larger switches controlling lights, larger numbers on clocks, and lever handles on doors and faucets. Offered by Comfort, Quality, Clarion, Sleep, Roadway, Econolodge and Friendship Inn motel chains.

Herbert J. Teison, editor, Travel Smart, *40 Beechdale Rd., Dobbs Ferry, NY 10522. Monthly. $44/yr.*

On the Road

■ **Vacation illness self-defense.** Get a list of family doctors in the states where you plan to travel. A list of members of the American Academy of Family Physicians is available free from the AAFP, 8880 Ward Pkwy., Kansas City, MO 64114.

American Guidance for Seniors by Ken Skala, advocate, lecturer, and author. The Career Press.

■ **Traveler's diarrhea self-defense basics.** Avoiding local water and uncooked foods isn't always enough. Travelers can still become infected by diarrhea-causing bacteria by eating *cooked* foods or swimming in pools, lakes, and rivers. If you get sick on a trip, increase your intake of salty soups to replace lost sodium and of fruit juice and bananas to replace lost potassium . . . eat a high-carbohydrate diet of bread, rice, potatoes, or salty crackers . . . take a nonprescription antidiarrheal medication that contains *loperamide.*

M. J. G. Farthing, M.D., professor of gastroenterology, St. Bartholomew's Hospital, London, writing in the British Medical Journal, *Tavistock Square, London WC1H 9JR, England. Weekly. $137/yr.*

■ **Better, healthier eating on the road.** Use travel time as dieting time . . . drink lots of water and avoid alcohol . . . never use travel as an excuse to overeat . . . pay closer attention to what

• **Adapt to local time as quickly as possible.** *Example:* If you land in Paris the morning after an all-night flight, have no more than a brief 90-minute nap —then stay awake until it's 9 or 10 P.M. in Paris.

Schedule nonstressful activities and eat light, refreshing meals on your arrival day. Pack a swimsuit and use the hotel's pool or hot tub to help you relax.

SAFE FOOD AND DRINK

Regions of the world fall into three "tiers":
- Europe, North America, Australia.
- Israel and the Caribbean.
- The rest of the Middle East, most of Africa, the Far East, and other developing regions.

Anytime you travel to the second or third tier, you must be especially vigilant about what you eat and drink. *Self-defense:*

• **Eat cooked food while it is still hot.** Make sure meats are well-done. Throughout developing countries, undercooked beef and pork are major sources of tapeworms and other parasites. Likewise, all poultry, seafood, and vegetables should be fresh and thoroughly cooked.

• **Avoid peeled fruits (and those with broken skin).** Watch out for raw vegetable salads, too. They can be contaminated with bacteria from food preparer's hands or from the water used to rinse the vegetables.

• **Avoid custards, pastries, and other baked desserts.** These foods are often contaminated with microbes that trigger gastric distress, especially if improperly refrigerated. *Exception:* Served still hot from the oven, these foods are generally safe. If you want dessert, stick to wrapped candy or fresh fruit that you peel yourself.

• **Stick to bottled or canned beverages.** And watch out for ice cubes, which might be contaminated. Avoid milk, milk products, and foods prepared with them unless you're sure they have been properly pasteurized.

• **Avoid bread left lying in open baskets.** It may have been exposed to flies and other disease-bearing insects. If you're not certain whether bread has been properly stored, remove the crust and eat only the interior of the loaf.

WATCHING OUT FOR INFECTIOUS DISEASES

If you're planning a trip to the tropics, ask your doctor about protecting yourself against malaria, yellow fever, schistosomiasis, and other potential threats. If you'll need immunizations, get them at least a month before your departure. Frantic, last-minute efforts to obtain "shots" only compound the ordinary stress occasioned by an overseas journey. And multiple immunizations require several shots over a period of days or weeks.

A 24-hour hotline run by the Centers for Disease Control and Prevention (CDC) provides recorded messages outlining immunization requirements and recommendations for international travel. Call 404-332-4559.

Health information for overseas travelers is also available from some medical schools and teaching hospitals. For a list of regions where war or political strife might jeopardize travelers, contact the U.S. State Department at 202-647-5225.

Malaria—probably the most serious of all the infectious diseases found in the tropics—used to be easily controlled with medications. *Now:* In many parts of the world, there are drug-resistant strains of malaria. Chloroquine and other antimalarial drugs are virtually useless against them.

A new drug called *mefloquine* (Lariam) is often effective against drug-resistant malaria, but even this medication is losing strength in Southeast Asia and parts of Africa. *Doxycycline* can combat stubborn strains but should not be taken by children or pregnant women.

To avoid malaria, ask your doctor about taking prophylactic drugs. These must be taken one week before you travel to ensure that adequate blood levels of the drug are reached before you arrive—and that any adverse reactions occur while you're still at home. For more information, contact the CDC's 24-hour malaria hotline at 404-332-4555.

Ultimately, no matter where you travel, common sense should prevail. Medications and inoculations

goes into your mouth . . . exercise regularly . . . don't try to eat exactly as you do at home—this will only lead to frustration and more overeating.

Healthy, Wealthy, & Wise: A Step-By-Step Plan for Success Through Healthful Living by fitness consultant Krs Edstrom, MS. Prentice-Hall.

In the Air

■ **Airplane hijackers.** If airplane hijackers demand passports, citizens of the United States should delay presenting them as long as possible. Keep your passport in hand luggage or in the pocket of a coat in an overhead compartment. If terrorists force you to leave your seat, you will not have it with you. If the hijacking continues, you will eventually have to produce it—but the terrorists' initial show of force may be over by then.

The Safe Travel Book by Peter Savage. Lexington Books, Inc.

■ **Loss-proof luggage.** List items contained in each bag . . . and your home address inside . . . carry a photo of your luggage for easy identification . . . check bags at least 30 minutes before domestic and an hour before international flights . . . never leave bags unattended . . . always put valuables and a spare set of clothing in a carry-on. *Extra theft protection:* Use a security belt or wallet . . . when waiting, stand with your back against the wall to discourage pickpockets.

The Senior Citizens' Guide to Budget Travel in Europe by Paige Palmer. Pilot Books.

■ **Thieves at airport parking lots.** Airport parking lots are a prime target for car thieves and vandals. *Self-defense:* Choose a spot not by how safe it looks when you arrive, but by how it will look when you return . . . park under a light or where there's a lot of nearby activity. *Example:* The cashier's gate or a shuttle bus stop. *Practical alternatives:* Public transportation, cab or limo service to the airport—or have someone drop you off.

Advice from the National Safety Council, cited in *The New York Times.*

■ **Standby basics.** Once a standby passenger boards a plane, he/she has many—but not all—of the same rights as a regularly ticketed passenger. In rare cases, he may be bumped if the regularly scheduled passenger has a series of international connections to make and cannot travel at any other time. Rather than asking the standby passenger to leave, however, most airlines will probably make an announcement asking for volunteers. When a standby passenger is asked to relinquish his seat, it is not required that he be offered compensation—only travelers with confirmed reservations have that right.

Roundup of travel industry experts, reported in *The New York Times.*

■ **Easier travel with children.** Many hotels have begun catering to families with infants and children. Many will allow up to two children to stay free in their parents' room. *Also:* Rooms are child-proofed and kits with toilet-lid locks, night lights, and door alarms are often available to parents . . . changing tables have been installed in all (men's and women's) public rest rooms . . . diaper pails, strollers, and cribs are usually available free of charge. Many hotels also run on-site "camps" with adult-supervised, age-appropriate activities

are no substitute for adequate rest during a trip, for avoiding excesses in eating and drinking or for following basic hygiene. With these precautions in mind, you should always be able to travel in comfort—and good health.

Secrets of a Much More Comfortable Flight

Randy Petersen

Airline travel may be fast, but it is not always comfortable. Too often, travelers, especially those seated in coach, are crammed into confining seats, fed factory-produced meals, and confronted with delays or lost luggage. Flights can be made more bearable, however, if you know how to work the system.

GETTING A GOOD SEAT

Most travelers don't want to sit in the middle seat of a row. But if you're late checking in for a crowded flight, you're almost certain of getting one. *Problem:* Airlines automatically assign aisle and window seats first, even if the two passengers in a row are traveling together.

You can improve your chances of getting an end seat by asking the agent at the check-in counter to search the passenger list for two travelers with the same last name in the same row. Request the middle seat in that row. Chances are the other two passengers are related and will want to sit together, leaving you either the window or aisle seat.

Randy Petersen, who travels up to 400,000 miles a year and is editor of *Inside Flier*, a magazine for frequent fliers, 4715-C Town Center Dr., Colorado Springs, CO 80916.

STORING LUGGAGE

Finding room for your carry-on luggage is always challenging. It is best, however, not to wait until you arrive at your seat to store your bags. Instead, put them in the first overhead compartment after you pass through the first-class cabin.

These compartments will likely be empty, since they are for the last passengers that board. In addition, you won't have to carry your bags to your seat as you enter or to the front as you exit the plane.

BETTER BAGGAGE HANDLING

Bags that have first-class or priority tags attached are usually first to come off the plane into the baggage claim area. Even if you're traveling in coach, you can benefit from this quick service by getting one of these tags.

Sometimes the airlines will give you a first-class tag if you ask for it. If not, try to find an old one from any airline. You can even make one up in advance by having a brightly colored card stamped with the word "priority" and laminated at a local printer. This will attract the attention of the baggage handlers.

GETTING AN UPGRADE

Just because you have enough frequent-flier miles to qualify for a better seat doesn't always mean you'll get one, especially if the flight is crowded.

In fact, you may actually stand a better chance of getting one if the flight is overbooked. In this situation, airlines commonly offer free tickets to passengers turning in their tickets. If you hear this announced, immediately notify the check-in personnel that you're still interested in upgrading.

Reason: A surprising number of first-class travelers give up their seats for free tickets, opening up space in the forward cabin.

A MORE COMFORTABLE FLIGHT

Strong sunlight is a common problem that travelers face when flying during the day. It often forces

FAMILY TIME

for children. *Note:* Cost and availability vary by hotel.

Good Housekeeping, 959 Eighth Ave., New York, NY 10019.

■ **When booking an unaccompanied child** on a connecting flight, avoid the last flight of the day. *Trap:* If the plane fails to take off, the child may spend the night alone in a strange city.

Travel Holiday, 28 W. 23 St., New York, NY 10010.

OVERSEAS TRAVEL

■ **Proof of citizenship requirements** are becoming increasingly stringent in the Caribbean, Bahamas, and Mexico. A driver's license alone is no longer sufficient identification for an American tourist to enter some of those places. *Also:* While most islands will accept a birth certificate accompanied by a photo ID, they'll reject a voter's registration card. *Self-defense:* Consider "proof of citizenship" to mean that a passport is required.

Travel adviser Arthur Frommer, writing in *Travel Holiday,* 28 W. 23 St., New York, NY 10010.

■ **Better outdoor-market shopping on international trips:** Do not carry valuables or your passport on your person. Bring just the cash that you plan to spend. *Men:* No wallets in side or back pockets. *Women:* No handbags slung behind or at the side. *Also:* Dress conservatively—no beachwear or shorts. Be careful to eat only cooked foods, and only in the cleanest-looking places. Make sure the person handling the food is not also responsible for handling the money.

Diana Kennedy, writing in *Condé Nast Traveler,* 360 Madison Ave., New York, NY 10017.

■ **Jet lag smarts.** To minimize jet lag, schedule important activities for when you will likely have the most energy. *High-energy times:* Evenings after jetting east . . . the next morning after jetting west.

Jet Smart by Diana Fairechild, former flight attendant, Flyana Rhyme, Inc., Box 300, Makawao, Maui, HI 96768.

TRAVEL SAVINGS

■ **Airfare-bargain traps.** Airfare "bargains" are often not what they seem. *Example:* One airline recently offered a discount on companion tickets, but the base fare rate was higher than normal. *Self-defense:* Find a smart travel agent with access to reservation computers that can track prices . . . and delay buying a ticket until 14 days before your flight, *except during holiday periods.* For holiday travel, book early to be sure of getting a seat. Insist that your travel agent continue to inform you about all deals that become available to your destination.

Herbert J. Teison, editor, *Travel Smart,* 40 Beechdale Rd., Dobbs Ferry, NY 10522.

■ **Frequent fliers traveling on free tickets** are not guaranteed the same treatment as paying passengers. If their flight is delayed or cancelled, the airline is less likely to endorse the ticket over to another carrier. A stranded traveler may not receive amenities such as hotel and meal vouchers. *Self-defense:* Make sure the gate agent knows you're a *very* frequent flier. Airlines generally go to great lengths to placate their best customers. Ask to be placed on standby for the carrier's next flight out. If you don't receive the treatment you think you deserve, complain in writing to the airline's customer service department.

Condé Nast Traveler, 360 Madison Ave., New York, NY 10017.

you to travel with the shade down. To avoid the sunny side when traveling eastbound, request an A, B, or C seat. When traveling westbound, request a seat on the other side of the cabin.

Great Vacations That Won't Break the Family Budget

Paige Palmer

Family vacations can be more than just fun in the sun. Trips that combine adventure, learning, meeting new people, and experiencing new cultures are enriching in many ways. And vacations that bring all this together can be the most inexpensive.

Involve the whole family in vacation planning . . . particularly the kids. It helps them grow and learn. And people won't feel forced to go somewhere they'd rather not be.

POSSIBILITIES*

• **Nature hikes and bird watching.** Most national parks and many state and local parks offer wildlife tours headed by experienced guides.

• **Festivals and fairs.** There's hardly a city in the country that doesn't have at least one annual celebration—from Mardi Gras in New Orleans to the Poteet Strawberry Festival in Poteet, Texas. Most feature music, local delicacies, and educational exhibits.

• **Museum field trips.**

• **City walking tours.** Sightsee at your own pace on self-guided tours that highlight architecturally significant buildings, historical sites, and other points of interest.

Paige Palmer, author of 15 travel books, including *The Senior Citizen's Guide to Budget Travel in the United States and Canada.* Pilot Books.

• **Cemetery tours.** Historically educational as well as fascinating. Not just for the ghoulish.

• **Factory tours.** Many factories, both large and small, offer formal and informal tours. *Bonus:* Many finish with free samples of the factory's product. Contact the company directly or call the local chamber of commerce for a listing of factories that run tours.

• **Washington, DC.** All government-run museums and monuments are admission-free, making the nation's capital a bargain traveler's paradise.

• **Hostels.** Now open to families, they offer hotel-style lodging at a fraction of the cost of a typical hotel.

• **Budget hotels.** Many hotel chains now cater to families. If you know where to look, you can stay at a wonderful hotel for very little money.

*For more information on a particular vacation, contact the local state or city tourism bureau or the local chamber of commerce. Listings, including toll-free phone numbers, are available at most libraries.

QUICK FIXES

■ **Keep within your credit limit when traveling** by using *two* credit cards and splitting expenses between them—for example, one for hotels, the other for car rentals and other expenses.

Peter Savage, author of *The Safe Travel Book,* writing in *International Living,* 824 E. Baltimore St., Baltimore, MD 21202.

■ **"Environmentally clean" hotel rooms** are not only smoke-free, many also contain filtration systems that remove odors, dust, and pollen from the air and impurities from the water. More than 200 hotels in North America and Europe offer these rooms at $5 to $10 above the standard room rate.

Katryna Glettler, senior editor, *Travel Holiday,* 28 W. 23 St., New York, NY 10010.

Best Places to See Animals in the U.S.

Tim O'Brien

• **Alaska Zoo.** The northernmost zoo in the world. Includes just about every species of animal that can survive Alaska's cold arctic climate . . . from the Glacier Blue Bear to the Bearded Musk Ox. The only species that aren't native to Alaska are an Asian and an African elephant—one paints pictures sold in the gift shop while the other is learning to play harmonica and drums.

Alaska Zoo, 4731 O'Malley Rd., Anchorage, AK 99516. 907-346-3242.

Tim O'Brien, author of *Where the Animals Are: A Guide to the Best Zoos, Aquariums and Wildlife Sanctuaries in North America.* The Globe Pequot Press.

TRAVEL SMARTS

■ **Do-it-yourself traveler's diarrhea relief.** In one glass, mix eight ounces fruit juice . . . ½ teaspoon honey . . . a pinch of salt. In a second glass, mix eight ounces purified water . . . ¼ teaspoon baking soda. Alternate sips from each glass until you've consumed them both.

U.S. Public Health Service, reported in Natural Health, *17 Station St., Box 1200, Brookline Village, MA 02147.*

■ **Quick metric conversion basics.** To convert a two-digit kilometer number into miles, multiply the first digit by six. *Example:* On a road where the speed limit is 90 kilometers per hour, multiply nine times six to get 54 miles per hour...if the kilometer figure is three digits, multiply the first two by six. *Example:* To convert 100 kilometers per hour, multiply 10 times 6 to get 60 miles per hour. *To convert Celsius to Fahrenheit:* Double the Celsius figure and add 30 degrees. *Example:* If it's four degrees Celsius, double that to eight and add 30 to get 38 degrees Fahrenheit. *Important:* While these figures are not exact, they are usually close enough. Four degrees Celsius is actually equal to 39 degrees Fahrenheit.

Travel Smart, 40 Beechdale Rd., Dobbs Ferry, NY 10522.

■ **If your flight is canceled** after you reach the airport, find a phone and call the airline's reservation number. Ask to be rebooked on the next scheduled flight to your destination. This avoids waiting in long lines of passengers trying to rebook. *Alternative:* Go to the desk personnel at one of your carrier's other gates, where there is no line. All desks tie into the same computer system—you need not wait at the designated gate.

Travel & Leisure, 1120 Avenue of the Americas, New York, NY 10036.

• **Audubon Park and Zoological Garden.** Situated right along the Mississippi River. *Outstanding:* Louisiana Swamp Exhibit complete with boardwalks, docks, bridges, lush tropical gardens, and the world's only known family of white alligators.

Audubon Park and Zoological Garden, 6500 Magazine St., New Orleans, LA 70118. 504-861-2537.

• **International Wildlife Park** (also known as the Bronx Zoo). Situated on 265 acres bordering the Bronx River in New York City, it is the largest urban zoo in the United States. More than 4,000 animals are displayed here in both indoor and outdoor naturalistic habitats. *Highlights:* JungleWorld, Himalayan Highlands, Wild Asia, and World of Birds.

The Bronx Zoo/International Wildlife Park, Fordham Rd. and Bronx River Pkwy., Bronx, NY 10460. 718-367-1010.

• **Brookfield Zoo.** Situated on 215 acres surrounding Indian Lake in a suburb of Chicago. Features more than 2,500 animals. *Highlights:* Tropic World, Aquatic Bird House, Seven Seas Panorama, Habitat Africa! and the Walkabout in Australia House.

Brookfield Zoo, 3300 Golf Rd., Brookfield, IL 60513. 708-485-0263.

• **Busch Gardens.** A zoo and amusement park in one. Last year it added the Myombe Reserve—the Great Ape Domain, the most state-of-the-art Gorilla exhibit in the world. The animals are fed right up next to the viewing window and the setting is a simulated rain forest complete with mist swirling around.

Busch Gardens, 3000 Busch Blvd., Tampa, FL 33674. 813-987-5082.

• **San Diego Zoo.** Constructed on two levels —"mesas" and "canyons"—connected by moving sidewalks. *Highlights:* Australian koalas, wild Przewalski's horses from Mongolia, rare Sichuan takins from China, long-billed New Zealand kiwis, and the world's largest collection of parrots and parrot-like birds.

The San Diego Zoo, Zoo Place and Park Blvd., San Diego, CA 92122. 619-234-3153.

Advice for Solo Travelers

Natalie Windsor

Traveling alone by air can have its advantages. You don't have to think about anyone but yourself, you can relax, watch a movie, read a book, or work in peace. Or can you? What if the traveler next to you won't stop talking? What if your wallet or purse disappears? *For trouble-free trips . . .*

- **Don't travel without telling someone.** Contact a friend or family member. Give him/her your itinerary so someone knows how to find you.
- **Streamline your wallet or purse.** Avoid having to replace everything—if it's lost or stolen—by only carrying identification and those cards that you may actually use.
- **Don't wear fine jewelry.** It's dangerous to put it in your luggage, so leave it home.
- **Travel light.** An overloaded traveler is a vulnerable traveler. Ship bulky items in advance.
- **Keep an inventory of items**—and put a copy of it and your personal identification inside your suitcase, and keep a copy, too. You'll know by checking the inventory if something's missing and you will increase the odds that you'll see it again if it's lost.
- **Wear a wedding ring.** You'll discourage unwanted advances.
- **Wear headphones.** You don't even have to plug them in, but you'll politely tune out chatterers.
- **Avoid the bulkhead**—the area that separates first class from coach. If there's an unescorted child on board, that's where he/she is most likely to be.
- **Have single bills handy.** You won't have to get change and attract the wrong kind of attention, and you'll speed your progress through the airport if you need to give a tip.

Natalie Windsor, author of *How to Fly—Relaxed and Happy From Takeoff to Touchdown*. CorkScrew Press.

CHEAPER AIR TRAVEL

■ **Travel on Tuesdays, Wednesdays or Thursdays**—low traffic days on which airlines often discount their tickets.

Departure times can also make a big difference in ticket prices. Look for competitive routes involving low-fare carriers—big airlines may match the fares.

Example: One major airline charged $800 for all round-trip Miami-Los Angeles flights—except between 5 pm and 6pm, when it had to go head-to-head with a low-fare carrier that was charging $300. For that flight, the major carrier matched the $300 price.

Randy Peterson, editor of *Inside Flyer*, 4715 C Town Ctr. Dr., Colorado Springs, CO 80916. Monthly. $33/yr. 800-767-8896.

SELF-CONTROL

■ **When you feel negative emotions**, ask yourself why you are feeling them . . . what you can do about them now . . . whether this is the right time to feel emotional pain. If it is not, take conscious control of the emotions and change them. *Important:* Treat feelings and emotions as messengers, not controllers. They are like internal eyes and ears, reporting how your body is handling a situation. Learn to control your responses to feelings—not be controlled by them.

Toughness Training for Life by James Loehr, Ed.D., president, Loehr-Groppel Sport Science, Wesley Chapel, FL. E. P. Dutton.

■ **Rely on *internal* cues**—not external factors—to stay on your diet. Scales may be unreliable—weight can change daily for anyone...and exercise builds muscle, which weighs more than fat. A compliment on how good you look provides temporary reinforcement but can lead you to backslide if you do not get another one soon. *Better:* Look inside yourself. Take responsibility for your actions and thoughts. Only you can decide how you feel.

Emotional Weight by Colleen Sundermeyer, Ph.D., nutritionist and eating-disorder counselor, Rancho Murieta, CA. The Putnam Publishing Group.

How to Know Yourself Much, Much Better

M. Scott Peck, M.D.

W e each make our own path through life. To succeed and better understand our behavior, we must be prepared to ask where we are at every stage of the journey. Then we can better decide where we want to go—and how to get there.

Here are guideposts to some of the most important issues we face and questions to ask as we meet life's challenges . . .

GROWTH

The main purpose of life is emotional and spiritual growth. No one really ever becomes fully grown-up. Most people are actually emotional children walking around in adults' clothing.

Growth involves pain. Many of us would like to go back to earlier times in our lives—even infancy—when we were protected from the challenges of adult life. That desire causes people to remain fixed in second childhoods—self-centered, whiny, and dependent. To know whether you have the basic prerequisite for growth, ask yourself, "Do I accept the impossibility of returning to childhood?"

COURAGE

Emotional and spiritual growth demands that you meet the challenges with which life continually con-

M. Scott Peck, M.D., psychiatrist, management consultant and founder of the Foundation for Community Encouragement, 109 Danbury Rd., Suite 8, Ridgefield, CT 06877. His most recent book is *Further Along the Road Less Traveled: The Unending Journey Toward Spiritual Growth*. Simon & Schuster.

fronts you, despite your fear of painful new experiences. Taking on these challenges in the face of such fear requires courage.

When you feel uneasy about an uncomfortable situation, ask yourself, "Will I be better off avoiding—or meeting—this challenge?" If you act only when your inner voice tells you it is the right thing to do, you are truly on the road to growth and maturity.

ANGER

Anger is a necessary emotion and an important self-defense mechanism. But we need to know when anger is appropriate and how to express it.

When a situation provokes you to anger, there are at least five different ways to express it. *Ask yourself:*

• *"Should I apologize?"* My initial reaction was mistaken . . . I was at fault.

"Should I ignore it?" What the other person did was an accident . . . it was not his/her fault.

• *"Should I minimize my anger?"* The other person did insult me a little . . . but it wasn't important.

• *"Should I express my anger?"* I will think about it for a few days. If it is clear that the other person seriously wronged me, I will complain to him/her.

• *"Should I lose my temper?"* The other person wronged me so badly that I have to express my anger strongly—on the spot.

You can assess your own stage of life's journey to maturity by how often you step back, think through your anger and express it appropriately.

JUDGMENT

It is impossible to go through life without making judgments about people—whom you should marry, how much freedom to give your children, whom you should hire or fire. How well you make those judgments is critical to the quality of your life. Before you judge someone else, you should judge yourself.

Example: You have to fire an unsatisfactory employee. *It has to be done but ask yourself:*

• *Was I sufficiently concerned with the employee earlier?*

SELF-CONTROL

■ **Clarify your life values** by determining what will make your life more worth living. *Ask yourself:* What would you like to have accomplished by the end of your life . . . what biographical information would you like the newspaper to include in your obituary . . . what would your spouse, friends, boss, or enemies add to that obit? *Also:* In only one or two sentences, describe how you want to be perceived and remembered.

From Stress to Strength: How to Lighten Your Load and Save Your Life by Robert S. Eliot, M.D., F.A.C.C., director, Institute of Stress Medicine in Denver. Bantam Books.

CRITICISM: DO'S & DONT'S

■ **Only expressing criticism**, anger and bitterness to your spouse is counterproductive. Break the negative-feedback cycle by spending 10 to 15 minutes alone with your partner, providing each other with honest, positive feedback. *Examples:* Tell your partner three things you like about the way he/she looks . . . his three greatest personality or character strengths . . . at least two things he does particularly well.

Lethal Lovers and Poisonous People by Los Angeles psychologist Harriet Braiker, Ph.D. Pocket Books.

■ **Giving and receiving feedback** is tricky, even for the most happily married couples. *Helpful:* A "feedback contract" negotiated and signed by both partners. *Useful questions:* Are you open to feedback at all times? . . . Do you want to be asked first, "Do you want feedback about this?" . . . Would it be more empowering for each of you to ask for feedback rather than to wait for it? Once you've made the agreement, write it down and put it some-

CRITICISM: DO'S & DON'TS

place visible, like on the bathroom mirror or the refrigerator.

Centering and the Art of Intimacy Handbook: A New Psychology of Close Relationships by Colorado Springs psychotherapists Gay Hendricks, Ph.D., and Kathlyn Hendricks, Ph.D. Fireside Books.

■ **Get rid of "should" statements** by asking who says you should do it. This makes you aware that you are criticizing yourself unnecessarily. Once you realize you are making your own rules, you can change them. Reformulate "should" statements into more realistic, less critical ones. *Example:* Instead of "I should be able to make my wife happy," say, "It would be nice if I could make her happy."

Feeling Good: The New Mood Therapy by David Burns, M.D., psychotherapist and University of Pennsylvania professor. Avon Books.

■ **Self-nurturing** means stopping . . . looking at where you are and accepting it . . . connecting with your inner needs . . . then taking steps to grow and get better. This is very different from self-pity, which looks to others to make us feel better . . . or self-indulgence, which denies and suppresses current bad feelings—guaranteeing that they will reappear.

Take Time for Yourself: Meditative Moments for Healthy Living by Ruth Fishel, cofounder of a healing program for women in Cape Cod, MA (Health Communications/$8.95)

• *Did I speak to him/her as soon as I could have or did I avoid confrontation until it was too late to solve the problem?*

If you answer such questions honestly, you will know how to act in the future to prevent the need for similar painful results.

UNCERTAINTY

Life is a series of decisions—and there is an easy way and a difficult way to make each of these decisions.

Easy way to decide: Always follow a rigid rule.

Example: Your teenage daughter wants to stay out on Saturday night until 1 A.M. Your response may always follow the rule "No! You know that your curfew is 10 P.M." or the rule "Of course. Whatever you do is fine."

Difficult way: Analyze every situation as thoroughly as you can.

Example: You think to yourself, "She does have a 10 P.M. curfew, but we set it two years ago. She is responsible and we trust her but we aren't sure about the boy she's going with."

Then you try to decide the most appropriate reply —"no," "yes" or a compromise, such as coming home by 11 P.M.

The *easy way* avoids thinking and allows quick decision-making.

The *difficult way* leaves you in doubt but admits there is no magic formula for the correct answer in every situation. If you take the difficult way, you know that you take life seriously.

WILL

How much you achieve in life depends on how strong a will you possess and on how well you can control it.

A *weak will* is like a little donkey in your backyard. It can't do very much work, and about the worst damage it can cause is to eat your flowers.

A *strong will* is like a dozen Clydesdales. If those massive beasts are trained, disciplined and harnessed, they can help you move mountains. But if you let them run wild, they may knock down your house.

To harness your will, voluntarily subject it to a power higher than yourself. The nature of that power is defined by your religious and moral beliefs.

To understand your role in life, ask yourself, "Am I undisciplined and selfish—or willing to go where I am led by the higher power in which I believe?"

SELF-LOVE

Army psychiatrists once studied the personalities of 12 people in the service. All were very successful in their jobs, their families, and their social relationships. They were asked to list the three most important things in their lives.

While they disagreed on their second and third most important priorities, every one of those successful people named the same top priority—*myself*.

This reply did not mean these people were exceptionally selfish. All were loving spouses and parents and caring supervisors. They stressed their self-love because they truly appreciated the value of life and felt a corresponding responsibility to make the most of it, which is why they were successful.

Self-love is consistent with a sense of *humility*, defined by a 14th-century monk as "a true knowledge of oneself as one is."

If you can attain humility—the ability to realistically evaluate both your virtues and your faults—then you own the best compass for guiding yourself along the winding highway of life.

Problems: Big and Small

Gordon Flett, Ph.D.

Little things wear people down because there is less support to help handle them. At times of major trouble, like death or divorce, most people seek and receive significant emotional and practical help from others.

But people rarely seek or are offered help in handling the grind of traffic jams, noise, and difficult coworkers.

Result: Those little things become wearing.

Self-defense: Simply talk to someone—either about what is bothering you or about something else to take your mind off the irritation. If problems persist, do not rule out the possibility of seeking professional help.

Gordon Flett, Ph.D., psychologist, York University, Toronto, Canada, and leader of a study of people's responses to big and small life problems.

■ **Schedule worry time for yourself.** Allow 30 minutes a day for exploring your concerns in detail. Focusing on your problems this way will help you solve them—or make you realize they are not worth worrying about. Setting aside time also lets you tell yourself that minor problems that crop up throughout the day will have to wait for "worry time." *Result:* The rest of your day stays relatively worry-free.

Michael Vasey, Ph.D., assistant professor of psychology, Ohio State University, Columbus, OH.

■ **Better decisions.** When you are faced with a big decision—to make a major purchase, change jobs or careers—ask yourself if what you have decided to do will get you closer to your goal. If not, think twice about doing it.

Questioning yourself will keep you focused on long-term success, not short-term gratification.

Grace Butland, editor, *ImageMatters*, Box 246, Riverton, CT 06065.

■ **"Exercise" your brain.** In much the same way physical exercise builds muscle mass, developing mental substance and stamina through resistance training builds character and allows us to learn how to better overcome obstacles. It's getting through the little steps that's most important.

Diamond in the Rough by Barry J. Farber, president, Farber Training Systems, Florham Park, NJ. Berkley Books.

■ **Music may boost intelligence.** Three-year-olds who learn keyboards for at least 15 minutes each week and who have daily sing-alongs show increased intelligence. And 18- to 22-year-olds who listen to Mozart for just 10 minutes a day show a similar but lesser short-term intelligence-boosting effect. *Intriguing:* The type of intelligence raised most in the three-year-olds is called *spatial intelligence*—the ability to visualize, rotate, and assemble objects. It is considered a key to math, engineering, and science.

Research led by Frances Rauscher, Ph.D., research psychologist, University of Wisconsin, Oshkosh, and Gordon Shaw, Ph.D., professor emeritus of physics, University of California, Irvine, CA.

■ **Feeling forgetful:** Boost your memory by deciding what you need to remember most and focusing on it . . . paying close attention to anything you want to memorize . . . learning to remember in little bits over time, not trying to remember a large amount of information at once.

How to Take Charge of Life Problems You Thought You Couldn't Change

Richard J. Leider

Most people have difficulty coping with change. But in today's world, change is inevitable—and if you do not take charge of your own life, change will take charge of you. Even if you are content with things as they are, you have to prepare for change since situations shift frequently today.

Performing your job well is not really a defense. If your company decides to downsize or is put up for sale—no matter how well you have mastered your current position—you may need a different set of skills to meet the needs of the future. In the 1990s, life planning is a survival skill.

AVOIDING CHANGE

People who cannot face change are in a state that I call *Inner Kill*. Prime symptoms include:
- Always taking the safe way.
- Reacting instead of taking risks.
- Avoiding decisions.
- Daydreaming and talking rather than taking action.

Inner Kill is closely related to fatigue, which may result from overwork and a pressure-filled life or underwork and too little engagement in life. *Examples:*

Richard J. Leider, a partner in the Inventure Group, a personal growth and team-effectiveness consulting firm, 8500 Normandale Lake Blvd., Minneapolis, MN 55437. He is the author of *Life Skills: Taking Charge of Your Personal and Professional Growth*. Pfeiffer and Company.

• **Middle-aged people** are often under intense pressure. They must juggle overwhelming work schedules and personal and financial responsibilities that may include aging parents and growing children.

Result: Some middle-aged people just go through the motions of their daily activities—fatigued and unable to think about where they are headed.

Early retirees who have unexpectedly and involuntarily been removed from the workforce may find themselves bewildered and unable to respond to life meaningfully—especially if they never took time during their careers to define themselves in ways other than their occupation.

Result: Many of these early retirees become ill within two years of their retirement.

• **Young adults** graduating from college and beginning their careers rarely think through what their talents and interests are best suited for. Many allow events to control them.

Result: Five, 10, or 20 years down the road, they find themselves in a rut and wonder how they ever got into it.

HOW TO FACE CHANGE

• **Take the initiative.** To engage life, you must take the initiative when facing change. That requires overcoming a number of very common fears—of criticism, rejection, betrayal, failure, even success. You must rescript yourself to trust both your own judgment and that of other people who can help you.

• **Accept that change is inevitable and impossible to avoid.** Decide to change, instead of escape—use change for personal and professional growth.

• **Be prepared to take risks.** It is better to choose the calculated risk of a positive decision for change than to let outside events force other less-welcome risks on you. Prudent risk-taking requires excellent information, so the first step is to acquire the information you need.

• **Take stock.** Before creating a vision of where you want to go in life and how you can get there, you must know yourself. Answer the ques-

Also helpful: Designate a *memory spot* in your home where you leave things, so you don't have to bother remembering where you put the car keys . . . or use a pocket notebook or file cards to help jog your memory.

Barry Gordon, M.D., Ph.D., behavioral neurologist, cognitive neuroscientist and experimental psychologist at Johns Hopkins University, Baltimore, MD, and author of *Memory: Remembering and Forgetting in Everyday Life.* MasterMedia.

Meditation: The Basics

Lawrence LeShan, Ph.D.

Meditation is a form of mental exercise in which you develop your ability to concentrate. And just like any exercise, the more you work at it, the easier it gets—and the greater the benefits.

If you practice meditation, your thinking will become more organized and disciplined. By routinely meditating, you will strengthen your will, sense of purpose, goal-oriented behavior, and ability to bar distractions.

There are many different meditation techniques, but at their core—wherever they originated—they are based on the same principles. Choose a technique with which you are comfortable, and change techniques if necessary.

The basics:

• **Commit to 10 to 15 minutes per day,** five to seven days per week for the first two weeks, then increase to 20 to 30 minutes.

• **Set a timer** or put a clock within easy view.

• **Pick a quiet place** and get into a comfortable position.

STRESS BUSTING

- **Anytime you become aware of stray thoughts** interrupting the meditation, push the thoughts aside and resume the technique.
- **Close your eyes.**

Three techniques:

- **The Meditation of Breath Counting**—Methodically, count to four and repeat, again and again, slowly.
- **The Meditation of the Bubble**—Visualize yourself at the bottom of a crystal-clear lake where bubbles are rising slowly to the surface. Each bubble contains one isolated thought, feeling, or perception as it drifts into and out of range. Switch to another bubble roughly every seven seconds, about the time it takes for the bubble to pass from view.
- **The Mantra Meditation**—Create a one or two syllable word and repeat it quietly aloud.

Examples: *Om, shareem, tooray.*

For personal instruction or to explore other forms of meditation techniques, check the Yellow Pages under "Meditation Instruction." Ask your doctor. Ask at a health food store. Check local papers.

Lawrence LeShan, Ph.D., author of *How to Meditate* (Bantam Books). *Meditating to Attain a Healthy Body Weight* is also by Dr. LeShan.

tions "Who am I? Why am I here? Where am I going?" Finding the truth about yourself requires courage. You must think seriously and answer a series of questions to assess your quality of life in ten fundamental areas.

- **Time.** What is your daily schedule? Do you have time for your real priorities? What is your most important need now?

Suggestion: Keep a journal of your activities, and review it at least quarterly. If your schedule is not consistent with your priorities, be prepared to change it.

- **Values.** What are your top three values now? Can you describe one risk you have taken recently because of your values?

Suggestion: Ask yourself why you do the things you do. Consider what values your actions express and whether you agree with them.

- **Vitality.** How do you spend your leisure time? Do you have fun? If you are tied to a routine and never enjoy spontaneous fun, you are suppressing an important part of yourself.

- **Purpose.** Why do you get up in the morning? Do you have a sense of purpose?

Suggestions: Consider what you would like your epitaph to say. If you learned that you had only two years to live, how would you spend your time?

- **Career.** How did you get where you are? Did you choose your career—or did it choose you? At what point did you come to love what you are doing, and why? If your current job does not match your needs and wants, the mental and physical costs can be high. True career progress requires not continual promotion but continual growth.

- **Talents.** What natural talents do others see in you? Which talents do you most enjoy using?

Suggestions: Consider your ability to handle facts, figures and concepts, deal with people, manipulate objects, etc. Consider keeping a *talents inventory.*

- **Spirituality.** Do you set aside time for contemplation? What principles govern your actions? You will live a more satisfying and fulfilling life if you know you are here for a higher purpose—not just to satisfy your material wants and compete in a rat race.

• **Health.** How is your health and your energy level? Do you exercise enough, relax, smoke, drink? If you take care of your health, you can expect a longer, better life.

• **Relationships.** Do you have friends? To whom do you talk? Do you talk about what is important to you? The single most important source of meaning in our lives is our connection with the people we love—spouse, family, and friends. Reflect on how well you are able to communicate with those closest to you.

• **Money.** What annual income do you need to support your lifestyle? How is your financial health? Do you have written financial goals and plans? If your current situation is unsatisfactory, decide whether the appropriate change is to make more money or to need less.

Important: You cannot take stock by yourself. Discuss the questions with the people who know you best.

TAKING CHARGE

After taking stock of your current activities and setting your priorities, you are equipped to decide the changes you want to make for a better future.

• **Write a master dream list** of all the things you would like to do throughout your life.

• **Talk with your partner**—or your family—and make a joint list.

• **Choose four major goals to pursue for the next 12 months**—one each for your personal life, your work, your relationships, and your finances. *Key questions to ask yourself:*

• *Do the people who matter to me support me?*

• *Do I have enough time and enough money?*

• *Am I willing to sacrifice any lower-priority items that conflict with a more important one?* If you can answer each question with a "yes," tell others about your plan to increase your motivation.

• **Develop an action plan for each goal—with deadlines.** Break the plan down into small, measurable steps. Put a date on each step to track

Five Days to an Organized Life

Lucy H. Hedrick

Grab just a few moments each day for the next five days, or one day a week over the course of the next five for an organized way to get organized:

• **Day one.** Develop a list of rewards for yourself—15-minute rewards, two- to three-hour rewards, all day rewards. *Examples:* Phone a dear friend, hike a favorite trail, or play 18 holes of golf.

• **Day two.** Write down goals. Dissect them into manageable, bite-size bits, and develop a plan of action that may include communicating with people, getting more education, or doing research. *Example:* A new job might require interviewing friends, taking a résumé workshop, and/or doing research at the library.

• **Day three.** Transfer every task to a pocket notebook, but divide the tasks into calls, errands, things to do and things to write. *Examples:* Call a career counselor, order stationery, set up files, draft a résumé.

• **Day four.** Buy a pocket calendar and record specific appointments and deadlines, "must do" tasks from your notebook as well as time for planned rewards. *Example:* Thursday: 7:30/breakfast with Ted. 9:30/staff meeting. 10:45/draft new marketing plan. 12:30/lunch in the park.

• **Day five.** Create a short, daily "to do" list by choosing a few reasonable tasks from your notebook and scheduling them when there is a break in your calendar schedule. *Example:*

7:30/breakfast with Ted. Stop by the post office. 9:30/staff meeting.

Lucy H. Hedrick, time-management consultant and author of *Five Days to an Organized Life*. Dell Publishing.

How to Break Bad Habits

William Knaus, Ed.D.

To break a problem habit, you need to create a *will to change*—not an attempt to restrain yourself. Self-restraint against bad habits rarely works.

Example: Dieters usually gain back the weight they have lost. But a *will to change* is a command effort that allows experimenting with change, accepting its difficulty and moving ahead again even after inevitable backsliding.

Helpful: Deflect your attention from the habit to something else.

Example: Keep a pitcher of water in the refrigerator. Whenever you have a habit urge—of any kind—pour and slowly sip two glasses of ice water. This will often allow time for the urge to pass.

William Knaus, Ed.D., author of *Change Your Life Now: Powerful Techniques for Positive Change*. John Wiley & Sons.

■ **Procrastination *adds* stress.** To get things done, write down the benefits of completing a task . . . break it into smaller parts . . . make appointments with yourself to accomplish specific tasks . . . keep those appointments—accomplish what you promise yourself you will . . . reward yourself when the task is finished.

Making the Most of Change (When Change Is Making the Most of You) by Roz Turner, motivational consultant, Issaquah, WA. Hara Publishing.

your progress. Your action plan will put you on the road to meaningful change.

How to Develop a Positive Attitude . . . How to Maintain a Positive Attitude

Wolf J. Rinke, PhD

For success in all areas of life, *attitude* is much more important than *aptitude*. People who cultivate consistently positive attitudes expect great things, work hard for those things and are likely to achieve them.

In fact, research by psychologist Martin Seligman of the University of Pennsylvania revealed that optimistic people are happier, healthier, and more successful than those with a negative outlook on life.

HEALTH

A new branch of medicine—*psychoneuroimmunology*—studies the relationship between mental attitude and health. Physicians have found that a positive attitude can result in faster recovery from surgery and burns, more resistance to arthritis and cancer and improved immune function.

Reason: Brain-produced substances—*neuropeptides*—transmit chemical messages that direct the immune system. When you think positively, these

Wolf J. Rinke, Ph.D., president of Wolf Rinke Associates, a human-resources development and management consulting firm in Clarksville, MD, and adjunct associate professor at Johns Hopkins University and the University of Maryland. He is the author of *Make It a Winning Life: Success Strategies for Life, Love and Business*. Achievement Publishers.

messages are more emphatic. When you are depressed, they tell your body, "Why bother?"

SUCCESS

When you think positively about yourself, you work harder at what you want to do—and give up less easily. You make a better impression on others, which encourages them to help you.

When you think more positively about your colleagues, employees, spouse, and children, you build stronger and more productive relationships—leading to greater success at work and at home.

Lesson: If you think you would be happier with your life if you were more successful, you have things backward.

DEVELOPING A POSITIVE ATTITUDE

A positive attitude does not pop into your mind by itself. How you feel is a decision you make every day. If you don't automatically feel upbeat, look around and find something to feel good about. *Aim:* Start out each day in a positive way:

- **Use a clock radio** that plays music that is soft and pleasant to wake up to. *Don't* use a loud alarm clock.
- **Allow yourself enough time** to prepare for the day's activities at a civilized pace. *Don't* get up at the last possible moment.
- **Think about the positive things** you expect to accomplish today. *Don't* listen to news of the world's problems or worry about your own problems while you are dressing.
- **Eat a healthy breakfast.** *Don't* drug yourself with coffee or cigarettes.
- **Discuss your plans for the day** with your partner. *Don't* bury your face in the newspaper.
- **Each day, find some positive feature** about your partner and compliment him/her on it.

As you go about your day's activities, always expect the best.

OBSTACLES

The common obstacles to developing a positive attitude are the types of negative thinking that dis-

BREAKING BAD HABITS

■ **Better use of time:** Turn off the TV for one full week . . . and you will suddenly find yourself with a lot more time to do things that you did not think you would ever have a chance to do.

Mental Pullups by Karen Boscaljon, a motivational speaker in Marshalltown, IA. Sta-Kris, Inc.

SMARTER LIVING

■ **Secret to living longer** is not all in the genes . . . it's attitude, too. *Key to longevity:* Stay productive, whether that means continuing to work, volunteering or taking up a hobby you enjoy . . . work hard to improve your marriage—such a relationship provides a buffer against the vagaries of life . . . live a healthy lifestyle, including eating a low-fat diet and exercising regularly.

Deborah Wingard, professor of epidemiology in the department of family and preventive medicine at the University of California, San Diego, School of Medicine.

Smarter Living

When life feels chaotic, take better care of yourself. It is tempting to say you do not have time for proper eating, regular exercise, and adequate sleep—but it is in times of chaos that you need these most.

During intense periods of change, listen to negative, fear-driven things you may be telling yourself. When you catch yourself thinking negatively, tell yourself, *I can handle it.*

Be proactive—create options for your future. Avoid thinking that maybe the change will not affect you. Assume it will, and plan to deal with it.

Making the Most of Change When Change Is Making the Most of You by Roz Turner, motivational consultant, Issaquah, WA. Hara Publishing.

■ **For a much better life.** Use a notebook to record each day's activities, and designate the day as an up one or a down one. After a few weeks, you should notice a pattern. It may turn out that specific events at work invariably create bad days. If so, and if you *must* do those activities, try to do them in the fewest days possible—so more days can be good.

Creativity for Leaders by Gary Fellers, Ph.D., a quality-management consultant and trainer in Central, SC. Pelican Publishing.

■ **Laughter is social glue.** Most of the things people laugh at in daily life are not especially insightful or clever. It is just social banter. Laughter is harder to fake than a smile. It may be more closely related to animal calls—which help groups of animals bond—than it is to speech.

Robert Provine, Ph.D., professor of neurobiology and psychology, University of Maryland, Baltimore County, MD.

■ **Five-minute energy boosters:** Call a friend on the phone to chat. Do a yoga stretch. Look at the sky. Look at family pictures. Pet a cat or dog. Browse through travel magazines. Visualize being at the beach or in the mountains. Wash your face. Plan an after-work treat. Sing. Watch tropical fish.

Marcia Yudkin, Ph.D., editor, *The Creative Glow*, Box 1310, Boston, MA 02117.

tort your evaluation of situations. Here they are, and how you can turn them around:

• **Exaggerating.** Overestimating problems and underestimating abilities.
Example: "I'm always late for meetings."
Replace with: "I make it to most meetings on time."

• **Overgeneralizing.** Taking an isolated event and assuming it always happens.
Example: "I'm stupid."
Replace with: "This time I made a wrong turn, but I usually do get where I'm going easily."

• **Personalizing.** Thinking everything revolves around you.
Example: "Everyone noticed that I wore the same dress twice."
Replace with: "I like this outfit, and I am properly dressed for the occasion."

• **Either/or thinking.** Seeing things as mutually exclusive, even when they're not.
Example: "Either I get the promotion or I'm a failure."
Replace with: "My performance has been exceptional, and I have a good chance of getting promoted. If I don't get it this time, there will be other opportunities."

• **Jumping to conclusions.** Drawing conclusions from limited information.
Example: "I wasn't assigned the project because I wasn't at my desk when my manager called."
Replace with: "I'll ask my manager if there's a way I can help out with the assignment."

• **Ignoring the positive.** Focusing on one negative and forgetting about all the positives.
Example: "I did not make my sales quota last month."
Replace with: "I hit my sales goals for 11 of 12 months, and I will hit it again."

SETTING YOURSELF UP FOR SUCCESS

Nothing enhances a positive attitude more than *success*, so regard success as the normal state of affairs—and the lack of success as the exception.

• **Avoid perfectionism.** Very few things are perfect in this world, so try to recognize that falling short of perfection is not failure.

Helpful approach: Remember that there is no such thing as failure—only outcomes. If your efforts produce an outcome that is less successful than you had hoped, don't say, "I'm a failure." Instead, say, "I'll change what I did wrong and next time I'll do better."

• **Focus on the future.** You can't change the past, but if you decide where you want to go in the future, you will give yourself the best chance of getting there. Always aim high, and you too will make it a winning life.

Now Is a Very Good Time to Reinvent Your Life and Escape Lifetraps

Jeffrey E. Young, Ph.D.

Many people go through life repeating the same self-destructive behaviors. They may keep forming attachments to the wrong people or sacrifice themselves so much to others that they neglect their own needs or regard themselves as unworthy, no matter how much they achieve.

While these people say that they would like to live more fulfilling lives, they seem unable to change these patterns, which I call *lifetraps*.

Jeffrey E. Young, Ph.D., founder and director of the Cognitive Therapy Centers of New York City and Fairfield County, CT. He is a faculty member of the Department of Psychiatry at Columbia University in New York and author of Reinventing Your Life: How to Break Free of Negative Life Patterns. *Dutton.*

LIFE SAVERS

■ **Better quality of life.** Give yourself a time-out when events seem overwhelming. Go someplace where you can be alone to think over the situation. *Helpful:* When making to-do lists, do not schedule every minute of the day. Allow time for unexpected problems. When you feel stuck and unable to do anything, write down 10 choices you have for getting unstuck . . . pick three of them . . . and take action.

Making the Most of Change When Change Is Making the Most of You by Roz Turner, motivational consultant, Issaquah, WA. Hara Publishing.

■ **No more blues.** Cure the blues by doing something for someone else . . . for yourself . . . or for your home. *Examples:* Invite some friends over to dinner—and use the good china . . . take three upbeat friends to lunch . . . plan a vacation . . . volunteer at a local soup kitchen . . . talk about your feelings to a good friend—or a good therapist . . . take a class . . . sing—even if you think you don't have a good voice.

Liz Carpenter, former White House press secretary, quoted in On the Edge of Darkness: Conversations about Conquering Depression by Kathy Cronkite. Delta Books.

TAKING CONTROL

■ **Take charge of your life** by saying "no" more often. You cannot do everything that everyone wants you to do. Unwanted socializing, interruptions, crisis management, and attempting too much at one time can all be solved by saying "no." *Important:* Learn to say "no" tactfully: *I would love to, but I have a rush project that must come first . . .* or *I am afraid I would do a very poor job for you, because . . .*

Richard Leider is a management consultant who specializes in executive career development, Minneapolis, MN, and author of *Life Skills.* Pfeiffer & Co.

■ **Tension triggers:** Tension can be set off by authoritarians who make you feel meek and childlike . . . anger that makes you feel out of control . . . other people's anger that frightens you . . . loud people . . . being teased . . . speaking in public . . . fear of appearing foolish . . . fear of making mistakes . . . a lull in a conversation during which you tend to babble . . . insecurity around strangers. *Self-defense:* Visualize the worst scenario in one of these moments, and imagine yourself overcoming the adversity. Knowing you can deal with the worst will give you the confidence to succeed.

Hit the Ground Running: Communicate Your Way to Business Success by Cynthia Kreuger, communications consultant in Wheaton, IL. Brighton Publications.

Lifetraps are developed in response to emotional damage caused during childhood. Repairing that damage requires three steps:

• Learning to recognize the patterns.

• Understanding what their origins were in childhood.

• Working determinedly to confront and change the destructive behavior.

ORIGIN OF LIFETRAPS

Lifetraps begin when our parents or others stronger than ourselves repeatedly mistreat us in some way. We become emotionally accustomed to the situations, no matter how unsatisfactory they may be. Then, as adults, we continue to create similar situations because that is all we know.

Example: Heather's parents, Holocaust survivors, were terrified that something might happen to their daughter and discouraged her enjoyment of everyday activities by continually warning her of remote dangers like being trapped in the subway, drowning or pneumonia.

Result: At age 42, Heather was a self-imposed prisoner in her own home, dependent on tranquilizers and paralyzed by fear of the outside, and her husband was losing patience.

ELEVEN COMMON LIFETRAPS

Lifetrap: Vulnerability. Do you live in fear that disaster—whether natural, criminal, medical, or financial—is about to strike? Do you tend to exaggerate the danger in everyday situations? As a child, you were probably overprotected by parents who constantly warned you about dangers.

Lifetrap: Defectiveness. Do you feel flawed—like there is something wrong with you? This is found in those who were constantly criticized as children and never given respect. As adults, they still expect rejection and, therefore, fear love.

Lifetrap: Subjugation. Do you sacrifice your needs and desires in favor of other people's needs for fear that they will reject you or because you will feel guilty if you please yourself instead? This lifetrap stems from childhood subjugation or from a parent who was needy.

Lifetrap: Unrelenting standards. Do you always strive for unrealistically high standards and never feel satisfied with yourself or others? You were probably told as a child that nothing you did was good enough and that anything less than the best was failure.

Lifetrap: Entitlement. Do you feel that you should have whatever you want right now? Impatient adults who disregard others were likely spoiled children who never learned self-discipline.

Lifetrap: Emotional deprivation. Do you feel that nobody truly understands or loves you? This lifetrap affects people whose parents gave them inadequate nurturance. As adults, they tend to be attracted to others who are cold and ungiving or may even act that way themselves. In either case, they form relationships that only fulfill their negative expectations.

Lifetrap: Failure. Do you believe your achievements are inadequate? This lifetrap develops in children who are constantly told—often by their fathers—that they are inferior and are tagged stupid, lazy, and untalented. As adults, they tend to act in ways that make them fail, and they cannot admit or identify their actual successes.

Lifetrap: Abandonment. Are you constantly fearful that those close to you will desert you—or die? These fears are a response to loss or separation from a parent at an early age or to an emotionally remote mother or father. People caught in this lifetrap are drawn to partners who are likely to abandon them, and their fear often makes them cling so tightly that they drive partners away.

Lifetrap: Mistrust. Do you expect to be hurt or abused? Mistrustful adults were often abused—physically, sexually or psychologically—during childhood. As adults, they are drawn to abusive or untrustworthy partners, and with good partners, they may themselves be angry or abusive.

Lifetrap: Dependence. Do you feel unable to handle everyday events and problems without a lot of help? This develops in those who were made to feel incompetent whenever they tried to demonstrate independence during childhood. As adults, they seek out strong figures to rule their lives and shrink from showing any initiative.

TAKING CONTROL

Use Past-Positives To Feel Better Today

Donna Rae Smith

Think back to childhood successes like climbing a tree, riding a bike, getting the best grade on a test or getting picked for a team.

Think about how good you felt. Recall that feeling repeatedly—and use it to counter any thoughts of negative self-worth.

Most people internalize parental criticism, then spend their adult lives unhappily recalling it. Instead, remember your childhood emotional highs, and call on them when you feel unworthy.

Donna Rae Smith, personal-effectiveness consultant, Chagrin Falls, OH, and author of *The Power of Building Your Bright Side: Five Surprising Renewal Strategies to Personal and Business Success.* Wynwood Books.

OPPORTUNITIES

■ **When you are criticized:** Separate criticism that you receive from any decision you have to make before you take action on it. First, understand what is said—then decide what to do about it. Search through the content of the feedback for helpful information. Try not to get defensive—that becomes a barrier to taking in information that could be useful.

Ken Blanchard, chairman, Blanchard Training & Development, Escondido, CA, and coauthor of *The One-Minute Manager.* Berkley.

■ **Rejection opportunity.** Being turned away by someone with whom you've been in a relationship should be viewed as positive—a chance to move forward with your life. While the rejection may sting, such a positive attitude will prevent you from obsessing over *the one that got away*. Instead, you'll spend your time more productively . . . and find others who will appreciate you for the great person you are.

How to Attract Anyone, Anytime, Anyplace: The Smart Guide to Flirting by Susan Rabin, MA, relationship therapist, New York. Plume.

■ **Cope with a painful situation** by giving yourself an *I can* message—telling yourself you can handle things even if, at the moment, you do not know how. Ask yourself what you can learn from the problem . . . how you can have power over the pain and loss . . . what could be a great outcome. *Example:* Not being bowled over by adversity again . . . or someday teaching or writing about your pain to help others handle their own pain. *Helpful:* Tell yourself you will recover and go on with your life—no matter what.

Judy Tatelbaum, M.S.W., psychotherapist, Carmel, CA, and author of *The Courage to Grieve* and *You Don't Have to Suffer*. HarperCollins.

Lifetrap: Social exclusion. Do you feel different from other people or ill at ease in group surroundings? As a child, you may have felt rejected by others because of some difference. As an adult, though you might feel comfortable in intimate settings, you still may feel uncomfortable in groups.

HOW TO BREAK FREE

You can escape from lifetraps. Negative patterns formed in childhood can be changed, provided you make a conscious decision to confront your problem. But you must first decide what positive life goals you are seeking.

When you identify your own needs and aspirations—not those forced on you as a child—you will realize how the negative patterns locked in by your lifetraps prevent you from fulfilling your goals. Then you are ready to change.

STEPS

• **Identify and address the childhood source.** Try to relive the pain you felt as a child—imagine you are that child once again, experiencing a particularly painful event. As a mature adult, reassure your inner child that there are other ways to cope.

Example: Danielle, trapped in the abandonment pattern, had a father who ran away and an alcoholic mother who paid little attention to her. She recalled a typical childhood scene when her mother was drunk and Danielle was trying vainly to get her attention.

The adult Danielle imagined herself entering the scene, taking the child Danielle on her lap and telling her, "Don't worry. Your parents aren't here when you need them, but I will stay with you and help you come out okay."

• **Express your pain.** Write a letter expressing your feelings to the parent or person who helped cause your lifetrap, even if you tear it up or put it away in a drawer.

• **Break the pattern.** Identify specific examples of negative behavior that you repeat frequently and work on changing them, one at a time.

Example: Heather, whose vulnerability lifetrap was discussed earlier, noted that before she went to sleep at night, she checked every possible source of danger—the children's room, garage, stove, microwave, toaster, even the hair dryer—five times.

With thought and effort, Heather learned how to estimate more realistically these and other fears of remote risks that were trapping her. She gradually began to engage in more activities, which improved her marital relationship and allowed her to enjoy life.

Important: Don't be afraid to ask for help from friends or therapists.

• **Confront yourself.** Look realistically at your behavior, write down specific ways in which you surrender to your lifetrap, then use rational thought to counteract them.

Example: Frank, trapped in mistrust, was intensely suspicious of his wife, Adrienne, and constantly accused her of betraying him. When asked to list the evidence, he could cite only one specific circumstance—before they were married, Adrienne had lunch with an old boyfriend without telling Frank. Adrienne had long since explained it was only to say good-bye to the former boyfriend. When he looked at this event realistically, Frank realized that his suspicion was unjustified.

Helpful: Write a reminder on a flash card explaining why the lifetrap is false. Put it in your wallet, and consult it frequently.

Example: After Danielle realized her fears of abandonment were unrealistic, she wrote a flash card saying, "It's not true that everyone will abandon me. I just feel that way because when I was a child my parents abandoned me."

• **Keep trying.** Breaking a lifelong pattern of behavior is not easy, but the rewards make persistence well worth it.

INNOVATIVE THINKING

■ **Tomorrow brings exciting new possibilities.** The past is not changeable, but we can learn from it and move forward. See tomorrow as a chance for well-laid plans and untried beginnings. Try to leave past problems in yesterday—and not carry them into tomorrow. If there is something in your past that has loose ends extending into the present, tie up the loose ends, close the past off and move on to the future.

The Self-Talk Solution by Shad Helmstetter, chairman, Self-Talk Institute, which develops motivational programs for schools and businesses. Simon & Schuster.

■ **Never ridicule ideas,** no matter how outlandish they seem. A permissive atmosphere is crucial to innovation because it encourages people to take intellectual risks. But employees must know that they and their ideas will not be ridiculed . . . and that they will not be penalized for honest mistakes or ideas that turn out to be bad ones. *Helpful:* Invite innovative ideas with a statement encouraging wide-ranging thinking.

Andrew Dubrin, Ph.D., professor of management, College of Business, Rochester Institute of Technology and author of *Reengineering Survival Guide: Managing and Succeeding in the Changing Workplace.* Thomson Executive Press.

■ **Better thinking.** Choose TV shows carefully, focusing on news and information programs . . . play bridge instead of bingo, blackjack instead of slot machines . . . do jigsaw and crossword puzzles, and play word games like Scrabble or anagrams . . . start something new—take an art class.

K. Warner Schaie, Ph.D., director of the Gerontology Center, Pennsylvania State University, University Park, PA.

A HAPPIER, HEALTHIER YOU

Happiness To-do List

Elaine St. James

• **Choose to ignore an insult.** Doing so prevents you from being consumed by negative energy.

• **Break your routine once in a while.** Try new ways of getting ready in the morning . . . new roads to drive to work . . . new strategies to organize your time. This will open you up to new ways of solving problems.

• **Stop judging others.** It will only distance you from people and result in little spiritual gain.

• **Do the things you fear.** Whenever you avoid dealing with something, ask yourself why. If it's because you fear failure or how you will look to others, force yourself to try it. There are valuable lessons to learn.

• **Get rid of your anger.** Channel your excess energy by running, working out, or writing in a journal. Understand why you're angry . . . learn from it . . . then move on.

• **Learn to forgive.** Don't let past negative experiences hinder you from moving ahead with your life and relationships.

• **Smile more.** If you're doing all of the above, smiling will become a natural part of your life and make you more approachable.

Elaine St. James of Santa Barbara, CA, who conducts nationwide seminars on how to reduce clutter and live simply. She is author of *Simplify Your Life* and *Inner Simplicity*. Hyperion.

Winning Words of Wisdom

Michael Levine

• **Live your life** in the manner that you would like your children to live theirs.

• **You know you're doing something right** when you start being copied.

• **Extraordinary people** are most often ordinary people with extraordinary determination.

• **Many important battles** in life have to be fought more than once to be won.

• **We must train ourselves** not to see the world only through our own eyes.

• **In terms of choosing a career**, the trick is to find a job that you would do for free if life afforded you that opportunity.

• **The job of a manager** is not to do everything—it is to make sure that every task gets done.

• **The only job security** in the world is to be more talented tomorrow than you are today.

• **Nothing is as stressful** as trying to be a different person from who you are.

• **A pessimist** is someone who complains about the noise when opportunity knocks.

• **As a leader**, you must constantly change the definition of winning. Keep moving the goal posts.

Michael Levine, president of Levine Communications, one of Hollywood's top entertainment public relations firms. He is author of several books, including *Lessons at the Halfway Point: Wisdom for Midlife* (Celestial Arts) and *The Address Book: How to Reach Anyone Who's Anyone* (Perigee).

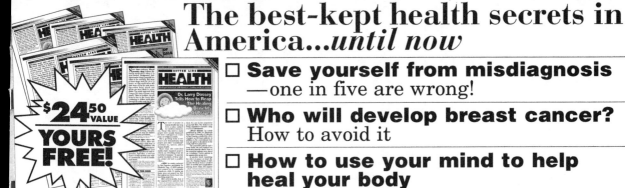